Monographs in Aerospace History **No. 57**

Science Advice
to NASA

Conflict, Consensus, Partnership, Leadership

Joseph K. Alexander

National Aeronautics and Space Administration

Office of Communications
NASA History Division
Washington, DC 20546

NASA SP-2017-4557

Library of Congress Cataloging-in-Publication Data

Names: Alexander, Joseph K., author.

Title: Science advice to NASA : conflict, consensus, partnership, leadership / Joseph K. Alexander.

Description: Washington, DC : National Aeronautics and Space Administration, Office of Communications, NASA History Division, 2017. | Series: Monographs in aerospace history ; no. 57 | "NASA SP-2017-4557." | Includes bibliographical references.

Identifiers: LCCN 2016049788 | ISBN 9781626830332 (pbk.)

Subjects: LCSH: Astronautics and state—United States. | Science and state—United States. | Scientists in government—United States. | Government consultants—United States. | United States. National Aeronautics and Space Administration.

Classification: LCC TL789.8.U5 A635 2017 | DDC 629.40973—dc23 LC record available at *https://lccn.loc.gov/2016049788*

This publication is available as a free download at *http://www.nasa.gov/ebooks*.

ISBN 9781626830332

90000 >

9 781626 830332

Table of Contents

Preface

The National Aeronautics and Space Administration (NASA) has a long history of interacting closely with and inviting advice from the
scientific community. This tradition is integral
to the culture of the Agency's scientific programs
and can be traced back to NASA's predecessor,
the National Advisory Committee for Aeronautics (NACA). Several authors have examined the
history of these relationships, both in the days of
NACA and following NASA's formation in 1958
up through the early 1980s, but there has been
no comprehensive treatment of the evolution of
NASA's scientific advisory activities for the Agency's second three decades. Nevertheless, the latter
period has seen important developments that are
worth attention, and so this monograph both
fleshes out aspects of the early advisory history
that have not been treated in much depth and then
follows that history forward into the mid-2010s.
Aspects of the advisory process have changed over
the past few decades, and there are sure to be more
changes in the future. For example, the aftereffects
of congressional enactment of the Federal Advisory Committee Act in 1972 and its amendment
in 1997 are still impacting the way that NASA can
obtain timely advice.

History, of course, has a more important role
than just recitation of a chain of events. NASA history is important as a way to help understand the
technological and societal implications of the space
age. Furthermore, in looking at NASA's use of outside scientific advice, we seek to understand what
good has come from it, whether it has had significant impacts, and if so, in what ways. The answers
to such questions, of course, address the question
of when NASA should seek outside advice. We ask
how well has the advisory process worked, what
efforts worked well, what fell flat, and why? Are

there common attributes or recurring themes that
help distinguish between effective efforts and run-
of-the-mill communications? What are the distinctions between different sources of outside advice
and are those distinctions relevant and important?
Finally, given past experiences and trends, can one
count on the process working as well in the future,
or are there obstacles to be anticipated and overcome? How might, or should, the advisory ecosystem adapt to be an asset to space research in the
future, and are there any fundamental principles
that need to be heeded going forward?

From a broader perspective, there are aspects
of NASA's advisory relationships with the outside
scientific community that are arguably exemplary
and even unique and provide useful lessons for
anyone interested in how government science and
technology agencies can benefit from independent
external scientific advice.

Consequently, the purpose of this book is to
document highlights of NASA's interactions with
outside scientific advisors over the Agency's full
lifetime and to draw lessons from that history for
research managers, decision makers, and scientists.
The intended audience is broad and ambitious. It
includes not only persons interested in the history
of the U.S. space program but also current and
future NASA officials, managers in other government research and development (R&D) agencies, federal R&D overseers and decision makers
in the Executive Office of the President and in
Congress, and of course, members of the scientific
community. Officials and scientists involved in
similar programs outside the United States might
even find it interesting to see how and where this
nation has tried to leverage its scientific brain-
power to guide space research in the country. Perhaps, equally importantly, ordinary citizens have a

right to understand how priorities and directions for space research in the United States—it's their program, after all—are determined.

The book is divided into three parts—the first two focus on history and the third on synthesis and analysis. Part 1 briefly examines early forerunner activities at NACA and in the decade leading up to NASA's formation; it then considers NASA's use of outside advice during its first three decades. Part 2 picks up the story in 1988 and follows it up to 2016. Part 3 examines a sampling of case studies, discusses recurring characteristics of notably successful advisory activities, and provides a glimpse of what past experience might imply for the future of scientific advice at NASA. The last two chapters provide big-picture summaries of themes that have emerged from earlier discussions. In particular, chapter 19 recaps conclusions to be drawn from the history and case studies, and chapter 20 takes a forward look to speculate on how the advisory environment might evolve in the future.

Research for the book utilized three main sources. The first—archival research—drew on material in the archives of the NASA History Division and the National Academy of Sciences (NAS) as well as other publicly available documents. The bibliographic essay in the appendix highlights some of the most important of these. The NASA and NAS archives were especially useful for records and correspondence relevant to Part 1. There are also abundant Internet sites where one can obtain copies of past reports and government documents, information about legislative activities, articles on specific events, and the like. The second research resource has been the author's own personal notes, which cover activities at NASA Headquarters from 1980 until late 1994 and then at the National Research Council Space Studies Board from 1998 until 2012.

The final, and in many ways most interesting, research component is a collection of interviews that the author conducted with current and former government officials and with scientists from outside NASA. Many chapters of the book quote directly from the interviews, and in a great majority of cases those quotations illustrate a point or theme that other interview subjects also raised. Thus, in a sense the book tells the story from the perspective of many more people than just the author. A full list of the interviews appears in the bibliographic essay, and a subset of the interview transcripts will be available to the public through the NASA Oral History Program. (Footnotes in the text to quotations from oral history interviews include the page number(s) where the quotation can be found in the interview transcripts.)

The scope of NASA's science programs has included wide-ranging research in both the physical and biological sciences, but this book focuses on the former. The disciplines of interest include all the areas that are covered under NASA's Science Mission Directorate as of 2016—namely, space astronomy and astrophysics, planetary science, solar and space physics, and Earth science and applications—all of which are conducted primarily via robotic spacecraft. NASA's research programs in space life sciences and micro-gravity physical sciences, which are conducted primarily via laboratories with astronaut crews, are also worthy subjects, but their distinct history, community culture, and modes of operation make them better suited for a separate treatment. Therefore, they are not treated here.

One form of advisory activities that the monograph will not examine in any detail is the use of peer reviews of proposals from scientists seeking agency funding for research projects. Proposal peer reviews do represent a form of advisory activity, but their task is very specific to competitions in the procurement process. Although some agencies, notably the National Science Foundation as chapter 13 explains, do use the proposal peer review process as a measure of the views of the scientific community, peer reviews at NASA are a regular formal process apart from the broader questions of gathering scientific advice. Nevertheless, many of the attributes that make other advice effective will apply to peer reviews as well.

Also for the sake of keeping the discussion focused, the book looks mainly at scientific advisory committees established by NASA (deemed *internal* committees) and bodies established by the National Research Council (deemed *external* committees), especially the Space Science Board, its successor the Space Studies Board (SSB), and their cousins, the Space Applications Board and the Aeronautics and Space Engineering Board. Several other NRC boards—notably the Board on Physics and Astronomy, the Board on Atmospheric Sciences and Climate, the Board on Earth Sciences and Resources, and the Board on Life Sciences—have organized important advisory studies for NASA. While the monograph's discussions do not ignore those bodies, the work of the SSB has been sufficiently extensive that the lessons from the SSB-NASA experience should be more broadly applicable to the rest of the NRC in terms of advice on NASA space and Earth science.

Finally, there have been other entities besides NASA's formally established internal committees and separate groups operating under the aegis of the National Research Council that have provided advice from time to time about the Agency's science programs. Examples include the National Academy of Public Administration, scientific societies such as the American Astronomical Society and the American Geophysical Union, public interest groups such as The Planetary Society, and a few "blue-ribbon" committees commissioned by the government. The advisory roles of these bodies and their cousins have been rather more ad hoc and much less ubiquitous than the NASA and NRC committees. Given that lessons from the large body of experience with the latter are quite likely to be relevant to the former, the monograph will not dig into the history of scientific advice from groups other than those formed by NASA and the NRC.

Acknowledgments

This book would not have been possible without the help of many people. I want to begin with special thanks to individuals at NASA—William Barry of the NASA History Division, Jens Feeley and Max Bernstein of the Science Mission Directorate, and Susan Keddie of the NASA Research and Education Support Services office—who considered my proposal for the project and then guided me through the process of securing financial support, via Grant NNX13AL26G, to defray the costs of interviews and logistics. I am also grateful to NASA History Division archivists Jane Odom, Colin Fries, and Elizabeth Suckow and to National Academy of Sciences archivists, Janice Goldblum and Daniel Barbiero, all of whom helped me find records about early events of interest to the project. My former NRC colleagues, Porter Coggeshall and Janice Mehler of the Report Review Committee and Betty Guyot and Tanja Pilzak of the Space Studies Board, helped me track down aspects of the institution's history that were not well documented except in their remarkable memories. I am also thankful for e-mail conversations with scientific colleagues Stephen Fuselier and Megan Urry who helped me understand some important events along the historical trail. Stephen Garber was the NASA History Division project manager for the book, without whose expertise and efforts this project would never have been completed.

Thanks also go to the Communications Support Service Center (CSSC) team of talented professionals who brought this project from manuscript to finished publication. Chinenye Okparanta carefully copyedited the text, Michele Ostovar did an expert job laying out the design and creating the e-book version, Kristin Harley performed the exacting job of creating the index, and printing specialist Tun Hla oversaw the production of the traditional hard copies. Supervisors Barbara Bullock and Maxine Aldred helped by overseeing all of this CSSC production work.

Perhaps the most illuminating and valuable aspect of the project was the opportunity to conduct one-on-one interviews with more than 50 experts in space science and/or political science and to get their candid perspectives on how the NASA advisory process works or has worked. The list of interview subjects is too long to reproduce here, but I encourage readers to consult the bibliographic appendix that contains the full list. They shared their time generously and gave me new insights every time I conducted a new interview. When interview subjects are quoted by name in the text, I have tried to ensure that I have quoted them accurately and true to their intent, but I take responsibility for any misstatements.

No matter how many times I reviewed my draft text and refined it, novel ways to make it obscure or worse still lurked in the text. Consequently, I want to give most sincere thanks to my colleagues Len Fisk, George Paulikas, and Marcia Smith who read early drafts and helped me try to make the text more intelligible, complete, and accurate. Finally, I want to thank my wife, Diana, for her patience, encouragement, and eagle-eyed reading of early drafts and my son, David, for his extraordinarily insightful critique of key chapter drafts.

PART I

The First Three Decades

CHAPTER 1

Advisory Precedents before NASA

Imagine the government of a young nation that is still organizing itself and is confronted with important decisions about issues involving science and technology, but that lacks the expertise to make those decisions or to convince its citizens of the right path forward. Or imagine an established government that suddenly faces alarming national security threats that call for scientific or technological expertise that is not available from inside its own corridors. Or imagine, if you will, a government that is heavily invested in science but that needs the best ideas scientists can provide to make decisions about where to place those investments. Those are the situations and some of the pressing reasons that call for outside scientific advice.

The practice of soliciting advice from citizen experts has been a feature of the federal government throughout its history. Some historians attribute the first advisory committee to President George Washington who, in 1794, created a commission to try to negotiate a settlement between the government and western Pennsylvania farmers who were violently protesting a new tax on distilled spirits. The commission's attempts at peaceful negotiations were not as successful as the government's threats of military action, thereby setting a precedent for having advisors provide political cover

even when the advice might have limited grasp.[1] Nevertheless, the founders of the U.S. government are credited with creating and nurturing a system that was more open to outside advice and scientific input than many other countries at that time.

In March 1863, Congress enacted and President Lincoln signed a bill creating the National Academy of Sciences (NAS) as an independent, non-government entity. The action reflected the fact that the government needed an organized way to get assistance in evaluating the many ideas being proposed for technologies and devices to help fight the Civil War. Hence, the legislation spelled out the Academy's advisory role "whenever called upon by any department of the government, [to] investigate, examine, experiment, and report upon any subject of science or art."[2] Among the first tasks for the new organization were a study to recommend a uniform system of weights and measures and coins for the United States and a separate study on how to improve the performance of magnetic compasses on iron ships. The former effort is interesting in that it took nearly three years to complete, thereby being the first example of the Academy's sometimes glacial pace in delivering advice, as well as in the fact that no one heeded the advice to adopt the metric system, thereby demonstrating that

---

1. Bruce L. R. Smith, *The Advisers: Scientists in the Policy Process* (The Brookings Institution, Washington DC, 1992), pp. 14–15.

2. Quoted in National Research Council, *The National Academy of Sciences: The First Hundred Years, 1863–1963* (Washington, DC: The National Academies Press, 1978), p. 53. The same article cites the early NRC studies that are mentioned in this paragraph.

recommendations are not always implemented. The latter study on magnetic compass corrections was completed in eight months, and it proved to be very helpful to the Navy Department.[3]

By 1916, with the First World War erupting in Europe, it became clear that the relatively small NAS could not handle the volume and variety of scientific and technical studies being requested by the government. Consequently, the Academy created the National Research Council (NRC) as its operating arm through which research and advisory activities were organized and conducted.[4] When the United States entered World War II in 1939, the federal government recognized that research at both government and academic laboratories needed to be expanded to a whole new level. Consequently, the Academy-Research Council assisted in organizing a wide array of research projects at universities across the country, the vast majority of which were directed towards addressing military technology needs.[5] The expansion of NRC activity continued after the war, especially due to the impact of the Vannevar Bush report, "Science, the Endless Frontier," which advocated strongly for government support of science and the subsequent establishment of several new federal scientific

organizations.[6] NRC funding for government contracts jumped from $4 million in fiscal year 1949–1950 to $10.6 million in fiscal year 1959–1960.[7] The NAS-NRC staff grew from 186 employees in 1946 to 643 in 1960.[8]

The institution's post-war organizational structure had a few precursors to what would become a science advisory structure to NASA. For example, the NRC Division of Physical Sciences had a Research Committee on the Physics of the Earth, and the Division of Geology and Geophysics was the home for more than 25 topical technical committees. The NAS established an Advisory Committee on Meteorology in 1956, and it became the Advisory Committee on Atmospheric Sciences from 1958 until 1960. Aside from hosting the U.S. institutional membership in the International Astronomical Union, the only formal attention to astronomy in the late 1940s and early 1950s was an Advisory Committee on Astronomy for the Office of Naval Research.[9]

One important post-war policy change within the NAS was agreement that the NAS charter to provide assistance "whenever called upon by any department" needn't be interpreted literally. Instead of having to wait for a request, the institution could

---

3. National Academy of Sciences. *The National Academy of Sciences: The First Hundred Years, 1863–1963* (The National Academies Press, Washington, DC, 1978), p. 81.

4. National Academy of Sciences. *The National Academy of Sciences: The First Hundred Years, 1863–1963* (The National Academies Press, Washington, DC, 1978), pp. 200–241.

5. The phrase "Academy-Research Council" was used to refer to the new two-unit organization. The National Academies today also includes the National Academy of Engineering (established in 1964) and the National Academy of Medicine (established in 1970 as the Institute of Medicine and renamed in 2015), which also utilize the NRC to conduct advisory studies. See *The National Academy of Sciences: The First Hundred Years, 1863–1963* (The National Academies Press, Washington, DC, 1978), pp. 382–432.

6. Vannevar Bush, "Science, the Endless Frontier" (U.S. Government Printing Office, Washington, DC, 1945). For example, the Atomic Energy Commission and the Office of Naval Research were created in 1946, and the National Science Foundation was established in 1950.

7. The figures are from the Annual Report of the National Academy of Sciences for fiscal years 1949–1950 and 1959–1960, respectively (available at NAS Archives, Washington, DC). When adjusted for inflation, they correspond to $41 million in 1949 and $87 million in 1959 in 2016 dollars. For comparison, the total National Academies federal contract payments in 2014 were approximately $226 million in 2016 dollars.

8. Rexmond C. Cochrane, *The National Academy of Sciences: The First Hundred Years, 1863–1963* (National Academy of Sciences, Washington, DC, 1978) p. 563. This book provides a comprehensive history of the NAS over this period.

9. NRC Organization and Members Directory for fiscal years 1939–1940, 1944–1945, 1948–1949 and 1956–1960; available at NAS Archives, Washington, DC.

actively communicate its availability and propose to federal agencies to conduct advisory studies.[10] The National Academy of Sciences became accustomed to, and accepted as, the premier source of expert recommendations on science and technology.

As the space age began to emerge after World War II, government agencies turned to both the Academy-Research Council and ad hoc groups of scientists to help guide the directions of new space technologies. This chapter will examine a few examples of those predecessor advisory experiences to see what effect they had on NASA's later approach to collecting outside scientific advice.

The NACA: Advisory Committee Was Its Middle Name

Part of NASA's openness to outside advice can be traced to the fact that Congress also created NASA's predecessor, the National Advisory Committee for Aeronautics (NACA), in the form of an advisory entity, and that the NACA retained much of that structure even when it grew to be a major research institution.

In 1911, a handful of aviation and aeronautical engineering enthusiasts came together to form the American Aeronautical Society. Noting the more organized and vigorous approach to this fledgling field that Europeans were taking compared to the relative inaction in the United States, some of the Society's members saw a need to establish a national aeronautical research entity in the country. Navy Captain W. Irving Chambers initially developed a substantive proposal along those lines, and it was subsequently refined by others. It entailed creation of a laboratory modeled on European establishments that would involve substantial facilities, staff,

and budget, all of which would be overseen by an appointed advisory committee or board. In spite of efforts by American advocates of the idea, a combination of classic Washington, DC, turf battles (involving the Navy, the Army, the Smithsonian Institution, and the Bureau of Standards) and political skepticism about whether the new area of aviation was to be taken seriously effectively stalled progress towards the creation of such a laboratory.[11] It would be hard to miss the irony in the fact that similar obstacles often plague technological progress more than a century later.

After several years of unsuccessful efforts, Charles D. Walcott, Secretary of the Smithsonian Institution, hit upon a successful strategy in 1914. Rather than creating an operational laboratory, Walcott simply proposed the creation of an advisory committee "to supervise and direct the scientific study of the problems of flight with a view to their practical solution, and to determine the problems which should be experimentally attacked and to discuss their solution and their application to practical questions."[12] The committee was to be comprised of seven representatives from relevant government agencies and up to seven other experts in aeronautical science and engineering. The committee would have an annual budget of only $5,000 and only a single full-time employee. Walcott's proposal was tucked into the naval appropriations bill where it was approved in the waning days of Congress in March 1915, roughly a dozen years after the Wright brothers' first flights in Kitty Hawk, North Carolina. Thus, the committee's creation represented a classic example of adept political timing and getting the camel's nose under the tent.

Notably, the entity that was later to become NASA began as an advisory committee—the

---

10. Rexmond C. Cochrane, *The National Academy of Sciences: The First Hundred Years, 1863–1963* (National Academy of Sciences, Washington, DC, 1978), p. 473.

11. For an excellent summary of efforts to create a national aeronautical laboratory in the period 1910–1915, see Alex Roland, *Model Research* (NASA SP-4130, NASA History Division, Washington, DC, 1985), vol. 1, chap. 1.

12. "Naval Appropriations Act, 1916," Public Law 271, 63d Cong., 3d sess., passed 3 March 1915 (38 Stat. 930).

NACA. By 1925, a decade after its establishment, the NACA was operating a national laboratory at Langley Field, Virginia, that had about 100 employees and utilized a significant number of wind tunnels and research aircraft.[13] One constant of the organization, however, was the continued presence of a broad oversight committee and a system of subordinate, discipline-oriented subcommittees. Shortly before the creation of NASA in 1958, the NACA organization chart showed the national committee, four technical committees, an industry consulting committee, and a special committee on space technology, all in line *above* the agency's director and its program officers and field installations.[14]

Several issues that were prominent during the NACA's history were harbingers of issues that remain significant in NASA today. First, there was continuing tension over whether the NACA would be a scientific or an engineering entity. That is, should the character of the organization be primarily influenced by basic research in the aeronautical sciences, or should it be driven by more practical problems in aeronautical engineering? This debate reflected early competition between the Smithsonian Institution, which was seen as a scientific organization, and the military, where practical engineering problems were considered paramount.[15] The debate was rekindled after World War II over differing views about whether the NACA's emphasis should revert to fundamental aeronautical science following the expansion of applied research and development in support of military needs during the war.[16]

A second issue involved advisory committee members' independence from conflicts of interest. The NACA's framers believed that the committee should not be vulnerable to the special interests of private or commercial influences. Rather, they believed the NACA's priorities should be the service of the interests of the federal government. Therefore, the membership of the NACA was intentionally set to be dominated by government representatives, and a handful of experts from academia rounded out the original committee.[17] Of course as time went by, the NACA policy on avoiding the influence of special interests did not prevent the research from producing important benefits for industry.

A third issue involved the roles and character of involvement of the technical committees and their subcommittees under the policy-setting national committee to which the NACA Director reported. There appears to have always been some level of tension between advocates of independent outside oversight and direction, on the one hand, and those (especially in the NACA laboratories) who sought more internal independence and authority. In 1950, soon after Hugh L. Dryden became the NACA Director, a document was issued that clarified the committees' roles. Specifically, they were responsible for (a) reviewing research progress, (b) recommending problems to be investigated, (c) aiding in research program formulation and coordination, and (d) communicating about research progress and directions.[18]

Dryden was a particularly important force in shaping the transformation of the NACA into

---

13. For an excellent summary of the early years of the NACA, see Roger E. Bilstein, *Orders of Magnitude: A History of the NACA and NASA, 1915–1990* (NASA SP-4406, NASA History Division, Washington, DC, 1989), ch. 1.

14. Management Processes Branch, *The Evolution of the NASA Organization* (NASA Office of Management, NASA Headquarters, Washington, DC Nov. 1983), p. viii; also available online at *http://history.nasa.gov/orgcharts/orgcharts.html#1958*.

15. Alex Roland, *Model Research* (NASA History Division, NASA Headquarters, Washington DC, NASA SP-4130, 1985), pp. 11–13.

16. Alex Roland, *Model Research* (NASA History Division, NASA Headquarters, Washington, DC, NASA SP-4130, 1985), pp. 196–197.

17. Alex Roland, *Model Research* (NASA History Division, NASA Headquarters, Washington, DC, NASA SP-4130, 1985), pp. 23–24.

18. Alex Roland, *Model Research* (NASA History Division, NASA Headquarters, Washington, DC, NASA SP-4130, 1985), vol. 1, p. 232.

NASA. A brilliant student who received his doctorate from Johns Hopkins University at age 20, he joined the National Bureau of Standards in 1918 and moved to the NACA in 1939. He earned national and international recognition at both institutions for his research and leadership in aerodynamics. Dryden served as Director of the NACA from 1947 until he became NASA's first Deputy Administrator in 1958, and he held that position until his death in 1965. Dryden had served on numerous scientific advisory committees, including the Scientific Advisory Committee to the President, the Interdepartmental Committee for Scientific Research and Development, and others that advised U.S. and international military R&D organizations. His experience with these advisory bodies and his views about the roles of the NACA committees after he became the NACA Director very probably influenced NASA's early thinking about the same kinds of relationships.[19]

Thus the scene was set for NASA's forerunner—the NACA—to create a tradition and culture in which the agency's operations were guided by an independent advisory body. In practical terms, the NACA's operations were not always determined by the oversight committee. Freelancing often did occur in the NACA's laboratories, and the discipline subcommittees could be co-opted by laboratory self-interests. (That aspect of the culture is not unheard of in NASA today, of course.) Nevertheless, the advisory-committee structure persisted throughout the NACA's history. This practice was a springboard for advisory relationships in NASA's early organization.

Rocket Panel

The work of 19th century science fiction writers and early 20th century visionaries such as Russian mathematician Konstantin E. Tsiolkovskiy, American physicist Robert H. Goddard, and German space pioneer Hermann J. Oberth stimulated thinking about the possibilities of spaceflight.[20] Tsiolkovskiy developed the theoretical basis for rocketry, including a theory of multi-stage rockets, around the turn of the century. Goddard conducted groundbreaking experimental tests of liquid-fueled rockets in the 1920s and 1930s. Oberth contributed to the foundations of astronautics for four decades starting in the 1920s, and he later collaborated with Wernher Von Braun in developing the German V-2 rocket. By the 1940s, scientists were using balloons and small sounding rockets to carry research instruments to study the upper atmosphere and cosmic rays.[21] After technologies for missile systems, electronic communications, and radar were developed for the military in World War II, the visions of spaceflight began to seem achievable, albeit probably costly. Furthermore, many scientists who detoured from their academic research to apply their skills to the war effort returned to academia after the war and applied what they had learned and developed to advancing technologies for basic research.

In 1945, officials at the U.S. Naval Research Laboratory (NRL) formed a new Rocket Sonde Research Section to explore and develop capabilities to study the upper atmosphere. Soon afterward, in early 1946, the U.S. Army sought to identify

---

19. For a concise but thorough biography of Dryden, see Michael H. Gorn, *Hugh Dryden's Career in Aviation and Space* (Monographs in Aerospace History, No. 5, NASA History Division, NASA Headquarters, Washington, DC, 1996).

20. For a nice summary of early work, see Homer E. Newell, *Beyond the Atmosphere: Early Years of Space Science* (NASA SP-4211, NASA History Division, NASA Headquarters, Washington, DC, 1980), chapter 3.

21. Cosmic rays are high-energy, electrically charged fragments of atoms that move at a significant fraction of the speed of light. Their origin was not understood in the 1950s, but they are now known to come from the Sun and from stellar explosions in the Milky Way galaxy and other galaxies.

scientific experiments that could be carried on flights of V-2 rockets that had been captured from Germany at the end of the war.[22] The NRL team organized discussions amongst university and military scientists to respond to the Army's invitation, and the discussions led to empanelment of a small group of scientists to assist in advising the Army. The panel's name changed over time, beginning as the V-2 Upper Atmosphere Research Panel, then becoming the Upper Atmosphere Rocket Research Panel (UARRP), and finally the Rocket and Satellite Research Panel, reflecting the evolution of the panel's scope of attention. Thus began a tradition of involving outside scientists in providing specific advice on scientific uses of space vehicles.[23]

The members of the ad hoc rocket panel elected NRL physicist Ernst H. Krause as the panel's first chair, and he was succeeded in 1947 by physicist James A. Van Allen from the Johns Hopkins University's Applied Physics Laboratory. Van Allen, who returned to the University of Iowa in 1951, served as chair until the time of NASA's formation in 1958. Mathematician and theoretical physicist Homer E. Newell from NRL, and later NASA, succeeded Van Allen and served as chair until 1961. Van Allen and Newell each played key roles in setting the scientific course for the U.S. space program—Van Allen as a member of the outside scientific community and Newell as an insider.[24]

Van Allen was an Iowa native who spent most of his career there. After working at the Carnegie Institution of Washington and then the Johns Hopkins University's Applied Physics Laboratory (APL) from 1939 to 1942 and a tour as an officer in the U.S. Navy, he joined the University of Iowa faculty in 1951 to become the long-time chair of the physics department. His research focused on studies of the upper atmosphere and cosmic rays; the origin of the latter was still a mystery at the time. Van Allen and his colleagues used V-2 rockets and a newly designed Aerobee sounding rocket to carry their instruments into the upper atmosphere, and then his Iowa team experimented with a scheme to launch small rockets from high-altitude balloons. In January 1958, Wernher von Braun's U.S. Army team launched Explorer 1 carrying Van Allen's Geiger counter instrument that led to discovery of the band of magnetically trapped radiation particles around Earth, and subsequently, to fame for the discoverer of the "Van Allen Belts."[25] Van Allen made extraordinary contributions not only via his groundbreaking research, but also as a thoughtful member of nearly all key advisory panels in the formative years of the space program—starting with the rocket panel and extending through service on the NACA Special Committee on Space Technology that was formed in 1958 to advise the agency on how it could make the transition from being an aeronautics research institution to the nation's space agency.

Homer Newell was a mathematician who earned a doctorate degree in 1940 from the University of Wisconsin. After a teaching stint at the University of Maryland, he joined NRL in 1944 where he became head of the rocket sonde group in 1947 and then acting superintendent of the Atmosphere and Astrophysics Division and scientific coordinator of Project Vanguard in 1954. Newell joined

---

22. "Sonde" is the French word for "probe." The "V" in "V-2" comes from "Vergeltungswaffe" or "vengeance weapon." For a full account of early involvement of scientists in using the V-2's, see David H. DeVorkin, *Science with a Vengeance: How the Military Created the U.S. Space Sciences after World War II* (Springer-Verlag, New York, NY, 1993).

23. For a concise summary of scientists' interactions during this period see John E. Naugle, *First Among Equals: The Selection of NASA Space Science Experiments* (NASA SP-4215, NASA History Division, Washington, DC, 1991), ch. 1.

24. Homer E. Newell, *Beyond the Atmosphere: Early Years of Space Science* (NASA SP-4211, NASA History Division, NASA Headquarters, Washington, DC, 1980), ch. 4.

25. For a comprehensive biography of Van Allen see Abigail Foerstner, *James Van Allen; The First Eight Billion Miles* (University of Iowa Press, Iowa City IA, 2007).

NASA at its formation, and he held successively more responsible leadership positions in space science, becoming Associate Administrator for Space Science and Applications in 1963. From 1967 until his retirement in 1974, Newell was NASA Associate Administrator—the number three position in the Agency—where he played a key policy-making and advisory role on all types of issues regarding NASA science. It is no exaggeration to say that his interactions with the outside scientific community on behalf of the government were pivotal in ensuring that outside advice was heard and applied. He was involved in establishing NASA's early advisory committee structure, he met often with NASA's internal committees and with the external Space Science Board, and he was a steady source of advice to NASA's senior leadership about the importance of maintaining constructive relationships with the scientific community[26] (See chapter 3).

Although the NRL's ad hoc rocket panel had no formal charter and was largely self-governed, it provided a broad array of advice to the Navy and Army on topics such as scientific opportunities and priorities for sounding rocket flights, rocket instrument payloads, performance requirements for rockets and flight support systems, alternatives and successors to the V-2, reference standard atmospheric properties, and the potential impacts of (unsuccessful) efforts to impose security classifications on atmospheric research. The panel also served as a forum for communication amongst scientists about the results of sounding rocket research. The panel ceased operations in 1961.[27] The relationships between the rocket panel and other complementary advisory bodies during the same period are illustrated in figure 1.1.

International Geophysical Year Committee

A small gathering of scientists at a dinner party hosted by Van Allen in April 1950 played a key role in the genesis of U.S. space science. The guests discussed and embraced an idea proposed by Lloyd V. Berkner of the Carnegie Institution of Washington for a third International Polar Year from 1957 to 1958.[28] Berkner and others subsequently stimulated international support for the idea, which became known as the International Geophysical Year (IGY), and in 1952 the International Council of Scientific Unions created a special Committee for the International Geophysical Year (referred to as CSAGI after its French name, Comité Special de l'Année Geophysique Internationale). Soon afterward, in 1953, the U.S. National Academy of Sciences formed a U.S. National Committee for the International Geophysical Year (USNC-IGY) to represent the United States in IGY activities.[29]

Also during 1952 the members of the NRL rocket panel began to discuss the idea of sounding rocket launches from a high-latitude site at Fort Churchill, Canada, as a part of the IGY. The proposal took hold, and in late 1953 the USNC-IGY created a Technical Panel on Rocketry to lead an IGY Sounding Rocket Program. Rocket panel chair Van Allen formed a special committee for the IGY

---

26. John D. Ruley, *The Professor on the Sixth Floor: Homer E. Newell, Jr. and the Development of U.S. Space Science* (University of North Dakota M.S. Thesis, Grand Forks, ND, 2010); available in NASA Historical Reference Collection, NASA Headquarters, record #61484.

27. Newell's book provides a good summary of the history of the rocket panel; see Homer E. Newell, *Beyond the Atmosphere: Early Years of Space Science* (NASA SP-4211, NASA History Division, Washington, DC, 1980), ch. 4.

28. The first International Polar Year was a collaborative effort between scientists from 11 nations who organized geophysical studies in the Arctic and Antarctic from 1882 to 1883. The second International Polar Year, from 1932 to 1933, expanded the collaboration to 40 nations and emphasized studies in meteorology and geomagnetism.

29. The National Academy of Sciences maintains a collection of records from the IGY at *http://www.nasonline.org/about-nas/history/archives/milestones-in-NAS-history/the-igy.html* (accessed 18 October 2016).

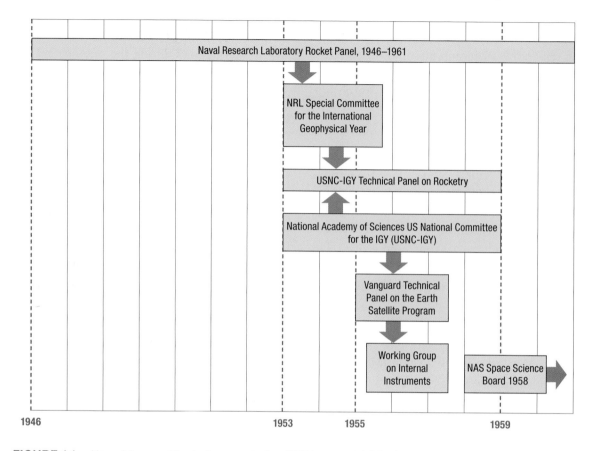

FIGURE 1.1   Key advisory entities in the years before NASA was established

(SCIGY), chaired by Homer Newell, to organize and coordinate the Fort Churchill launch campaign on behalf of the rocket panel in early 1954. SCIGY was subsequently transferred to operate under the auspices of the USNC-IGY, where it was merged with the Technical Panel on Rocketry.[30]

The IGY was a seminal effort for U.S. space research for several reasons. First, it became the initiative to which the first U.S. artificial satellite program was tied, thereby making the program a scientific endeavor open to international view rather than a closed military effort. Second, it was an activity planned and conducted by scientists, with the National Academy of Sciences playing the lead role in the United States. Third, especially

because the IGY predated any formal U.S. government space agency, U.S. IGY leaders saw themselves as being in charge of U.S. participation and, thereby, providing a logical precedent for how a national space research program might be expected to emerge.

Vanguard Selection Committee

In 1955, President Dwight D. Eisenhower announced that the United States would develop and launch several scientific satellites as part of the IGY. The Navy's proposed Vanguard rocket was chosen to be the launch vehicle, and the Vanguard Program was to be supported by the

---

30. Homer E. Newell, *Beyond the Atmosphere: Early Years of Space Science* (NASA SP-4211, NASA History Division, NASA Headquarters, Washington, DC, 1980), pp. 45–46.

National Science Foundation (NSF), Navy, Army, and Air Force. Joseph Kaplan, chair of the USNC-IGY, formed a new Technical Panel on the Earth Satellite Program (TPESP) that was responsible for planning the scientific program and selecting participating scientists for Vanguard. Kaplan named Richard W. Porter of General Electric as TPESP chair and charged the panel to

a. formulate the scientific program to be carried out by means of artificial satellites as part of the U.S. program for the International Geophysical Year;

b. delegate and direct the execution of this program; and

c. establish policies and formulate procedures related to the program in the fields of (i) budget, (ii) information policy, and (iii) institutional relationships.[31]

The TPESP subsequently created a working group on internal instrumentation with Van Allen as chair. In 1956, the working group established criteria for selecting experiments to be launched aboard Vanguard, reviewed proposals, set priorities for experiments to be selected, and recommended specific selections to the TPESP. Thus, the TPESP and its working group were considerably more than advisory groups. Rather, they provided direction to the government agencies about how to carry out the scientific aspects of Vanguard.[32]

While Vanguard was still in development in preparation for launch, the Soviet Union captured world attention with its launch of the Sputnik I satellite in October 1957.

Space Science Board

The surprise and sense of alarm in the United States that accompanied the successful launch of Sputnik I and the launch of Sputnik II in November set off a period of intense activity regarding space research. Vanguard I failed to achieve orbit in December. In the same month, the renamed rocket panel issued its own ideas for a new space agency in a report titled "National Space Establishment: A Proposal of the Rocket and Satellite Research Panel."[33] The U.S. Army's Jupiter-C rocket successfully launched the Explorer 1 satellite (developed by the Jet Propulsion Laboratory in California and carrying Van Allen's cosmic ray experiment) in January 1958, the Eisenhower administration submitted legislation to transform the NACA into NASA in April, Van Allen's team announced the discovery of trapped radiation belts around Earth in May, and Congress passed and the President signed the National Aeronautics and Space Act in July. All in all, it was a breathtaking sequence of events.

Action by the National Academy of Sciences was also prompt and direct. In response to a request from the National Science Foundation, the NACA, and the Department of Defense Advanced Research Projects Agency (DARPA), NAS President Detlev W. Bronk formally established the Space Science Board (SSB) on 4 June 1958, and appointed geophysicist Lloyd Berkner to serve as chair. At the time, Berkner was president of Associated Universities, Inc., president of the International Council of Scientific Unions, and a member of the President's Scientific Advisory

---

31. Minutes of the First Meeting, Technical Panel on Earth Satellite Program, 20 October 1955, NAS Archives, IGY Series, Washington, DC.

32. John E. Naugle, *First Among Equals: The Selection of NASA Space Science Experiments* (NASA SP-4215, NASA History Division, NASA Headquarters, Washington, DC, 1991), pp. 7–12.

33. J. A. Van Allen, "National Space Establishment: A Proposal of the Rocket and Satellite Research Panel," 27 December 1957, reproduced in Logsdon, John M., ed., with Amy Paige Snyder, Roger D. Launius, Stephen J. Garber, and Regan Anne Newport, *Exploring the Unknown: Selected Documents in the History of the U.S. Civil Space Program, Volume V, Exploring the Cosmos* (NASA SP-4407, NASA History Division, Washington, DC, 2001), p. 87.

Council.[34] In a 26 June letter to Berkner, Bronk set down the charge to the SSB as follows:

[W]e shall look to the Board to be the focus of the interests and responsibilities of the Academy-Research Council in space science; to establish necessary relationships with civilian science and with government scientific activities, particularly the new Space Agency, the National Science Foundation, and the Advanced Research Projects Agency; to represent the Academy-Research Council in our international relations in this field on behalf of American scientists and science; to seek ways to stimulate needed research; to promote necessary coordination of scientific effort; and to provide such advice and recommendations to appropriate individuals and agencies with regard to space science as may in the Board's judgment be desirable.

As we have already agreed, the Board is intended to be an advisory, consultative, correlating, evaluating body and not an operating agency in the field of space science. It should avoid responsibility as a Board for the conduct of any programs of space research and for the formulation of budgets relative thereto. Advice to agencies properly responsible for these matters, on the other hand, would be within its purview to provide.[35]

Bronk's direction to the SSB to confine its roles to advisory rather than operational matters marked a significant departure from the earlier roles of bodies such as the NACA technical committees,

the rocket panel, and the Vanguard selection committee.

Lloyd Berkner was an engineer and physicist who earned a baccalaureate in electrical engineering from the University of Minnesota in 1927. He never received a Ph.D., but he was the recipient of a dozen honorary degrees in recognition of his technical and scientific leadership accomplishments. After graduation, Berkner worked as an engineer at the U.S. Bureau of Lighthouses, the National Bureau of Standards, and the Carnegie Institution of Washington. While on active duty in the Navy during World War II he became responsible for all naval electronics engineering, especially including airborne radar systems for navy fighter aircraft. He returned to Carnegie after the war to become chair of the Section of Exploratory Geophysics of the Atmosphere. However, his time there was often interrupted as he took on assignments as executive secretary of the Research and Development Board established by the Departments of War and Navy, special scientific assistant to the Secretary of State, and leader of a National Academy of Sciences study on science and foreign relations.[36] As one of the nation's scientific leaders who was known for being especially persuasive and energetic, who had argued for the creation of a civilian rather than military space agency, and who had been involved in many interagency and international scientific and technical negotiations, Berkner was an ideal choice to be the founding chair of the SSB.

The original board had 15 members, including distinguished physicists, chemists, and engineers, plus a biologist, a meteorologist, and a psychologist.[37] Nearly all of the members were then or would

34. Homer E. Newell, *Beyond the Atmosphere: Early Years of Space Science* (NASA SP-4211, NASA History Division, NASA Headquarters, Washington, DC, 1980), p. 30.

35. Logsdon, John M., ed., with Amy Paige Snyder, Roger D. Launius, Stephen J. Garber, and Regan Anne Newport. *Exploring the Unknown: Selected Documents in the History of the U.S. Civil Space Program, Volume V, Exploring the Cosmos* (NASA SP-4407, NASA History Division, NASA Headquarters, Washington, DC, 2001), p. 100.

36. Anton L. Hales, "Biographical Memoir of Lloyd Viel Berkner" (National Academy of Sciences, Washington DC, 1992).

37. Homer E. Newell, *Beyond the Atmosphere: Early Years of Space Science* (NASA SP-4211, NASA History Division, NASA Headquarters, Washington, DC, 1980), App. F.

become elected members of the National Academy of Sciences, and the membership included one current and two future Nobel laureates.[38] The SSB held its first meeting on 27 June 1958, and after that meeting a geophysicist was added to the roster. All of the early members were men.[39]

During its first year of operation, the SSB established eleven ad hoc committees to carry out the Board's work, widely circulated an invitation to U.S. scientists to propose scientific experiments to be conducted in space, utilized its committees to provide an initial set of recommendations (to NASA, NSF, and the Advanced Research Projects Agency) for specific experiments to be selected, collaborated with NASA to hold a seminar to stimulate interest in space science,[40] and published an article in *Science*[41] to encourage scientific interest in space research.

Although Bronk and Berkner sought to keep attention focused on the SSB's advisory and planning roles, some members still hoped that the Board would have more to say about operational decisions. This issue was put to rest when NASA prescribed a statement of work for the Board's contract renewal for fiscal year 1960. In it, NASA made clear that it sought "thoughts, ideas, and recommendations…on the broad overall objectives" and that "Guiding principles are needed, rather than a detailed program formulation…."[42] However, as we shall see, a certain vagueness about where to draw the line between strategic advice and programmatic guidance continued to give the SSB openings and challenges in the years to come.

Post-War Precedents for Technical Agencies and Advisors

The immediate post-war period saw a flurry of new government scientific and technical organizations and accompanying advisory bodies, and these very probably influenced the heads of the National Science Foundation, the NACA, and the Department of Defense Advanced Research Projects Agency when they asked Bronk to create the SSB. For example, the Army Air Force Scientific Advisory Board, which had been formed in 1944 and later became the USAF Scientific Advisory Board, served as an advisor to the Office of Air Research starting in 1948, and it became the top-level advisory body for the Air Force Office of Scientific Research in 1951. The Office of Naval Research and its Naval Research Advisory Committee were formed together in 1946. The Atomic Energy Commission, which was a predecessor to the Energy Research and Development Administration and then the Department of Energy, also was created in 1946, and its General Advisory Committee was established the next year. When the National Science Foundation was created in 1950, the National Science Board was legislatively established to be both the governing entity of the Foundation and a source of science policy advice to the government. As a consequence of these and other precedents, there was a degree of shared experience across the government regarding the interactions of science and technology agencies and their advisors. Not only were government

---

38. Harold C. Urey (1934), Joshua Lederberg (1958), and Haldan Keffer Hartline (1967), respectively.

39. The SSB did not have its first female member—astronomer E. Margaret Burbidge—until 1971.

40. John E. Naugle, *First Among Equals: The Selection of NASA Space Science Experiments* (NASA SP-4215, NASA History Division, NASA Headquarters, Washington, DC, 1991), pp. 31–34.

41. Space Science Board, "Research in Space" *Science Magazine* 130, no. 3369 (24 July 1959): p. 195.

42. See John E. Naugle, *First Among Equals: The Selection of NASA Space Science Experiments* (NASA SP-4215, NASA History Division, NASA Headquarters, Washington, DC, 1991), p. 72.

officials familiar with the process, but there was enough overlap between membership in the various committees, including space program committees, to ensure a degree of continuity across the whole U.S. R&D scene.

Impact of the Pre-NASA Committees

Looking back on the lineage of the many advisory bodies that operated before NASA was established, it is easy to see the list as confusing and convoluted. But, in fact, the membership of these entities gave them coherence and continuity. For example, James Van Allen was among the first members appointed to the rocket panel and he served for many years as its chair; he served on the Vanguard selection panel and was chair of its working group on internal instrumentation; and he served on the SSB from 1958 to 1969. Richard Porter chaired the Vanguard selection panel, sat on the working group for internal instrumentation, and was a charter member of the SSB. Homer Newell served on the rocket panel, chaired the Scientific Committee for the IGY, was a member of its Vanguard selection panel, and framed much of the policy about the operation of NASA's early science organization. Berkner was chair of the USNC-IGY and original chair of the SSB. Another important member of these early entities was Fred L. Whipple, a Harvard astronomer, who served on the first rocket panel and was a member of the Vanguard selection panel. Consequently, these scientists, among others, helped ensure that ideas and concerns were well understood across the scientific advisory ecosystem.

Indeed, one can view some of the major players who helped develop independent scientific advice for an embryotic NASA as visionaries similar, in their own way, to Tsiolkovskiy, Goddard, and Oberth. The latter created a technical foundation for later spaceflight. The former were movers and shakers who brought the scientific community and the government together to make a space science program feasible and to put it in motion. Dryden, who was a member and home secretary of the NAS, helped ensure that the NACA's technical committees had meaningful roles, and he carried that tradition to NASA. Berkner had the vision and the drive to ensure that the idea of the IGY took hold internationally, and he guided the launch of the SSB. Van Allen used his capacity for innovation and leadership to create a sustainable scientific enterprise.

One important point to draw from the experience of the advisory forerunners to NASA is that while their control of decision making (e.g., about flight payloads) would diminish when NASA was established, their importance would not. Indeed, the tradition of utilizing outside scientific advisory panels had become ingrained in the early culture of space science. Scientists came to expect, and NASA understood, that their voices would be heard. (See box on the following page.)

The process by which scientists' views would be heard in the future NASA continued to be influenced by some of the same issues that weighed on the framers of the NACA. In particular, issues of advisors' independence versus conflicts of interest and of the operational reach of advisory committees' recommendations continued to color the character of the advisory process for years to come.

The Scope of Space Science Then and Now

Early planners for research in space had a very broad vision of the scientific potential of a national space program. At the first meeting of the Space Science Board, chairman Berkner identified seven disciplinary areas—astronomy and radio astronomy, geochemistry of space and exploration of moon and planets, geodesy, ionospheres of Earth and planets, meteorological aspects of satellites, physics of fields and particles in space, and psychological

ADVICE 101: THE PRINCIPAL MEANS AND MEDIA FOR OUTSIDE ADVICE

NASA often received advice via both formal and informal routes. The Agency regularly established formal, standing, advisory bodies that served over the time for which they were chartered and ad hoc groups that served just long enough to perform a specific task. (See chapter 3.) NASA also turned to outside entities, especially the National Research Council (NRC), to formally empanel independent advisory bodies, sometimes also on a continuing basis and sometimes for one-of-a-kind projects. The Space Science Board (SSB) and its standing committees are the premier example of the former, and committees to advise on specific planetary protection protocols are examples of the latter. (See chapter 2.) NASA also established ad hoc advisory groups that operated outside the constraints of federal advisory committee rules and regulations, and these groups usually focused on lower-level tactical issues of concern to individual program managers. There also was no lack of informal advice from individuals and special interest groups who would not hesitate to catch a NASA official's ear whenever the opportunity, and occasionally the invitation, appeared. These informal advisors most often approached NASA at their own initiative rather than at NASA's.

The advice itself came in many forms. Starting with the most comprehensive, some of NASA's formally chartered committees and nearly all NRC committees have delivered their advice via full-length (i.e., 30 to 300 page) *study reports* that often include summaries and analyses of data or information collected by the committee plus the committee's conclusions, generally in the form of specific findings and recommendations. Other advisory reports may take the form of position papers (NASA calls them *white papers*) that outline salient aspects of an issue, possibly including alternative perspectives and options for action, but that do not make explicit recommendations. An NRC version of this type of document is the *workshop report* that summarizes discussions by experts assembled to chew over an issue without offering consensus recommendations on the subject.

There are also options for shorter, more concise advisory documents that are presented in the form of a letter to NASA. Such *letter reports* were often used by the SSB up through the 1990s, and they have been a common vehicle for NASA's internal committees to communicate their views. In a few instances, an advisory body will deliver its advice simply by briefing the appropriate Agency officials without any accompanying document, except perhaps for copies of the briefing charts.

Finally, there is an option for airing advisory perspectives that involves no documents at all. Instead, the advisory group may simply engage in an informal discussion with the NASA official so that the latter can hear from the former in real time but without any formal documentation. The NRC employs this vehicle, which it calls a *round table*, as a means of convening experts for discussions with agency officials without going through the process of endorsing the discussions as formal advice from the NRC.

and biological research—around which to form ad hoc committees.[43] These areas constituted the SSB's first definition of the scope of space science. NASA's first standalone Office of Space Sciences emerged in 1961 with Homer Newell as Director. He had three science-discipline offices—bioscience, geophysics and astronomy, and lunar and planetary programs—which covered most of the same territory as the early SSB science categories.

If we fast-forward to 2016, there were both similarities and interesting differences in what one finds under the rubric of space sciences. As of this writing, the Space Studies Board (the Space Science Board's successor in the National Academies structure) has standing committees in astronomy and astrophysics, astrobiology and planetary science, Earth science and applications, and solar and space physics. That structure mirrors the four science program offices in NASA's 2016 Science Mission Directorate.

But behind the simple differences between the names of modern SSB committees and NASA organization charts and their predecessors more than five decades ago is a story of revolutionary advances and accomplishments across all fields. "Astrophysics" in the nomenclature for the contemporary space astronomy program reflects the explosion in new knowledge brought about via measurements from space across the full electromagnetic spectrum from millimeter waves to gamma rays. The planners of the 1950s could hardly imagine how dramatically space astronomy would open up new research areas such as high-energy astrophysics, observational cosmology, and detection of extrasolar planets.[44] The coupling of "astrobiology"[45] and planetary science reflects the emergence of searches for evidence of life, or its origins, in solar systems as a maturing field.

Perhaps the biggest change in the inventory of major areas of space science is the development of Earth science and applications as a mature, vibrant, and societally important research field. Neither the original SSB nor NASA's early science offices fully anticipated the potential of measuring Earth from the remote perspective of space. The combination of in-situ atmospheric measurements and remote sensing of the land, oceans, biosphere, and cryosphere have had revolutionary impacts on topics such as global change, climate, land use, oceanography, and ecosystems management. Thus, as these capabilities evolved, Earth science became very much a part of space science—when the latter term is used in its broadest sense.

All of the contemporary science fields cited above have been pursued through the use of robotic spacecraft. Two other science areas—space life sciences and microgravity physical sciences—have developed primarily along a different track. Both the life sciences, which includes the study of biological processes in cells, plants, and animals (including humans), and study in areas such as materials science, fluid physics, combustion, and fundamental physics have been pursued mainly in space laboratories staffed by in-flight astronaut crews. These space laboratory sciences are certainly appropriate categories of science in space, but they are distinctly different from the other fields mentioned above in terms of the manner in which they have been conducted and the character and traditions of the space research communities that pursue work in these fields.

Henceforth, this book will focus on the areas that have been pursued primarily through robotic spacecraft—astronomy and astrophysics, Earth science and applications, planetary science (including astrobiology), and solar and space physics. The discussion will consider the laboratory sciences in microgravity only when there is a need to compare the latter with the former.

---

43. Space Science Board, "Minutes of the First Meeting, 27 June 1958," reproduced in John M. Logsdon, *Exploring the Unknown, Vol V: Exploring the Cosmos*, (NASA History Division NASA Headquarters, Washington, DC, 2001), pp. 99–113.

44. Extrasolar planets are planets that orbit stars other than the Sun.

45. In the early decades of space science, this research was known as "exobiology."

CHAPTER 2

The Space Science Board Goes to Work

After organizing itself in 1958, the SSB lost no time in getting to work. During its first three years of operation, the SSB developed guidance to the U.S. delegation to the United Nations regarding international cooperation in space activities; prepared a major strategic review of prospects and opportunities for science in space; and delivered letters to senior NASA officials regarding policies for human space exploration and basic research in space science, data exchange policies, and tracking and orbit computation services.[1]

Thus, a spectrum of products and services emerged that responded to Bronk's original charge. Namely, the Board conducted advisory studies and organized workshops, both to gather information and perspectives for use by its study committees and to promote communication about space science across the government and non-government scientific communities. It began to produce three kinds of advisory reports: (a) broad-based reports on strategic issues, (b) more narrowly focused study reports on specific topics about which the government (mainly NASA) needed advice, and (c) brief letter reports that communicated a perspective or set of recommendations developed by the Board on a more rapid time scale than was required to complete study reports.

The SSB's relationship with NASA gained heightened visibility beginning with an agency reorganization initiated by NASA's second Administrator, James E. Webb, in 1961. Webb's organization chart included a dotted-line (i.e., advisory) connection between "Research Advisory Committees" and the Administrator's office.[2] The arrangement probably reflected the ideas of Deputy Administrator Dryden, who had blocked out similar arrangements in potential organizational schemes for NASA while he was still the NACA Director.[3] By November 1962, this dotted-line advisory position on the NASA organization chart was specifically identified with the "Space Science Board of National Academy of Sciences." (See figure 2.1.) The special advisory role of the SSB was explicit in NASA's organization charts until 1967 when the role was expanded to encompass the National Academy of Sciences and the National Academy of Engineering. Three national academies—NAS, NAE, and the National Academy of

---

1. All reports prepared by the Space Science Board, the Space Studies Board, and the committees of the boards are listed in the annual reports of the Space Studies Board (see *http://sites.nationalacademies.org/SSB/SSB_051650*), and they are all available at the SSB Web site: *http://sites.nationalacademies.org/SSB/index.htm*.

2. See *The Evolution of the NASA Organization* (Office of Management, NASA Headquarters, Washington DC, March 1985) *http://history.nasa.gov/orgcharts/orgcharts.html* for a complete compilation of NASA organization charts.

3. The NACA, "A National Research Program for Space Technology," a staff study of the NACA, 14 January 1958, Model Research, NASA SP-4103 Volume 2, Appendix H, no. 45.

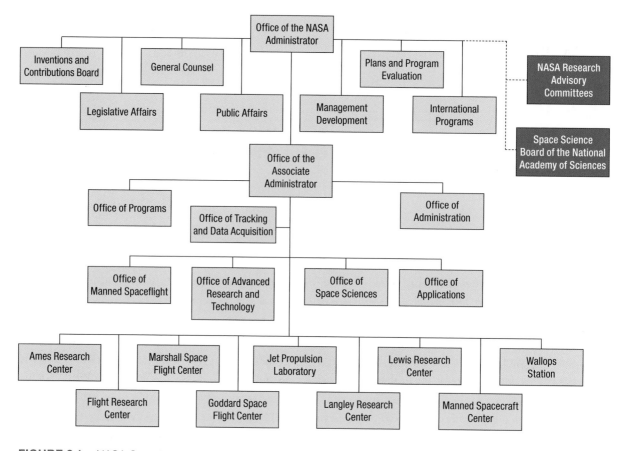

FIGURE 2.1   NASA Organization Chart as of August 1962[4]

Public Administration—were included in 1968–1976 versions. A specific relationship with the national academies no longer appeared in the final organization charts issued under Administrator James C. Fletcher in 1976.[5] Nevertheless, the SSB and its counterparts experienced a remarkable 16-year period of responsibility during which NASA portrayed them as integral elements of the process of obtaining advice for the Agency. After 1978, the SSB's advisory activities for NASA continued without change, even though the Agency no longer called attention to its relationships with the

academies as adjunct elements of the NASA organizational structure.

While the SSB and NASA officials communicated freely and often with each other, the NAS guarded its independence resolutely. For example, Harvard planetary scientist Richard Goody, who chaired the SSB from 1974 to 1976, recalled that when he was recruited to become Board Chair, Administrator Fletcher objected because he was concerned that Goody would not be a supporter of the proposed Large Space Telescope. (In fact, Goody turned out to be an active supporter.)

4. Adapted from 17 August 1962 NASA Headquarters organization chart presented in "The Evolution of the NASA Organization" (Office of Management, NASA Headquarters, Washington DC, March 1985); also available at *http://history.nasa.gov/orgcharts/evol_org.pdf*.

5. Office of Management, *The Evolution of the NASA Organization* (NASA Headquarters, Washington DC, March 1985); also available at *http://history.nasa.gov/orgcharts/evol_org.pdf*.

Fletcher appealed directly to the president of the NAS, Philip Handler, to stop Goody's appointment. In a classic show of the Academy's independence, Handler ignored Fletcher's plea. Goody recalled how the episode played out:

> What happened was that the President of the Academy simply said nothing about it. He let them come and see him and make their objection, but he did nothing, didn't say a word to me, didn't tell me that they had visited him or anything. As far as he was concerned, their statements didn't exist. When I look back I realize that he had no choice, because the Academy has to act on its own and not on the behest of others. I mean, it can accept requests, but it doesn't accept orders…. This was purely a NASA problem, which we at the Academy had no intention of taking any notice of.[6]

Homer Newell described this event from his inside-NASA perspective in his 1980 book:

> But in the early 1970s the Academy of Sciences began to show great concern over questions of conflict of interest and potential charges of being captive to those it advised. Thus, when a new chairman was needed for the Space Science Board, instead of consulting with NASA on possible choices as had been the custom, the Academy unilaterally—as it had every right to do—selected a candidate. James Fletcher, the fourth NASA administrator, had doubts about the choice—doubts that were shared by the author—since the proposed chairman had previously shown little evidence of giving thought to the negative effect that his outspoken criticism of various space science projects could have on NASA's efforts to defend its budget on the Hill. NASA objected to the choice; the Academy stood firm; and Fletcher gave serious thought to withdrawing NASA's financial support from the board and relying on NASA's own committees for advice. In the end NASA fortunately did not sever the relationship with the board, and the new chairman did an excellent job.[7]

Standing Committees

When Berkner formed seven discipline-oriented, ad hoc committees at the SSB's first meeting, he also established five other implementation-oriented, ad hoc committees covering future vehicular development, international relations, near-term issues and problems, long-term space project planning, and general engineering services. Before retiring as SSB chair in 1962, Berkner led a reorganization of the Board in which the original set of ad hoc committees was replaced by a new executive committee and eight standing committees with the following areas of responsibility:

- Earth's Atmosphere,
- Environmental Biology,
- Exobiology,
- Geodesy,
- High Altitude Rocket and Balloon Research,
- International Relations,
- Man in Space, and
- Physical Contamination of Space.[8]

---

6. Goody interview, p. 2. All footnotes that cite NASA Oral History Program transcripts include the page number for the interview quotation cited in this text.

7. Homer E. Newell, *Beyond the Atmosphere: Early Years of Space Science* (NASA History Division, NASA Headquarters, Washington, DC, NASA SP-4211, 1980), p. 214.

8. Memorandum from Berkner to NAS President Detlev Bronk dated 5 January 1961, "Reorganization of the Space Science Board," NAS Archives, Washington, DC.

Interestingly, the old ad hoc committees covering astronomy, lunar and planetary exploration, meteorology, and physics of fields and particles in space were dissolved, because Berkner argued that their work was completed and NASA's plans were well underway in those fields. Of course, all those areas came home to roost and merited renewed attention just a few years later.

Throughout the SSB's first three decades, the work of the Board was often carried out by its standing committees or by ad hoc, topical committees, which often operated with oversight by the standing committees. Besides organizing and conducting advisory studies, the standing committees regularly met with senior NASA officials who were responsible for programs in the committees' areas of interest to stay abreast of program developments and plans and to promote communication between NASA and the interested scientific community. A full set of discipline-oriented standing committees was re-established in 1974 under Richard Goody as chair, and they were the same in 1988 when Thomas M. Donahue completed his six-year term as chair three decades after the SSB was formed, as follows:

- Committee on Earth Sciences from Space
- Committee on Space Astronomy and Astrophysics
- Committee on Data Management and Computation
- Committee on Planetary Biology and Evolution
- Committee on Planetary and Lunar Exploration
- Committee on Solar and Space Physics
- Committee on Space Biology and Medicine

This committee organizational structure largely reflected the way members of the research communities were organized and interacted with each other (or didn't). Astronomers belonged to the American Astronomical Society, and they rarely interacted with the Earth scientists who had their own professional societies. Likewise, the solar and space plasma physicists probably never interacted with the biologists, and their interests overlapped with relatively narrow sub-segments of the astronomy and Earth sciences communities. But the committee assignments made sense then in terms of scientific expertise, experience, and interests. The broadening of scientific perspectives occurred at the level of the SSB where all relevant disciplines came together. Later chapters will show how advisory activities began to take on more cross-disciplinary perspectives as the space science program evolved.

Science Strategies and Focused Reports

By 1988, the Board and its committees prepared more than 100 advisory reports for NASA. Of those, approximately 40 percent were major strategic reports, about 30 percent were focused topical reports, and 30 percent were letter reports to the NASA Administrator or other senior officials. Table 2.1 presents an abbreviated list of examples of reports of each type during the period.

The science strategies are particularly notable. The Board began with studies that outlined major scientific opportunities and broad priorities for the full range of fields in space science (e.g., the 1966 report "Space Research: Directions for the Future"[9]) and then revisited and updated that comprehensive look across all of space science in 1971 and 1988. The SSB also used its standing committees or formed specialized study committees to prepare more detailed examinations and to recommend scientific directions in a specific discipline (e.g., a 1968 study on "Planetary Exploration

---

9. National Research Council, *Space Research: Directions for the Future* (The National Academies Press, Washington, DC, 1966).

TABLE 2.1   Illustrative examples of SSB reports, 1958–1988*

Strategic Reports
A Review of Space Research (1962)
Space Research: Directions for the Future (1966)
Physics of the Earth in Space — A Program of Research: 1968–1975 (1968)
Planetary Exploration 1968–1975 (1968)
The Outer Solar System — A Program for Exploration (1969)
Priorities for Space Research: 1971–1980, Report of a Study on Space Science and Earth Observations Priorities (1971)
Space Plasma Physics — The Study of Solar System Plasmas (1978)
A Strategy for Space Astronomy and Astrophysics for the 1980s (1979)
Solar System Space Physics in the 1980s: A Research Strategy (1980)
Space Science in the Twenty-First Century — Overview (plus six discipline-specific volumes, 1988)

Focused Reports
The Atmospheres of Mars and Venus (1961)
Biology and the Exploration of Mars: Report of a Study Held Under the Auspices of the Space Science Board, National Academy of Sciences-National Research Council, 1964–1965 (1966)
Scientific Uses of the Large Space Telescope (1969)
Sounding Rockets: Their Role in Space Research (1969)
Institutional Arrangements for the Space Telescope — Report of a Study at Woods Hole, Massachusetts, July 19–30, 1976 (1976)
Recommendations for Planetary Quarantine for Mars, Jupiter, Saturn, Uranus, Neptune and Titan (1978)
Data Management and Computation — Volume I: Issues and Recommendations (1982)
The Role of Theory in Space Research (1983)
The Explorer Program for Astronomy and Astrophysics (1986)

Letter Reports
Policy Positions on (1) Man's Role in the National Space Program and (2) Support of Basic Research for Space Science (27 March 1961)
Report of the Ad Hoc Committee on NASA/University Relationships (1962)
Space Science Board Assessment of the Scientific Value of a Space Station (1983)
Space Telescope Science Issues (1983)
On the Continued Development of the Gravity Probe B Mission (1983)
The Categorization of the Mars Orbiter Mission (1985)
On the Balance of Shuttle and ELV Launches (1986)
Assessment of the Planned Scientific Content of the LGO, MAO, and NEAR Missions (1986)
On Mixed Launch Fleet and Policy Option (1987)
Assessment of Planned Scientific Content of the CRAF Mission (1987)

*All SSB reports are available at *http://sites.nationalacademies.org/SSB/index.htm*. The SSB also tracks the history of its advisory activities in its annual reports, which are posted at *http://sites.nationalacademies.org/SSB/SSB_051650*. One particularly useful feature of the annual reports is a set of diagrams that display timelines and relationships for SSB reports in each scientific discipline area.

1968–1975"[10] and a 1978 study on "Space Plasma Physics—The Study of Solar System Plasmas"[11]). All of the science strategies focused on scientific priorities, and they usually stopped short of addressing programmatic aspects such as implementation of spaceflight missions or research facilities. Thus, the science strategies stayed mostly true to NASA's request in 1960 that the Board concentrate on broad overall objectives and not be concerned with detailed program formulation. Nevertheless, they were especially important guides for NASA's scientific priorities, and they were forerunners of the decadal science strategy surveys that followed in later decades (see below and chapter 11).

However, it was not unusual for the SSB's focused study reports and letter reports to move into implementation issues. Sometimes these reports were prepared at the Board's initiative without receiving a request from NASA. For example, SSB chair A. G. W. Cameron established a committee on data management and computation in 1978, and the committee published its first report, "Data Management and Computation—Volume I: Issues and Recommendations,"[12] in 1982. In his Foreword to the report, Cameron wrote

> The present report on data management and computation was *prepared in response to our perception* [emphasis added] that data problems were pervasive throughout the space sciences. The data chain from satellite to ground to processing to principal investigator to reduction and analysis and archiving is central to all of space-science results. Yet it has suffered

from inefficiencies all along the line, ranging from inadequate funding and application of advanced technologies to indifference on the part of management and scientist alike. The present report of the SSB Committee on Data Management and Computation (CODMAC) systematically addresses these issues and makes recommendations for improved treatment all along the data chain.[13]

Thus, the report's 21 recommendations included a list of specific technologies that NASA needed to address as well as recommendations for organizational changes that, in CODMAC's view, were needed (specifically, creation of a software organization to support NASA's efforts). While the report heightened consciousness about these issues inside NASA, actions in response to the committee's specific recommendations were few and slow to develop. Andrew Stofan, who was Associate Administrator for the newly reorganized Office of Space Science and Applications, did create an Information Systems Office to focus on data system issues.[14]

A second example of a Board-initiated letter report is the February 1987 letter from SSB chair Donahue to NASA Administrator Fletcher regarding the Board's views on launch vehicles for space science missions. Prior to the Space Shuttle Challenger accident in February 1986, NASA had been pursuing a policy whereby the Shuttle was to be the primary launch vehicle for all NASA missions. Donahue expressed concerns about the lack of near-term robustness in NASA's launch

---

10. National Research Council, *Planetary Exploration: 1968–1975* (The National Academies Press, Washington, DC, 1968).

11. National Research Council, *Space Plasma Physics: The Study of Solar-System Plasmas* (The National Academies Press, Washington, DC, 1978).

12. National Research Council, *Data Management and Computation—Volume I: Issues and Recommendations* (The National Academies Press, Washington, DC, 1982).

13. National Research Council, *Data Management and Computation—Volume I: Issues and Recommendations* (The National Academies Press, Washington, DC, 1982), p. vii.

14. Alexander document files from the 19 November 1981 SESAC meeting, NASA HRC.

capabilities as the Agency began to consider a post-accident strategy that would employ a variety of expendable launch vehicles (ELVs) in addition to the Space Shuttle. The letter urged NASA to have "back up modes of launching"[15] upcoming science missions to alleviate possible schedule delays if future Shuttle launches were delayed in the years before the mixed-fleet strategy could be implemented. The letter went on to specifically recommend that:

- ELVs be acquired to launch ROSAT [German-U.S.-U.K X-ray observatory] in 1989; Mars Observer in 1990; EUVE [Extreme Ultraviolet Explorer] in 1991; and Wind, Geotail, and Polar [part of the multi-spacecraft International Solar-Terrestrial Program] in 1992.
- At least one backup Titan IV, with conversion hardware, be acquired to guard against failure to launch one of the three major 'planetary' missions, Galileo, Magellan, and Ulysses, during the 1989–1990 opportunities. We urge that an effort be made to launch both Galileo and Ulysses in 1989.
- The backup ELVs be used for later missions, such as CRAF [Comet Rendezvous and Asteroid Flyby], if they are not required for one of these missions.[16]

Donahue's letter implicitly acknowledged that there were budgetary implications accompanying the Board's proposal, but there was no reference to whether the Board had considered the budgetary realism of the SSB plan. In the end, all six spacecraft mentioned in the first point were launched on ELVs between 1990 and 1996, and Galileo, Magellan, and Ulysses remained on the Shuttle for successful launches from 1989 through 1990. While CRAF was cancelled later for other reasons, NASA did not pursue the Board's ideas about purchasing backup rockets.

On other occasions, such implementation-specific letters responded to a question for which NASA sought a quick authoritative answer. Such was the case with the 1962 "Report of the Ad Hoc Committee on NASA/University Relationships,"[17] in which a committee appointed by Berkner conducted a short study to answer NASA officials' questions about whether, and if so how, it would be appropriate to establish programs at universities to address national needs for a skilled science and engineering work force. This particular interaction between NASA and the SSB brought together NASA's interest in finding ways to satisfy its needs for a space-oriented workforce and the academic community's interest in creating new opportunities for research support. NASA Administrator Webb translated his interest in engaging universities in the space program into action by creating the Sustaining University Program,[18] and the SSB letter helped him make the case. The idea of a fundamental NASA commitment to universities was to become a recurring theme of advice from the scientific community, and NASA's response was sometimes supportive

15. Space Science Board letter report, "On Mixed Launch Fleet Strategy and Policy Option," Thomas M. Donahue to James E. Fletcher, 11 February 1987 (National Research Council, The National Academies Press, Washington, DC, 1987), p. 1.

16. Space Science Board letter report, "On Mixed Launch Fleet Strategy and Policy Option," Thomas M. Donahue to James E. Fletcher, 11 February 1987, p. 1.

17. National Research Council, Report of the ad hoc Committee on NASA/University Relationships (The National Academies Press, Washington, DC, 1962).

18. See W. Henry Lambright and Edwin A. Block, "Launching NASA's Sustaining University Program" (Inter-university Case Program, Syracuse NY, 1969) and also John M. Logsdon, Exploring the Unknown: Selected Documents in the History of the U.S. Civilian Space Program, Vol. II: External Relationships, NASA History Division, NASA Headquarters, Washington DC, 1996), pp. 420–421.

and sometimes indifferent, especially at the very highest levels of the Agency.

A 1985 letter from the chair of the Board's Committee on Planetary Biology and Chemical Evolution on "The Categorization of the Mars Orbiter Mission" is another example of a prompt response to a specific question from NASA. NASA needed quick guidance regarding appropriate planetary protection[19] provisions for the mission. In this case, the committee reviewed NASA's plans on 15 and 16 May 1985 and made specific recommendations for clean-room standards and risk assessment limits in a letter to NASA on 6 June.[20] NASA was able to meet its September deadline for completing the final planetary protection plan for the mission and to comply with the committee's recommendations.[21]

Finally, the SSB also prepared several reports that made implementation recommendations as a follow-up to prior science strategy reports. For example, in the 1980s the SSB Committee on Planetary and Lunar Exploration (COMPLEX) prepared several science strategy reports for aspects of the planetary sciences, and COMPLEX then followed up on its strategy recommendations by reviewing the programs that NASA subsequently proposed in response to the strategy. One such review was the committee's 1985 "Assessment of Planned Scientific Content of the CRAF [Comet Rendezvous and Asteroid Flyby] Mission,"[22] in which the COMPLEX provided its views about how NASA intended to act on recommendations from the committee's 1980 "Strategy for the Exploration of Primitive Solar System Bodies—Asteroids, Comets, and Meteoroids: 1980–1990."[23] In the opening of the 1985 report, COMPLEX made its approach clear:

As you know, it is the practice of COMPLEX to assess the scientific content of a mission, as it nears proposal as a new-start candidate, in order to measure how well the agency has responded, in a mission context, to the committee's science strategy. The conclusions of the assessment are a measure of the support of the committee and the Space Science Board for the proposed planetary mission. The committee intends to make further Assessments during the development period of the mission leading to launch.[24]

The phrase "a measure of the support of the committee and the Space Science Board" above illustrates an interesting aspect of the SSB's clout during the 1970s and early 1980s. NASA and the scientific community regularly sought SSB blessing for new-start candidates, and here COMPLEX was saying that this report would render a verdict on CRAF.

19. Planetary protection involves the prevention of biological contamination of other solar system bodies by spacecraft from Earth and of terrestrial contamination by samples returned to Earth.

20. Letter from Harold P. Klein, chair of the Committee on Planetary Biology and Chemical Evolution, to Arnauld E. Nicogossian, Director of Life Sciences, "On Categorization of the Mars Orbiter Mission: Letter Report"(National Research Council, The National Academies Press, Washington, DC, 6 June 1985).

21. Michael Meltzer, When Biospheres Collide: A History of NASA's Planetary Protection Programs (NASA History Division, NASA Headquarters, Washington, DC, NASA SP-2011-4234, 2011), p. 372.

22. National Research Council, Assessment of Planned Scientific Content of the CRAF Mission Letter Report (The National Academies Press, Washington, DC, 1985).

23. National Research Council, Strategy for the Exploration of Primitive Solar-System Bodies—Asteroids, Comets, and Meteoroids: 1980–1990 (The National Academies Press, Washington, DC, 1980).

24. Space Science Board, Assessment of Planned Scientific Content of the CRAF Mission, Letter Report (National Research Council, The National Academies Press, Washington, DC, 1985), p. 1.

Another example of a strategy follow-up report is the 1985 report by the Board's Committee on Solar and Space Physics, "An Implementation Plan for Priorities in Solar-System Space Physics."[25] That report built on the committee's 1980 report, "Solar System Space Physics in the 1980s: A Research Strategy,"[26] and it recommended missions and mission priorities, launch rates, and supporting research programs and facilities and discussed budget levels and decisions that would be required to accomplish the recommended program. Then in 1991, the committee followed up on its follow-up with "Assessment of Programs in Solar and Space Physics,"[27] which examined the state of NASA's responses to the NRC's advice over the preceding decade. The 1991 report is an interesting forerunner to what later became a regular series of legislatively mandated SSB assessment reports (see chapter 11). It is also notable as an example of the SSB's occasional collaboration with other units of the NRC. In this case, the report was prepared jointly with the Committee on Solar-Terrestrial Relations of the Board on Atmospheric Science and Climate. The two committees worked together routinely starting in 1990.

The 1986 letter report by COMPLEX, "Assessment of the Planned Scientific Content of the LGO, MAO, and NEAR Missions,"[28] provides an interesting example of interactions between the SSB and NASA's internal advisory committees. In 1978, COMPLEX produced a "Strategy for the Exploration of the Inner Planets: 1977–1987,"[29] which included the committee's recommendations for the primary scientific objectives of studies of Mars and the Moon. A complementary 1980 COMPLEX report, "Strategy for the Exploration of Primitive Solar-System Bodies—Asteroids, Comets, and Meteoroids: 1980–1990,"[30] outlined similar priorities for those bodies. Then in 1983, NASA's own Solar System Exploration Committee (See chapter 5 for a discussion of NASA internal committees.) recommended three moderate-scale missions in a report entitled "Planetary Exploration Through the Year 2000: A Core Program."[31] Thus, the 1986 COMPLEX report was an SSB-sponsored evaluation of the response by a NASA committee to an earlier, SSB-sponsored, science strategy. This approach of linking science strategy recommendations to implementation plans to implementation assessments was repeated in several forms in ensuing years. (See chapter 11.)

Letter Reports

Both kinds of regular study reports (i.e., strategic and topical) were generally developed after a period of information collection by the study committee, consultations with additional experts,

25. National Research Council, *An Implementation Plan for Priorities in Solar-System Space Physics* (The National Academies Press, Washington, DC, 1985).

26. National Research Council. *Solar-System Space Physics in the 1980's: A Research Strategy* (The National Academies Press, Washington, DC, 1980).

27. National Research Council, *Assessment of Programs in Solar and Space Physics—1991* (The National Academies Press, Washington, DC, 1991).

28. National Research Council, *Assessment of Planned Scientific Content of the LGO, MAO, and NEAR Missions: Letter Report* (The National Academies Press, Washington, DC, 1986). LGO was Lunar Geoscience Observer; MAO was Mars Aeronomy Observer; and NEAR was Near Earth Asteroid Rendezvous.

29. National Research Council, *Strategy for Exploration of the Inner Planets: 1977–1987* (The National Academies Press, Washington, DC, 1978).

30. National Research Council, *Strategy for the Exploration of Primitive Solar-System Bodies—Asteroids, Comets, and Meteoroids: 1980–1990* (The National Academies Press, Washington, DC, 1980).

31. Solar System Exploration Committee, *Planetary Exploration through the Year 2000: Part 1: A Core Program* (NASA Advisory Council, NASA Headquarters, Washington, DC, 1983).

and internal committee discussions. However, the letter reports were often "eminence-based." That is, they were founded upon the collective expertise and experience of the Board members themselves and drafted in a few months or less. The Board's first initiative of this type was a 1961 letter from Berkner to NASA Administrator Webb, in which Berkner outlined two policy positions that the Board wished to communicate to NASA. The first position addressed "Man's Role in the National Space Program" and stated that "scientific exploration of the Moon and planets should be clearly stated as the ultimate objective of the U.S. space program for the foreseeable future."[32] Such a bold piece of advice to the leader of NASA—telling him not only what should be the principal goal of the nation's new space program but also that the goal should be communicated broadly and with fanfare—reflected the confidence with which the SSB embraced its early role. Chutzpah, one might say. NASA did continue to support a strong science program, thanks in no small measure to vigilant efforts by Homer Newell and other insiders (see chapter 3), but science never rose above the Apollo program as the Agency's flagship endeavor.

The second issue in Berkner's 1961 letter, which "represented careful discussions over a period of some three years," concerned NASA support for basic research. Here the letter articulated a set of principles for a basic research program, "quite aside from current flight-package and related research," that the SSB viewed as essential "for the long-range success of our national space efforts."[33] This point, about the importance of the basic scientific underpinnings of the program, was a theme that has remained central to SSB advice throughout its history. It is also reminiscent of the earlier NACA debates over emphasis on basic aeronautical science versus applied research.

As time went by, members of the Board became especially interested in the option of preparing letter reports, and, sometimes, NASA also found this approach to be preferred. Both the SSB and NASA appreciated the Board's ability to prepare a brief report with specific recommendations quickly and with minimal bureaucratic overhead. The letter reports were usually drafted by the members of the Board itself and communicated to the appropriate agency official by the Board (or standing committee) chair. Thus, they drew on the collective experience of the members, all of whom were usually distinguished experts from across the scientific, technical, and policy spectrum for space science. When NASA needed a prompt answer to a specific question, usually about policy rather than detailed technical issues, the SSB could respond via a letter report. Of course, there were also times when NASA might just as well have preferred not to receive a report at all. The Board sometimes prepared letter reports at its own discretion without receiving a request from NASA, and these reports also carried the full weight of the SSB and the NRC when they were delivered. [See chapter 9 for more discussion of the introduction of specific NRC policies on letter reports in the 2000s.]

In addition to formal letter reports, which were produced by the Board or an authoring study committee, the Board chair himself also prepared letters to NASA officials from time to time. For example, in 1983 SSB chair Donahue wrote to NASA Administrator James M. Beggs to forward recommendations regarding "Space Telescope Science Issues." In this letter, while applauding NASA for its leadership and commitment to the program, Donahue also voiced concerns about (a) how NASA was obtaining scientific advice for use in the Space Telescope program, (b) whether there were adequate provisions for testing telescope

32. National Research Council, *Policy Positions on (1) Man's Role in the National Space Program and (2) Support of Basic Research for Space Science* (The National Academies Press, Washington, DC, 31 March 1961), p. 2.

33. National Research Council, *Policy Positions on (1) Man's Role in the National Space Program and (2) Support of Basic Research for Space Science* (The National Academies Press, Washington, DC, 31 March 1961), p. 1.

instruments, and (c) the need to protect other high-priority science missions from the impacts of possible Space Telescope development problems.[34]

Donahue was a space scientist whose specialty was the study of planetary atmospheres. His research career began with the use of high-altitude sounding rockets and moved into space flight missions to the Moon, Venus, and the outer solar system. Donahue was a gregarious leader who guided the SSB through a notably active and occasionally confrontational period. The use of letter reports and letters from the chair expanded during Donahue's tenure from 1982 to 1988, during which time the SSB sent 25 letters or letter reports to NASA.[35] During that time he also worked closely with his scientific colleague Frank McDonald, who was NASA chief scientist over the same period, to maintain a continuing dialog between the SSB and the NASA Administrator's office. On more than one occasion Donahue and McDonald collaborated on initiating SSB studies to advise NASA and to elicit NASA commitments on behalf of space science.

Summer Studies

One of Berkner's actions during the 1962 reorganization of the SSB was initiation of a series of nearly annual summer studies. The Board's first summer study was hosted by Van Allen at the University of Iowa over an eight-week period from 17 June to 10 August 1962. It was a massive undertaking with

over 100 outside scientists as full- or part-time participants, along with scientists and managers from NASA and representatives from the Department of Defense, Atomic Energy Commission, National Science Foundation, and National Bureau of Standards. The study's findings and recommendations, some of which were rather general, and others of which were quite detailed, covered topics that ranged from flight program science and technology to administrative and policy matters and international cooperation to the social implications of space activities. These outcomes and the summaries of the work of the various topical working groups from which the conclusions were derived were published together in a single SSB document, "A Review of Space Research," in 1962.[36]

The practice of conducting summer studies remained a staple of the SSB's activities through the 1970s. During the period 1962 to 1978, the Board sponsored 15 summer studies, some of which ran concurrently and which covered topics ranging from biology and human physiology to solar system exploration to scientific uses of the Space Shuttle.[37] The major summer study effort of the mid-1980s compared with or exceeded the scope of the original summer study in 1962. In early 1984, NASA Administrator Beggs asked Donahue to undertake a long-range study to identify the major new scientific advances in space research, as well as necessary technology advances that could be expected during the period from about 1995 to 2015.[38] This study was subsequently organized

34. Space Science Board, *Space Telescope Science Issues: Letter Report* (National Research Council, The National Academies Press, Washington, DC, 1983).

35. See National Academies of Sciences, Engineering, and Medicine, *Space Studies Board Annual Report 2015* (The National Academies Press, Washington DC, 2016), pp. 83–85.

36. Space Science Board, *A Review of Space Research* (National Research Council, The National Academies Press, Washington, DC, 1962).

37. SSB files, NAS Archives, Washington, DC.

38. Letter from Beggs to Donahue, 7 February 1984, NAS Archives, Washington, DC. The letter was quite possibly drafted by Frank McDonald after consultation with Donahue. It probably represented McDonald's effort to ensure that space science received appropriate attention at a time when much of NASA's attention was on completing development of the Space Shuttle and securing a go-ahead for the Space Station program.

for the summer of 1984, and work continued on it through 1986. The results were published in 1988 in a seven-volume report, "Space Science in the Twenty-First Century: Imperatives for the Decades 1995 to 2015."[39]

Summer studies subsequently waned as a feature of SSB activities and products, partly due to the budget constraints of the SSB's principal sponsor, NASA, and partly due to increasing time constraints being felt by many potential summer study participants. The latter limitation reflected an increasing demand for experts' time for their own research, responsibilities at their home institutions, and increasing demand for service in other advisory functions (e.g., NASA in-house committees, proposal peer reviews, etc.) One might also suspect that the SSB members and staff were simply exhausted after the 1984–1988 effort.

International Activities

The original charge to the SSB included responsibility to follow international aspects of space research and "to represent the Academy-Research Council in our international relations in this field on behalf of American science and scientists."[40] When the International Council of Scientific Unions formed the Committee on Space Research (COSPAR) in 1958 to promote and exploit international opportunities for scientific activities in space, the SSB became the official U.S. National Committee to COSPAR.

The Board's studies on planetary protection had a unique international impact. NASA regularly forwarded SSB recommendations on planetary protection standards and protocols to COSPAR where they usually were adopted as international standards.

In addition to COSPAR, the Board also established other formal and informal international links. Its standing committees on solar and space physics and on planetary and lunar exploration often invited European liaison representatives to participate in committee meetings. After the European Science Foundation established the European Space Science Committee (ESSC) in 1975 as the closest equivalent to the SSB in Europe, the SSB and the ESSC began a long-standing liaison relationship. There were also occasional joint projects, including a 1976 workshop on international views about space observatories[41] and a 1983 international workshop on solar and space physics.[42] The former helped build the case, which was still somewhat controversial at the time, for the Large Space Telescope that eventually became the Hubble Space Telescope, and the latter helped develop momentum for what eventually became the International Solar-Terrestrial Physics program. The SSB and the ESSC followed up on the 1976 workshop with a 1978 review (and endorsement) of the proposed focal plane instruments that NASA and the European Space Agency had selected for the Space Telescope.[43]

---

39. National Research Council, *Space Science in the Twenty-First Century: Imperatives for the Decades 1995 to 2015, Overview* (The National Academies Press, Washington, DC, 1988).

40. Bronk letter to Berkner, 26 June 1958.

41. Space Science Board and European Science Foundation, *An International Discussion of Space Observatories: Report of a Conference Held at Williamsburg, Virginia, 26–29 January 1976* (National Research Council, The National Academies Press, Washington DC, 1976).

42. National Research Council, *An International Discussion on Research in Solar and Space Physics* (The National Academies Press, Washington, DC, 1983).

43. Space Science Board and European Science Foundation, *Space Telescope Instrument Review Committee: First Report* (National Academy of Sciences, The National Academies Press, Washington DC, 1978).

Report Peer Review

During the SSB's early years, reports issued under SSB auspices were usually drafted by a few members and then reviewed by the full Board membership. When authoring committees completed a draft report, the draft was forwarded to the Board for members to read and comment upon. Reports that were to be issued by the Board itself were prepared during discussions at Board meetings, or by a small drafting group, or sometimes by the chair with NRC staff assistance. In each case, the whole membership had an opportunity to review the draft. This was an efficient process that was sometimes accomplished in a matter of a few weeks. On the other hand, the review process could be criticized for being insular, not sufficiently broad and independent, and potentially biased.[44]

By the early 1970s, the Board often permitted senior NASA officials to sit in on meetings where they would reach some agreement on items being discussed, after which the Board chair would send a letter to the NASA Administrator describing what they had agreed upon. None of these letters subsequently appeared in official listings of SSB reports. Richard Goody, who became SSB chair in 1974, described provisions for independent review of informal board reports when he took office as "really weak at that time."[45]

Some members of the National Academy of Sciences began to question the wisdom of such an unfettered approach to interacting with government agencies in an advisory capacity. In response to these kinds of concerns all across the institution, the National Research Council created a Report Review Committee (RRC) in 1972 to oversee independent, expert, peer review of all NRC reports. The first chair of the RRC was George Kistiakowsky, a Harvard physical chemistry professor who had served as President Eisenhower's science advisor and who was vice president of the NAS.

At first, the new RRC process of report review may have had little impact other than to ensure that the boards could no longer operate totally independently. Goody recalled the approach to report review leading up to formation of the RRC:

> It was my impression that the structure of report review was pretty chaotic at that time. Then the President of the Academy decided that it needed a stronger hand at the helm.... It was later that the Report Review Committee became what it is today.... But it is a fact that when we issued reports, we would review them ourselves … and often there wasn't much in the way of review outside of that.[46]

Goody also noted that when he became SSB chair in 1974 the RRC chair warned him that the SSB was not to send letters to the NASA Administrator without approval.

The new RRC did establish guidelines and a process for report review that remained largely unchanged from that time forward. Those guidelines require that before a report can be delivered to a sponsor and released to the public on behalf of the authoring group and the NRC, it must be reviewed by experts who have had no role in the drafting of the report and who are asked to examine the report for quality, objectivity, evidentiary credibility, and adherence to the study charge. The authoring group must consider and provide some response to (but not necessarily comply with) all reviewers' comments. A member of the RRC or a person selected to serve on the RRC's behalf oversees the review process and is empowered to recommend approval of the report once the review is completed. Only then does the

---

44. Goody interview, pp. 3–4.

45. Goody interview, p. 3.

46. Goody interview, p.4

RRC recommend that the report be given a final NRC approval.[47]

Astronomy Decadal Surveys

The SSB was the principal source of scientific advice to NASA, but one other advisory activity had a particularly important impact during NASA's first few decades, and its impact grew even greater later. In 1962, the National Academy of Sciences Committee on Science and Public Policy (COSPUP) formed a panel on astronomical facilities to assess the status and future needs for new ground-based astronomical facilities in the United States. The committee's 1964 report[48] considered the state of observing facilities as well as trends in graduate student enrollment in astronomy and their implications for demand for astronomy facilities in the country. The panel confined its attention to needs and priorities for ground-based facilities even though it recognized the emerging opportunities for space astronomy in the U.S. space program.

Five years later, COSPUP formed a new Astronomy Survey Committee that had a substantially broader and more ambitious charge — namely, to review the state of U.S. astronomy, identify the most important scientific problems in the field, and recommend priorities for both ground-based and space astronomy for the coming decade. The scope of the new study[49] — reviewing progress over the past decade and recommending priorities for the next decade — led to the study being popularly called a "decadal survey."

Subsequent astronomy and astrophysics decadal surveys were completed approximately every ten years through 2010 under joint leadership of the NRC Board on Physics and Astronomy and the SSB. The fact that the decadal surveys were developed with broad input from the astronomical community and that they recommended explicit priorities made them extraordinarily persuasive with government decision makers. Chapter 11 will discuss the evolution, expansion, and impacts of the decadal surveys in detail.

Aeronautics and Space Engineering Board

In 1967, the NRC created an Aeronautics and Space Engineering Board (ASEB), both to cover the first "A" in NASA and to serve as a sister unit to the SSB covering space engineering and technology.[50] The ASEB's charter emphasized aerospace engineering topics such as space transportation and propulsion systems research, human spaceflight systems engineering and risk analysis, and the full panoply of technological areas that were not focused on fundamental science in and from space.[51] As time went by, the ASEB and SSB conducted a few studies jointly, especially with respect to identifying needs for advanced technology development, but they largely worked independently though the 1970s and 1980s.[52]

---

47. See a description of the NRC study process, including report peer review, at *http://www.nationalacademies.org/studyprocess/index.html#st4*.

48. Committee on Science and Public Policy, *Ground-Based Astronomy: A Ten-Year Program* (National Academy of Sciences-National Research Council, National Academy Press, Washington, DC, 1964) stated in the report's Foreword.

49. Astronomy Survey Committee, *Astronomy and Astrophysics for the 1970s* (National Academy of Sciences, National Academy Press, Washington, DC, 1972).

50. ASEB files, NAS Archives, Washington, DC.

51. A complete list of ASEB reports dating from 1977 to the present is available on the Board's Web site: *http://sites.nationalacademies.org/deps/ASEB/index.htm*.

52. In 2007, the NRC staffs of the two boards were merged under a single staff director. The arrangement promoted closer coordination between the two boards, but their roles and responsibilities remained unchanged.

Space Applications Board

The SSB and the ASEB were not the only elements of the NRC to provide advice to the government on space research. There were early advocates for the practical applications of space as well as for basic scientific studies, and NASA began to explore such opportunities in parallel with its initial efforts to develop a scientific satellite program. The first meteorological satellite, TIROS-1,[53] was launched in 1960, and several Advanced Technology Satellites were launched beginning in 1966 to develop and test technologies for space-borne communications and Earth-imaging systems. As interest in space applications grew, so did the need for NASA to seek outside expert advice about these opportunities.

In late 1966, Administrator Webb asked the NRC to study the useful applications of Earth-oriented satellites, and that request led to a series of summer studies conducted under the auspices of the NRC Division of Engineering in 1967 and 1968. The project was chaired by physicist, mathematician, and engineer Deming Lewis, who was President of Lehigh University. Deming's central review committee drew on the work of 13 topical panels that were organized around particular application areas such as forestry, agriculture, and geography; oceanography; and point-to-point communications; as well as on cross-program topics such as economic factors and cost-benefit relationships. The study report appeared in two parts—first, a summary of the panel findings and recommendations, and, second, an overview report from the central review committee.[54]

The project had one interesting hiccup that illustrates the effects of the Cold War environment of the times. All of the study activities were conducted in an open, unclassified setting. One of the technical panels was organized around geodesy and cartography, and the panel produced its summer study report just like all the other panels. That report was sent to NASA in early 1968 as part of an interim report on the project, during which NASA conducted security clearance reviews of all the reports. To the NRC's surprise, NASA requested that the geodesy and cartography panel report be given a Secret security classification, and so the NRC staff recalled all the existing copies and had them destroyed, albeit well after numerous copies had been circulated amongst the study participants. In the end, the name of the geodesy and cartography panel was included in the list of study panels, but its report was not mentioned and did not appear in the final reports. The NRC staff never learned why the panel report was classified, and participants were told that the only person at the NRC who had sufficient clearances to know the answer was NAS President Frederick Seitz.[55] One can make a reasonable guess that the open discussion of advanced capabilities in those scientific areas might have been threatening to classified military intelligence gathering programs that depended on precise satellite orbit determination and camera pointing systems.

Nevertheless, all the rest of the reports were released, and the principal conclusions were very positive about the prospects for space applications. They made useful recommendations about potential applications projects, needs for advanced technology R&D, and expectations for cost-benefit impacts, and they recommended that NASA increase its investments in the area by a factor of two or three above its $100 million annual level in 1969.

---

53. TIROS was an acronym for Television Infrared Observation Satellite.

54. Summer Study on Space Applications, *Useful Applications of Earth-Oriented Satellites* (National Research Council, National Academy of Sciences, Washington, DC, 1969).

55. Letter from L. R. Daspit, study executive director, to John S. Coleman, NAS executive officer, regarding how to handle the geodesy and cartography report, 7 August 1968, NAS Archives, Washington, DC. The author is not aware of any classified SSB reports.

One consequence of the 1969 workshops was that in late 1971 NASA indicated its support for the formation of a space applications board to operate in parallel with the SSB, and the President of the National Academy of Engineering commissioned an organizing committee in 1972. The committee, chaired by Allen E. Puckett, who was executive vice president and assistant general manager of Hughes Aircraft Company, submitted its report recommending creation of the board in early 1973, and the Space Applications Board (SAB) was formally established in December 1973. The original areas covered by the SAB included the applications topics that had been covered by the earlier workshops—communication services, Earth resources services, and environmental services—and also one more that had not been covered in the 1967–1968 workshops—manufacturing and materials processing in space.[56] Puckett was appointed as the first SAB chair and amongst the initial members were Daniel J. Fink of General Electric Corporation and William A. Nierenberg of Scripps Institute of Oceanography, both of whom later served as chairs of the NASA Advisory Council.

One of the SAB's first actions was to organize a more broadly ranging 1974 successor to the prior summer studies. The report of that effort—"Practical Applications of Space Systems"[57]—made recommendations about improving federal institutional arrangements to encourage and set policies and priorities for meeting non-military space applications needs, roles for the Space Shuttle in space applications programs, and important applications areas such as hazard monitoring and prediction and land-use management.

In 1982, the SAB organized a new summer study in response to NASA's request for advice on conducting applications research on the Space Station. As with the earlier summer studies, the SAB utilized several topical panels—for example, on Earth resources, environmental measurements, and materials science and engineering—to carry out the task. In addition to highlighting opportunities and technology development needs in each area, the final report[58] made three interesting broader recommendations. First, it suggested that the Space Station program include a multi-instrument polar-orbiting platform for Earth remote sensing. This idea helped spawn the concept of a Space Station polar platform, but the concept eventually died as it became clear that any real connections with the low-orbit-inclination Space Station program were bogus. The second overarching conclusion was that NASA should expect to devote as much attention to developing equipment to *use* the Space Station as to constructing the Station itself. And finally, the report concluded that there were important opportunities for having people on the ground to operate systems on the Station via telepresence and without needing an on-orbit crew.

One more report is notable as an example of the SAB's activities. In 1983, the Board formed the Committee on Practical Applications of Remote Sensing from Space to examine the U.S. civil remote sensing program and determine why it was not prospering as it should. Ralph Bernstein, who was a digital image processing expert and senior technical leader at IBM, chaired the 22-person committee. After working for more than a year, the committee submitted its (largely technical) draft report to the SAB for review, but the Board declined to accept the report because SAB members believed the problems were due to policy and institutional issues, not technical ones. The Board wrote its own

---

56. See report of the Organizing Committee for the Space Applications Board submitted to the President of the NAE, 5 February 1973, NAS Archives, Washington, DC.

57. Space Applications Board, *Practical Applications of Space Systems* (National Research Council, National Academy of Sciences Press, Washington, DC, 1975).

58. Space Applications Board, *Practical Applications of a Space Station* (National Research Council, National Academy Press, Washington DC, 1984).

report, drawing on material from the committee, but developing a long list of findings and recommendations that stemmed from the Board's views of the policy problems.[59] Thus, the report's recommendations had to do with fixing an unacceptably incoherent and uncoordinated federal program, resolving rigid and divisive relationships between NOAA and NASA, and moving NOAA out of the Department of Commerce. Over the next two decades (not exactly an example of prompt government action), many of the NOAA-NASA roles and responsibilities issues were fixed, but as chapter 11 will show, a major 2005 SSB study found that the U.S. program was still suffering from many of the ills that the SAB highlighted two decades earlier.

In September 1988, NASA Associate Administrator Lennard A. Fisk met with NAS President Frank Press and suggested that the NRC consider eliminating the SAB and consolidating the three space research boards into just two—one of which could be primarily science oriented and the other engineering oriented. Fisk was not reacting to the critical conclusions of the 1985 SAB report above; rather, he had done a similar thing when he merged his three internal NASA advisory committees into a single committee for his office. Fisk also hoped that such a consolidation would reduce the overall costs to NASA of NRC advice.[60]

The idea was attractive to senior NRC officials, and David L. Bodde, who was executive director of the NRC Commission on Engineering and Technical Systems, was charged to develop a plan for the transition. Bodde's plan provided for dissolving the SAB when its NASA contract expired in February 1989 and moving responsibilities for studies and advice on Earth remote sensing, materials sciences in microgravity, and data systems for space research and operations to the SSB. Other former SAB roles in the areas of space communications, microgravity manufacturing and materials processing, engineering technology, and space commercialization in general would be moved to the Aeronautics and Space Engineering Board.[61]

When word got out about impending NRC plans to dissolve the SAB, there were not unexpected objections from some members and supporters of the space applications community. SAB chair, former DOD and aerospace industry executive Richard D. DeLauer, supported a change, but he appealed to Press to keep the SAB responsibilities all together and transfer them wholly to either the SSB or the ASEB so as to avoid subordination of applications. DeLauer also gave Press a sense of the community pushback when he quoted one anonymous correspondent who said, "This is an overt attempt by the science fraternity to deemphasize applications and thereby reduce the competition for the limited funds."[62]

The NASA Advisory Council, which was NASA's primary internal advisory body comprised of outside experts (see chapter 5), also raised a red flag about the NRC plans. Council chair John L. McLucas, a former Secretary of the Air Force and former president of the COMSAT Corporation, wrote to NASA Administrator Fletcher to say that at its 21 November 1988 meeting the Council was concerned that "the proposed termination of the Space Applications Board of the National Research Council may be seriously detrimental to the

59. Space Applications Board, *Remote Sensing of the Earth from Space: A Program in Crisis* (National Research Council, National Academy Press, Washington DC, 1985).

60. E-mail message from NRC Executive Officer Phil Smith to Executive Director of the Commission on Engineering Systems and Technology David Bodde, "ASEB – SAB – SSB," 9 September 1988, NAS Archives, Washington, DC.

61. E-mail from David Bodde to Frank Press, Phil Smith, and NAE President Robert White, "Game Plan for Space Applications Board," 26 September 1988, NAS Archives, Washington, DC.

62. Letter from Richard DeLauer to Frank Press on transferring functions and responsibilities of the SAB to the SSB, 29 November 1988, NAS Archives, Washington, DC.

Nation's programs of space applications."[63] Fletcher had already indicated his support for the change, but perhaps to mollify the Council, he wrote to Press urging the NRC to "assure that the realignment satisfies the total range of NASA programs receiving National Research Council advice" and also to "be sensitive to the views of other external bodies, including the Congress."[64]

Press, however, was convinced that the reorganization was the right way to go. He had become concerned about the relatively low level of SAB activity in recent years, and he had full confidence that the new chair of the SSB, Louis Lanzerotti from AT&T Bell Laboratories, could deal effectively with a board having combined scientific and applications interests.[65] Press may also have felt that the way to resolve the SAB's occasional struggles to walk an appropriate line between providing advice on technological issues for space applications versus advocating on behalf of commercial space applications interests would be to put the SAB's responsibilities in units that had clear scientific and technological charters. Press formally announced the realignments along the lines of Bodde's plan in March 1989.

At about the same time as the NRC discussions of dissolution of the SAB, physicist Louis Lanzerotti succeeded Tom Donahue as SSB chair. He was a past SSB member and had chaired its Committee on Solar and Space Physics, and he also had served on key NASA science committees (see chapter 5). Upon taking office, Lanzerotti initiated a board self-assessment in which the SSB consulted widely with government agency and congressional representatives and members of the space research community about future directions for the Board and engaged in its own review of the structure and future priorities for the Board. This process facilitated a smooth integration of former SAB responsibilities into the SSB. The SAB's work on Earth remote sensing was assimilated under the SSB's Committee on Earth Sciences, and a new Committee on Microgravity Research was formed to cover the former SAB attention to materials processing and science in space. Recognizing that the SSB's most recent science strategy reports were still timely and that NASA's Office of Space Science and Applications had just created its own comprehensive strategic plan (see chapter 7), the Board decided to hold further science strategy studies in abeyance. Instead, the SSB would focus for the next five years on monitoring NASA's progress in pursuing those strategies and also turn its attention to issues related to human spaceflight, cross-disciplinary priority-setting, and needs for technology development for future science missions.[66]

The SSB made one other change that might have appeared to be cosmetic but that communicated an important transition in the character of the Board. It changed its name from Space Science Board to Space Studies Board, thereby acknowledging its new, expanded roles after the SAB termination. Thus, as NASA marked the end of its first three decades, the Space Studies Board stood ready to continue to provide advice on the full range of NASA science activities. The next few chapters will examine some key concurrent developments that affected the overall climate for scientific advice in NASA's first 30 years.

63. Letter from NAC chair John McLucas to NASA Administrator James Fletcher communicating the NAC statement on the "Proposed Termination of the Space Applications Board," 19 December 1988, NAS Archives, Washington, DC.

64. Letter from NASA Administrator James Fletcher to NAS President Frank Press regarding "impending reassignment of the former functions of the SAB to the SSB and ASEB, 21 November 1988, NAS Archives, Washington, DC.

65. E-mail from Frank Press to National Academy of Engineering President Robert White, "Gameplan for Space Applications Board," 6 October 1988, NAS Archives, Washington, DC.

66. SSB files, NAS Archives, Washington, DC.

CHAPTER 3

NASA's Internal Advisory Committees

At the same time that the young NASA invited scientific advice from the Space Science Board, and even included the SSB on its formal organization charts, the Agency also formed its own internal advisory committees. These committees continued the long established practice of the NACA and the work of the rocket panel and its successors at the Naval Research Laboratory (NRL). This action also reflected, in part, the fact that while NASA inherited many aeronautical science experts from the NACA, its early in-house staff had relatively less expertise in the space and geophysical sciences. The latter scientists had come mainly from NRL's rocket and Vanguard teams and had transferred to NASA Headquarters or to the new Beltsville Space Center (later to become the Goddard Space Flight Center) in Maryland. NASA's formation of internal advisory committees involving outside scientists also served to promote more communication between NASA and the outside scientific community. In addition, it gave that community an added sense that NASA was open and sensitive to the views of the outside community. Homer Newell described a sometimes rocky relationship between NASA and its advisory committees, especially in the late 1960s and early 1970s.[1] Committee members often shared the concerns of much of the outside scientific community that NASA science would be subordinated to the larger and more costly Gemini and Apollo human spaceflight programs. There was also an undercurrent of concern that NASA officials would not always take the outside advice seriously.

The dual advisory structure, with both NASA-inside and SSB-outside advisors, was obviously subject to some overlaps in the responsibilities of the two advisory entities. But the two approaches reached an approximate equilibrium. (See figure 3.1 for an overview of some key advisory body milestones.) The NASA committees were often tasked to address issues that were more tactical in nature and that required relatively fast responses, and the SSB more often was tasked to address longer-term issues. However, as we shall see below, NASA's own suite of internal committees grew into a tiered structure in which lower-level committees often reported to more senior committees that did, indeed, delve into advice for NASA about long-range goals, etc. And the previous chapter showed that the SSB was not especially shy about digging into implementation matters when that seemed to be required.

---

1. Homer E. Newell, *Beyond the Atmosphere: Early Years of Space Science*, (NASA History Office, Washington, DC, NASA SP-4211, 1980), ch. 12.

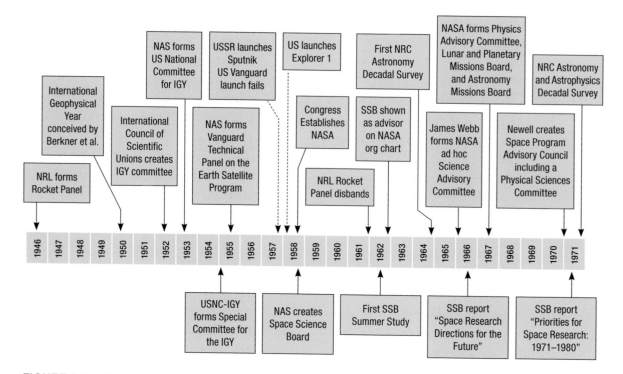

FIGURE 3.1   Timeline of key advisory events, 1946 to 1971

Early Ad Hoc Committees

Some of NASA's first ad hoc advisory bodies were discipline-oriented subcommittees formed to assist the all-NASA-employee Space Science Steering Committee in planning future programs and in evaluating proposals and recommending selections of investigations for space flight missions.[2] However, according to Newell, many of the outside scientists were concerned about whether they were able to have a broader impact on NASA's overall space science program, how NASA dealt with conflicts of interest as it solicited advice, and generally how NASA should deal with universities and university scientists. In early 1966, NASA Administrator Webb invited Harvard professor Norman F. Ramsey to lead an ad hoc science

advisory committee that would have a much broader mandate than experiment selection and that would examine a wide range of space science program implementation issues.[3]

Ramsey earned a doctorate in physics from Columbia University in 1940 after studying at the Cavendish Laboratory at Cambridge University, where he met many of the leading figures in physics at the time. During World War II, Ramsey was intimately involved in operational aspects of the Manhattan Project. After the war, he returned to Columbia. In one of history's many interesting turns, Ramsey's first graduate student at Columbia, William A. Nierenberg, later became chair of the NASA Advisory Council under NASA Administrator Robert Frosch. Ramsey joined the Harvard University faculty in 1947. There his

---

2. See Naugle chapter 6 for a full discussion of this process, also Newell chapter 12.

3. Homer E. Newell, *Beyond the Atmosphere: Early Years of Space Science* (NASA History Office, Washington, DC, NASA SP-4211, 1980), pp. 217–218.

research focused on development of highly accurate atomic measurement standards, which led to the hydrogen maser and, subsequently for Ramsey, a Nobel Prize in Physics.[4]

The Ramsey committee provided recommendations on topics such as NASA's relations with universities and university scientists, establishment of a lunar science institute, and even the character of NASA advisory committees. The latter recommendation created a stir in NASA when the Ramsey committee proposed to create a general advisory committee

> for advice and counsel on the initiation of new programs, on the wisdom of continuing ongoing activities, on the quality of effort at laboratories and Centers, on the assignment of managerial responsibility, on allocation of resources, and on the best means for improving international cooperation in space programs.[5]

This idea did not sit well with senior NASA officials, who argued that the roles for the proposed committee were properly responsibilities of senior management and, therefore, not to be delegated to outsiders. Furthermore, while the committee was understood to be an advisory body, there was concern that under a weak administrator, sometime in the future the committee could become a governing board instead. Finally, NASA officials argued that the proposed committee roles had considerable overlap with those of the NRC SSB and ASEB. Consequently, NASA declined to accept the recommendation.[6]

The event did illustrate a significant characteristic of scientists as advisors. Namely, when given sufficient latitude, scientific committees will not hesitate to provide broad advice that can stretch the limits of their charters. The SSB displayed the same boldness (or brashness) early in its lifetime with the 1961 letter to NASA Administrator Webb in which the Board offered its views on what should be the principal goal and message of the nation's space program.[7] (See discussion of SSB letter reports in chapter 2.)

The Missions Boards

Not long after declining to accept the Ramsey committee's recommendation for a new general advisory committee, NASA did establish three broad science program advisory bodies—the Physics Advisory Committee (PAC), the Lunar and Planetary Missions Board (LPMB), and the Astronomy Missions Board (AMB).[8] These bodies were charged with looking across the full range of topics within their respective fields and recommending integrated programs for their segments of space science. Hence, the missions boards had complementary, and probably sometimes competing, roles with respect to the science strategy studies of the SSB. For example, the SSB produced four science strategy reports related to planetary science in the same period.

---

4. Daniel Kleppner, "Biographical Memoir of Norman F. Ramsey" (*Biographical Memoirs*, National Academy of Sciences, Washington DC, 2015).

5. NASA Ad Hoc Science Advisory Committee, "Report to the Administrator," mimeographed, 15 August 1966, Historical Reference Collection folder 18437, History Division, NASA Headquarters, Washington, DC.

6. These points where outlined in NASA's 7 June 1967 interim response to the Science Advisory Committee report of August 1966, Historical Reference Collection folder 18435, History Division, NASA Headquarters, Washington, DC.

7. National Research Council, *Policy Positions on (1) Man's Role in the National Space Program and (2) Support of Basic Research for Space Science*, (The National Academies Press, Washington, DC, 31 March 1961).

8. NASA Management Instruction 1156.10—"NASA Physics Advisory Committee," 3 January 1967; NASA Management Instruction 1156.12A—"NASA Lunar and Planetary Missions Advisory Board," 1 May 1967; and NASA Management Instruction 1156.16—"NASA Astronomy Missions Advisory Board," 25 September 1967.

Both NASA and the NRC encouraged good communications between their respective bodies by inviting and involving representatives in each other's meetings. In fact, on at least one occasion the SSB and the LPMB organized a joint summer study on outer solar system research priorities,[9] and the SSB and LPMB also co-authored a letter to the NASA Administrator regarding scientific options and preferences for the Apollo Program.[10]

While the three science bodies were clearly only chartered to provide advice and to operate under direction from the Associate Administrator for Space Science and Applications (Homer Newell), they enjoyed remarkable access to what would be called insider information today. For example, at the September 1968 meeting of the LPMB, NASA officials shared NASA's interim operating plan (i.e., a budget document that was being negotiated with Congress) with the Board. Even more interesting, the minutes of the March 1969 LPMB meeting include the following gem:

> [Henry J.] Smith distributed a memorandum from the Associate Administrator enclosing a copy of a memorandum from the Administrator to the White House to Board members, not including the Executive Director. The information was discussed in considerable detail. Board members were told that this was privileged information not to be discussed outside of the Board meeting.[11]

Such intimacies were examples of NASA's efforts to work closely with the Board in those days, along the lines that Newell and Naugle hoped to nurture, but they would be seen as scandalous in NASA today.

The Physics Advisory Committee was established in January 1967 with astrophysicist William A. Fowler of Caltech as its first chair. "Willy" Fowler was typical of the kind of distinguished scientists that NASA sought as leaders of its advisory groups. He earned a doctorate degree in nuclear physics from Caltech in 1936, and he spent his entire career there until retiring in 1982. During a sabbatical year at Cambridge University in 1954–1955, he began collaborating with British astrophysicists Fred Hoyle and Margaret and Geoffrey Burbidge, and that led to their groundbreaking 1957 paper on atomic nucleosynthesis in stars. His continued work on this subject became the basis for the 1983 Nobel Prize in Physics, which he shared with Subrahmanyan Chandrasekhar.[12] Fowler also served on the NSF National Science Board from 1968 to 1974, and he became a member of the SSB on two occasions—1970–1973 and 1977–1980.

Fowler's committee was charged to consider opportunities and problems across the broad spectrum of physics disciplines that might be relevant to space science and to recommend experiments that might be undertaken in these fields.[13] The committee's early efforts identified three such areas: a test of the special theory of relativity, potential methods to study gravitational radiation, and the

---

9. Space Science Board *The Outer Solar System: A Program for Exploration* (National Research Council, The National Academies Press, Washington DC, 1969).

10. Charles H. Townes and John W. Findlay to Thomas O. Paine, 24 August 1970, cited in Barry Rutizer, "The Lunar and Planetary Missions Board," 30 August 1976, NASA Historical Document Collection folder HHN-138, History Division, NASA Headquarters, Washington, DC, p. 31–32.

11. Summary minutes of the meeting of the Lunar and Planetary Missions Board, 11 and 12 March 1969, NASA Historical Reference Collection, History Division, NASA Headquarters, Washington, DC, digital record no. 31371.

12. William A. Fowler, "William A. Fowler – Biographical" Nobel Media AB 2014. Web. 9 August 2016. *http://www.nobelprize.org/ nobel_prizes/physics/laureates/1983/fowler-bio.html*.

13. See NASA Management Instruction 1156.10—"NASA Physics Advisory Committee," 3 January 1967.

study of extremely high-energy cosmic radiation. Notably, all three topics remained on NASA's plate, and versions of two actually have been launched. The Gravity Probe B mission was developed over a period of more than 40 years and launched in 2004 to test predictions of general relativity[14] (see chapter 18). NASA has studied a Laser Interferometer Space Antenna mission and several alternative, potentially lower-cost, future gravitational wave detection flight missions; and NASA now collaborates with the European Space Agency as a junior partner in planning for a future space mission to search for gravity waves.[15] In addition, an instrument (the Alpha Magnetic Spectrometer, see chapter 18) designed to search for antimatter and dark matter and to measure ultra-high-energy cosmic rays was developed with Department of Energy support and installed on the International Space Station in May 2011.[16]

NASA formed the Lunar and Planetary Missions Board in May 1967. Its first chair was John W. Findlay of the National Radio Astronomy Observatory. Findlay was a puzzling choice to chair the LPMB. He had earned a baccalaureate degree in physics from Cambridge University in 1937, and then after serving in the Royal Air Force to install radar systems during the war, he returned to Cambridge to complete his doctorate. His research efforts focused on use of radio-wave techniques for studies of the ionosphere, but there is scant evidence of his engagement in lunar or planetary research. However, his work in ionospheric research had introduced him to Lloyd Berkner, who shared the same interests, and Findlay visited the United States in the early 1950s for collaborations at the Carnegie Institution of Washington. Shortly

afterward, Berkner, who was then the President of Associated Universities, Inc., and who was tasked by the NSF to study the feasibility of a national radio astronomy observatory, invited Findlay to come to the United States to join in building the observatory. Findlay was amongst the first few employees of the National Radio Astronomy Observatory, and he subsequently became a senior technical manager and a leader in the design and construction of some of its major telescopes.[17] In addition to his service as chair of the LPMB from 1967 to 1970, Findlay also served on the SSB from 1961 to 1970. Altogether, there were five SSB members on the original LPMB.

The LPMB's charge covered scientific planning for all planetary and lunar missions.[18] During its first few years of operation, the LPMB made recommendations for missions to Mars, Venus, Jupiter, and Mercury; developed a set of specific scientific questions for the study of Mercury; and addressed problems of lunar exploration, including recommending guidelines for continued Apollo program studies on the lunar surface. The Board devoted considerable attention to some very specific issues such as priorities and sequencing for Apollo lunar surface activities, draft proposal solicitations for science investigations on planetary missions, guidelines for creating a lunar science institute, and policy for release of photographs from early planetary missions. The Board maintained an unwavering position about the importance of a balanced solar system exploration program, including small missions that would protect against letting emphasis in one area sacrifice progress in other areas. This view led to their vigorous opposition to a class of large outer solar system

---

14. See Stanford University's Gravity Probe B project Web site at *http://einstein.stanford.edu/index.html.*

15. See *http://pcos.gsfc.nasa.gov/studies/L3/* and *http://sci.esa.int/lisa-pathfinder/.*

16. See *http://ams.nasa.gov/* or *http://cyclo.mit.edu/ams/.*

17. Interview with John W. Findlay (Papers of Woodruff T. Sullivan III: Tapes Series, National Radio Astronomy, 14 and 18 August 1981), available at *http://www.nrao.edu/archives/Sullivan/sullivan_transcript_findlay_1981_1.shtml.*

18. See NASA Management Instruction 1156.12A, "NASA Lunar and Planetary Missions Advisory Board," 1 May 1967.

missions that would use the Saturn-V rocket and nuclear propulsion systems and to abandonment of Apollo lunar missions in order to start a space station program.[19]

The latter position above ended with one of the panel's most interesting, albeit unsuccessful, efforts. In August 1970, NASA Administrator Thomas Paine wrote to both the LPMB and the SSB to invite their input on how to shorten the Apollo program and reduce the number of missions to the Moon. Administration budget constraints called for reductions in Apollo flights in order to move forward with the Skylab space station program.[20] The two advisory bodies met and sent a joint reply to Paine within a matter of weeks.[21] Paine did not select either of the advisors' two preferred options. Nevertheless, the episode illustrates an interesting difference about concerns over preserving an image of independence for the internal and external advisory bodies then and later. The LPMB and the SSB did not hesitate to collaborate directly in the face of an urgent, high-profile issue.

The Astronomy Missions Board rounded out the suite of early program-oriented advisory bodies. Formed in September 1967, the AMB was initially chaired by Harvard astronomer Leo Goldberg, who was also a charter member of the SSB, on which he served through 1963. Goldberg was an expert in solar physics and astronomical spectroscopy, who held successive directorships at McMath Observatory in Michigan (1946 to 1960), Harvard College Observatory (1960 to 1971), and Kitt Peak National Observatory (1971 to 1977). He was also offered the directorship of the National Radio Astronomy Observatory in 1956 and the NASA Goddard Space Flight Center in 1965, but he declined both. Goldberg advocated establishment of an active space astronomy program at Michigan, but was rebuffed. He then helped build a highly successful one at Harvard. He was especially respected for his administrative and leadership skills, willingness to assist students, and diplomatic acumen when he negotiated the handling of International Astronomical Union membership for the Peoples Republic of China (already a member) and the Republic of China (Taiwan, seeking membership) in 1958.[22]

The AMB was charged to provide advice on objectives, strategies, and priorities for NASA's astronomy program,[23] and it undertook a particularly ambitious agenda. The Board prepared recommendations on a flight program rationale and long-range plan, suborbital sounding rockets for astronomy, flight instrument development, ground-based astronomy in support of the flight program, particles and fields research in the context of astrophysics, and even specific experiments to be flown. The AMB devoted nearly two years to developing a long-range plan for space astronomy, and the effort involved more than 50 scientists spread amongst the board and nine panels and working groups. The plan presented both a "minimum balanced program" and an "optimum program." Both described a set of spaceflight missions and launch schedules for astronomical research across the full electromagnetic spectrum (including X- and gamma-rays and infrared and radio wavelengths), and both included planetary and solar

---

19. The activities of the LPMB are summarized nicely in Barry Rutizer, "The Lunar and Planetary Missions Board," 30 August 1976, NASA Historical Reference Collection, History Division, NASA Headquarters, Washington DC, document HHN-138.

20. Rutizer, p. 31.

21. Charles H. Townes and John W. Findlay to Thomas O. Paine, 24 August 1970, cited in Barry Rutizer, "The Lunar and Planetary Missions Board," 30 August 1976, NASA Historical Document Collection folder HHN-138, History Division, NASA Headquarters, Washington, DC, pp. 31–32.

22. Lawrence H. Aller, "Biographical Memoir of Leo Goldberg" (*Biographical Memoirs*, National Academy of Sciences, Washington, DC, 1997).

23. See NASA Management Instruction 1156.16—"NASA Astronomy Missions Advisory Board," 25 September 1967.

astronomy and atomic particles and fields measurements of relevance to astrophysics.[24] While the AMB recommended a space astronomy program for the period from 1971 through the mid-1980s, many of the mission concepts actually came to fruition only decades later, and some of the recommended missions never materialized.

As Newell's book discusses, relationships between NASA and the two mission boards were not always smooth and simple,[25] but NASA officials were remarkably sensitive to the science advisors' concerns. For example, Goldberg had written to Newell in March 1968 expressing the concerns of the AMB over the robustness of NASA's space astronomy program. Newell directed NASA's Associate Administrator for Space Science, John Naugle, to find ways to address those concerns and to prepare a reply to Goldberg. Newell was committed to building a program that was responsive to the astronomers' advice. Thus, he ended his note to Naugle quite explicitly, saying "We must find a number of means to make better use of our resources and to provide more astronomers more opportunities to carry out investigations in space."[26]

Nevertheless, members of the boards sometimes doubted that NASA took their advice seriously. Over time, the LPMB became increasingly concerned and vocal about NASA's emphasis on engineering programs at the expense of science and about what was seen to be indifference to LPMB views on the part of the office responsible for the Apollo program. One particularly difficult situation arose after President Nixon had charged Vice President Agnew in February 1969 to lead a small group—the Space Task Group—to recommend directions for the U.S. space program after Apollo. The group—consisting of Secretary of the Air Force Robert C. Seamans, Acting NASA Administrator Thomas O. Paine, and Science Advisor to the President Lee A. DuBridge—delivered its report in September 1969. The task group outlined several options, including either parallel or sequential development of a space shuttle and a large space station followed by a human Mars mission. Upon seeing the report, members of the LPMB felt that NASA's input to the effort had ignored or significantly strayed from recommendations of the LPMB, particularly regarding the board's recommendations for sustaining a balanced program that included small missions as well as large missions.[27] In October, John Findlay sent a letter to Paine saying that some members of the Board were beginning to feel that "their intelligence, experience, and efforts are in fact being wasted, or perhaps—even worse—being used as a screen or cover for plans they do not approve."[28]

---

24. "A Long-range Program in Space Astronomy, Position Paper of the Astronomy Missions Board," NASA, edited by Robert O. Boyle, Harvard College Observatory, July 1969, NASA SP-213, reproduced in Logsdon, John M., ed., with Amy Paige Snyder, Roger D. Launius, Stephen J. Garber, and Regan Anne Newport. *Exploring the Unknown: Selected Documents in the History of the U.S. Civil Space Program, Volume V, Exploring the Cosmos.* (NASA History Office, NASA Headquarters, Washington, DC, NASA SP-4407, 2001), p. 602.

25. Homer E. Newell, *Beyond the Atmosphere: Early Years of Space Science*, (NASA SP-4211, NASA History Office, NASA Headquarters, Washington, DC, 1980), pp. 218–219.

26. Memorandum from Homer Newell to John Naugle, dated 9 April 1968, on "Response to letter dated March 22, 1968 from Dr. Leo Goldberg, Chairman, Astronomy Missions Board," Historical Reference Collection folder 4490, History Division, NASA Headquarters, Washington, DC.

27. Homer E. Newell, *Beyond the Atmosphere: Early Years of Space Science*, (NASA SP-4211, NASA History Office, Washington, DC, 1980), pp. 218–219.

28. Letter from Findlay to Paine, 20 October 1969, NASA Historical Document Collection, folder 13052, NASA History Office, NASA Headquarters, Washington DC. For a more complete discussion of these events, see Barry Rutizer, "The Lunar and Planetary Missions Board," NASA Historical Reference Collection, NASA History Office, NASA Headquarters, Washington, DC, document HHN-138, August 1976.

As further evidence of the stress between outside advisors and NASA, AMB chair Leo Goldberg telephoned Homer Newell in late 1969 "to express concerns about…the role of the Astronomy Missions Board and about the possible danger that…the Astronomy Missions Board is going to fold up."[29] The issue involved an AMB discussion of mission priorities for consideration in NASA's fiscal year 1971 budget—namely, continuation of the Orbiting Astronomical Observatory (OAO) series of missions via development of OAO-D versus initiation of a new High-Energy Astrophysics Observatory (HEAO) mission for X- and gamma-ray astronomy and cosmic ray measurements. On the basis of preliminary assessments of the budget environment, NASA officials had led the AMB to believe that OAO-D was likely to go ahead and that board members were only being asked whether they endorsed HEAO as the next astronomy mission start. After endorsing HEAO as the top AMB priority, the budget outlook turned much worse, and there were fears that the White House Office of Management and Budget would terminate OAO to make room for HEAO. This, according to Goldberg, was not the AMB's intention. Board members were up in arms over being ill-informed and misdirected, and Goldberg was hearing talk in parts of the scientific community that "AMB is getting credit for killing OAO."[30]

In the end, OAO-D did go forward to be launched in 1972, and the first HEAO was eventually launched in 1977. But the damage was done. As Goldberg put it to Newell,

[I]t is all very well to advise the group to tighten their belts and go on with long-range planning in the expectation that things will get better, but when [a] whole major part of a program gets cut out involving a considerable number of people who have been associated with the program ever since NASA began in 1958, and have a stake in it—well it is pretty hard to avoid bitterness on their part.[31]

In September 1968, NASA replaced the ad hoc Science Advisory Committee that had been chaired by Ramsey with a more formal Science Advisory Committee, chaired by University of California at Berkeley Chancellor Roger Heynes.[32] The PAC, LPMB, and AMB nominally reported to the Science Advisory Committee, but they delivered most of their advice through letters to the Associate Administrator for Space Science and through face-to-face discussions with NASA science officials.

The 1970 Reorganization

By the spring of 1970, officials in NASA's Office of Space Science and Applications (OSSA) were becoming concerned about a need to reorganize the internal advisory structure to streamline it and to reduce duplication of effort. OSSA Associate Administrator John Naugle played a key role in this assessment, along with Homer Newell (see chapter 1). Naugle had an enormous impact on framing and preserving NASA's policies towards science and science management. He had earned a Ph.D. degree in physics from the University of

29. "Notes on telephone call" from Leo Goldberg to Homer Newell, 10 December 1969, NASA Historical Reference Collection, History Division, NASA Headquarters, Washington, DC.

30. "Notes on telephone call" from Leo Goldberg to Homer Newell, 10 December 1969, Historical Reference Collection, Alexander folder, History Division, NASA Headquarters, Washington, DC.

31. "Notes on telephone call" from Leo Goldberg to Homer Newell, 10 December 1969, NASA Historical Reference Collection, History Division, NASA Headquarters, Washington, DC.

32. See NASA Management Instruction 1156.18—"Science Advisory Committee," 12 September 1968.

Minnesota in 1953, after having served in the U.S. Army during World War II, during which he was a German prisoner of war and later participated in the cleanup of Dresden after the end of the war. Naugle carried out research on the upper atmosphere and high energy magnetospheric particles, using high altitude balloons and sounding rockets. After working a few years at the Convair Scientific Research Laboratory, he joined NASA in 1959. He became director of physics and astronomy in 1960 and then science Associate Administrator in 1967. In 1971, Naugle succeeded Newell as NASA Associate Administrator; later, he was chief scientist before retiring to become chairman of Fairchild Space Co.[33] As a senior manager, Naugle was respected because he had been a working scientist, he understood scientists' motivations, and he was trusted to be fair in weighing the competing interests of different groups and institutions.

Naugle and his headquarters staff were certainly convinced of the importance of an advisory process, noting that outside advisors were needed to ensure that NASA had a *national* program and not just a NASA program. Furthermore, they emphasized that an important role of an advisory structure was to strengthen education and communications between NASA and the outside technical communities by providing for outside participation in project and program development, selection of specific scientific investigations, and solutions to technical problems in projects.[34] Given that commitment to

an advisory process, Naugle proposed that NASA's science programs rely on five entities:

1. An internal,[35] senior-level Planning Advisory Committee that would report to and advise top Agency management;
2. A set of seven internal program-oriented advisory committees that would report to the PAC and provide program planning advice to the OSSA Associate Administrator and program directors; and
3. The internal Space Science and Applications Steering Committee and its discipline-oriented panels that would continue to advise the OSSA Associate Administrator on individual investigation selections; as well as
4. The SSB that would provide external advice on national program goals and priorities between disciplines and conduct major studies and overviews of NASA programs and goals; and
5. The ASEB that would serve as an external source of NASA's major studies in civil aeronautics, provide advice on technology needs for the Space Shuttle, provide advice on civil aeronautical R&D policy, and provide ad hoc advice to the Department of Transportation.[36]

NASA officials began to describe the ideas for a reorganization of the advisory structure in the late spring and summer of 1970, but they did not receive particularly enthusiastic endorsement.

---

33. Interview of John E. Naugle by David DeVorkin on 20 August 1980, Niels Bohr Library and Archives, American Institute of Physics, College Park, MD, available at *http://www.aip.org/history-programs/niels-bohr-library/oral-histories/4793*, accessed 18 October 2016.

34. Unsigned and undated briefing charts from Office of Space Science and Applications staff discussion, Historical Reference Collection file 7481, NASA History Division, NASA Headquarters, Washington, DC. Handwritten annotations on the charts by Margaret B. Beach, secretary to the Space Science and Applications Steering Committee dated 15 May 1970, suggest that they were from that general period.

35. "Internal" meaning a committee organized and managed by NASA but with members from outside NASA.

36. Unsigned and undated briefing charts from Office of Space Science and Applications staff discussion, Historical Reference Collection folder 7481, History Division, NASA Headquarters, Washington, DC. Handwritten annotations on the charts by Margaret B. Beach, secretary to the Space Science and Applications Steering Committee, dated 15 May 1970, suggest that they were from that general period.

For example, AMB Chair Goldberg wrote to Administrator Paine[37] to object strenuously to what he saw as treating all disciplines as if they were the same and neglecting the unique needs of astronomy. He also objected to whether the purported cost savings of the reorganization were credible, whether the reorganization would inappropriately distance astronomers from access to the Administrator's level in NASA, and whether it would reduce the effectiveness of advice. Concluding that he felt the proposal represented "a down-grading of the importance of astronomy in the NASA program," Goldberg proposed to resign as AMB Chair.[38] Members of the LPMB were no less upset. Board member George Pimentel described the change as a "rather shabby dismissal of LPMB and the misguided plans for recasting NASA's advisory structure."[39] The resistance from the astronomers and planetary scientists illustrates a common trait that is shared by most scientific communities. Namely, no one wants to give up multiple seats at the table or yield his advantage to other, potentially competing, points of view.

One aspect of the proposal that drew considerable opposition was that NASA employees would be considered for membership on the program-oriented advisory committees or panels that would report to the PAC. Both Newell and Naugle had long sought to build the in-house scientific competence of the NASA field centers so that the Centers could better cooperate with outside scientists in conducting space missions. Therefore, Center scientists would be able to participate in the same ways as scientists from academia. Members of the LPMB and AMB, among others, argued against having NASA employees (especially Headquarters officials or field center managers) on the panels, because that would constitute a clear conflict of interest in which NASA staff members would be advising themselves. There was an underlying attitude that even NASA scientists who were not managers would have an unfair competitive advantage over outside scientists and that the NASA scientists probably also were not of the same caliber as those academic scientists who served on the advisory bodies.[40]

In September 1970, NASA Associate Administrator Newell largely implemented the reorganization of OSSA advisory bodies. In doing so he cited the successful history of the NACA advisory structure before NASA, reaffirmed the Agency's commitment to advisory committees, and noted the need to have a process that was responsive to the increasingly cross-disciplinary character of NASA programs. Newell announced creation of a Space Program Advisory Council (SPAC—a change in name from the proposed PAC) that would take an interdisciplinary view and integrate across NASA's science and applications activities. Four committees were to report to the SPAC: one each for physical sciences, life sciences, space applications, and space systems. The discipline committees could have NASA members, who would be working scientists, up to a maximum of 25 percent of the membership. This arrangement helped recognize in-house scientists as competent members of the scientific community while also ensuring that NASA employees would not

---

37. Leo Goldberg to Thomas O. Paine, 5 June 1970, NASA Historical Reference Collection, Alexander folder, History Division, NASA Headquarters, Washington, DC.

38. Leo Goldberg to Thomas O. Paine, 5 June 1970, Historical Reference Collection, Alexander folder, History Division, NASA Headquarters, Washington, DC.

39. Letter from George C. Pimentel to Findlay dated 13 July 1970, quoted in Barry Rutizer, *The Lunar and Planetary Missions Board* (NASA Historical Reference Collection, History Division, NASA Headquarters, Washington DC, document HHN-138, August 1976), p. 33.

40. For example, see memo from F.B. Smith to Naugle, "Notes on 23 March 1967 STAR meeting at Newark Airport," 27 March 1967, Historical Reference Collection folder 009993, History Division, NASA Headquarters, Washington, DC.

dominate the advisory process. The old SAC, PAC, LPMB, and AMB were to be dissolved. In parallel with the SPAC, Newell retained a Research and Technology Advisory Council (RTAC) and its committees that had been addressing NASA's aeronautical program and some aspects of spaceflight technology.[41]

Thus, when it was formally established in 1971, the SPAC had an even broader mandate than its predecessors. The Council was charged with looking across all NASA programs, including technology development, engineering, and the human spaceflight program, as well as space science. Consequently, the SPAC became the forerunner of the NASA Advisory Council.[42] The Lunar and Planetary Missions Board and the Astronomy Missions Board were folded into the new SPAC Physical Sciences Committee (PSC), thereby consolidating NASA's advisory structure into a slightly smaller number of entities.

In December 1971, Newell prepared a memo for NASA Administrator James Fletcher in which he cogently outlined the issues over NASA's relations with the scientific community and in which he advised the Administrator about working effectively with the SSB. Newell offered three basic conclusions about the environment at the time. First, he noted that NASA's Space Task Group had proposed such ambitious future missions as to make recommendations by the LPMB and AMB no longer affordable within NASA's overall resources or even consistent with scientific priorities. Newell reported that "our Lunar and Planetary Missions Board threatened to resign en masse" and that "this kind of concern ... was also expressed by the Astronomy Missions Board."[43]

Newell also emphasized the need to help improve communications between NASA and both its own advisory bodies and the SSB, especially since many new members were not well-informed about the real-world budgetary, political, and technical issues that NASA managers had to confront day-in and day-out. He noted that if and when NASA's adversaries became familiar with NASA's problems, they would be more likely to become NASA's partners.

Then Newell made seven recommendations to the Administrator:

1. Provide "more exposure on both sides to the give and take of problems and alternatives being considered on the other side"[44]—more insight, more openness, less retreat into one-sided closed discussions.
2. Involve the SSB chair, and maybe some committee chairs, in off-the-record discussions with senior NASA officials during the last weeks of budget decisions to detect whether decisions might be going off the tracks.
3. Provide better support for SSB studies to help the Board carry out its responsibilities.
4. Work with the SSB to help ensure that long-range plans considered by the SSB and NASA have staying power and that commitments can survive over the long haul.
5. Be sensitive to and supportive of the SSB's urging that NASA's program be balanced both in terms of project size and disciplinary mix.
6. Ensure that there are adequate numbers of small projects to sustain a robust research community during the parallel development courses of longer-term large projects.

---

41. Homer E. Newell, "NASA Advisory Structure," memo for the record, 4 September 1970, Historical Reference Collection folder 17481, History Division, NASA Headquarters, Washington, DC.

42. See chapter 5 about formation of the NAC.

43. "Relations with the Scientific Community and the Space Science Board," Homer E. Newell memo to James C. Fletcher, 3 December 1971, Historical Reference Collection folder 4247, History Division, NASA Headquarters, Washington, DC.

44. "Relations with the Scientific Community and the Space Science Board," Homer E. Newell memo to James C. Fletcher, 3 December 1971, Historical Reference Collection folder 4247, History Division, NASA Headquarters, Washington, DC.

7. Restore an environment in which the scientific community is urging NASA to do things rather than to not do things. Build on emerging community enthusiasm for new initiatives rather than outrunning support before it has materialized.

Newell's memo to Fletcher was remarkably perceptive and constructive. His support of more openness, attention to staying power and commitments, and attention to programmatic balance and robustness very directly reflected concerns of the scientific community. His advice to involve the SSB chair in off-the-record conversations about budgets and budget decisions may have been realistic in the 1970s, but it became problematic from the perspectives of both the government and the NRC in later years. Nevertheless, his advice rings true today. Whether it is, or can be, heeded in today's climate, in which disclosure of ongoing budget decisions and non-public discussions with advisory groups is strongly prohibited, is another question.

The 1973 Reorganization

In 1973, yet another assessment of the advisory structure played out. In a memorandum for the record, Newell again summarized senior management views about advisory committees, reaffirmed NASA's satisfaction with the SSB, and continued to keep the SPAC and RTAC as separate entities.[45] Newell also noted some Agency dissatisfaction with the effectiveness of the SPAC, and his memo prescribed efforts that needed to be made to improve SPAC's attention to Agency-level issues that were raised by its committees and to maintain closer contact with the SSB and ASEB.

Newell's memo also presented NASA's views about the explicit roles of each body. For the SSB, the list was as follows:

1. To serve as an independent source, clearly not under the control of NASA, of advice and criticism on the nation's space science program.
2. Advise on space science goals and objectives.
3. Advise on programs, missions, and priorities, to meet space science goals and objectives.
4. Advise on needs of scientists and institutions engaged in the space program.
5. Advise on international aspects of the space science program.
6. Advise on persons to work on space science and to serve on advisory committee and working groups.
7. Assist in generating an understanding of and support for the space science program in the scientific and other communities.[46]

Newell indicated that the SPAC was expected to "go more in depth than the Space Science Board on matters of programing and NASA in-house planning and studies."[47] His list of roles for the SPAC was as follows:

1. Advise on goals and objectives of the space program.
2. Advise on programs, missions, technologies, and capabilities, and on priorities among these, to meet the space program goals and objectives.

45. Homer E. Newell, "Advisory Committees," memo for the record, 30 May 1973, Historical Reference Collection folder 17481, History Division, NASA Headquarters, Washington, DC.

46. Homer E. Newell, "Advisory Committees," memo for the record, 30 May 1973, Historical Reference Collection folder 17481, History Division, NASA Headquarters, Washington, DC.

47. Homer E. Newell, "Advisory Committees," memo for the record, 30 May 1973, Historical Reference Collection folder 17481, History Division, NASA Headquarters, Washington, DC.

3. Serve as a forum through which the chairmen of the committees of SPAC can develop the total perspective for guiding their respective committees.

4. Advise on the needs of persons and institutions engaged in the space program.

5. Advise on relations with other agencies and institutions.

6. Advise on persons to work on space programs and to serve on advisory committees and working groups, particularly on memberships of the SPAC committees.

7. Assist in generating an understanding of and support for the space program, and serve as one channel of communication between outside communities and NASA.

8. Facilitate appropriate interaction with the Space Science Board, Aeronautics and Space Engineering Board, and Scientific Advisory Board.[48]

There were some differences in the details of the roles for the SPAC compared to the SSB's and considerable overlap as well. The major difference was reflected in the statements about the SSB's independence from NASA and the SPAC's charge to go "more in depth,"[49] as well as the by-now familiar sense that the SSB would focus on strategic perspectives and NASA's committees would be more attentive to shorter-term, tactical issues. Nevertheless, the extent to which the document stopped short of drawing sharper role distinctions is a puzzle.

While Newell's memo focused on the roles of NASA's advisory committees (i.e., what they should do), the Federal Advisory Committee Act that had been enacted in 1972 laid out a process for how they should do it. The next chapter summarizes the origins, main elements, and NASA's response to that legislation.

---

48. Homer E. Newell, "Advisory Committees," memo for the record, 30 May 1973, Historical Reference Collection folder 17481, History Division, NASA Headquarters, Washington, DC.

49. Homer E. Newell, "NASA Advisory Structure," memo for the record, 30 May 1973, Historical Reference Collection, History Division, NASA Headquarters, Washington, DC.

CHAPTER 4

Congress Weighs in on Advice — The Federal Advisory Committee Act

The passage of the Federal Advisory Committee Act (FACA) was a major milestone in the evolution of how the government obtained and used outside advice. The Act responded to wide-ranging interests in making the process more orderly, more uniform, more cost-effective, and more open and balanced. The end result was largely successful, and it had a significant impact across the federal government, including NASA. Presidents and congresses before and after the 1972 enactment of FACA have refined the advisory process, but the passage of the original FACA legislation was a seminal event.

Legislative Origins

While NASA was assessing and reorganizing its advisory committee structure in the late 1960s and early 1970s, both Congress and the Nixon administration were looking at broader aspects of government advisory committees. There was general agreement that an advisory process was valuable and needed. However, congressional attention reflected wide concerns over proliferation of advisory bodies that were duplicative, costly, and often ignored; that continued to operate long after they had fulfilled the need for which they were formed; that conducted their business out of public view and with no means for public insight or input; and that operated with little or no over-sight.[1] In opening a November 1971 House of Representatives hearing to consider new legislation to address these concerns, Rep. John S. Monagan of Connecticut, Chair of the Legal and Monetary Affairs Subcommittee of the House Committee on Government Operations, said

> To point to problems in the advisory com-mittee system is certainly not to suggest that all advisory committees should be abolished. There are many advisory committees per-forming useful and even necessary roles in our government, and we seek to increase their use-fulness and effectiveness. At the same time we must seek to eliminate those advisory bodies which serve no useful function and in their ineffectuality demean the functions of the useful advisory committees.[2]

---

1. Wendy R. Ginsberg, "Federal Advisory Committees: An Overview" (Congressional Research Service, Washington DC, CRS report R40520, 16 April 2009), p. 2. In his book, *The Advisors: Scientists in the Policy Process* (The Brookings Institution, Washington, DC, 1992, p. 24), Bruce L. R. Smith provides a detailed account of how controversy of USDA and EPA handling of reviews of the herbicide 2,4,5-T may have been a tipping point regarding the openness of advisory committee activities.

2. Committee on Government Operations' Subcommittee on Legal and Monetary Affairs, *Advisory Committees*, Hearings, 92nd Cong, 1st sess., 4 November 1971, U.S. Government Printing Office, Washington, DC.

NASA advisory committees were not singled out by Congress other than to acknowledge that NASA and other agencies that issue research grants needed to exempt peer review panel discussions of individuals' competence and character from public disclosure. In what may have been a rare reference to the space program in the more than two years of congressional reviews of advisory committees, Rep. Monagan summarized his concerns (and perhaps his understanding of space technology) by saying,

> Advisory committees seem to me sort of like satellites. They go out into outer space but they keep circling around and no one really knows how many there are or what direction they are going or what duplication there is.[3]

The House Committee on Government Operations initiated a survey of advisory committees across all federal agencies in 1969 to collect information about the establishment, charters, lifetimes, membership, accomplishments, costs, and staffing levels of more than 1,500 advisory bodies. The committee held hearings in 1970 and 1971 to support the drafting of the House version of the Federal Advisory Committee Standards Act (HR 4383). The bill, which was introduced by Rep. Monagan, was approved by the full House on 9 May 1972 by a vote of 357 to 9.[4] The vote count clearly illustrates that the effort drew strong bipartisan support.

By that time, congressional frustration with executive branch attention to the advisory committee process had become palpable. This was particularly evident in the following passage in the April 1972 House report on HR 4383:

On March 17, 1970, the Assistant Director of OMB, Mr. Dwight Ink, testified before the Special Studies Subcommittee. He recognized the need for a permanent office having responsibility for the control of advisory committees. He also stated that OMB had developed a draft revised OMB Circular A-63, which would be released soon.

Nearly 15 months later, on June 10, 1971, OMB Associate Director Arnold Weber, responding to the committee's request for views on H.R. 4383, stated that a plan to improve Federal committee oversight had been developed and a directive implementing that plan would be ready for issuance in three weeks.

On November 4, 1971, nearly 4 months later, the promised directive had not yet been issued. Mr. [Frank] Carlucci, who had replaced Mr. Weber as Associate Director of OMB, stated that OMB hoped to have the directive out within 60 days.

Over 5 months later the directive had not been issued. Thus, nearly 25 months after OMB first promised a new directive regarding the use of advisory committees, no directive has been forthcoming.

Even if OMB does produce a directive soon, the need for H.R. 4383 will not be mitigated. In spite of continued congressional pressure OMB has been unable to assign more than one man to the task of managing advisory committees and coordinating their use by Federal agencies. There is not even any assurance that this one OMB staff man will be assigned to this function on a full-time basis.[5]

---

3. Ibid.

4. Wendy R. Ginsberg, "Federal Advisory Committees: An Overview" (Congressional Research Service, Washington DC, CRS report R40520, 16 April 2009), pp. 5–7.

5. Excerpt from House Report (Government Operations Committee) No. 92-1027, 25 April 1972 [To accompany H.R. 4383].

The White House had tasked all department and agency heads, in the spring of 1969, to review and evaluate the roughly 3,000 public advisory boards and commissions.[6] In June 1972, the President issued the promised executive order that required advisory committees to hold meetings open to the public so as to allow for public participation.[7] Thus, the executive order trailed behind passage of the House bill by one month.

The prevailing view of members of Congress was that the White House executive order was a case of too-little-too-late. The executive order did provide for public access to advisory committee meetings, and so congressional concerns about openness were at least partially addressed. However, other congressional priorities such as provisions for coverage of Presidential committees as well as agency committees, congressional oversight, comprehensive review by OMB, opportunities for public submission of views (more than just attendance) at advisory committee meetings, and availability of meeting transcripts were not covered in the executive order.

The Subcommittee on Intergovernmental Relations of the Senate Committee on Government Operations held its own hearings in 1970 and 1971 (including a long 12-day series of hearings in 1971). While the House drew heavily on the results of its survey of a large number of advisory committees, the Senate delved more deeply into case studies of a handful of specific examples of advisory committees. Three versions of a bill were introduced in 1971—one each from Democrat Sen. Lee W.

Metcalf of Montana and from Republicans William V. Roth of Delaware and Charles H. Percy of Illinois—and the final Senate version (S. 3529) was a consolidation of the three bills. The Committee on Government Operations unanimously approved the bill, and the full Senate passed its version of the Act by a voice vote on 12 September 1972, about three months after President Nixon issued his executive order.[8]

A conference committee resolved differences between the House and Senate versions of the bill within a few days after Senate passage, and President Nixon signed the Federal Advisory Committee Act on 6 October 1972.[9]

Legislative Provisions

The law defined an advisory committee as "any committee…or similar group…which is established or utilized by the President, or…one or more agencies in the interest of obtaining advice or recommendations for the President or one or more agencies."[10] The bill exempted from coverage under the law any committees composed entirely of officers or employees of the federal government and committees formed or used by the Central Intelligence Agency or the Federal Reserve System. According to the House-Senate conference report, the law would "not apply to persons or organizations which have contractual relationships with Federal agencies nor to advisory committees not directly established by or for such agencies."[11] The bill also did not apply to committees having operational rather than advisory

---

6. Peter M. Flanigan, Assistant to the President, "Review of Boards and Commissions," memo to NASA Administrator and other agency heads, 4 June 1969, and John C. Whitaker, Secretary to the Cabinet, memo to department heads, same subject, 21 May 1969, Historical Reference Collection folder 17481, History Division, NASA Headquarters, Washington, DC.

7. Richard M. Nixon, "Committee Management," Executive Order 11671, The White House, 5 June 1972.

8. Wendy R. Ginsberg, "Federal Advisory Committees: An Overview" (Congressional Research Service, Washington DC, CRS report R40520, 16 April 2009), pp. 5–7.

9. Federal Advisory Committee Act (FACA); 5 U.S.C. Appendix—Federal Advisory Act; 86 Stat. 770, as amended.

10. Ibid.

11. "Federal Advisory Committee Act, P.L. 92-463," House Conference Report No. 1403, 18 September 1972 [To accompany H.R. 4383]

responsibilities and this became an important distinction later at NASA.

The new law specified both executive branch and legislative branch responsibilities and provisions for establishing, managing, and evaluating advisory committees. These included continuing review in which congressional committees were charged to examine whether each advisory committee under their jurisdiction had a clearly defined purpose that could not be served by another existing committee, had fairly balanced membership in terms of the advisory committee members' points of view, and had provisions to prevent inappropriate influence that would compromise the committee's independence. The law also authorized the President to delegate responsibility for evaluating and acting on recommendations of presidential advisory committees and provided for an annual report to Congress, and it called for a new Committee Management Secretariat in the Office of Management and Budget (OMB)[12] to establish uniform committee management procedures and to conduct a comprehensive annual review of each advisory committee. The law required each agency to establish uniform guidelines and management controls for its advisory committees. With respect to the operation of advisory committees, the law prescribed procedures for establishing committees, provided for termination of all committees two years after their formation unless they were formally renewed, required that meetings be open to the public (except where material to be discussed, such as personnel matters, is exempt from disclosure under the Freedom of Information Act), required that meeting agendas include opportunities for public comments, and required that any meeting transcripts or minutes be made available to the public.

NASA's Response

In February 1974 President Nixon issued an executive order that rescinded the June 1972 order and directed all departments and agencies to comply with the FACA legislation,[13] and the next month OMB issued a revised version of guidance that provided more detailed instructions. NASA formally incorporated the requirements of the law into its set of Agency management instructions in June 1974.[14]

The NASA directive incorporated all the provisions of the law for advisory committee establishment, management, and operations. It noted that the requirements did not apply to "the National Academy of Sciences and its various committees," because they fell in the category of "organizations which have contractual relations with NASA."[15] The directive also indicated that "no advisory committee shall be used for functions which are not solely advisory," thus making it clear that government officials had the discretion to accept or decline the advice and also setting up an argument for keeping operational committees out from under FACA.

Among the explicit provisions regarding committee membership, the management instruction made two important points:

> Non-Government members of advisory committees will be selected on the basis of professional competence and not as representatives of the organization with which they are affiliated, [and]
>
> The membership of an advisory committee shall, to the extent practicable, be fairly balanced in terms of the professional perspectives represented and the committee's functions. In selecting members, an effort should be made

---

12. This responsibility was transferred to the General Services Administration in a 1977 amendment to FACA.

13. Richard M. Nixon, "Advisory Committee Management," Executive Order 11769, The White House, 21 February 1974.

14. "Establishment, Operation, and Duration of NASA Advisory Committees," NASA Management Instruction 1150.2C, 19 June 1974.

15. Ibid.

to include individuals representing different points of view and types of employment—e.g., university, industry, etc., and without discrimination on the basis of race, age, color, sex, religion, or national origin.[16]

The NASA management guidance was also quite explicit about openness of the committee's activities, with provisions including the following:

- "Committee meetings shall be open to members of the public," except when agenda items were determined to fall under exemptions listed in the Freedom of Information Act.
- Except when "public notice of a committee meeting would be inconsistent with national security," a notice of each meeting should be published in advance.
- "Any member of the public who wishes to do so shall be permitted to file a written statement with the committee, before or after the meeting" and "to present oral statements at the meeting," within certain constraints that could be set by the committee chair. However, "Questioning of committee members will not be permitted except in accordance with procedures established by the chairman."
- "Detailed minutes shall be kept of each advisory committee meeting," and "Subject to the provisions of [the Freedom of Information Act], committee records shall be available for public inspection and copying."[17]

An aspect of the advisory process that loomed large, both in terms of practicality and legality, was the use of committees whose roles were more operational and practical than strategic and advisory. As the previous chapter notes, NASA had often assembled a tiered array of advisory bodies with major committees that spawned and utilized subordinate layers of subcommittees and more discipline-specific panels. As one went down the advisory food chain, each lower layer tended to delve into increasingly more detailed aspects of program or mission operations and to assist NASA managers in making more detailed technical decisions. The structured and sometimes bureaucratic process that governed advisory committees could be an impediment, even a deal breaker, to the effectiveness of the lower-level operational committees.

Therefore, NASA and other agencies having similar needs made a case for distinguishing between advisory committees that functioned at a strategic level and groups that dug into the nitty-gritty of a program or project manager's operational trade-offs. In NASA, the term for the latter entity was a Management Operations Working Group (MOWG), and such bodies were deemed to be outside the constraints of FACA.

In November 1973, John Naugle, Associate Administrator for Space Science and Applications, provided his own guidance regarding how to distinguish between FACA-relevant advisory committees and other more operational entities.[18] Naugle defined an advisory committee as

A committee composed of persons other than full-time officers or employees of the Federal Government whose function is to provide advice or make recommendations on goals,

---

16. Ibid.

17. "Establishment, Operation, and Duration of NASA Advisory Committees," NASA Management Instruction 1150.2C, 19 June 1974.

18. John Naugle to staff, "Implementation of Federal Advisory Committee Act, Public Law 92-463 and Related Activities," 15 November 1973, Historical Reference Collection folder 17481, History Division, NASA Headquarters, Washington, DC.

objectives, program or mission content, or policy matters.[19]

In contrast, Naugle drew on guidance from NASA's lawyers to define a MOWG as

A committee whose primary function is to assist NASA management in working out program or mission parameters or otherwise participate in carrying out what has been decided upon.

Naugle's definition of an operational committee emphasized attention on "current work and assistance with operational aspects of programs, projects, and missions."[20] That distinction has largely persisted to the present day, although the use of MOWGs has varied over the years. As chapter 12 will show, NASA's lawyers employed an increasingly stringent interpretation of the leeway available to MOWGs and their successors in the 2000s, and so their utility and flexibility began to shrink.

Nevertheless, after 1972 FACA largely ruled agencies' formation and use of advisory committees. The law put structure in the process and ensured that committees operated in ways that were open to public view. For many years, the process was generally invisible to committee members except for an obligatory annual ethics briefing. And as the next chapter will show, NASA's FACA committees had significant impacts on the progress of Earth and space science over the next few decades.

---

19. John Naugle to staff, "Implementation of Federal Advisory Committee Act, Public Law 92-463 and Related Activities,"
    15 November 1973, Historical Reference Collection folder 17481, History Division, NASA Headquarters, Washington, DC.
20. Ibid.

CHAPTER 5

The NASA Advisory Council and Its Committees

Government-wide or Agency-wide re-evaluations of advisory committee structure remind one of a brood of cicadas; they re-emerge every few years, create a fuss for a few months, and then disappear until the next time they are due to surface. Such was the case in 1977, when President Carter introduced his zero-base approach to government management and budgeting. In February, the president called for "a government-wide, zero-base review of all advisory committees, with the presumption that committees not created expressly by statute should be abolished except those (1) for which there is a compelling need; (2) which will have truly balanced membership; and (3) which conduct their business as openly as possible, consistent with the law and their mandate.[1]

In November 1977, after prolonged internal NASA discussions, the Space Program Advisory Council and its companion body, the Research and Technology Advisory Council, were abolished to be replaced in 1978 by a new Agency-wide NASA Advisory Council (NAC). Thus, the Ramsey committee's 1966 recommendations for a general advisory committee (see chapter 3) were finally implemented, albeit with clear guidance under FACA that the NAC's role was to be advisory and not managerial. NASA Administrator Robert A. Frosch also established subordinate NAC standing committees in each of the following areas:[2]

- aeronautics,
- history,
- life sciences,
- space and terrestrial applications,
- space sciences and technology, and
- space systems.

Frosch recalled that NASA's response to the Carter administration's directive to reduce the number of advisory committees was straightforward but creative:

[W]hen I came in there were a bunch of in-house committees and non-academy committees and Academy committees. And as far as I could tell from sampling what I could hear and see, they were being useful, there weren't many of them, nobody was complaining about it, everybody was saying we get lots of good advice and some of it we take…. [I]t seemed to

---

1. From "Zero-Base Review of Advisory Committees," John E. Naugle memo to Distribution, 22 March 1977, NASA Historical Reference Collection folder 17481, History Division, NASA Headquarters, Washington, DC.

2. "Establishment of NASA Advisory Committees," Robert A. Frosch memo to Acting Associate Administrator for External Relations, 9 November 1977, NASA Historical Reference Collection folder 17481, History Division, NASA Headquarters, Washington, DC.

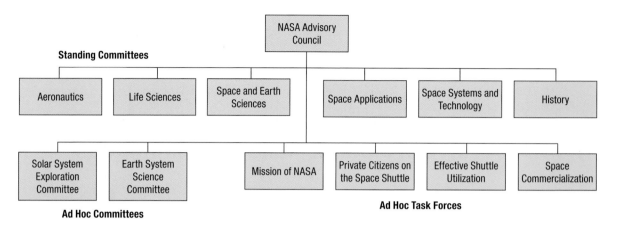

FIGURE 5.1   NASA Advisory Council and committees in 1983[3]

me to be a functional system.... So it was just fine with me, and I left it alone.

Then somebody in the office of mumbling bumblers (OMB) got it into his head, for reasons of some other department, "We are wasting a lot of money on the outside committees." So they made a policy rule—no agency could have more than two committees. This didn't apply in the Academy committees, because you could contract for that. But in terms of direct advice, you could only have two committees.... I don't know how many we had, but it was a lot more than two.... And then we read the policy directive and said, "Okay we're going to have only one committee. We are going to have, which we didn't have at the time, the Administrator's own outside advisory committee, which by the way would have a lot of subcommittees, but they don't count."

So we reorganized it that way. And essentially after we had the structure in place we slid the committees we wanted in under it...as the NASA Advisory Council.[4]

The new NAC was chaired by physicist and director of the Scripps Institute of Oceanography William A. Nierenberg, and its members included University of Arizona planetary scientist Donald M. Hunten (chair of the NAC Space Science Advisory Committee) and solar physicist John W. Firor from the National Center for Atmospheric Research (chair of the NAC Space and Terrestrial Applications Advisory Committee), plus at-large science members Harvard astronomer A.G.W. Cameron (then the SSB chair) and Harvard astrophysicist George B. Field. Figure 5.1 shows the organizational structure of the NAC in 1983, which was typical of that period.

At the beginning of the 1980s, the Space Science Advisory Committee's (SSAC's) meetings followed a familiar pattern that reflected NASA's difficult budget times. Budgets tightened at the end of the Carter administration in 1980, but they got even more so at the beginning of the Reagan administration in 1981. The Office of Space Science, which had been aiming to start a major new flight mission each year from 1981 through 1985, found itself facing a best-case possibility of no new starts

---

3. From "NASA Advisory Council and Related Committees," NMI 1156.34D, 30 September 1983, NASA Historical Document Collection folder 16712 and "NASA Advisory Council Recommendations and Actions," 1 August 1983, NASA Historical Document Collection folder 16710, NASA History Division, NASA Headquarters, Washington, DC.

4. Frosch interview, pp. 3–4.

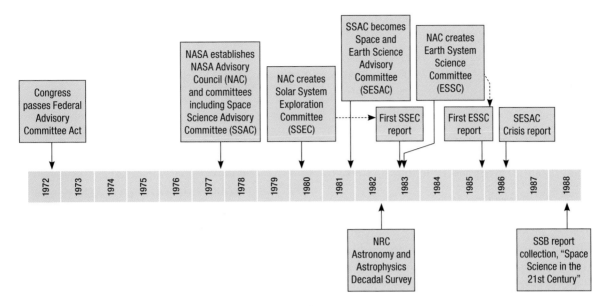

FIGURE 5.2   Timeline for key advisory events, 1972 to 1988

until 1983 and then only one in 1983 and another in 1984, corresponding to a four-year hiatus since the Hubble Space Telescope and Galileo mission to Jupiter were initiated in 1978. At each SSAC meeting, the Associate Administrator for Space Science summarized the status of the program, noted ongoing budget and mission schedule problems and threats, and described the glum (administration and congressional) outlook for initiating new flight missions in the near future. SSAC then discussed needs for protecting program balance, coping with the new-start logjam, and setting priorities and making hard decisions. Finally, they prepared statements deploring the budget impacts on the space science program and reviewed and recommended priorities for new starts in the coming year.[5]

In December 1981, NASA reorganized to create the Office of Space Science and Applications (OSSA), and SSAC became the Space and Earth Science Advisory Committee (SESAC). NASA's executive secretary for SESAC, OSSA Assistant Associate Administrator Jeffrey D. Rosendhal, had

become concerned over the scientific community's increasingly adversarial relationships with NASA. He worked with SESAC chair, planetary geophysicist Lawrence A. Soderblom, to try to focus the committee's attention towards constructive and actionable directions. That effort continued under the leadership of Soderblom's successor as chair, Louis J. Lanzerotti. SESAC undertook several internal projects, including a review of the health of the research and analysis grants programs and an assessment of scientific opportunities on the Space Station. Beginning in 1983, SESAC identified review of new-start candidates as a regular agenda item for every June meeting.[6] Two of the committee's most important efforts were the formation of the Earth System Science Committee and a study leading to the SESAC Crisis report, both of which are described below. See figure 5.2 for a timeline of key advisory activities from 1978 to 1988.

While the committee meetings were mostly serious and steeped in NASA technology and jargon, they were not without their revealing moments of

---

5. Alexander document files from SSAC meetings, NASA HRC.

6. List of initiatives for the early 1980s is derived from the Alexander document files of SESAC meetings in 1982 and 1983.

misguided policy, candor, and levity. During 1981 SSAC meetings, NASA officials admonished the committee that "Programs that avoid use of the Space Shuttle will be in jeopardy."[7] And a White House Office of Science and Technology Policy official added that "The Shuttle is here to stay,"[8] and that projects that use it will have an advantage. Five years later, NASA would be completely revising its policy after responding to the impacts of the Challenger accident.

As for candor, at a November 1982 SESAC meeting, OSSA Associate Administrator Burton I. Edelson exposed the ambiguity between his own authority and that of NASA Chief Scientist Frank B. McDonald when he advised SESAC, "If you are going to write letters about supporting your program, don't send them to me, send them to Frank McDonald."[9] The humor surfaced in a later comment not related to Edelson's at the same meeting when McDonald characterized the rosy views espoused by NASA's leadership by describing the Administrator's suite at NASA headquarters as "a hospice for the incurably optimistic."[10]

The same meeting provided evidence that at least some decision makers in Congress were attentive to the committee's activities. While speaking with the committee, House of Representatives Subcommittee on Space Science and Applications staff member Radford Byerly inquired as to whether SESAC members felt free to make comments or whether they were constrained by NASA to follow the Agency's agenda. Byerly went on to ask whether SESAC would prefer to have statutory support for its work. He apparently received satisfactory answers to his questions, because there

was no effort to create specific legislative authority for SESAC.[11]

SESAC Crisis Report

The early-to-mid 1980s were a trying time for space science. Reagan administration cancellations or indefinite deferrals of Carter administration space science mission initiatives (see below) were alarming developments that foretold the possibility of a long dry spell between the last major mission new starts in the late 1970s and any prospects for new missions until the mid-to-late 1980s. To make matters more challenging, missions that had been started—notably Space Telescope and the Galileo Jupiter orbiter—and proposed future missions such as the Cassini Saturn orbiter and other Great Observatories to follow the Space Telescope collectively required a very different long-term budget profile. The fact that all these missions would require significant budget commitments to cover their operation and data analysis for a decade or longer meant that there could be no funds left in NASA's coffers to permit new missions.

In spite of these challenges to the size and shape of the budget, OSSA managers and many in the scientific community continued to hope for and push for ambitious new mission starts. For example, in a May 1983 SESAC meeting, OSSA Associate Administrator Edelson presented NASA's "best internal thinking" for fiscal years 1985 to 1989 new-start goals corresponding to a rate of two to three new starts per year.[12] Edelson acknowledged that would probably oversubscribe the budget annually by 50 percent, but he apparently considered it to

---

7. Alexander document files on the 29 June 1981 meeting of the Space Science Advisory Committee, NASA HRC.

8. Alexander document files on the 19 November 1981 meeting of the Space Science Advisory Committee, NASA HRC.

9. Alexander document files on the 18 November 1982 meeting of the Space and Earth Science Committee, NASA HRC.

10. Ibid.

11. Ibid.

12. Alexander document files from the 24 May 1983 meeting of the Space and Earth Sciences Advisory Committee, NASA HRC.

be an appropriately aggressive strategy. SESAC members expressed growing frustration over the annual new-start logjams, unproductive annual competitions, and unclear decision-making process. They also declined to endorse Edelson's set of new-start priorities.

On top of these daunting prospects for the future, SESAC members continued to worry about the overall health of the research and analysis program that provided the basic scientific and technological underpinnings of the space sciences and about declines in the launch rate of small, principal-investigator-led Explorer missions that kept a portion of the research community involved in space investigations even when there were no new major flight missions. They also grappled with the broadened and commensurately more complex content of the program after the space and Earth sciences offices had been merged.

On top of all the explicit programmatic challenges that confronted OSSA, there was an undercurrent of concern about OSSA's leadership. Edelson was an expert in satellite communications and a former director of Comsat Laboratories, but he came to NASA with scant familiarity with space science or the space research community. Those were obstacles that he never completely overcame, and they bred a lack of confidence amongst the community of scientists who depended on NASA support and who were the program's advocates and advisors.

Louis Lanzerotti, who succeeded Larry Soderblom as SESAC chair in 1984, was an expert in space plasma physics and geophysics at Bell Laboratories. He had served earlier on the Physical Sciences Committee when Noel Hinners was Associate Administrator for Space Science and Applications, and he later served as chair of the SSB and chair or member of many important NRC and other advisory bodies. He and Rosendhal led

SESAC in undertaking a broad-based evaluation of the problems confronting the space and Earth science programs. The committee's two-year effort culminated in a final report that was provocatively titled, "The Crisis in Space and Earth Science: A Time for a New Commitment."[13]

The Challenger Space Shuttle accident occurred while the committee was completing its study, and the impacts of launch delays and budget uncertainties following the accident only heightened the sense of urgency. The committee's report outlined the principal concerns about stresses to NASA's program and made a compelling argument for why SESAC felt that the vitality of U.S. space and Earth science was threatened. Then the report described SESAC's views about what should be the key elements of a healthy program, thereby outlining metrics by which remedies could be evaluated, and it analyzed trends that had contributed to stresses. Finally, the report presented and explained a set of recommendations to NASA to restore program vitality, including (1) continuing program diversity and breadth, (2) ensuring that space mission decisions be driven by scientific requirements, (3) using orderly and realistic planning to underpin program plans and budgets, and (4) applying "clear and specific criteria" to setting priorities and making research project and mission decisions.[14]

Lanzerotti's successor as SESAC chair was MIT astrophysicist Claude R. Canizares, who was a member of SESAC when the Crisis report was prepared. Canizares recalled that the report had impacts both with its intended policy-making audience and with the space science community:

> But I think one value of those kinds of reports is actually what it does for the community. It really brings the community together around the common sense of being able to send their

---

13. Space and Earth Science Advisory Committee, *The Crisis in Space and Earth Science: A Time for a New Commitment*, (NASA Advisory Council, Washington, DC, November 1986).

14. Ibid.

message. I guess my sense is that people paid attention—people on the [Capitol] Hill and others. Whether it really changed the course of events, one can't know.... I think one of the challenges with these committees is that they're in some sense sort of representing the community. But they're also where the factions all meet around the table and arm-wrestle with each other. Starting to bring in more of a strategic planning mindset helped to alleviate that.[15]

The report was generally well received when it was released in late 1986. Certainly SESAC used its own report as guidance as it advised OSSA over the next few years. When Lanzerotti completed his tenure as SESAC chair in 1989, he moved to become chair of the Space Science Board, and so the principles and approaches outlined in the Crisis report very likely influenced Lanzerotti's approach to leading the SSB.

Shortly after the report was released, Lennard A. Fisk succeeded Edelson as OSSA Associate Administrator. Fisk quickly took actions to address the issues of program balance, diversity, planning, priority-setting, and decision-making that were consistent with the SESAC report (See chapter 7.).

Solar System Exploration Committee

In addition to its standing committees, the NAC occasionally established ad hoc committees for special tasks. The Solar System Exploration Committee (SSEC) was a notable example.[16] At the time, NASA's planetary science program was reeling from two major threats to its very existence. After a relatively robust period of activity in the

1970s, with launches of the Viking missions to Mars, Pioneer missions to Venus and Jupiter, and two Voyager outer solar system missions, there was only a single new start for solar system science slated for the 1980s—the Galileo orbiter mission to Jupiter. A proposed mission to intercept Halley's Comet failed to gain sufficient political traction, and a mission to send a radar imaging spacecraft to Venus was approved late in the Carter administration but then cancelled by the incoming Reagan administration. Reagan's budget director David A. Stockman also proposed to cancel either the Hubble Space Telescope, Galileo, or the U.S. part of the ESA[17]—NASA International Solar Polar Mission (ISPM). Indeed, Stockman made a serious proposal to terminate the entire planetary exploration program, and Administrator Beggs put this idea forward during negotiations over the NASA fiscal year 1983 budget. In the end, ISPM fell but Galileo survived.

The planetary program's near-death experience led NASA to create the SSEC to formulate an overall strategy for solar system exploration. The SSB had recommended separate science strategies for the inner planets and for primitive bodies (asteroids, comets, and meteoroids), and it had published a short treatise on the science and goals of planetary exploration. But what NASA lacked was a coherent, integrated, programmatic strategy for a sustained, but affordable, program. John Naugle, then having left NASA to become an executive at Fairchild Space Company, served as the SSEC's first chair from 1980 to 1981, to be followed by Noel Hinners (Director of the National Air and Space Museum at the time) from 1981 to 1982, and subsequently University of Hawaii astronomer David Morrison in 1983.

---

15. Canizares interview, p. 2. Canizares also served as Chair of the Space Studies Board from 1994 to 2000.

16. See "The Survival Crisis of the U.S. Solar System Exploration Program" by John M. Logsdon in *Exploring the Solar System: The History and Science of Planetary Exploration*, edited by Roger D. Launius (Palgrave Macmillan, 2013, pp. 45–76) for a comprehensive discussion of the origins of the SSEC.

17. ESA is the European Space Agency.

The SSEC's report, "Planetary Exploration Through Year 2000: Part One: A Core Program,"[18] appeared in 1983. The report embraced and drew on the scientific goals developed earlier by the SSB and its Committee on Planetary and Lunar Exploration.[19] The NASA committee outlined a specific sequence of core missions to Venus, Mars, a comet, and Saturn's satellite Titan. But perhaps more importantly, the report recommended a new strategy based on modest-scale missions—Planetary Observers modeled after the Explorer program in space physics and astronomy—and a new larger-scale class of missions that would utilize a standard modular spacecraft design concept—the Mariner Mark II. The strategy emphasized principles of affordability and program stability. Finally, the committee recommended an augmented program that would go beyond the core program "as soon as national priorities permit," and part II of the committee's report, issued in 1986,[20] outlined recommendations for the expanded program.

The SSEC report had a significant positive impact and helped NASA gain support to put the planetary exploration program back on track, in spite of the fact that the specific recommendations for new classes of missions never completely materialized. The idea for a Planetary Observer class of missions translated into a Venus Radar Mapper (later to be called Magellan), but the second mission in the proposed series—Mars Geoscience/Climate Orbiter (later called Mars Observer)—experienced serious cost growth and schedule delays. The Planetary Observer spacecraft were expected to be derived from commercially manufactured busses developed for operation in

Earth orbit, but the concept proved to be flawed because adapting a commercial spacecraft for use in one-of-a-kind planetary science missions was costly and complex. More tragically, Mars Observer suffered a catastrophic failure during its entry into Mars orbit and never collected any scientific data. The first two Mariner Mark II missions were slated to be the Cassini Saturn orbiter and the Comet Rendezvous/Asteroid Flyby (CRAF) mission. Cassini was launched, along with its piggybacked ESA Huygens Titan probe, in 1997 and went on to become a roaring success in its observations of the Saturn system. However, CRAF was terminated due to NASA budget problems in 1993, thereby marking the end of a real Mariner Mark II program. The SSEC idea of developing a standard spacecraft design and re-flying it for a variety of large planetary missions was not realistic.

In spite of the fact that the specific programmatic ideas espoused by the SSEC failed to be fully implemented, the committee's efforts to right the ship and outline a more realistic approach to planetary exploration saved the day by outlining an approach that, at the time, appeared to be fresh and pragmatic. Thus, it bought NASA managers time and provided a foundation on which NASA could build going into the late 1980s.

Earth System Science Committee

Another NAC committee, the Earth Systems Science Committee (ESSC), played a critical role in the formulation of NASA's Mission to Planet Earth program and the U.S Global Change Research Program. The committee's origins go at

18. Solar System Exploration Committee, *Planetary Exploration Through Year 2000: Part One: A Core Program* (NASA Advisory Council, Washington, DC, 1983).

19. National Research Council, *Opportunities and Choices in Space Science* (The National Academies Press, Washington, DC, 1975), pp. 115–146; National Research Council, *Strategy for Exploration of the Inner Planets: 1977–1987* (The National Academies Press, Washington, DC, 1978); and National Research Council, *Strategy for the Exploration of Primitive Solar-System Bodies—Asteroids, Comets, and Meteoroids: 1980–1990* (The National Academies Press, Washington, DC, 1980).

20. Solar System Exploration Committee, *Planetary exploration through year 2000: an augmented program: part two of a report by the Solar System Exploration Committee of the NASA Advisory Council*, (NASA Advisory Council, Washington, DC, 1986).

least as far back as 1982, when Harvard scientist Richard Goody led a NASA-sponsored workshop to address "long-term global changes that can affect the habitability of the Earth."[21] Following on Goody's influential, but politically sensitive, report, the NRC convened a workshop led by physicist Herbert Friedman that led to a proposal for a broadly based, interdisciplinary International Geosphere-Biosphere Program.[22]

NASA Associate Administrator Edelson wanted to translate those ideas into a comprehensive NASA program—which became NASA's Mission to Planet Earth—and so, at SESAC's urging, he arranged for formation of the ESSC in 1983 under the auspices of the NAC. His idea was to repeat the success that the Solar System Exploration Committee was enjoying at the time, and the ESSC surpassed that success.

The committee was chaired by theoretical meteorologist Francis P. Bretherton, who was director of the National Center for Atmospheric Research from 1974 until 1980, when he moved to the University of Wisconsin. The committee met over a period of five years. The seminal aspect of its first report[23] was a diagram that illustrated the complex web of interactions between natural physical climate and biogeochemical components and processes, external forces, and human activities. The diagram, and the committee's accompanying discussion, became a classic tool for illustrating the concept of how Earth and all the components of its global environment—atmosphere, oceans, cryosphere, biosphere, and lithosphere—comprise an integrated, highly interactive system (the Earth system). The report also made a compelling case for how the Earth system, and all its components, needed to be studied together in an integrated fashion.

The committee argued for using space observations to tackle this ambitious challenge, outlined specific missions spanning a period of more than a decade to accomplish the recommended research, and called for an advanced information system to facilitate use of the new data. The ESSC also recommended that NASA take the lead in the space-based observing program, proposed roles for NOAA and NSF, and discussed opportunities for international participation.

The ESSC report gained widespread attention in the scientific community, and scientists largely embraced the committee's scientific arguments in spite of the ambitious scale of the proposed program. A catalyst for building support in Congress came from another report, which was primarily driven by a single NASA employee.[24] In late 1986, NASA astronaut Sally K. Ride volunteered to NASA Administrator James Fletcher to come to Washington and lead an in-house NASA effort to articulate new directions for the Agency to help get it back on track after the Space Shuttle Challenger accident. Her report, "NASA Leadership and America's Future in Space,"[25] outlined four possible central goals:

1. Mission to Planet Earth
2. Exploration of the solar system
3. Permanent lunar outpost
4. Humans to Mars

21. Richard Goody, *Global Change: Impacts on Habitability—A Scientific Basis for Assessment* (Jet Propulsion Laboratory document JPL D-95, NASA Contractor report CR-169174, Pasadena CA, 7 July 1982).

22. National Research Council, *Toward an International Geosphere-Biosphere Program: A Study of Global Change* (National Academy Press, Washington, DC, 1983).

23. Earth System Sciences Committee, *Earth System Science: Overview, A Program for Global Change*, (NASA Advisory Council, NASA, Washington DC, 1986).

24. Author's interview with former Congressional Research Service staff member Marcia Smith highlighted the impact of the Ride report in stimulating congressional interest in Mission to Planet Earth.

25. Sally K. Ride, *NASA Leadership and America's Future in Space: A Report to the NASA Administrator*, NASA, Washington, DC, August 1987.

Ride's report did not propose that NASA single out one of them, but rather that the Agency pursue several or even all of them together or sequentially. Like so many post-Apollo planning efforts, senior NASA managers and government space-policy makers proved unable or unwilling to pick up the ball and run with it. The report received plaudits but no substantive follow-up attention. An exception was that the cachet of Ride's having highlighted Mission to Planet Earth as one potential major goal for the civil space program helped build support for that program in Congress.[26] Thus, it helped advance the ideas presented in the ESSC report.

NASA's interest in Mission to Planet Earth benefitted from another boost beyond those derived from the ESSC and Ride reports. Senior OSSA managers understood, through OMB, that President George H. W. Bush supported the program. For example, the chief of the OMB Science and Space Programs Branch Jack Fellows commented to SESAC's successor, the Space Science and Applications Advisory Committee, in February 1989 that the newly inaugurated President wished to pursue a strong emphasis on global change and environmental issues, including support for Mission to Planet Earth.[27] Consequently, the program enjoyed a favored position until the conflict between NASA ambitions and the political reality of federal budgets intervened.

The Mission to Planet Earth concept envisioned by the ESSC and proposed by NASA was the subject of multiple reviews, restructurings, and downsizings in subsequent years, all stimulated or guided by science and engineering advisory panels.[28] Many of the reviews were commissioned by NASA and conducted either by NASA committees or NRC committees; one was organized by the NRC at the request of Congress.

One such review was established by NASA at Administrator Daniel S. Goldin's request, and it had a notable impact on NASA's plans and on congressional views about the program's progress and cost. The EOS (Earth Observing System) Engineering Review Committee was chaired by physicist Edward A. Frieman, who was director of the Scripps Institution of Oceanography at the time. Frieman's report recommended reducing the scope of the program, focusing more on climate change, and shifting to multiple small-to-moderate-size satellite platforms instead of large, heavy, and heavily instrumented platforms, as had been previously planned.[29] Advisory committee recommendations are relatively rarely incorporated in presidential orders and directives, but a 1992 National Space Policy Directive signed by President Bush assigned lead agency responsibilities to NASA for Space-Based Global Change Observation System activities, including Mission to Planet Earth, and directed NASA to carry out the EOS program according to the recommendations of the Frieman committee.[30] The program survived, and much of the impetus for the program that did emerge, beginning with launch of the Terra satellite in December 1999, can be traced back to the work of NASA's ESSC and to subsequent advisory body reviews.

26. The idea of a global study of planet Earth also emerged in the Paine Commission report (National Commission on Space, *Pioneering the Space Frontier*, Bantam Books, 1986), but it failed to get traction then. A member of the Office of Space Science and Applications staff, Dixon M. Butler served on Ride's committee and played a big role in developing the Mission to Planet Earth ideas in the Ride report.

27. Alexander document files from the February 1989 SSAC meeting, NASA HRC.

28. For a comprehensive treatment of the advisory origins and assessments of NASA's Mission to Planet Earth Program, see National Research Council, *Earth Observations From Space: History, Promise, and Reality*, (The National Academies Press, Washington, DC, 1995).

29. EOS Engineering Review Committee, *Report of the Earth Observing System (EOS) Engineering Review Committee*, Edward Frieman, Chair, (NASA, Washington, DC, 1991).

30. "Space-Based Global Change Observation," NSPD-7, The White House, Washington, DC, 28 May 1992.

CHAPTER 6

The Advisory Environment in the 1980s: A Critical Assessment

Concluding Ideas

The work of advisory bodies during NASA's first three decades played an important role in the Agency's development and in the content and successes of its scientific programs. By the mid-1980s, NASA was drawing on a well-established system of both internal and external advisory bodies that utilized scientists and technologists from academia, industry, and federal laboratories to recommend scientific priorities and program plans and to assist NASA managers in decision making about the Agency's space and Earth science program. This sometimes complex and often hierarchical network of providers and users of advice (see figure 6.1) comprised an advisory ecosystem in which the various components interacted, sometimes cordially and sometimes under stress. Nevertheless, the process was a positive one, and through it, the scientific community that the advisors represented, NASA, and the nation's space program were all well served. In this chapter, we look back at some key factors that contributed to the advisory ecosystem as NASA approached its 30th anniversary.

NASA BEGAN WITH A CULTURE THAT ACCEPTED OUTSIDE SCIENTIFIC ADVICE.

When NASA was established in 1958, it inherited a structure that accepted and incorporated input from outside technical advisors. Use of advisory committees was part of the NACA's culture. When the NACA Director Hugh Dryden became NASA's

first Deputy Administrator, it was natural for him to see value in integrating outside advisory bodies into NASA's operations. Homer Newell brought the same approach to research planning when he moved from NRL, where he had served on and chaired the rocket panel and key International Geophysical Year (IGY) committees, to take on leadership roles in NASA's science program. NASA's early leaders also recognized that in a field as broad and diversified as space science, there was relatively little in-house expertise compared to the vaster pool of expertise outside the Agency.

THE EARLY SPACE SCIENCE BOARD DREW STRENGTH FROM THE STATURE OF THE NATIONAL ACADEMY OF SCIENCES AND INDEPENDENCE FROM ITS RELATIVE FREEDOM FROM BUREAUCRATIC OR PROCEDURAL CONSTRAINTS.

The advisory tradition influenced by the NACA history and IGY-era committees, plus the fact that the SSB was in place before NASA was established, meant that the SSB was running when the infant NASA was just taking its first steps. Consequently, the SSB did not hesitate to interpret its charter very broadly. It asserted initiative to provide advice on the most fundamental issues (e.g., its view of the basic purpose of the U.S. civil space program) and to direct that advice to the very top of the Agency. The Board initiated studies on topics that it deemed important and did not always wait for NASA to come seeking advice. It developed a product mix

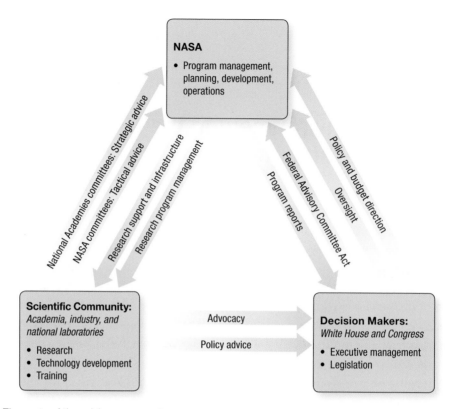

FIGURE 6.1   Elements of the advisory ecosystem

that included long-range science strategies, technical studies, and program assessments based on in-depth analyses. The Board also delivered short letter reports that were prepared and delivered quickly and that were based on Board or committee members' existing experience and expertise.

The Board and its committees interacted often with NASA officials and with NASA's internal committees. Indeed, on a few occasions in the 1960s and early 1970s, NASA committees and the SSB conducted joint studies for NASA. Movement of individual scientists between serving on SSB entities and NASA committees was not unusual, thereby contributing to cross communications and continuity at the expense of total independence of perspective between the two sets of advisors.

An interesting test of the independence of NASA's Space and Earth Science Advisory

Committee and the SSB from each other occurred while SESAC was completing its Crisis report. SSB members shared the concerns that had driven SESAC to undertake its study, and the impacts of the Challenger accident greatly increased the sense of urgency at the SSB, just as they had with SESAC. Consequently, SESAC chair Lou Lanzerotti had discussions with SSB chair Tom Donahue about the possibility of the two bodies issuing a joint statement outlining their concerns, and a draft of such a statement had been prepared. However, at an April 1986 meeting of the NASA Advisory Council, Lanzerotti reported that National Academy of Sciences president Frank Press would not permit the issuance of a joint statement.[1] Press's refusal to go along with the idea was, presumably, not because he disagreed with the points to be raised, but because he would not sanction any actions that could be interpreted as evidence that the SSB was

---

1. Alexander document files on the 29 April 1986 NAC meeting, NASA HRC.

not acting independently and on its own. Soon afterwards, the SSB did send two of its own letter reports to the NASA Administrator citing SSB concerns, especially regarding the need to restore a mixed fleet of launch vehicles that would reverse NASA's heavy dependence on the Space Shuttle.

NASA'S INTERNAL ADVISORY COMMITTEES EVOLVED IN PARALLEL WITH THE INDEPENDENT SSB.

The Agency's first scientific committees with external members were the discipline-specific subcommittees and panels serving under the Space Science Steering Committee. But these were more operational than strategic, because they assisted NASA managers in making selections amongst competing experiment proposals for flight missions. Hence, their primary purpose was to assist NASA in the procurement process rather than to establish goals and objectives or mission and program priorities.

Beginning with the formation of the Physics Advisory Committee and the Lunar and Planetary Missions Board and Astronomy Missions Board there was always a set of advisory committees organized around certain scientific disciplines to advise senior managers in NASA's science office. The disciplinary breadth of their portfolios would change over time, but the internal committees became a fixture operating in parallel with the SSB. Their operating style was often more informal and somewhat more person-to-person than that of the SSB. Hence, the internal committees capitalized on strengths of accessibility and quickness of response to complement the SSB's strengths of stature and greater independence.

NASA program managers often developed close working relationships with the internal advisory committees and relied heavily on them. Former senior NASA executive Noel Hinners noted that when he became Associate Administrator for Space Science in 1974, he viewed the Physical Sciences Committee (PSC) as "my committee."[2] In comparing the PSC with the SSB, Hinners found the former to be more useful because the members were inclined to be more responsive to issues that concerned the Agency. The SSB, in contrast, tended to act as a group of purists who had their own agenda and who were not as likely to be cognizant of constraints under which NASA was operating.

The internal advisory structure also grew into a hierarchical network in which lower-level, more narrowly focused panels—Management Operations Working Groups (MOWGs)—provided advice across the science organization. The MOWGs at the lower end of the food chain advised program or project managers; the next level up advised discipline division directors; and each level of advisory group reported to the level above. A key attribute of the MOWGs was the fact that they could provide increasingly more specific advice about operational questions as one went down the food chain. NASA discipline managers were especially appreciative of the capacity of the MOWG system to help them stay keenly aware of the interests and views of their research communities.[3] Former OSSA Associate Administrator Lennard Fisk described MOWGs as follows:

> I thought that was one of the great constructs of all time, because it really created paths of information internal to NASA for internal people. Suppose you are a branch head, and you don't think your division chief is listening to you. So you talked to your advisory committee, and usually someone on those MOWGs served on the division director's committee. So we really

2. Hinners interview, 11 December 2013.

3. Science Definition Teams (SDTs) worked in a fashion that was similar to MOWGs. SDTs would be formed for the specific purpose of advising a program manager about recommended scientific goals and instrument payloads during the early study phase of a new flight project.

had this wonderful flow of information [to NASA] and to the community.[4]

Former NASA Director of Astrophysics Charles Pellerin, who became a management consultant after leaving NASA, put it this way: "I don't think there's any system anywhere to get as close to this aspect of customers in any business I've ever seen."[5]

THE NRC HAD BECOME THE PRINCIPAL SOURCE OF ADVICE ABOUT MAJOR SCIENTIFIC STRATEGIES, AND INTERNAL COMMITTEES WERE THE MAJOR SOURCE OF PROGRAM IMPLEMENTATION STRATEGIES.

Beginning in the 1960s and continuing into the 1980s, the SSB prepared a series of major science strategy reports that covered all subfields of space science and also Earth science from space. These studies concentrated on long-range scientific goals and priorities, and they were usually supported by extensive, and often scholarly, discussions of the scientific basis for the study conclusions. NASA managers and internal advisory committees could, and often did, use the SSB reports as starting points or reference points from which to develop program strategies and priorities for specific missions or mission sets. For example, between 1969 and 1980 the SSB's Committee on Planetary and Lunar Exploration completed science strategy studies for the outer planets, the inner planets, and primitive solar system bodies.[6] The NASA Advisory Council's Solar System Exploration Committee used those reports as a scientific basis for its recommendations for the planetary exploration program through year 2000.[7] Similarly, the NAC Earth System Science Committee drew on reports that were prepared by the SSB's Committee on Earth Studies[8] and on the results of Herbert Friedman's International Geosphere Biosphere Program workshop[9] as the ESSC developed its reports in 1986 and 1988.[10]

In addition, the SSB filled at least two unique roles. First, in its capacity as the U.S. National Committee for COSPAR, the SSB was the principal representative of the United States in international discussions between scientists about space research. Second, the SSB was the source of expert advice to NASA and to COSPAR on standards and approaches for planetary protection (i.e., prevention of biological contamination of solar system bodies by terrestrial microbes or terrestrial biological contamination by extraterrestrial organisms).

For all these reasons, the SSB had become established as a major source of scientific advice for NASA and the rest of the U.S. space community.

4. Fisk interview, p. 5. Fisk also served as SSB Chair from 2003 to 2008.

5. Pellerin interview, p. 4.

6. National Research Council, *Outer Planets Exploration: 1972–1985* (The National Academies Press, Washington, DC, 1971); National Research Council, *Strategy for Exploration of the Inner Planets: 1977–1987* (The National Academies Press, Washington, DC, 1978); and National Research Council, *Strategy for the Exploration of Primitive Solar-System—Asteroids, Comets, and Meteoroids: 1980–1990* (The National Academies Press, Washington, DC, 1980).

7. Solar System Exploration Committee, *Planetary Exploration Through Year 2000, Part One: A Core Program* (NASA Advisory Council, Washington, DC, 1983).

8. National Research Council, *A Strategy for Earth Science from Space in the 1980s—Part I: Solid Earth and Oceans,* (The National Academies Press, Washington, DC, 1982), and *A Strategy for Earth Science from Space in the 1980s and 1990s—Part II: Atmosphere and Interactions with the Solid Earth, Oceans, and Biota* (The National Academies Press, Washington, DC, 1985).

9. National Research Council, *Toward an International Geosphere-Biosphere Program: A Study of Global Change* (National Academy Press, Washington, DC, 1983).

10. Earth System Sciences Committee, *Earth System Science: Overview, A Program for Global Change* (NASA Advisory Council, NASA, Washington DC, 1986).

FACA CREATED AN ORDERLY ADVISORY SYSTEM MANAGEMENT PROCESS AND ENSURED PUBLIC ACCESS.

Enactment of the Federal Advisory Committee Act in 1972 provided a layer of order, standardization, rigor, and oversight to advisory activities across the government. Perhaps most importantly, it provided for more substantive public information about and access to advisory activities. From all accounts, NASA made its advisory committee members more aware of the requirements, but FACA did not otherwise especially constrain the advisory process. It was largely invisible to most participants in the 1970s and 1980s.

And importantly, both NASA's MOWGs and the boards and committees of the National Academies were not required to operate under FACA requirements and constraints. MOWGs were exempted because their work was viewed as directed at the operational implementation of policy decisions that had already been made. National Academies' advisory studies were exempted because the law did not apply to government contractors.

AN ENVIRONMENT OF CONSTRUCTIVE TENSION REMAINED.

NASA's relationship with its outside advisors, regardless of whether they were serving on NASA's internal committees or bodies under the National Academies, were always characterized by some level of constructive tension. Members of the scientific community believed that the U.S. space and Earth science program was *their* program and that NASA was charged to organize and conduct it on behalf of the scientific community. Consequently, the scientific community did not hesitate to view the advisory process as a means to give NASA direction and to take the Agency to task when it did not appear to be responsive or able to meet outside expectations. Everyone on both sides of the conversation understood that advisory bodies' statements were only recommendations and that NASA still had the final authority to make and execute decisions. But that did not make advisors any more bashful.

This cultural tradition began at the time of NASA's birth when the SSB sought to assume full responsibility for planning space research missions and selecting the experiments to be flown and the investigators to conduct them. The SSB ambitions were put to rest when NASA made it clear that the Board's role was to be confined to advising on broad objectives and was not to involve detailed program formulation (See chapter 1). Nevertheless, the SSB never hesitated to advise the NASA Administrator and other NASA officials about the Board's views on topics as disparate as the fundamental purpose of the U.S. space program or what the recommended mix of launch vehicles for scientific missions was to be.

Likewise, NASA's internal advisory committees rarely hesitated to engage their NASA sponsors in vigorous debate and to voice concerns about the content, pace, or direction of NASA's science programs. At times the tension could become palpable, as was the case when conflicts about the direction of the program pushed both the Astronomy Missions Board and the Lunar and Planetary Missions Board to threaten to resign en masse in 1969 and 1971, respectively (See chapter 3).

For their part, NASA science officials considered the advisory process essential and mostly took the flak philosophically. They recognized that the process was a key means to promote communication between NASA and the research community and that, in the long run, a strong advisory process helped foster a stronger program. More to the point, advisory committees often helped Agency managers find real solutions to real problems. NASA's commitment to this point of view was clear as the Office of Space Science and Applications planned to reorganize its advisory committees in 1970 and as NASA Associate Administrator Homer Newell advised Fletcher about relations with the SSB in 1971 (See chapter 3).

NASA officials generally accepted, and often encouraged, vigorous debate and constructive criticism from their advisory bodies. For example, former OSSA director of astrophysics Charles Pellerin recalled his experience with the astrophysics subcommittee of SESAC:

"That was where almost all the advice that I personally received came from…. I liked putting the program out there and debating issues with them, because I liked the people. I liked working with them. Riccardo [Giacconi, then Space Telescope Science Institute Director] and I would go nose to nose, so nothing short of fisticuffs, but at the end of the day we liked each other…. We just both like to argue points vigorously."[11]

While debates were vigorous and criticisms could be sharp, the process was usually constructive and civil. On the other hand, when times were tough, for example when budgets were shrinking, relationships could develop sharp edges and combative tones. Former SSAC and SESAC executive secretary Jeffrey Rosendhal recalled that his first exposure to the advisory community in the 1970s evidenced a particularly adversarial tone in which the attitude of the advisory committee was one of coming to meet at NASA so as to dump on the Agency.[12]

The tension was not always drawn between advisory committees and NASA. Rather, there were often natural tensions between committee members or blocs of members. For example, Claude Canizares described the environment in the early 1980s thusly:

"I think one of the challenges with these committees is that they're in some sense representing the community. But they're also basically where the factions all meet around the table and arm-wrestle with each other…. So the committee itself was hardly a unified committee. It was an assemblage like the *loya jirga;* it was all the tribes were getting together…. There were attempts to get people to think big and think agency-wide. But it was a place where these tensions between the different parts of the community as well as between the community and NASA were inevitable. We would unify around how are we going to try to get space science high in the NASA agenda but then would struggle over who was going to get the new start."[13]

The challenge of getting the members of the scientific community to reach shared positions and present united views was put most succinctly by former NASA Associate Administrator Noel Hinners when he said, "There's no one mind of the infamous science community. It's only a community when an enemy shows up."[14]

A Need for Leadership

As NASA turned thirty, one could describe the advisory ecosystem as steeped in history, thoroughly woven into the fabric of space and Earth sciences, largely open and visible to all stakeholders, and energized by constructive tension between NASA and the scientific community. The environment was also increasingly stressed for a number of reasons. Austere budgets during the end of the

11. Pellerin interview, p. 8.

12. Rosendhal interview.

13. Canizares interview, p. 2.

14. Hinners interview, 18 August 2010, p. 19, NASA Headquarters Oral History Project, *http://www.jsc.nasa.gov/history/oral_histories/NASA_HQ/Administrators/HinnersNW/HinnersNW_8-18-10.pdf.*

Carter administration and the beginning of the Reagan administration put pressure on the program as a whole. The near-death experience of the planetary science program, which was an extreme example of the budget stresses, led to formation of the Solar System Exploration Committee. Apprehension over threats to the vitality of the program overall and frustration with an unpredictable NASA decision-making process for priorities subsequently led to SESAC's report on the Crisis in Space and Earth Sciences. And on top of all those issues, the Challenger accident had the potential to make matters worse across all of NASA.

Thus, the situation urgently called for leadership that could help reinforce the strengths of what had been a remarkably successful science program for three decades, restore the program, and provide some stability going forward. Over the ensuing two and a half decades, three key players—NASA, Congress, and the advisory community—all took actions that were relevant to this need. The chapters that follow in Part II will examine how each player dealt with the need for leadership.

Advice in NASA's Second Three Decades

CHAPTER 7

NASA Creates Its Own Strategic Plan

Confronting a Crisis

As chapter 5 explains, the mid-1980s were a time of multiple stresses for NASA. Budget cuts in the early years of the Reagan administration had severely constrained the space and Earth science programs. Then the impacts of the January 1986 Space Shuttle Challenger accident spread across the entire Agency. All launches planned for the Shuttle, which at the time reflected the Agency's policy to make the Shuttle the primary launch vehicle, were grounded and indefinitely deferred. Launches of the Space Telescope and the Galileo Jupiter orbiter were put on hold, as were the launches of the planned European Space Agency Ulysses mission to pass over high-latitude regions of the Sun and the NASA Cosmic Background Explorer (COBE). COBE was subsequently modified to move to a Delta expendable rocket launch. Plans for a Shuttle-based Solar Optical Telescope mission were canceled.

To make matters worse, the United States experienced Titan rocket launch failures in August 1985 and April 1986, a failure of the tried-and-true Delta rocket in May 1986, and an Atlas Centaur launch failure due to a lightning strike in March 1987. For all practical purposes, the U.S. space program was completely grounded in 1987.[1]

The dismal state of the U.S. space launch fleet exacerbated broader threats to the space and Earth science program that had been laid out in the SESAC Crisis report. And in a rather more profound sense, the combined effect of the U.S. launch stand-down and the fact that NASA had not launched or started a major new space science mission since the late 1970s left room to argue that the United States was no longer an international power in space exploration.

A Change in Leadership

In April 1987, Lennard Fisk succeeded Burton Edelson as Associate Administrator for Space Science and Applications. Fisk had been an astrophysicist at the Goddard Space Flight Center from 1969 until 1977, when he joined the physics department faculty at the University of New Hampshire (UNH). At UNH he rose through the academic ranks and then undertook administrative assignments to become director of the Space Science Center, then director of research, and finally vice president for research and financial affairs until he moved to NASA Headquarters.[2] He was well

---

1. James Gleick, "Errant U.S. Rocket Destroyed by Ground Control," *New York Times*, 28 August 1986, available at *http://www.nytimes.com/1986/08/28/us/errant-us-rocket-destroyed-by-ground-control.html* (accessed 11 August 2016).

2. Interview of Lennard A. Fisk by Rebecca Wright, NASA Oral History Program, 8 September 2010.

known as a working scientist, but his professorial demeanor concealed unusual skills at dealing with both the management and political environments of NASA Headquarters.

Fisk's first exposure to the political side of science came when he led efforts in the United States to gain support for a U.S.-European mission to send a pair of spacecraft over high-latitude regions of the Sun—the International Solar Polar Mission. The initial campaign succeeded in securing a budget new start during the Carter administration, but then the U.S. component fell victim to budget cuts during the near-death experience for planetary science early in the Reagan administration.[3] While that experience was no doubt painful, Fisk applied what he learned to serve as chair of the steering committee of the Space Science Working Group, which was a lobbying activity organized through the American Association of Universities on behalf of space science in the United States. In the 1980s, Fisk also served on SESAC and its predecessor, SSAC, as well as on the Earth System Science Committee and the SSB. Thus, when Fisk assumed his new role at NASA, he was able to bring first-hand scientific, institutional management, and political experience and insight to the job.

At his first meeting with SESAC, only one month after taking office, Fisk outlined four priorities:

1. providing for an orderly progression of new mission starts,
2. supporting an orderly buildup of Space Station laboratory science investigations,
3. securing necessary advanced technology funding to enable the start of the Earth Observing System in fiscal year 1991, and
4. ensuring the health of the scientific community, including the succession of the current generation of researchers, via a

strong program of research and analysis and small missions and the like.[4]

Among Fisk's first actions to pursue these priorities was the commissioning of an Office of Space Science and Applications strategic plan. He argued that, based on his experience at UNH, the need for real-life strategic planning was a given: "How do I know whether I succeed, if I don't know what I am supposed to be doing?"[5] The new OSSA strategic plan ended up changing relationships between NASA's science office and its advisory committees, the research community, and decision makers in Congress and the administration.

Elements of a New Strategy

Fisk had several objectives as he set out to formulate a strategic plan. He wanted a clear and well-understood process for setting priorities and making decisions. He expected to replace the annual new-start shoot-outs that had clouded OSSA planning and been a source of frustrations highlighted in SESAC's Crisis report. He also wanted to instill a sense of stability and dependability about the directions of the program so that the scientific community, students preparing to enter the community, and aerospace industry could be more confident about what were, and were not, likely prospects for future years.

The way in which the principal elements of the new strategic plan came into focus sounds almost too quaint to be true. Early in his time as Associate Administrator, Fisk traveled to Japan for a meeting on international space program cooperation. While there, he took advantage of some free time to sit contemplatively with a pen and notepad in a quiet Japanese garden. There, he jotted down the framework for the strategy.

---

3. Ibid.

4. Alexander document files from May 1987 SESAC meeting, NASA HRC.

5. Fisk interview, p. 8.

One of the beauties of the strategy was its simplicity. It could be explained in a way that lent itself to the one-hand rule—that is, the strategy involved three key elements, each of which could be outlined by enumerating points on the fingers of one hand.

The strategy itself would consist of five actions:

1. Establish a set of programmatic themes.
2. Establish a set of decision rules.
3. Establish a set of priorities for missions and programs within each theme.
4. Demonstrate that the strategy can yield a viable program.
5. Check the strategy for technology readiness and resource realism.[6]

Action number one produced five themes or structural elements:

1. the ongoing program,
2. leadership through major and moderate missions,
3. increased opportunity with small missions,
4. the transition to Space Station (when and where it offered unique opportunities), and
5. the research base.

Action number two produced five decision rules by which mission priorities and sequencing would be determined:[7]

1. complete the ongoing program,
2. initiate a major or moderate mission each year,

3. initiate small missions in addition to major and moderate missions,
4. move aggressively, but sensibly, to build science instruments for the Space Station, and
5. seek research base augmentations whenever they are warranted.

Each annual update of the strategic plan then presented specific initiatives for the coming year as well as an explicit five-year queue for missions and facilities planned for the near-term future.

When the strategic plan was introduced in the late 1980s, NASA had escaped the budget doldrums of the early 1980s and was enjoying annual budget growth. In 1984, NASA Administrator James Beggs made a commitment to SSB chair Thomas Donahue that NASA would budget "at least 20 percent of NASA R&D funds for space science and applications, and [would] protect these funds from the demands resulting from Space Station development."[8,9] With NASA's budget growing to support the Space Station development, plus the costs of returning the Space Shuttle to flight after the Challenger accident, science could count on growing in proportion to the total budget. The Fisk plan took note of that and was predicated on such continuing growth. However, the strategy also was meant to provide flexibility to adjust priorities within and among the five programmatic themes in response to changing budgetary, and other, circumstances.

An aspect of the strategy that was somewhat controversial was the fact that the second highest priority decision rule was to start a major or

---

6. This list of actions and the two lists below (themes and decision rules) are from the Office of Space Science and Applications, *Strategic Plan* 1988 (NASA, Washington, DC, 1988).

7. Decadal surveys prepared in 2010 (and later) used their own versions of decision rules, not to outline how overall mission priorities and sequencing would be determined, but to recommend how NASA should deal with unforeseen implementation problems. See chapter 11.

8. James M. Beggs to Thomas M. Donahue, 9 May 1984, Space Studies Board Archives, National Research Council, Washington, DC.

9. When Beggs made his 20 percent commitment, the science budget did not include launch vehicle costs, which were carried elsewhere in NASA's budget. After adding the costs of science mission launches, the fraction allocated for science was more in the neighborhood of 30 percent of the Agency budget.

moderate mission every year, so long as resources permitted. Given that the NASA and OSSA budgets were recovering from the lean times of a few years earlier, Fisk was convinced that this was an important way for the United States to recover from the interruptions caused by the Challenger accident and other launch system incidents and to demonstrate the robustness of the civil space program:

> I felt because we were getting decent support from the government—from the Congress and administration and the agency—that we had to make a bold statement. We had to demonstrate that the space program was alive and well and was coming back rapidly. And one of the ways to do that was show that we were going to start major new programs. So I viewed this in a much more global, national, strategic context than just dealing with backlogs of missions or things like that. It was simply a matter of trying to make as bold a statement as quickly as we could that the space program was back on its feet.[10]

Executing the Strategy

The strategic plan drew its scientific priorities from relevant SSB science strategy reports, and thus it was rooted in a foundation of National Academies scientific advice. But the development of the implementation strategies and priorities was very much a NASA effort. Fisk had a clear sense of where the SSB should hand off responsibility to NASA:

> I mean we basically said, "Okay you have given the advice on what we should be doing, and this is our plan for how we are doing it. That's our business; that's our side of the

equation."… It wasn't as if we sort of made up our own priorities. We didn't ask them to say which goes first—AXAF or CRAF/Cassini or EOS—but each one of them had some blessing by an Academy committee someplace. And it was our job to see how to make a budget out of this thing, and I think that's a reasonable division of labor.[11]

Once the plan was drafted, OSSA did present it to its internal advisory committees and invite comments and suggestions for improvements. But NASA never sought formal feedback from the SSB or its committees on the plan. When the draft strategy was first introduced to OSSA's own division directors, there was some pushback over concerns that they had not been sufficiently involved in formulation of the basic elements of the strategy. Fisk acknowledged this and avowed that while the themes would not change, the decision rules could be evaluated annually to determine whether the environment mandated an adjustment.[12] After the plan began to take hold, OSSA's discipline divisions embraced the strategy and engaged their discipline sub-committees of SESAC and their MOWGs in refining discipline strategies that provided input to the plan.

Fisk made it clear to the OSSA staff and advisory committees that the plan would be the guiding policy for the program and that it would, indeed, be utilized. At the first OSSA budget review after the plan was issued—a review of division proposals for the NASA fiscal year 1990 budget request in the summer of 1988—he arranged for a placard that sat in front of the meeting room saying that proposals for new initiatives that were not in the plan would not be in the budget. The message couldn't be simpler or more to the point, and the actual budget preparation was true to that directive.

---

10. Fisk interview, p. 14.

11. Fisk interview, pp. 21–22.

12. Alexander document files, NASA HRC.

The new strategic plan was a quick success. OSSA's advisory committees lauded the plan, although there were some reservations about its success-oriented approach that relied on a growing resource envelope to support a succession of robust new program starts. The broader research community embraced the plan, because it put a sense of order in the new-start process and let advocates of new mission candidates know where they stood in the queue. Fisk often noted that, "They understood for the most part that they couldn't jump the queue, and therefore, they were going to help sell the mission in front of them, so they got their shot."[13] Aerospace industry firms liked the plan because they could invest more confidently in preparing to compete for new mission development contracts. Budget planning relations with OMB were substantially improved. In a February 1989 conversation with the Space Science and Applications Advisory Committee (SSAAC),[14] the chief of OMB's Science and Space Branch, Jack Fellows, told the committee that the strategic plan had "made OMB's job much easier."[15] Likewise, OSSA enjoyed good relations with key members of Congress and their staffs, because the plan provided a clear, and stable, articulation of program priorities.

The 1991 astronomy and astrophysics decadal survey committee (see chapter 11) said, "In contrast to the fruitful 1970s, ...leadership in areas the United States had pioneered, such as x-ray astronomy, moved to Europe, the Soviet Union, and Japan. The currently planned program in space astronomy, described in the *Strategic Plan* (NASA, 1988, 1989) for NASA's Office of Space Science and Applications, can reverse this trend."[16]

Indeed, the plan's top priorities did remain largely stable and unchanged from 1988 through 1991. All three top-priority major missions—the Advanced X-ray Astrophysics Facility, the Comet Rendezvous Asteroid Flyby and Cassini Saturn orbiter pair of missions, and the Earth Observing System—were successful in securing budget starts in 1989, 1990, and 1991, respectively. However all three underwent significant restructuring and downsizing in later years as OSSA's budget prospects tightened. The plan's top priority small missions—a low-cost, principal-investigator-managed line of Explorer missions (called Scout-class missions or SMEXs for "small explorers") and a similar line of low-cost Earth science missions called Earth Probes—received budget starts in 1989 and 1991, respectively.

At the November 1988 inaugural meeting of the newly established SSAAC, Fisk reported on the success and broad acceptance of the strategic plan to date. And he reported that OSSA could look forward to 35 flight mission launches over the next five years and a steady-state launch rate stemming from the strategic plan of as much as eight launches per year. Committee member Jeffrey Cuzzi noted that the upcoming 35 launches represented recovery from the earlier launch stand-down and that policy makers needed to appreciate that this was "a flood from a broken dam over a parched landscape" rather than a sign that all was well.[17]

13. Fisk interview, p. 9.

14. The three former OSSA NAC advisory committees were merged into a single Space Science and Applications Advisory Committee in late 1988.

15. Alexander document files on the 1 February 1989 SSAAC meeting, NASA HRC.

16. National Research Council, *The Decade of Discovery in Astronomy and Astrophysics* (The National Academies Press, Washington, DC, 1991), p. 63.

17. Alexander document files from the 3 November 1988 meeting of the Space Science and Applications Advisory Committee, NASA HRC.

The Strategy Faces a Changing Environment

Fisk had emphasized that the plan would be a living document that could adapt to changes in budgetary or other situations, and the challenges were not long in coming. While the fiscal year 1991 budget included a new start for the Earth Observing System, the prospects for more new mission starts in subsequent years were bleak. Thus, as early as the October 1990 meeting of SSAAC, Fisk warned of a constrained growth scenario. NASA Deputy Administrator J. R. Thompson worried that scientists were inclined to stack "too many bricks on the wagon," and he added, "If you can throw them off when you get in trouble, you can throw them off now."[18]

Then Fisk introduced the option of a significant change in the strategy: Should the priority order of the themes be changed to lead with small missions rather than major and moderate size missions?

The SSAAC agreed to hold a strategic planning workshop in the summer of 1991, and planning for the effort began at the committee's meeting in February 1991. Fisk explained that there were no major or moderate mission new starts in the administration's fiscal year 1992 budget proposal to Congress. He challenged the committee to think about whether the time had come to reevaluate the entire mission queue, particularly if fiscal year 1993 shaped up to be worse than 1992. The committee met again in June 1991 to prepare for its summer workshop. At that meeting, Fisk again cautioned about a tightening budget climate and said that the idea of making a major mission new start a big event in the budget needed to be changed and that the time had come to "think small."[19]

The July 1991 SSAAC strategic planning workshop in Woods Hole, Massachusetts, represented an important rethinking of the OSSA strategy. Reflecting, in part, the vigorous debates that comprised the meeting and the fact that there were inevitably winners and losers, the meeting also gained fame (or infamy, if you felt that you were on the losing end of the priority order) as the "Woods Hole shoot-out."[20] Led by SSAAC chair and University of New Hampshire global change expert Berrien Moore, the participants included members of SSAAC, some former advisory committee members, representatives from the SSB, and OSSA division directors and other senior staff. Fisk opened the meeting by emphasizing that the time had come for a different, bolder plan, because the tide was no longer rising; he added that growth rates would be less than half of what OSSA had been enjoying.[21]

Over a five-day period, participants assessed current plans, reviewed the latest SSB strategies, vigorously debated strategic themes and decision rules, and grappled with alternative new-start queues. The Woods Hole strategy represented a new direction, particularly regarding the idea of combining intermediate, moderate, and major-scale missions into a single queue. In the end, the workshop reached consensus on four new decision rules (others were considered but not widely agreed to):

1. Complete the ongoing program.
2. Establish a mission queue by consensus. SSAAC subsequently defined priorities for missions in the queue to be (1) small innovative missions, (2) intermediate or moderate-profile missions, and (3) flagship missions.

---

18. Alexander document files from the 1 November 1990 meeting of the Space Science and Applications Advisory Committee.

19. Alexander document files from the 5 June 1991 meeting of the Space Science and Applications Advisory Committee.

20. Congressional Office of Technology Assessment, *NASA's Office of Space Science and Applications Process, Priorities, and Goals* (An OTA Background Paper, NTIS order #PB92-152503, Washington, DC, January 1992), p. 20.

21. Alexander document files on the 29 July 1991 SSAAC strategic planning workshop.

3. Implement the queue following the by-year sequence.
4. Initiate all missions on a given year's line before proceeding to the next year's line.[22]

In January 1992 the congressional Office of Technology Assessment (OTA) held a one-day workshop (convened at the request of Representative George Brown, chair of the House Committee on Science, Space, and Technology) to evaluate OSSA's strategic planning process. The fifteen distinguished participants included University of Texas at Arlington Dean of Engineering John McElroy (chair), Princeton astrophysics professor and former astronomy and astrophysics decadal survey chair John Bahcall, oceanographer and former Bretherton committee member D. James Baker, MIT astrophysicist and future SSAAC chair Claude Canizares, former NASA Associate Administrator Noel Hinners, Bell Laboratories physicist and SSB chair Louis Lanzerotti, and George Washington University Space Policy Institute head John Logsdon.[23]

The OTA workshop participants concluded that OSSA's strategic planning process had been notably successful in helping secure funding for NASA's science programs, which had doubled between fiscal years 1982 and 1992. They applauded the planning process for the breadth of its outreach to the scientific community and the explicitness of its priority-setting decision rules, calling them "exemplary." However, the workshop also raised questions about the strategy's realism, noting that a strategy that always assumes rising funding lacks flexibility and resilience in the event that the success-oriented expectations can't be met. Even

after recognizing changes to the strategy that emerged from NASA's 1991 Woods Hole workshop, participants in the OTA workshop were concerned that the revised plan might require more resources than what might be realistically available.[24] In a way, the OTA workshop was remarkably prescient.

OSSA did prepare a 1992 version of the strategic plan that incorporated the new directions recommended by SSAAC's Woods Hole workshop. The new plan was never released, owing to other events at NASA, but it was used as a guiding document for the office's operations during the year.

On 1 April 1992, Daniel Goldin became NASA Administrator, succeeding Richard Truly. Goldin had been a senior executive at TRW Space and Technology Group, where he had responsibility for two of NASA's Great Observatories (the Advanced X-ray Astrophysics Facility and the Gamma-Ray Observatory) and a number of classified Department of Defense space missions (including the space segments of the Brilliant Pebbles and Brilliant Eyes projects under the Strategic Defense Initiative). Early in his tenure at NASA, he emphasized his interests in improving program efficiency, applying the principles of Total Quality Management, increasing adoption of new technologies in flight missions, and most notably, transitioning to a "faster-better-cheaper" approach to space missions. To incorporate his concept of faster-better-cheaper into the NASA culture, Goldin pressed hard on the Agency to find ways to reduce the cost of ongoing big projects by 30 percent[25] and to substantially increase the number of small, short-development-time missions. When reminded, for example at a November 1992 SSAAC meeting, that the revised OSSA strategic plan had

22. Alexander document files, NASA HRC.

23. Congressional Office of Technology Assessment, *NASA's Office of Space Science and Applications Process, Priorities, and Goals*, An OTA Background Paper, NTIS order #PB92-152503, Washington, DC, January 1992.

24. Congressional Office of Technology Assessment, *NASA's Office of Space Science and Applications Process, Priorities, and Goals*, An OTA Background Paper, NTIS order #PB92-152503, Washington, DC, January 1992.

25. Alexander document files from 18 May 1992 Office of Space Science and Applications senior staff meeting.

already anticipated the need to move in that direction, Goldin argued that the shift was not being applied sufficiently broadly across all space and Earth science disciplines and that there was still an imbalance between planning for major missions and small mission concepts.[26]

In October 1992, Goldin announced his intention to break OSSA into three pieces that would place space sciences (astrophysics, planetary science, and solar and space physics), Mission to Planet Earth, and micro-gravity life and physical sciences under three separate management offices. He explained to SSAAC during the November 1992 meeting that OSSA was too big and that Mission to Planet Earth was not able to get adequate public visibility inside OSSA. SSAAC voiced concerns about potential threats from the reorganization to the OSSA strategic planning process and urged that the process remain in place to provide an integrated approach to planning NASA science programs and that NASA embrace the results of SSAAC's Woods Hole planning workshop.[27] The reorganization was formally implemented in April 1993.

Goldin named Fisk NASA Chief Scientist with responsibilities for integrating scientific program quality control, planning, and community outreach across the Agency and for communicating about NASA science both to an interested public and to potential international partners. Goldin cultivated an image of being a visionary leader, but his brusque demeanor, aggressive and often chaotic management style, and explosive temper frequently neutralized the positives that he espoused. When an SSAAC member suggested that making Fisk a "roving ambassador without authority" was not likely to be accepted by the scientific community, Goldin replied, "I've said all I need to say."[28]

The main elements of the 1992 OSSA strategic plan remained in place during the transition to the new organizational structure and leadership, but each of the new offices was left to develop its own strategic plan in future years. Fisk left NASA in July of 1993 to become chair of the Department of Atmospheric, Oceanic, and Space Sciences at the University of Michigan. In 2003, he became chair of the Space Studies Board and was also selected to hold an endowed professorship at Michigan named in honor of Thomas M. Donahue, who had served as SSB chair in the 1980s.

Assessing the Impact of the 1988 Strategy

Daniel Goldin's reorganization of OSSA brought an end to the approach to strategic planning that had been in place since 1988, but the process had enduring impacts. First, the strategy was a key factor in realizing Fisk's goal of restoring a vigorous NASA space and Earth science program and reestablishing U.S. international leadership in space research. Second, it introduced an orderly process for making decisions about priorities and communicating those priorities to the outside world. Third, the strategy helped build a significant degree of shared ownership, coherence, and mutual support across a diverse scientific community that could otherwise easily resort to the behavior of warring factions. The net result of all these impacts was that NASA's overseers elsewhere in the executive branch and in Congress were more easily persuaded to be supportive of the Agency's science program proposals. In short, they believed that NASA's science office had its act together.

The process served the Agency and the space research community well during a period of

---

26. Alexander document files from the 5 November 1992 meeting of the Space Science and Applications Advisory Committee.

27. Alexander document files from the 5 November 1992 meeting of the Space Science and Applications Advisory Committee.

28. Alexander document files from the 5 November 1992 meeting of the Space Science and Applications Advisory Committee.

healthy budget growth. However, it proved to be more challenging, but not irrelevant, when a period of constrained resources returned.

The 1988 OSSA strategic planning process had another, arguably more profound, impact. Prior to that time, there had been no coherent internal strategic planning process that spanned the full range of NASA science programs. Agency managers relied, instead, on discipline-oriented science strategies that were usually developed by the SSB and its committees and/or program strategies recommended by the Agency's internal advisory committees. The approach often led to long-range plans that were not especially strategic, science priorities that were not necessarily translated into program priorities, and reliance on the SSB as the principal long-range player in the process. With the advent of the new OSSA strategic plan, the division of roles between NASA and the SSB changed significantly. NASA still relied on programmatic advice from its internal committees such as SESAC and on long-term scientific advice from the SSB, but NASA exercised more control over its future direction. This change did not diminish the importance of the SSB, as chapter 11 will show, but it did influence the overall division of responsibilities.

CHAPTER 8

Congress Issues a Mandate —
The Government Performance and Results Act

In 1993, Congress passed legislation that mandated the use of certain planning and performance evaluation processes in all federal departments and agencies.[1] One might not expect that a set of bureaucratic requirements imposed on NASA (and all other agencies) would have an impact on NASA's use of outside science advice, but it did. This chapter tells that story.

In the late 1970s, the California city of Sunnyvale began to use a performance-based planning and management system that integrated long-range planning, results-oriented budgeting, and performance measurement to run the city government and provide services to its citizens. One can imagine how the aerospace industry's project management culture in the area might well have spilled over into local government. As the system evolved, its successes won attention and plaudits from scholars studying municipal and regional government management, as well as from the Clinton administration Office of Management and Budget (OMB). Former Sunnyvale Mayor and

City Council member John Mercer was serving as Republican counsel to the Senate Governmental Affairs Committee in 1990 when he interested Senator William Roth of Delaware in applying Sunnyvale's process to performance-based management in the federal government. Roth, who was also author of one of the three bills that were merged in the Senate to form the FACA legislation, subsequently introduced legislation to adopt Mercer's ideas. Roth's bill ultimately received broad bipartisan congressional and Clinton White House support, and the Government Performance and Results Act (GPRA) was enacted in August 1993.[2]

GPRA applied to every federal department and independent agency. The law required agencies to prepare a five-year strategic plan that would be revised or updated every three years. It required annual performance plans that involved goals that were linked to the agency's strategic plan. The act also called for an annual report that provided a publicly available assessment of the agency's performance as measured against its goals.[3]

---

1. Government Performance and Results Act, Public Law No. 103-62, enacted 3 August 1993, *https://www.congress.gov/bill/103rd-congress/senate-bill/20/text*.

2. See Homer A. Neal, Tobin L. Smith, and Jennifer B. McCormick, *Beyond Sputnik: U.S. Science Policy in the Twenty-First Century* (University of Michigan Press, Ann Arbor, MI, 2008), p. 76. Also John Mercer, "The Government Performance and Results Act," Strategisys.com, 2016, at *http://strategisys.com/gpra*; William Matthews, "Giving life to GPRA" (Federal Computer Week, 9 December 2001) at *https://fcw.com/articles/2001/12/09/giving-life-to-gpra.aspx?m=1*; and Florence Olsen "Interview: John Mercer, government reformer" GCN.com, 27 July 1998, at *https://gcn.com/articles/1998/07/27/interview-john-mercer-government-reformer.aspx*.

3. Government Performance and Results Act, Public Law No. 103-62, enacted 3 August 1993, *https://www.congress.gov/bill/103rd-congress/senate-bill/20/text*.

From the perspective of NASA's use of external scientific advice, GPRA had at least two significant implications. First, the mandate to develop regular strategic and performance plans created a continuing opportunity for NASA to utilize its advisory bodies in helping to translate scientific priorities recommended by the scientific community into Agency plans. Second, there was an opportunity to enlist the assistance of advisory bodies in evaluation of agency performance as measured against those plans. The former process—scientific planning—was already a relatively well-established practice in NASA's science office. The latter process—short-term performance evaluation—posed a perilous challenge in the sense that scientific research is fundamentally a long-term, and often unpredictable, endeavor.

After GPRA had been in place for more than a decade, Congressman Henry Cuellar of Texas, along with Senators Tom Carper of Delaware and Mark Warner of Virginia, led an effort to update the legislation to reflect what had been learned during its first decade or more. That effort culminated in enactment of the GPRA Modernization Act (GPRAMA) of 2010,[4] which put those lessons into practice.

Among the most significant changes was a provision to require that agency strategic plans be prepared at four-year intervals (instead of three) and aligned with the dates of presidential administrations, thereby ensuring that the strategic plans would be less likely to become irrelevant when administrations changed during an interval between plan due dates and more likely to reflect administration policies. The new legislation also changed the interval covered by annual performance plans so that they spanned two-year intervals rather than only one year, and it required that the performance plans show how they relate to agency strategic goals and objectives.[5]

NASA's Response to GPRA

To comply with GPRA requirements, NASA established a strategic management system that set out Agency policies and procedures for formulating the required strategic plans and performance plans and reports and that defined the linkages between the Agency's annual planning, budgeting, and performance evaluation schedules.[6] Every NASA program office was expected to engage in strategic planning to support the requirement for triennial Agency strategic plans. Therefore, while NASA's science offices did not need to produce annual strategic plan updates as OSSA had done through 1991, they were expected to produce an up-to-date plan every three years. In view of the fact that the goals and objectives outlined in the strategic plan were often long-term, NASA established a process by which major program offices would also prepare program-element *roadmaps* that were intended to span the gap between long-range goals and annual GPRA performance plans and to provide more specific implementation details that would not be included in a strategic plan. In space and Earth science, discipline-level subcommittees of the NASA Advisory Council assisted in the road-mapping process.

For many years, the SSB had produced occasional assessments of NASA's responses to SSB scientific strategies. In 1997, Associate Administrator Wesley Huntress and strategic planning lead Carl

---

4. U.S. Congress, GPRA Modernization Act of 2010, Public Law 111-352, enacted 4 January 2011; available at *https://www.gpo.gov/fdsys/pkg/PLAW-111publ352/pdf/PLAW-111publ352.pdf*.

5. For a thorough summary of the provisions in GPRAMA and differences from GRPA, see John M. Kamansky, "GPRA Modernization Act of 2010 Explained," IBM Center for The Business of Government, Washington DC, *http://www.businessofgovernment.org/sites/default/files/GPRA%20Modernization%20Act%20of%202010.pdf*.

6. For example, see "NASA Strategic Management Handbook," (NASA Headquarters, Washington DC, NPG 1000.2) at *http://www.hq.nasa.gov/office/codez/plans/2000Handbook.pdf*.

Pilcher in NASA's Office of Space Science asked the SSB to conduct a formal review of the office's draft triennial strategic plan, and that review process was repeated through 2003. The Board organized a similar review for the Office of Earth Science in 2000 and 2003. After the two offices were recombined, the SSB also reviewed the draft 2006 and 2014 Science Mission Directorate science plans.

All of the SSB reviews of Agency science plans shared certain common findings and conclusions. They all reported that the NASA plans presented appropriate scientific goals and objectives that were generally consistent with science priorities and strategies recommended in earlier NRC reports. The reviews often raised some concerns about whether the NASA drafts provided adequate attention to balance between spaceflight missions and supporting investments in research, data analysis, and advanced technology development and also whether they addressed Agency responsibilities for helping to nurture future members of the aerospace research workforce.

However, the most notable conclusion that every SSB review highlighted involved concerns about the extent to which the NASA documents were genuinely strategic. For example, the Board's review of the 1997 Office of Space Science Plan, which was arguably the most favorable of all of the reviews, concluded that

[T]he document's utility as a strategic plan could be augmented by broadly strengthening its presentation of key strategic processes [including] a discussion of budget and schedules for accomplishing the science goals [that] would help demonstrate their realism, balance, and feasibility.[7]

The most scathing of all the reviews was the "Assessment of NASA's Draft 2003 Earth Science Enterprise Strategy," which found that, "The ESE draft document does not clearly and compellingly articulate the Earth Science Enterprise's rationale, scope, relationships, and programmatic approaches."[8] Consequently, the report recommended that NASA's plan be revised to address the following:

missing elements of a strategic plan, including information on schedules, milestones, and evaluation criteria and approaches. In particular, the ESE [Earth Science Enterprise] draft document should discuss the methodology and the criteria that will be used in establishing relative program priorities.[9]

If one fast-forwards to 2013, that SSB review went to considerable lengths over the need for NASA to clearly and directly communicate the basis for a realistic strategy in the face of tough times:

NASA finds itself faced with a number of challenges in the near and more distant future. One of the most fundamental challenges is the uncertain and apparently decreasing level of available funding for space science in real terms.... This fiscal reality makes it more important than ever for NASA to have a clearly articulated and consistently applied method for prioritizing why and how its scarce fiscal resources will be apportioned with respect to the science program in general and on a more granular level among component scientific disciplines. The rationale behind this apportionment needs to be transparently

7. Space Studies Board, *On NASA's Office of Space Science Draft Strategic Plan*, letter report from SSB Chair Claude Canizares to OSS Associate Administrator Wesley Huntress, 27 August 1997, p. 5.

8. Space Studies Board, *Assessment of NASA's Draft Earth Science Enterprise Strategy* (National Research Council, National Academies Press, Washington DC, 2003), p. 1.

9. Space Studies Board, *Assessment of NASA's Draft Earth Science Enterprise Strategy* (National Research Council, National Academies Press, Washington DC, 2003), p. 1.

communicated, both internally and externally.... Decisions that will cause a failure to achieve previously declared goals, or a loss of national capability and capacity, ought to be a deliberate and clearly communicated choice.[10]

In this case at least, NASA took heed of the thrust of the 2013 review. Marc Allen, who was then the Science Mission Directorate's Deputy Associate Administrator for Research, noted that some of the shortcomings reflected the fact that the draft NASA plan had been sent out for review prematurely. Nevertheless, he found that the review was still helpful:

> [T]he review was really valuable for several reasons. I mean, it showed us some things we need to fix up in a fundamental way and also kind of woke us up a little bit and made us realize that we really had to focus more on it. But you know, NASA manages the science program budget on behalf of the research community. And it's one of those things Harry Truman said, "In Washington, if you want a friend get a dog." It's not quite the same situation, but the funding agency that can't stand up in front of its constituencies and hear what they've got to say is no longer viable. You really have to be ready to make the decisions and then take the medicine.[11]

In its final version of the 2014 science plan,[12] NASA did add expanded discussions of the different kinds of challenges that confronted each of the Science Mission Directorate's discipline divisions. The revised document also added material that responded to SSB calls for expanded discussions of needs for advanced technologies for future missions and explicit mapping of how the SMD program would respond to priorities recommended by the SSB's decadal survey reports (see chapter 11). However, the plan probably stopped short of what the SSB reviewers wanted to see in terms of presenting explicit decision rules for coping with budgets that would be too lean to let the Agency meet its long-term science goals. NASA's hesitance to be more definitive probably reflected the fact that the science plan had to be developed in consultation with, and approved by, OMB officials who were rarely willing to tie the administration's hands about how future budget problems might be handled.

Although the SSB had conducted periodic assessments of NASA's programmatic progress as measured against SSB science strategies, the whole idea of GPRA-mandated short-term assessments of results or outcomes was a new concept. In the late 1990s, Office of Space Science representatives inquired informally about whether the Board would organize a process for evaluating and grading NASA's annual GPRA performance reports. The SSB was skeptical about the feasibility and meaningfulness of annual evaluations of research outcomes and declined to take on this role.

Consequently, GPRA created significant new opportunities for NASA's internal advisory committees. The cycle of producing strategic plans at three-year intervals and performing performance reviews every year presented a ready match for engaging internal advisory committees such as SSAC and its successors. Once GPRA processes were phased in, NASA did put its in-house advisory committees to work in reviewing the Agency's annual performance reports.

---

10. Space Studies Board, *Review of the Draft 2014 Science Mission Directorate Science Plan* (National Research Council, National Academies Press, Washington DC, 2013), p. 6.

11. Allen interview, 7 May 2014, p. 11.

12. NASA tried an experiment with the NASA 2014 Science Plan, by not producing printed copies and only posting the document on the Internet and also making it available for download. See *http://science.nasa.gov/media/medialibrary/2014/05/02/2014_Science_Plan-0501_tagged.pdf*.

Monitoring the performance of spaceflight mission development and operations can be relatively straightforward, because performance measures can be derived from key project milestones such as hardware deliveries and tests and spacecraft design and flight readiness reviews. To tackle the more complex job of measuring research program performance, NASA science discipline divisions (e.g., astrophysics or planetary science) frame their evaluations around key science questions that are linked to higher-order science goals in the office's strategic plan. The divisions prepare annual self-evaluations and then have those reviewed by the respective science discipline subcommittees of the science office's NAC committee. Through this process, the advisory committees play a direct role in development of the accountability reports that NASA submits to Congress.

NASA's Allen voiced his surprise that at least some advisory committee members found this to be an enjoyable exercise:

> They would basically have a conversation about events that had happened scientifically during the year and decide whether it was about what you'd expect for the amount of money that got spent or if there were disappointments or calamities…. And they go through these things and then grade them. It struck me as something that must be incredibly tedious, but I had more than one subcommittee member say it was the most enjoyable thing that they did, because it was the only time when they came to subcommittee meetings that they actually got to talk about scientific results.[13]

National Academies Views on GPRA

In 1998, the National Academies Committee on Science, Engineering, and Public Policy (COSEPUP) examined the GPRA process from the perspective of evaluating research activities. The committee reported two major conclusions:

- The useful outcomes of basic research cannot be measured directly on an annual basis, because the usefulness of new basic knowledge is inherently too unpredictable; so the usefulness of basic research must be measured by historical reviews based on a much longer timeframe.

- That does not mean that there are no meaningful measures of performance of basic research while the research is in progress; in fact, the committee believes that there are meaningful measures of quality, relevance, and leadership that are good predictors of eventual usefulness, that these measures can be reported regularly, and that they represent a sound way to ensure that the country is getting a good return on its basic research investment.[14]

The COSEPUP report made several recommendations that were particularly relevant to the advisory process:

- For basic research programs, agencies should measure quality, relevance, and leadership…. The use of measurements needs to recognize what can and cannot be measured. Misuse of measurement can lead to strongly negative results; for example, measuring basic research on the basis

---

13. Allen interview, 7 May 2014, p. 10.

14. Committee on Science, Engineering, and Public Policy, *Evaluating Federal Research Programs: Research and the Government Performance and Results Act* (National Academy Press, Washington DC, 1999), p. 2.

of short-term relevance would be extremely destructive to quality work.

- Federal agencies should use expert review (i.e., peer review) to assess the quality of research they support, the relevance of that research to their mission, and the leadership of the research. Expert review must strive for balance between having the most knowledgeable and the most independent individuals serve as members.

- Both research and mission agencies should describe in their strategic and performance plans the goal of developing and maintaining adequate human resources in fields critical to their missions both at the national level and in their agencies.

- The science and engineering community can and should play an important role in GPRA implementation. As a first step, they should become familiar with agency strategic and performance plans.[15]

In 2001, the National Research Council (NRC) followed up on its earlier study with a more in-depth look at government research agencies' implementation of GPRA, focusing on how five agencies—NSF, NIH, DOD, DOE, and NASA—operated under the law. The study report reemphasized the fact that evaluating research progress is difficult because one cannot easily measure the generation of knowledge. Nevertheless, it concluded that the five agencies had "made a good-faith effort" to comply with GPRA and that GPRA was having a positive effect on "some agencies," albeit at the expense of added workload.[16]

The NRC report also repeated earlier advice that "federally supported programs of basic and applied research should be evaluated regularly through expert review, using the performance indicators of quality, relevance, and, where appropriate, leadership."[17]

When the NRC looked explicitly at NASA, the committee found that meeting the requirements for program evaluation posed particular challenges. While proposal peer review provided a proven mechanism for evaluating the merit of individual principal-investigator-level research projects, it could not be directly adapted to broader projects and programs. Consequently, the NRC report noted that NASA had decided to institute a new level of reviews of clusters of research programs called senior reviews.[18] Although NASA had other reasons beyond GPRA for conducting the space mission senior reviews, it did represent an important step in the Agency's use of outside advisors in managing the science program.

Impacts of NASA GPRA Plans

The process of developing strategic and performance plans is often mentioned as being more valuable than the documents that emerge from the process. For example, former Office of Space Science Associate Administrator Wes Huntress described the NASA strategic planning process as follows:

> The planning process was key ... because what you had to do was create a consensus in the community that what NASA was strategically

---

15. Committee on Science, Engineering, and Public Policy, *Evaluating Federal Research Programs: Research and the Government Performance and Results Act* (National Academy Press, Washington DC, 1999), pp. 38–40.

16. Committee on Science, Engineering, and Public Policy, *Implementing the Government Performance and Results Act for Research: A Status Report* (National Academy Press, Washington DC, 2001), p. 2.

17. Committee on Science, Engineering, and Public Policy, *Implementing the Government Performance and Results Act for Research: A Status Report* (National Academy Press, Washington DC, 2001), p. 5.

18. Chapter 10 explains in detail how senior reviews used panels of outside experts to assess the post-launch scientific effectiveness and productivity of groups of spaceflight missions in particular scientific disciplines.

planning to do they could support. That when they talked to their representatives in Congress they would talk positively about it. And so the process was very, very important and involved getting out to the community and at their meetings, using key community members in the planning process. So the process was absolutely key.[19]

Seasoned NASA science managers have not always been as enthusiastic about the clout of the planning documents outside NASA. Former Science Mission Directorate Associate Administrator Ed Weiler was skeptical about the persuasiveness of the NASA plans compared to the externally developed strategies from the NRC:

You have to ask yourself a question. Have you ever gone back 10 years and looked at the roadmap for OSS and asked yourself where we are today, or go back 5 years and ask? I mean, they are interesting exercises, but with the vagaries of Congress, the vagaries of funding, the bigger picture with decadals [NRC decadal surveys] coming out, roadmaps tend always to be superseded by events. To be brutally honest, I found the decadals to be a better roadmap of what we should be doing than any other roadmaps … because they had more cachet. I mean, go use the NASA roadmap or the NASA strategic plan as a justification to Congress and see how far that will get you.[20]

Marc Allen took a pragmatic view of the role of NASA strategic plans:

If you look at the strategic plans that the science office has turned out under its various

names, the programs are described basically carefully segregated from one another, and the assumption is that their budgets are as well. In fact, a lot of the strategic planning gets done based on budgets and programmatics in the budget formulation process, and the strategic plan basically documents it … It's sort of like going to buy a car. You get a brochure with colored pictures. You have a section on the engines, and one on the luxury features, and one on the trim options, and so on. But the car is manufactured someplace else, so it's not manufactured using that brochure. It sort of explains what it has, why it has it, and why it's a good thing. I think of those strategic plans as being more or less like that.[21]

Marcia Smith, who was the primary expert on NASA in the Congressional Research Service for many years, summarized her assessment of the importance of the NASA plans as follows, although like Weiler's comment above, she did not entirely fault NASA:

[T]hey were not very useful or relevant. A lot of it is because it was just a bunch of words on paper. They are very nice thoughts, but the reality of implementing any of those never seemed to work out. And a lot of that was factors that NASA itself couldn't control. I think NASA's budget has been up and down and up and down and up and down so much. Doing any of those kinds of strategic planning exercises is really no more than checking a box — somebody requires you to do a strategic plan.[22]

But like Huntress, Smith acknowledged that the process alone had its own benefits:

19. Huntress interview, p. 9.
20. Weiler interview, p. 4.
21. Allen interview, 9 September 2013, p. 7.
22. Smith interview, p. 14. Smith also served as director of the SSB from 2006 until 2009.

My own view is that the product is not very worthwhile, but the process is. Getting people to sit down around a table and actually talk about "What are you trying to accomplish, how you are trying to accomplish it, what do you want to do?" I think that is a good thing to be doing all the time. And if they want to spit out a report every three years or four years, that's fine; maybe it's useful to have a product. But I have never found any of those products particularly useful.[23]

Not everyone inside NASA was happy with GPRAMA, because implementation of the new version of the legislation, at least as prescribed by the Office of Management and Budget, turned out to be quite a task. When NASA officials who were responsible for NASA's strategic plan briefed the NAC Science Committee about the process in July 2013, they reported that new requirements for performance plans and evaluations after the enactment of GPRAMA had led to "monstrous growth" in effort by the planning staff, which led to about five times as much work, but no additional planning budget compared to the past.[24]

GPRA in Context

It's interesting to look back at Sunnyvale, California, where it arguably all began more than thirty years ago. Sunnyvale still uses performance-based principles in preparing its 20-year financial plan, but the system has evolved just as federal agencies' application of GPRA has evolved. An early change was to shift from output-based measures to outcome-based measures, just as the federal government has. And Sunnyvale managers realized that they needed to avoid "world peace" metrics and become more practical and more nuanced in selecting metrics that reflected the diversity of kinds of city operations and services, much in the same way that federal R&D agencies needed metrics that reflect the distinctions between operations and research. So while Sunnyvale's contemporary approach to long-range budget planning still uses performance-based metrics to help instill financial discipline and the city government still takes a data-driven approach to its job, the performance-based system has become less of a driving force than it may have been decades ago.[25]

As Marcia Smith and others have noted, GPRA and GPRAMA have become relatively invisible or inconsequential to most people outside federal agencies. Furthermore, both government and outside assessments of the impacts of the legislation have produced rather lukewarm conclusions about how significantly GPRA improves agency performance.[26] And some federal staff members have felt that the law exacerbated an already heavily burdened culture that lived via paperwork rather than measurable results. GPRA did push agencies to be more organized and more transparent in their planning and more explicit in their performance measurement, but whether or how performance

---

23. Smith interview, p. 15.

24. Minutes of the NASA Advisory Council Science Committee meeting of 29 July 2013, p. 4.

25. Sunnyvale update based on the author's 14 August 2014 interview with Sunnyvale Director of Finance, Grace Leung.

26. For example, see "Managing for Results: Implementation of GPRA Modernization Act Has Yielded Mixed Progress in Addressing Pressing Governance Challenges," Government Accountability Office, Washington, DC, GAO report 15-819, 30 September 2015; Donald Moynihan, "The New Federal Performance System: Implementing the GPRA Modernization Act," IBM Center for the Business of Government, Washington DC, 2013, *http://businessofgovernment.org/sites/default/files/The%20New%20Federal%20Performance%20System.pdf*; and Beryl A. Radin, "The Government Performance and Results Act (GPRA) and the Tradition of Federal Management Reform: Square Pegs in Round Holes?," *Journal of Public Administration Research and Theory,* January 2000, 10, pp. 111–135.

assessment is used to manage is unclear. One can debate whether the mandated procedures achieved the goals of openness and performance-based management, but nevertheless both FACA and GPRA did press agencies to adhere to an explicit standard and to assess progress.

However, as the next chapter will show, the push to expand the principle of openness and accountability also spun off approaches that threatened to compromise, or even neuter, the attributes of flexibility, responsiveness, and agility that agencies often needed.

CHAPTER 9

Congress Drops Another Shoe — The NRC Gets Its Own FACA Section

An institution should never become overconfident or complacent about its standing or its clout. In the 1990s, the National Academy of Sciences and its operating arm and affiliated entities (the National Research Council [NRC], the National Academy of Engineering [NAE], and the Institute of Medicine [IOM]) were well-established and respected sources of independent, expert, science, and technology advice for the federal government. The institution had a long record, a reputation of impeccable stature, and remarkable freedom to operate as an independent, non-government entity. Following the creation of the NRC under an executive order by President Woodrow Wilson in 1916, Presidents Dwight Eisenhower and George H. W. Bush formally reaffirmed the importance of the NRC in their own executive orders in 1956 and 1993, respectively.[1]

While the institution's reputation and stature remained untarnished, the independence of the NRC and its sister organizations came under special scrutiny in the mid-1990s. The NRC had been exempt from procedures and constraints imposed by FACA, because the law was not interpreted to apply to committees established by government contractors or committees not established by the

government itself. The NRC usually did business as a government contractor and formed its study committees independent of any government control, so NRC studies were considered FACA-free. Furthermore, the NRC had long-established policies and procedures for dealing with such issues as potential committee member conflicts of interest, closed meetings for committee deliberations, and independent peer reviews of draft study reports. But those aspects of a study were conducted internally at the NRC and were not routinely shared with the outside world. That was about to change.

In 1994, the Animal Defense Legal Fund, joined by Psychologists for the Ethical Treatment of Animals and the Association of Veterinarians for Animal Rights, sued in Federal Court to require that the NRC be required to comply with FACA. The NRC had been contracted by the National Institutes of Health to revise the NRC's widely used "Guide for the Care and Use of Laboratory Animals,"[2] and the plaintiffs objected to how committee members were chosen. The plaintiffs also sought to require that all the committee's meetings be open to the public so that the public could have access to the committee's deliberations. The defendants in the suit were the Department of Health

---

1. Wilson signed Executive Order No. 2859 on 11 May 1918; Eisenhower amended it with Executive Order No. 10668 on 10 May 1956; and Bush further amended it via Executive Order 12832 on 19 January 1993.

2. The revised document did appear as National Research Council, *Guide for the Care and Use of Laboratory Animals* (The National Academies Press, Washington, DC, 1996).

and Human Services and the National Institutes of Health; the National Academy of Sciences joined in the defense. After an initial finding in favor of the defendants and a series of appeals court decisions, the last of which was in favor of the plaintiffs, the U.S. Supreme Court refused to reverse the appeals court decision against the government and let it stand. Consequently, the Supreme Court's action (or decision not to act) on 3 November 1997 put the NRC squarely under FACA.[3]

While the case was moving through the courts, officials at the National Academies had been working with members of Congress to provide a remedy to what was viewed as a potentially lethal threat to the institution's independence. Once the Supreme Court ruled, congressional action proceeded at a breathtaking pace. Amendments to FACA were introduced in the House of Representatives on 9 November; they were passed in the House by voice vote on 10 November and in the Senate by unanimous consent on 11 November; and they were signed by President Clinton on 17 December. The amendments were integrated into the Act as section 15—"Requirements relating to the National Academy of Sciences and the National Academy of Public Administration"—and became known familiarly as "FACA section 15."[4]

The FACA amendments had two key provisions. First, "any committee that is created by the National Academy of Sciences or the National Academy of Public Administration" was explicitly excluded from FACA requirements other than those in section 15. Second, federal agencies were forbidden from accepting advice from the National Academies unless they complied with the provisions of section 15. Notably, the NRC was required to

- post the names of proposed study committee members for public comment before appointments were finalized,
- publicly announce open meetings of committee meetings in advance,
- make material submitted to a committee by outside parties available to the public, and
- provide brief summaries of closed meetings to the public.[5]

On the other hand, the NRC was able to preserve its ability to hold closed committee deliberation meetings and to preserve the confidentiality of report peer reviews. Consequently, portions of the NRC study process became more open to the public, but key aspects that defined the NRC's independence were preserved. Nevertheless, the NRC's narrow escape from potentially devastating restrictions under FACA made the institution particularly gun-shy about ever getting into a situation that might take the matter back to Congress for another look.

---

3. The final appeals court decision and accompanying background details are presented in United States Court of Appeals, District of Columbia Circuit, "ANIMAL LEGAL DEFENSE FUND, INC., et al., Appellants, v. Donna E. SHALALA, et al., Appellees," No. 96-5011, Decided: 10 January 1997. That decision is available at FindLaw for Legal Professionals, "Animal Legal Defense Fund v. Shala," *http://caselaw.findlaw.com/us-dc-circuit/1054924.html* (accessed 3 August 2016). A summary of subsequent Supreme Court and Congressional actions is available at Reporters Committee for Freedom of the Press, "Congress exempts two public bodies from advisory committee act," 1 December 1997, *http://www.rcfp.org/browse-media-law-resources/news/ congress-exempts-two-public-bodies-advisory-committee-act* (accessed 16 November 2016). The organization Psychologists for the Ethical Treatment of Animals subsequently changed its name to the Society & Animals Forum, Inc.; it is not the same as People for the Ethical Treatment of Animals (PETA).

4. Federal Advisory Committee Act Amendments of 1997, Pub. L. 92–463, §15, as added Pub. L. 105–153, §2(b), 17 December 1997, 111 Stat. 2689.

5. Federal Advisory Committee Act Amendments of 1997, Pub. L. 92–463, §15, as added Pub. L. 105–153, §2(b), 17 December 1997, 111 Stat. 2689.

The NRC's Response

The NRC's response to the new legislation was sweeping. Immediately after enactment of section 15 in December 1997, there was a 29-page formal policy and checklist for complying with the law. The institution was both genuinely concerned about reinforcing the attributes of National Academies studies that had underpinned their stature and credibility and obsessively concerned about the risk of running afoul of Congress and losing the FACA exemptions. The checklist included items on the committee appointment process, open committee meetings, public access to materials used by committees, report review, and release of reports, all of which dealt with transparency in NRC activities. Responsibility for compliance was placed on the shoulders of the individual NRC study staff directors, accompanied by stern warnings:

> You will be required to file a certificate of substantial compliance for each report (including letter reports) issued in connection with the study. Noncompliance with this law could result in the study's sponsoring agency not being able to use your committee's report. In addition, you could face serious legal consequences as an individual, and the Academies could be subject to lawsuits as an institution, if your committee fails to comply.[6]

The principal impacts of the NRC's new procedures were to codify most processes already in place, to make some more rigorous, and to apply them more broadly and uniformly across most of the institution's activities.

However, one change had a particularly big impact on the way the SSB operated and on its relationships with its sponsors, especially NASA.

Throughout its history, the SSB occasionally prepared its own advisory reports, for which the members of the Board itself gathered relevant information, either in response to an Agency request or at their own initiative. The Board members debated the issues at hand, reached consensus on conclusions and recommendations to be forwarded to the government, and authored the report. In doing so, the Board drew on the considerable breadth of expertise and experience of its members to prepare a report that was respected for its legitimacy. Most major policy-oriented SSB reports, especially letter reports, were reports on studies undertaken by the Board and authored by the Board. Also from the very beginning, the Board's discipline-oriented, standing committees regularly wrote their own reports. (See chapter 2.) Most science strategy reports and assessment reports came from the standing committees. Like the membership of the Board, the members of the standing committees were selected on the basis of their scientific and technical breadth and experience and their stature in their communities.

In 2001, the SSB obtained verbal agreement from the presidents of the National Academy of Sciences and the National Academy of Engineering, who were respectively also the chair and vice chair of the NRC, that standing bodies could author advisory reports so long as their membership could be shown to be appropriately qualified, balanced, and free of conflicts of interest for the topic at hand. In the end, however, the NRC prohibited Boards and standing committees from authoring reports, unless the authoring body was first formally vetted and appointed to serve as a committee for the topic in question (i.e., the particular subject or issue about which a new report was to be prepared) and unless the preparation of the report followed the same procedures as were prescribed for ad hoc study committees.

---

6. National Research Council, "Checklist for Responsible Staff Officers for Compliance with Section 15 of the Federal Advisory Committee Act," 17 December 1997, edited 13 August 2009.

The effect of this policy was twofold. First, it prolonged the turnaround time between when NASA might present a question to the SSB (or the SSB might identify an urgent issue that needed attention) and when the SSB could respond. The process of obtaining NRC project approval and appointing a study committee (even one that already existed as a standing committee) typically added months to the process. The second issue was that the policy effectively weakened the Board and its standing committees. After a four-decade history of being the nation's principal source of outside advice on space research, the SSB was being relegated to being a committee of committees, none of which could act on its own without going through added bureaucratic procedures. Distinguished scientists in the space research community began to ask, "Why should I sit on the SSB or an SSB committee whose role(s) have been neutered?" This led some to ask whether NASA should even fund the board and committees at all.

An ancillary effect was to eliminate most letter reports from the SSB's product line. From his experience as a member of the NRC Report Review Committee, Robert Frosch recalled that up through the mid-1980s letter reports

> were reports of what the committee was up to. You know, "We've had three meetings in which we discussed whatsis. I'm not sure how it will come out, but it will sort of be in this direction so you might start thinking about stuff like that."… And [then] we began—from the RRC point of view—to see letter reports that

had findings and recommendations, somewhat concealed but pretty clearly you didn't have to worry much to get the idea the committee recommends even if it didn't say so.[7]

The SSB under the chairmanship of Tom Donahue and Lou Lanzerotti was not necessarily the worst offender in the NRC, but it had been amongst the most active sources of letters. Thus, senior RRC officials began to urge that the proliferation of letter reports be curtailed well before enactment of FACA section 15, especially to avoid cases of special pleading. In 1992, the SSB established its own guidelines saying that "letter reports should be limited to important and urgent topics where rigorously defensible recommendations can be briefly stated."[8] In 1994, still some years before enactment of FACA section 15, the NRC Report Review Committee issued further formal criteria[9] that would govern the authorization and review of letter reports.

One aspect of the new guidelines was precipitated in part by the SSB. In late 1992, the SSB wanted to send a letter to NASA Administrator Daniel Goldin to express concerns about his plans to break apart the Office of Space Science and Applications. Both the chair of the RRC, Peter Raven, and the chair of the NRC, Frank Press, felt that a letter that volunteered advice about how NASA was organized would not be appropriate, and Press put a stop to it before it could be delivered.[10] That experience, and a few other similar cases, led the RRC to require that all proposals for letter reports receive formal authorization before

---

7. Frosch interview, pp. 5–6.

8. NRC Report Review Committee, "Guidelines for Preparation of Letter Reports by Committees of the Space Studies Board," RRC archives, National Research Council, Washington DC, 19 June 1992.

9. Raven memo to NRC Governing Board, "New Policy for Authorization of Letter Reports, RRC archives, National Research Council, Washington DC, 25 October 1994.

10. Letter from RRC chair Peter Raven to chair of the NRC Commission on Physical Sciences, Mathematics, and Applications Richard Zare, 10 October 1994, RRC archives, National Research Council, Washington DC. In the end, the SSB did get to make its points about Goldin's actions after Senator Barbara Mikulski arranged to have the Board conduct a review of the management of science at NASA in 1995 (see chapter 16).

boards or committees could begin to prepare them. Nevertheless, letter reports continued to be an acceptable form of formal advice to federal agencies, but the guidance was meant to ensure that they would meet NRC standards for both quality and timeliness.

Letter reports had often been prepared to address an urgent, narrowly focused issue or to respond to a very specific question from NASA, which often had a pressing time constraint within which NASA needed an answer. Recipients valued the letter reports because of their quick availability. A 1995 letter from the Board to then-NASA Chief Scientist France Cordova is a particularly interesting example of a quick-response letter report that would probably be impossible under the NRC's section 15 procedures. Cordova had a discussion with the Board at its 1 March 1995 meeting, during which she outlined Agency concerns about possible budget-driven cutbacks in the scientific workforce at NASA field Centers. She asked the SSB to provide its views about the roles and missions of Center scientists so as to assist senior NASA managers as they weighed options for dealing with the budget challenges in advance of mid-May deadlines. The Board pursued the questions in discussions with other senior NASA officials and in its own internal discussions, both at the meeting and at a subsequent SSB executive committee conference call, and framed a response. The SSB letter was sent to Cordova on 29 March,[11] with an explicit caveat that acknowledged that the depth of the Board's commentary was limited by the urgency of NASA's schedule for seeking views.

Another example stemmed from an August 1998 request from Carl Pilcher, the Science Program Director in NASA's Solar System Exploration Division, for the SSB's standing Committee on Planetary and Lunar Exploration (COMPLEX) to assess the Agency's plans for Mars exploration so as to facilitate mission planning decisions for 2003 and 2005 launches. Pilcher asked for SSB input by 15 November 1998. COMPLEX was able to gather information from key NASA experts during a committee meeting in September and to draw on earlier studies by COMPLEX and other NRC committees and to provide a letter report to NASA on 11 November 1998 that responded to Pilcher's request.[12] While this was a case where COMPLEX was able to act in near-record time, it does illustrate the more general ability of standing committees to quickly respond to special Agency needs.

The SSB reviews of draft Agency science strategies (see chapter 8) were also conducted via letter reports prepared by the Board, often with standing committee input and often on short time scales. But under the new NRC policy requiring that the SSB assemble, vet, appoint, charge, and utilize a unique committee to prepare a letter report, the time by which NASA needed an answer had often passed. Subsequently, the NRC discouraged letter reports unless either the authors of the letter were first vetted as an ad hoc committee established under the provisions of FACA section 15 or the letter only used and restated material from prior section 15–compliant NRC reports.

Reactions to the NRC's Implementation of FACA Section 15

Senior NASA science executive Paul Hertz described the problem from the Agency perspective:

Every member of the community will give us advice, but how do we boil that down into something, which can inform our decision

---

11. Space Studies Board letter report, Claude Canizares to France Cordova, *On NASA Field Center Science and Scientists* (National Research Council, The National Academies Press, Washington DC, 29 March 1995).

12. Space Studies Board, *Assessment of NASA's Mars Exploration Architecture: Letter Report* (National Research Council, The National Academies Press, Washington, DC, 1998).

making? The value of having an advisory committee to weigh these inputs and then give us advice gives a level of value to a decision that, if we make it ourselves, seems arbitrary…. [I]f we can't root our decisions in the community, then we are just a bunch of arbitrary bureaucrats and we lose our … credibility, our legitimacy with the community.

The NRC has forbidden the standing committees … or the Space Studies Board itself from giving us findings, recommendations, or advice on anything. According to their rules as they stand at the moment, if we want advice on a subject we have to ask a specific question and then they have to formulate an … ad-hoc committee that is specifically put together to answer that question and has its conflicts of interest specifically balanced with regard to that question. And then they will undertake a quick study to answer the question, and then their response will go through the complete NRC and Academy review before we can receive it.

And so we no longer get responses to the kinds of questions that we used to ask the standing committees…. I don't get any kind of balanced consensus or trade-off between the various possibilities and options…. The NRC committees can't even come to a conclusion; they can only gather together senior members of the community to provide discussion and individual opinions.[13]

Len Fisk summarized the standing committees' handicaps, saying, "Yes, they meet with NASA people, and they get to have a dialog. But there is no power behind the dialog. There is no public statement that somebody can refer to that brings some clout to what the Board has to say."[14]

When Marcia Smith moved from the Congressional Research Service to become director of the NRC Space Studies Board and Aeronautics and Space Engineering Board, she got an insider's look at whether the National Academies responded appropriately and consistently to FACA:

I didn't realize that the Academies were under FACA until I was accepted for the job, and I started looking into it more thoroughly. The first thing I learned was that the NRC's regulations on FACA were *interim* and they had been *interim* for a long time before I went to work there…. So it was very hard to know exactly what that meant and exactly what was applied. And I found the NRC's implementation of FACA to seem capricious at times. Sometimes it seemed as though if the NRC did or did not want to do something, FACA would be used as the excuse. That may be harsh, it may even be untrue, but after three years that is what I walked away believing. As opposed to when I walked in the door, I thought, "Oh, good thing, I'm all for transparency and public accessibility and everything."… And the fact that people were resisting applying FACA was just people who were too set in their ways and who had been in their jobs for too long. But I walked out of there with a completely different idea.[15]

Claude Canizares held out hope that the NRC could find a path to resolution of the problems:

I think when the FACA lawyers got too close to things, I think some of what I'm describing about the effectiveness of the SSB was diminished … I'm not convinced that the Academies have been as forceful as would be warranted

---

13. Hertz interview, p. 5.

14. Fisk interview, p. 20.

15. Smith interview, p. 23.

to try to advocate for a sensible and effective position…. I wish there were ways to maybe vet the group in some public way. Have public discussions to say that we are doing that. Then have maybe even the surgeon general's warning on the letter that says this should be taken as advisory but not a firm recommendation but that still allows the government to hear this, because otherwise they won't hear it.[16]

Another SSB chair and former NASA official Charles Kennel shared his colleagues' feelings of dismay:

I will just say that as far as I am concerned, the infestation of FACA rules and quasi-FACA rules on a naive and unsuspecting Academy and panel process was, for the first 10 years, a complete disaster and hobbled the Space Studies Board in ways that are almost unspeakable.[17]

Nevertheless, Kennel held out hope that some of the most egregious problems could be overcome in the future, adding, "but we've gotten through that."[18]

There was some evidence that Kennel's hopes were beginning to be realized. As of early 2015, the staff director of the SSB and ASEB, Michael Moloney, indicated that the boards and standing committees were becoming more engaged in direct, informal discussions with NASA science officials, who regularly used the NRC groups as sounding boards with whom they could share issues and hear the experts' opinions. Moloney saw that as an important way for the NRC to fulfill its role as a forum for dialog between the government and the U.S. scientific community.[19] When NRC boards and standing committees are not meeting to respond to a formal request for advice, they are permitted to meet with government officials in closed sessions where there can be more candid discussions than might be acceptable in sessions open to the public. By late 2016, the NRC seemed to be moving towards a policy that would allow the SSB and its standing committees to issue statements or letters expressing consensus views or concerns, although those statements would be devoid of any formal advice to the government.[20]

From the perspective of the National Academies, the institution's FACA section 15 procedures could be viewed as examples of responsible behavior to protect the Academies and stay within the strict confines of the law. They kept the Academies more transparent and beyond any hint of conflict. But in the course of surviving the 1994 suit brought by the Animal Defense League and the 1997 federal court decisions, the Academies solutions also presented significant problems for the value and utility, not to mention the perception in the scientific community, of the SSB and its committees.

---

16. Canizares interview, p. 10.

17. Kennel interview, p. 4.

18. Kennel interview, p. 4.

19. Moloney, 18 March 2015 interview.

20. Moloney e-mail to the author 24 September 2016.

CHAPTER 10

NASA Senior Reviews

NASA's success with go-aheads for major missions such as the Cassini Saturn orbiter and the beginning of the Great Observatories program in the mid-1980s and then a robust series of new mission starts in the late 1980s and early 1990s came with a mortgage. Many of those missions were intended to operate over a long span of time—more than a decade—and others proved to be so well designed that they typically exceeded their "prime-phase" design lifetimes and continued to produce valuable scientific results for many years. Consequently, NASA found itself having to find ways to either pay for their operations and data analysis[1] activities at the expense of having funds to start new missions or be able to count on continuously rising budgets. The latter option proved unrealistic, and in fact impossible. SESAC recognized this challenge as it organized its study that led to the 1986 Crisis report. (See chapter 5.)

Associate Administrator Lennard Fisk described the challenge as one of his principal concerns when he met with SESAC's successor, SSAAC, in 1990.[2] NASA Administrator Daniel Goldin began to attack the problem in 1992 when he commissioned a set of review teams to look for ways to find efficiencies and budget reductions in various programs.[3] The Chief of the Astrophysics Division's Science Operations Branch Guenter Riegler began to press managers at the Goddard Space Flight Center, which handled most astrophysics mission operations, to reduce their costs or face the need to pull the plug on some missions altogether.

Riegler began his NASA career as an astrophysicist conducting research in x-ray astronomy at the Goddard Space Flight Center. He joined NASA Headquarters in 1987 and eventually served as Director of Research Program Management and then Executive Director for Science in the Office of Space Science. He moved from Headquarters to the Ames Research Center in 2002 to serve as Director of Astrobiology and Space Research at Ames until his retirement in 2005.

Riegler's initial efforts were partially successful, but NASA officials recognized that the problem was bigger than what could be accomplished by ad hoc approaches and simple belt-tightening. A major element of the solution rested in involvement of advisors from the outside scientific community.

---

1. Mission operations typically cover support for control centers where specialists manage tracking and orbit data computations, monitoring of spacecraft health, scheduling of changes to spacecraft status and instructions, and uploading of commands. Data analysis typically includes data processing and conversion of raw telemetry data into physical units, distribution and archival of data files for scientific use, and scientific analysis.

2. Alexander document files, NASA HRC.

3. Alexander document files from OSSA staff meeting on 18 May 1992.

Senior Reviews of Space Mission Operations

In 1992, Riegler was commissioned to organize a "senior review" of six currently operating astrophysics flight missions;[4] the process expanded to consider 11 astrophysics missions in 1993; and it was adopted subsequently across all of NASA's space and Earth science programs. The original process only considered mission operations (i.e., the effort devoted to monitoring and operating the spacecraft in flight), and it did not examine the scientific data analysis segments of ongoing projects.[5] The reviews assessed the progress and scientific accomplishments of ongoing missions and their objectives and plans for future (presumably more efficient) operations.

An expanded level of senior reviews, which assessed the requirements and value of both mission operations and data analysis funding, was initiated for solar-terrestrial physics[6] missions in 1997[7] and for astrophysics missions in 1998, and they were further expanded to consider planetary science flight mission programs in 2001.[8] In addition to helping NASA managers deal with the budget challenges noted above, the process offered an effective way for the Office of Space Science to meet some of its performance evaluation requirements under GPRA. Missions were ranked based on assessment of the scientific merit of their proposed operations for the next two years and on factors such as cost efficiency, expected new hardware or software development, and education and outreach plans. Each review panel was charged to recommend to NASA a strategy for which missions should be either

a. continued at their current levels of activity and support,
b. continued but with some budget enhancements or reductions compared to their current levels,
c. continued with "bare-bones" funding for operations and data handling amounting to about one half of the prime-mission levels but with no funds for science data analysis, or
d. terminated.

In 2007, the Earth Science Division of NASA's Science Mission Directorate formed a senior review panel to evaluate 13 operating Earth science missions, all of which were at or approaching the end of their planned prime mission lifetimes.[9] A second panel was convened in 2009. The panel was charged to make recommendations for mission extensions and funding levels for fiscal years 2010 and 2011 as well as preliminary recommendations for the subsequent two years, 2012–2013. The panel's approach was modeled closely on that

---

4. Logsdon, John M., ed., with Stephen J. Garber, Roger D. Launius, and Ray A. Williamson, *Exploring the Unknown: Selected Documents in the History of the U.S. Civil Space Program, Volume VI: Space and Earth Science* (NASA SP-2004-4407, NASA History Division, Washington DC, 2004), p. 173.

5. Guenter Riegler, Chief, Space Science Operations Branch, NASA Headquarters, "Charter: OSSA Operations and Data Analysis (MO&DA) Blue Team," 17 June 1992. Reproduced in Logsdon, John M., ed., with Stephen J. Garber, Roger D. Launius, and Ray A. Williamson, *Exploring the Unknown: Selected Documents in the History of the U.S. Civil Space Program, Volume VI: Space and Earth Science* (NASA SP-2004-4407, NASA History Division, Washington DC, 2004), p. 248–249.

6. The field of *solar-terrestrial physics* is also sometimes called *solar and space physics or heliophysics*.

7. See *http://science.nasa.gov/heliophysics/senior-review/*.

8. For an in-depth description of the senior review process as it had evolved by 2002, see Guenter Riegler, "The 'Senior Review' Process" (Office of Space Science, NASA Headquarters January 2002) in Alexander document collection, NASA History Division, Washington, DC.

9. Senior Review Committee, "NASA Earth Science Senior Review," (NASA Earth Science Division, Science Mission Directorate, NASA, Washington DC, 2007).

employed in earlier years for space science missions. NASA officials gave guidelines to each mission for out-year funding levels against which to prepare proposals for the review panel to evaluate, and the panel was asked to consider scientific productivity, contribution to national needs, technical status, and cost efficiency. Based on those factors, the panel was then expected to categorize each mission in terms of whether it merited

a. continued funding at the guideline level,
b. continued funding with some augmentation,
c. continued funding but at a level below the guidelines, or
d. preparation for termination.[10]

The Earth science panelists found that all 13 missions were still making important scientific contributions and were worthy of continuation in 2010 and 2011, but they concluded that two missions could be terminated during fiscal year 2012 or 2013. They also found that a third mission had become underutilized and recommended that extended operations in 2012 should depend on whether nearer-term efforts were successful to reduce costs, improve data access, expand data usage, and sustain data quality. Such a hopeful proposal for the nearer-term period, for which the panel failed to recommend any terminations, was probably not as helpful to NASA managers as they would have preferred, but the panel's detailed assessments of each mission did provide insights that could help NASA set more realistic priorities.

NASA Director of Astrophysics Paul Hertz described the senior reviews as:

a process by which NASA could make a reasoned decision as to when a mission had outlived its value, [and] to determine when it was no longer a good buy to continue paying the operation costs in exchange for the additional science you would get for additional operations.... All the operating missions would essentially submit proposals as to what science they predicted they would do over the next two years and what it would cost to keep the mission going to attain that science.[11]

And he emphasized the way in which the process facilitated orderly planning for future years:

But those are always revisited the next two years, and ... it allows us to make plans ... and the missions can start the process for soliciting their next cycle of science investigations. If a mission is going to be terminated, it gives us the rest of the fiscal year to terminate them before their funding ends at the end of the fiscal year.[12]

A key aspect of the senior reviews, and a major factor in their success and acceptance, is the involvement of outside scientists to conduct the reviews. The term "senior review" pertains to what Riegler called "the highest level of peer review within the space science program."[13] About a dozen review panelists from the outside community are selected based on their breadth of experience and expertise, especially regarding their familiarity with multiple missions being considered in the review and their knowledge of the relevant research areas. Each biennial review panel is asked to examine the

10. Senior Review Panel (Steven A. Ackerman, chair), "NASA Earth Science Senior Review 2009," Earth Science Division, Science Mission Directorate, NASA Headquarters, Washington DC, 2009.

11. Hertz interview, p. 1.

12. Hertz interview, p. 2.

13. Guenter Riegler, "The Senior Review Process," Office of Space Science, NASA Headquarters, Washington, DC, January 2002.

expected continuing scientific value of individual missions. However, it also becomes a comparative review that pits missions (and data centers) against each other and seeks to rank the expected returns of competing missions, assess their effectiveness, and recommend a strategy for continued operations within a specific disciplinary program.

Congress became so impressed with the value of the senior review process that it mandated regular use of the reviews by prescribing them in the NASA authorization bill for 2005:

SEC. 304. ASSESSMENT OF SCIENCE MISSION EXTENSIONS.

(a) ASSESSMENT.—The Administrator shall carry out biennial reviews within each of the Science divisions to assess the cost and benefits of extending the date of the termination of data collection for those missions that have exceeded their planned mission lifetime. In addition—

(1) not later than 60 days after the date of enactment of this Act, the Administrator shall carry out such an assessment for at least the following missions: FAST, TIMED, Cluster, Wind, Geotail, Polar, TRACE, Ulysses, and Voyager; and

(2) for those missions that have an operational component, the National Oceanic and Atmospheric Administration or any other affected agency shall be consulted and the potential benefits of instruments on missions that are beyond their planned mission lifetime taken into account.

(b) REPORT.—Not later than 30 days after completing each assessment required by subsection (a)(1), the Administrator shall transmit a report on the assessment to the Committee on Science of the House of Representatives and the Committee on

Commerce, Science, and Transportation of the Senate.[14]

While the senior reviews have become a particularly powerful example of NASA's reliance on outside advice for decision making, they also appear to have some soft spots. Astronomer and veteran member of the SSB and several decadal survey committees Marcia Rieke observed the challenge of forming truly balanced and objective review panels:

[O]ne thing that I have been concerned about is that if I look at the membership for the recent senior review panels and the suite of missions they're looking at, it didn't look to me that it was a balanced community group. And the missions that were recommended to be defunded, some of them successfully lobbied to get funding back. And those were the ones that didn't seem to have particular defenders on the committee, should we say. And so I really worry about how well that's working. The principle I think is still a good idea, but whether it's actually working as well as it might is another question.[15]

As NASA budgets became more constrained in later years, some review panels felt that they had very little room to maneuver. When NASA was able to set funding limitation guidelines for the panels that were seen to be reasonable, panels could embrace a program that recommended priority choices but kept scientifically valuable projects on a productive course—"Add money to mission A, keep mission B at its current level, cut back on mission C but keep it going, and plan to terminate mission D." Once NASA managers prescribed more severe limits under which the panels' reviews were framed, the reviews became what one

---

14. "National Aeronautics and Space Administration Authorization Act of 2005," section 304, PL 109-155, 30 December 2005.

15. Rieke interview, p. 55.

participant called "a blood bath with rather irrational decisions."[16] Even when senior review panelists thought they were being responsive to NASA guidance, there have been occasions when budget officials at OMB objected to the fact that some older missions received high scientific ratings, thereby running counter to OMB hopes to free up funds by terminating the old missions. This may have been the case when the administration's fiscal year 2016 budget request for NASA included no funding for the Opportunity rover on Mars and the Lunar Reconnaissance Orbiter, in spite of the fact that both missions received very high ratings in the 2014 senior review.[17] Congress refused to accept the proposed terminations and provided funds to keep both missions alive at least through fiscal year 2017.

In 2015, recognizing the various political and scientific pressures on the senior review process that had emerged over the years, NASA asked the SSB to conduct an assessment of the value of extended missions and of the senior review process itself. That assessment produced very positive conclusions about the value and overall effectiveness of the senior reviews, saying that the study committee reached "a strong consensus that NASA's approach to extended missions is fundamentally sound and merits continued support."[18] The study report also provided useful illustrations of the successes of extended missions and how the senior review process evolved over the years, and the report offered a number of recommendations about how to sharpen the process in the future. Thus, some 23 years after Riegler introduced the senior review concept, the process continued to be a valuable and effective model for using outside advice.

Senior Reviews of Scientific Research Programs

In 1999, the Office of Space Science prepared to add a second system of senior reviews to its management toolbox—this one to review the office's research and analysis (R&A) programs.[19] R&A is NASA's term of art for research programs (primarily funded via research grants to individual principal investigators) for new science instrument technology development, suborbital research flights on high-altitude aircraft and balloons and sounding rockets, analysis and interpretation of spaceflight data, development of theory and computer simulations, and ground-based telescopic and laboratory measurement in support of spaceflight investigations. Thus, R&A programs help bring spaceflight missions to scientific fruition, lay scientific and technological groundwork for future missions, and provide unique opportunities for training future space scientists and technical experts.

In 1998, two advisory studies had recommended that NASA implement a systematic process by which to evaluate its R&A programs. Both an internal committee operating as a task force under SSAC and an ad hoc committee of the SSB[20] called for such an effort. OSS responded by first

---

16. Correspondence from L. A. Fisk to the author, 21 February 2015.

17. For discussion of reactions to the proposal, see Casey Dreier, "Is the Opportunity Rover a Mission 'Whose Time Has Passed'? No," The Planetary Society Blog, 16 March 2015, *http://www.planetary.org/blogs/casey-dreier/2015/0315-is-opportunity-a-mission-whose-time-has-passed.html* and Leonard David, "NASA Moon Orbiter, Mars Rover Face Budget Chopping Block," Space.com, 27 March 2015, *http://www.space.com/28943-opportunity-rover-lro-nasa-budget.html.*

18. National Academies of Sciences, Engineering, and Medicine, *Extending Science—NASA's Space Science Mission Extensions and the Senior Review Process* (The National Academies Press, Washington, DC, 2016), p. 7.

19. Guenter R. Riegler, "Assessment of NASA's Space Science Research and Analysis Programs," (Office of Space Science, NASA, Washington DC, 28 June 2001), Alexander document files, NASA Historical Reference Collection, NASA Headquarters, Washington, DC.

20. See Space Studies Board, *Supporting Research and Data Analysis in NASA's Science Programs: Engines for Innovation and Synthesis*, (National Research Council, The National Academies Press, Washington, DC, 1998).

reorganizing its roughly 40 individual R&A programs into 11 topically related research clusters and then adapting the senior review process to conduct an assessment of the whole program in 2001.

At the first R&A review, the senior review panel was asked to examine the elements of the program in terms of scientific merit and relevance, appropriateness of the budget distribution across the elements, structure of the program in terms of best meeting long-term strategic goals, and highest-priority needs for new initiatives or budget augmentations. The panel was also asked to assess the distribution of funding across the program and to recommend whether adjustments were needed. The panel responded to this charge by assigning programs to one of four categories:

1. most deserving of more funding if an augmentation could be obtained,

2. deserving of continued support and some increase if an augmentation could be obtained,

3. areas in need of improvement and/or candidates for reductions, and

4. candidates for major reductions or termination.

The panel placed seven of the R&A clusters in category 1, three in category 2, one in category 3, and none in category 4. The panel presented detailed assessments for all of the program elements, thereby giving NASA useful information with which to manage the programs going forward.[21]

The Office of Space Science embraced the panel's recommendations by reducing the budget of the lowest-ranked program and charging its managers to develop a plan for progress improvement. Three of the high-priority initiatives received budget augmentations.[22]

In spite of repeated encouragement from advisory committees in 1998 and again in 2010,[23] NASA did not attempt more cross-program R&A senior reviews. In response to the 2010 SSB report, which had emphasized principles and metrics for evaluating and managing R&A program effectiveness and portfolio balance, NASA's Planetary Science and Astrophysics Divisions did organize ad hoc committees to examine the individual division's R&A programs. The panel reports addressed issues such as program structure, adequacy of funding, and portfolio strength and balance, but they did not recommend priorities or potential budget reallocations along the lines of the mission operations reviews and the 2001 R&A review.[24]

Having a group of outside scientists review, evaluate, and rate the scientific productivity and funding portfolios of research programs that spanned the full range of science disciplines proved to be too big a challenge. The task was controversial and subjective. The senior reviews of space mission operations, when conducted within the boundaries of a single disciplinary program such as astronomy, were challenging enough, but they proved successful even when they were painful. However, an effort to tackle the whole research program in a single gulp was not repeated.

21. See Guenter R. Riegler, "Assessment of NASA's Space Science Research and Analysis Programs," (Office of Space Science, NASA, Washington DC, 28 June 2001) in *http://science.nasa.gov/heliophysics/senior-review/*.

22. Memo from Guenter Riegler to R&A discipline scientists, "Recommendations and Decisions for the Space Science research and Analysis (R&A) programs," 2001 at *http://science1.nasa.gov/media/medialibrary/2010/12/27/RASR01_RESPONSE-NASA-HQ.pdf*.

23. Space Studies Board, *An Enabling Foundation for NASA's Space and Earth Science Missions* (National Research Council, The National Academies Press, Washington, DC, 2010).

24. See Supporting Research and Technology Working Group, "Assessment of the NASA Planetary Science Division's Mission-Enabling Activities," Planetary Sciences Subcommittee of the NASA Advisory Council, 29 August 2011 and Committee to Review Astrophysics Programs for Research, Analysis, and Enabling Technology, "NASA Astrophysics Research, Analysis & Enabling Technology 2011 Review Panel Comments," NASA Astrophysics Division, NASA Headquarters, Washington DC, 2011.

As chapter 16 will show, this was not the first time that the task of setting broad cross-disciplinary priorities exceeded advisors' reach. But first, the next chapter will examine particularly important additions to the SSB's portfolio of disciplinary advisory products that emerged at roughly the same time as NASA's senior reviews.

CHAPTER 11

Expansion of NRC Decadal Surveys and Performance Reviews

At a 2015 hearing of the House of Representatives appropriations subcommittee that approves NASA's budget, the committee chair said,

> I really want to see NASA focus on those decadal surveys, I really think that's the proper guide.… That's my North Star, just to make sure that we're following the recommendations of the best minds in the scientific community in each of these areas of specialty.[1]

The congressman's comment illustrates one of the greatest success stories in the history of outside advice to NASA.

The NRC decadal science strategy surveys—or more colloquially known as the *decadal surveys* or just the *decadals*—are the signature products of the SSB. There is probably no NRC space science advisory product that has earned the attention and reputation, year after year, or had an impact to rival that of the decadals. Various observers and users have called these reports "the gold standard for scientific advice"[2] and have described them as "incredibly valuable," "truly stunning," "in a class

by themselves in terms of congressional buy-in," and "the National Academies at their best."[3] How the decadal surveys gained such a unique place in the world of scientific advice provides an important lesson about the impact of broad engagement and commitment from the scientific community. The story of how the endeavor expanded from an activity conceived and pursued by a single community—U.S. astronomers—to an activity that spans all of space science marks an important milestone in the evolution of NASA's scientific advisory history. And as we shall see, the ability of the decadal survey process to evolve and adapt to a changing scientific, technological, programmatic, and political environment has been a continuing challenge.

Origins of the Decadal Survey Process

In 1962, the National Academy of Sciences Committee on Science and Public Policy (COSPUP) formed a panel on astronomical facilities and gave it a straightforward charge: examine needs for new ground-based astronomical

---

1. Congressman John Culberson quoted in "A Great Day on Capitol Hill: House Appropriations Hearing on fiscal year 2016 NASA Budget Request," *FYI: AIP Bulleting of Science Policy News*, 12 March 2015, Number, 34, American Institute of Physics.

2. Comment by William Atkins, former House Subcommittee on Space and Aeronautics staff director, at November 2006 SSB Decadal Science Strategy Surveys Workshop, Alexander document files, NASA HRC.

3. Paul Hertz at November 2012 SSB workshop on Lessons Learned in Decadal Planning in Space, Alexander document files, NASA HRC; Turner, Allen (9 September 2013, p. 9) and Weiler (9 September 2013, p. 3) interviews, respectively.

facilities in the United States, assess the likely costs of new facilities, and recommend priorities for facility construction over the ensuing decade.[4] Astronomer Albert E. Whitford, who was director of the University of California's Lick Observatory from 1958 to 1968, was appointed chair of the committee. He was a respected leader of the U.S. astronomy community, a member the National Academy of Sciences, and an important participant in the founding of the Kitt Peak National Observatory.

The eight-person Whitford committee included experts in both optical and radio astronomy, who represented many of the major astronomical institutions of the day. The committee's 1964 report briefly summarized the most notable and promising scientific questions in the field and assessed the status of U.S. astronomy compared to the rest of the world. This assessment considered the state of observing facilities as well as trends in graduate student enrollment in astronomy and the implications for demand for astronomy facilities in the United States. The committee confined its attention to needs and priorities for ground-based facilities to be supported by the NSF, Office of Naval Research, and NASA, even though it recognized the emerging opportunities for space astronomy in the nascent U.S. space program. NASA had already gained an image for its robust budget, and the committee emphasized that its recommendations represented a "prudent" program that would be "of the order of one half of one percent of that going into the space effort."[5]

Five years after publication of the Whitford report, COSPUP formed a new astronomy survey committee that had a substantially broader and more ambitious charge—namely, to review the state of U.S. astronomy, identify the most important scientific problems in the field, and recommend priorities for both ground-based and space astronomy for the coming decade.[6] The new committee, which was considerably larger—23 members—than the Whitford committee, was chaired by Jesse Greenstein of Caltech.

Greenstein was an astrophysicist who earned a Ph.D. degree from Harvard and who was elected to the National Academy of Sciences in 1957. He led the establishment of the graduate program in astronomy at Caltech and served as its chair from 1948 until 1972. In the 1950s, his earlier interest in radio astronomy reawakened, and that interest was reflected both in his seminal studies of quasars and his efforts to establish the Caltech Owens Valley Radio Observatory and the National Radio Astronomy Observatory.[7]

The Greenstein committee drew on input from about 100 experts who served on a dozen topically organized panels and working groups; thus, its conclusions reflected input from a significant fraction of the growing community of U.S. astronomers. The committee's 1972 report[8] included an extensive discussion of contemporary frontiers in astrophysics; an assessment of the state of U.S. astronomy and astrophysics in terms of manpower, funding, and facilities; explicit, prioritized recommendations for new investments for the next

4. Committee on Science and Public Policy, *Ground-Based Astronomy: A Ten-Year Program* (National Academy of Sciences-National Research Council, National Academy Press, Washington, DC, 1964).

5. Committee on Science and Public Policy, *Ground-Based Astronomy: A Ten-Year Program* (National Academy of Sciences-National Research Council, National Academy Press, Washington, DC, 1964) stated in the report's Foreword.

6. Astronomy Survey Committee, *Astronomy and Astrophysics for the 1970s* (National Academy of Sciences, National Academy Press, Washington, DC, 1972).

7. Robert P. Kraft, "Biographical Memoir of Jesse Leonard Greenstein" (National Academy of Sciences, Biographical Memoirs, vol. 86, The National Academies Press, Washington, DC, 2005).

8. Astronomy Survey Committee, *Astronomy and Astrophysics for the 1970's* (National Academy of Sciences, National Academy Press, Washington, DC, 1972).

decade and estimates of their likely costs; and principles to guide implementation of the report's recommendations. The survey's scope spanned the full range of astronomical subjects—including solar and planetary astronomy—and it considered all relevant federal funding agencies—including not only NASA and NSF, but also the Department of Defense and the Atomic Energy Commission (which later became the Department of Energy).

While the committee was entirely independent of the government agencies, there were connections that promoted communications with the agencies' own advisory committees. Notable from a NASA perspective was the fact that Leo Goldberg, who chaired NASA's Astronomy Missions Board (see chapter 3), was also a member of the Greenstein committee.

The general scope of the Greenstein committee's survey of astronomy and astrophysics served as a framework for all future decadal surveys, and it introduced attributes that became fundamental factors that endowed decadal surveys with extraordinary staying power. These included the following:

- broad disciplinary scope that covered an entire scientific field;
- a long time horizon that examined accomplishments and advances over the previous decade and scientific priorities for the next decade;
- inclusive participation by a large fraction of the relevant scientific community;
- explicit priorities for new projects and facilities, including consideration of their estimated costs and recommended schedules; and
- consideration of enabling capabilities such as workforce and training, computation

and data handling, institutional factors, and various dimensions of balance.

The committee recommended four "highest priority" initiatives followed by seven efforts that were "of high scientific importance," but not so important as to displace any in the top four. The top tier included one space program, which would be devoted to x-ray and gamma-ray astronomy and which rounded out the list at fourth position. The second-tier space recommendations included a proposed doubling of support for aircraft, balloon, and sounding rocket astronomy (#6 overall priority); continuation of the Orbiting Solar Observatory satellite series (# 7 priority); and "an expanded program of optical space astronomy…leading to the launch of a large space telescope at the beginning of the next decade" (#10 priority).[9]

The Greenstein report's treatment of the Large Space Telescope (LST, which later became the Hubble Space Telescope) was somewhat controversial. There were advocates for the LST, especially within NASA, but the survey committee declined to include it in its list of high priority programs. The committee was concerned that LST would be an especially expensive project and that it would be affordable only in a budget environment that supported more vigorous growth than was considered to be realistic. Therefore, the survey report cited the extraordinary potential of an LST and stated that "This program should be directed toward the ultimate use of an LST."[10] However, the report suggested that support for the LST in the 1970s should be limited to modest funding for technology development leading to consideration in the 1980s if funding increases materialized to support such a large project.[11] While that conclusion was hard to swallow within NASA, it probably improved the

9. National Research Council, *Astronomy and Astrophysics for the 1970s* (The National Academy Press, Washington, DC, 1972), p. 8.

10. National Research Council, *Astronomy and Astrophysics for the 1970s* (The National Academy Press, Washington, DC, 1972), p. 100.

11. Robert W. Smith, *The Space Telescope: A Study of NASA, Science, Technology, and Politics* (Cambridge University Press, New York, NY, 1989), pp. 131–134.

immediate credibility of the report by showing that the survey committee did stay true to its responsibility to be realistic and make hard choices.

The outcome of the Greenstein committee's measured support for LST provides an interesting story in contrasts between how the recommendations of this early decadal survey were treated by the community compared to the practically inviolable status of later surveys that are described below in this chapter. Two Princeton astronomers, John Bahcall and survey committee member Lyman Spitzer, mounted a full-court press to lobby both the members of the Greenstein Committee and Congress to accept the LST as an important and viable new initiative. Subsequently, Congress did begin to hear a more supportive perspective from the astronomical community. Also in 1974 the SSB initiated a new study of priorities for space science. Its 1975 report endorsed the LST as a new budget start for fiscal year 1976 saying that since the publication of the Greenstein report "the LST has moved to first place in priority among the large space projects under consideration by the astronomical community."[12] This was probably the last time that an NRC committee departed so explicitly from the position of a decadal survey. Although there were several more years of nail-biting experiences as the telescope made its way through the congressional approval process, it did survive and emerge as a successful program.[13]

The astronomy community followed up on the Greenstein report with decadal survey reports in 1982, 1991, 2001, and 2010.[14] Each of those surveys followed the general template that the Greenstein committee introduced in the 1969–1972 study. They also expanded the level of broad community participation by holding multiple town-hall meetings during regular conferences of the American Astronomical Society and at various universities and astronomy research facilities. Each of the survey reports enjoyed a positive reception in Congress and OSTP and supportive attention in NSF and NASA. A report's high-priority recommendations were not always affordable within the ten-year time span recommended by the committee, but in almost all cases the federal government was ultimately able to initiate the recommended projects. For example, the space x-ray telescope recommended in the 1982 survey was launched as the Chandra X-ray Observatory in 1999; a space infrared telescope recommended in the 1991 survey was launched as the Spitzer Space Telescope in 2003; a successor to the Hubble Space Telescope recommended in the 2001 survey is being built for launch as the James Webb Space Telescope (JWST) in 2018; and a successor to JWST recommended in the 2010 survey is in its formulation stage at NASA for a mid-2020's launch.

The 1991[15] and 2001[16] survey reports are good examples of how the surveys produced results. Box 11.1 illustrates the outcomes from recommendations for major investments in astronomy and astrophysics space missions. Seven flight programs—SIRTF, FUSE, SOFIA, medium-size Explorer satellites, JWST, GLAST, and SDO[17]—went forward

---

12. National Research Council, *Opportunities and Choices in Space Science* (The National Academies Press, Washington, DC, 1975), p. 40.

13. A full account of the aftermath of efforts to keep LST alive is presented in chapter 5 of Smith's book.

14. The 1991 survey was administered by the staff of the NRC Board on Physics and Astronomy, which was established in 1983 and which is a companion NRC board to the SSB. All subsequent astronomy surveys have been administered jointly by the BPA and SSB.

15. National Research Council, *The Decade of Discovery in Astronomy and Astrophysics* (The National Academies Press, Washington, DC, 1991).

16. National Research Council, *Astronomy and Astrophysics in the New Millennium* (The National Academies Press, Washington, DC, 2001).

17. SIRTF (Space Infra-Red Telescope Facility), FUSE (Far-Ultraviolet Spectroscopic Explorer), SOFIA (Stratospheric Observatory for Infrared Astronomy), JWST (James Webb Space Telescope), GLAST (Gamma-ray Large Area Space Telescope), SDO (Solar Dynamics Observatory).

Survey Recommendations	Outcome
The Decade of Discovery in Astronomy and Astrophysics (1991)	
#1 large initiative: Space Infrared Telescope Facility (SIRTF)	The redesigned free-flying SIRTF mission was approved in 1998 and launched in 2003 as the Spitzer Space Telescope.
#1 moderate initiative: dedicated spacecraft for the Far-Ultraviolet Spectrographic Explorer (FUSE)	FUSE was originally planned for a Space Shuttle launch but subsequently configured for launch on an expendable rocket and launched in 1999.
#2 moderate initiative: Stratospheric Observatory for Far-Infrared Astronomy (SOFIA)	SOFIA was initiated as a NASA-German Space Agency collaboration in 1996. The telescope first acquired astronomical images in 2010.
#3 moderate initiative: Delta-class Explorer program acceleration	Four Delta-class astronomy and astrophysics Explorers were launched in the 1990s compared to one in the 1980s.
#4 moderate initiative: Astrometric Interferometry Mission (AIM)	AIM was redesigned in the 1990s to become the Space Interferometry Mission (SIM), simplified further in 2002, but not recommended in the 2010 decadal survey, and discontinued.
#5 moderate initiative: international collaborations on space instruments	NASA continued to engage in international collaborations but without creating a separate budget line.
Astronomy and Astrophysics in the New Millennium (2001)	
#1 major initiative: Next Generation Space Telescope	Design studies for the renamed James Webb Space Telescope began in 2002 and construction began in 2004.
#2 major initiative: Constellation-X Observatory (Con-X)	After determining that Con-X would be too costly, NASA collaborated with ESA studies of an International X-ray Observatory, renamed the Advanced Telescope for High Energy Astrophysics (Athena). The mission has not yet been approved.
#3 major initiative: Terrestrial Planet Finder (TPF)	NASA selected two alternative TPF design concepts for study in 2002. Budget problems led to termination of the effort in 2006.
#4 major initiative: Single Aperture Far Infra-Red (SAFIR) Observatory	NASA initiated a mission concept study for Far-IR Surveyor mission in 2015 for consideration in the 2020 decadal survey.
#1 moderate initiative: Gamma-ray Large Area Space Telescope (GLAST)	GLAST was launched in 2008 and renamed the Fermi Gamma-ray Space Telescope.
#2 moderate initiative: Laser Interferometer Space Antenna (LISA)	NASA joined as a partner with ESA to prepare for a future LISA mission, leading to a technology test flight in 2015 and studies of a future gravity-wave space observatory.
#3 moderate initiative: Solar Dynamics Observatory (SDO)	SDO was launched in 2010.

BOX 11.1   Summary of outcomes from the largest recommended space program initiatives in the 1991 and 2001 astronomy and astrophysics decadal surveys

successfully. On the other hand, the 1991 survey's proposed planet-hunting Astrometric Interferometry Mission foundered, as did its successor, the Terrestrial Planet Finder, which was endorsed in 2001. Neither mission moved forward to development stage. The Con-X mission, LISA, and the SAFIR[18] observatory for infrared astronomy did not blossom in the 2000s, but they still remain alive as prospects for the 2020s.

---

18. Con-X (Constellation-X x-ray observatory), LISA (Laser Interferometer Space Antenna), SAFIR (Single Aperture Far Infra-Red observatory).

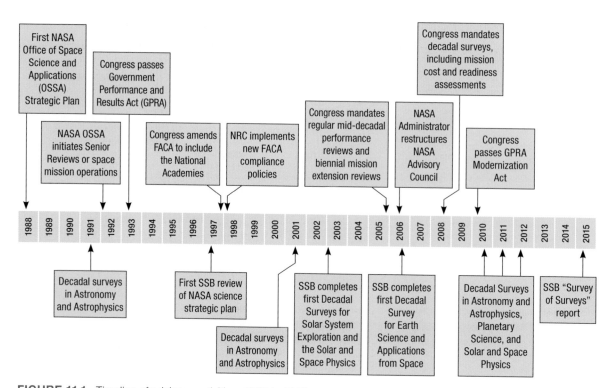

FIGURE 11.1 Timeline of advisory activities, 1989 to 2015

Expanding from Astronomy to All Space and Earth Science

In 2000, while the 2001 astronomy and astrophysics decadal survey report was in preparation, NASA Associate Administrator for Space Science Edward Weiler concluded that he should apply the decadal survey process to the other elements of NASA's space science program as well. Thus, a major expansion of the decadal surveys began in 2001. Responding to Weiler's requests, the SSB organized two new survey committees—the Solar and Space Physics Committee, chaired by physicist Louis Lanzerotti, and the Solar System Exploration Survey Steering Committee, chaired by astronomer Michael Belton. Following the astronomers' model, both surveys were organized around a main steering committee and an array of disciplinary and cross-disciplinary subpanels. Both surveys utilized town meetings at various locations across the United States to gather community member perspectives. The solar system survey committee also invited scientists to submit short papers that summarized proposals for new initiatives for consideration by the survey committee and its panels. These first two decadal surveys to reach beyond the field of astronomy and astrophysics were published in 2003.[19] (See figure 11.1.)

The 2003 planetary science survey[20] provides an interesting example of successes as well as of action delayed. Table 11.1 lists the survey committee's recommendations for major flight missions and NASA's response. Five candidate missions were recommended for NASA's medium scale New

---

19. Solar System Exploration Committee, *New Frontiers in the Solar System: An Integrated Exploration Strategy* (Space Studies Board, National Research Council, National Academies Press, Washington DC, 2003); Solar and Space Physics Survey Committee, *The Sun to the Earth – and Beyond: A Decadal Research Strategy in Solar and Space Physics* (Space Studies Board, National Research Council, National Academies Press, Washington DC, 2003).

20. National Research Council, *New Frontiers in the Solar System: An Integrated Exploration Strategy* (The National Academies Press, Washington, DC, 2003).

TABLE 11.1 Major flight programs recommended by the 2003 Solar System Exploration decadal survey

Survey Recommendations	Outcomes
#1 priority large initiative: Europa Geophysical Explorer	After exploring joint studies with ESA in 2007, NASA initiated new studies in 2011 in response to the 2011 decadal survey call for a simplified multiple-flyby mission to Europa. With congressional urging, the formulation phase began in 2015, and a lander was added to the mission concept in 2016.
#1 priority medium initiative: Kuiper Belt-Pluto Explorer	The New Horizons mission was selected as the first New Frontiers Program mission; it launched in 2006 and flew past Pluto in 2015.
#2 priority medium initiative: lunar South Pole-Aitkin Basin Sample Return	A lunar sample return mission was carried over for the next round of New Frontiers mission selections.
#3 priority medium initiative: Jupiter Polar Orbiter with Probes	The Juno orbiter mission (without probes) was selected in 2004 as the second New Frontiers mission and was launched in 2011 for a 2016 arrival at Jupiter.
#4 priority medium initiative: Venus In Situ Explorer	A Venus mission was carried over for the next round of New Frontiers mission selections.
#5 priority medium initiative: Comet Surface Sample Return	A comet sample return mission was carried over for the next round of New Frontiers mission selections.
#1 priority large Mars initiative: Mars Sample Return	NASA joined with ESA in 2009 to plan a sample return mission but withdrew in 2011, citing budget cuts. In 2012, NASA began new studies of a 2020 rover and sample-caching mission.
#1 priority medium Mars initiative: Mars Science Laboratory	MSL design began in 2004. It was launched in 2011, and the Curiosity rover landed on Mars in 2012.
#2 priority medium Mars initiative: Mars Long-Lived Lander Network	The InSight mission was selected as a one-node geophysical network to be launched in 2018.

Frontiers Program, and two were selected to proceed to development and then launched. The New Horizons mission to Pluto led the way and produced spectacular results at Pluto in 2015. The second mission in the program—Juno—was launched in 2011 and entered into an orbit at Jupiter in 2016.

Studies for the survey's only recommended large mission, which would explore Jupiter's satellite Europa, led to concepts that were initially unaffordably complex and ambitious. Consequently, the 2011 decadal survey report[21] said that the mission could not be endorsed unless it was simplified.

NASA began that simplification, and the revised Europa mission moved into formulation stage in 2016. Congressional enthusiasm for the mission, particularly the enthusiasm of Congressman Culberson, who chaired the relevant House budget appropriations subcommittee for NASA, made this a case study in going beyond the decadal survey's recommendations. Congress not only embraced the mission but also directed NASA to add a Europa lander element.[22]

The story for the outcomes of 2001 Mars program recommendations was also a mixed bag. The

21. National Research Council, *Vision and Voyages for Planetary Science in the Decade 2013–2022* (The National Academies Press, Washington, DC, 2011).

22. Eric Berger, "Congress: NASA must not only go to Europa, it must land," ArsTechnica, 16 December 2015, *http://arstechnica.com/science/2015/12/congress-nasa-must-not-only-go-to-europa-it-must-land/*.

committee's top-priority medium-scale mission—the Curiosity rover—was built, launched in 2011, and landed on Mars in 2012. The mission did grow significantly in scope and cost during development, thereby causing delays in subsequent Mars missions. The survey's top priority large mission—a Mars Sample Return—started out briefly as a collaboration between NASA and ESA, but NASA withdrew in 2011 due to budget problems. NASA then regrouped in 2012 and initiated studies for a surface rover and sample-collector mission that could be the first phase of a sample return mission in 2020 or later. A sample-caching rover was the top-priority recommendation of the 2011 decadal survey, and so NASA attempted to stay true to the survey's priorities.

In 2003, then SSB chair Lennard Fisk and the author, Joseph Alexander, met with NOAA Assistant Administrator for Satellite and Information Services Greg Withee and NASA Associate Administrator for the Earth Science Enterprise Ghassem Asrar to discuss the idea of further expanding the use of decadal surveys to the field of Earth observations and applications from space. The two officials agreed, and in 2004 the NRC established the Committee on Earth Science and Applications from Space.[23]

This survey was different from its predecessors in several ways. First, it encompassed a field that has a large applied science dimension that builds on and extends beyond the basic research aspects of the Earth sciences. The committee acknowledged this both in terms of how the survey's topical panels were organized and by focusing much of the committee's priority-setting on an assessment of potential societal benefits. Second, the Earth science community was considered to be significantly more diverse, both topically and culturally, than the space science disciplines that were considered in the prior surveys. Furthermore, the community was (a) demoralized by recent budget cuts in a Bush administration that was not especially supportive of the Earth sciences and (b) hesitant to embrace the idea of a decadal survey for the field. To begin to cope with such challenging aspects of the survey, the organizers held a planning workshop before the steering committee was appointed to initiate discussion and gather ideas about how to organize the survey. One of the survey's eventual successes was the fact that the undertaking did help bring the community together and get its members to take a more integrated view of their field. As a consequence of this impact, one might argue that the survey report was among the most important documents for the field, possibly ranking only behind the Bretherton report (see chapter 5).

Another important difference between the Earth science survey and its predecessors was that the survey's two sponsors, NASA and NOAA, and Congress asked the committee to prepare an interim report before the survey was completed in order to provide a heads-up on urgent issues that would require near-term attention. The committee complied with a report[24] delivered in 2005. Its central conclusion was that due to recent, persistent budget cuts, "the national system of environmental satellites is at risk of collapse." Lamentably, many of the concerns outlined in this report were not terribly different from the Space Applications Board's 1982 report, "Remote Sensing of the Earth from Space: A Program in Crisis," that is described in chapter 2. While such a stark description in the 2005 interim report garnered government and community attention, the survey committee did not see satisfactory

23. National Research Council, *Earth Science and Applications from Space: Urgent Needs and Opportunities to Serve the Nation* (The National Academies Press, Washington, DC, 2005).

24. National Research Council, *Earth Science and Applications from Space: Urgent Needs and Opportunities to Serve the Nation* (The National Academies Press, Washington, DC, 2005).

near-term progress, and it repeated its pessimistic assessment in the final survey report a little more than a year later.[25]

Applying Lessons Learned

In 2006, the SSB held a workshop to evaluate the effectiveness of the first round of surveys that had expanded the process to new scientific fields starting in 2001. Survey committees had often struggled with a tendency to underestimate the cost and technological risk of new-mission candidates and to rely on unrealistically optimistic cost estimates. In essence, the new surveys were giving credence to the kind of concerns expressed by the Greenstein committee in 1972 when it declined to give a high priority to LST because of worries about its potential budgetary impact on the rest of NASA's space astronomy program. Consequently, participants at the 2006 workshop recommended four steps for future decadal surveys:

1. include cost assessment and technology experts on survey committees,
2. obtain independent cost estimates and include cradle-to-grave life-cycle costs,
3. include cost uncertainty indexes to help define the risk of cost growth, and
4. use common costing approaches so that costs for different missions or facilities can be compared.[26]

Congress embraced the recommendations when it passed the NASA Authorization Act of 2008 and directed that future decadals include independent estimates of life-cycle costs and technical readiness of missions.[27]

The next round of surveys produced reports that were published in astronomy and astrophysics[28] and in planetary science[29] in 2011 and solar and space physics[30] in 2012. The new surveys all took heed of the conclusions from the 2006 workshop and incorporated an extensive process of independent cost and risk assessment that was aimed at enabling the survey committees to more rigorously evaluate and compare candidate missions. However, the survey reports were delivered in the midst of an unstable NASA budgetary and political environment. Consequently, NASA managers faced an uphill battle to implement the surveys' recommendations even though they often wished to follow them.

University of Chicago theoretical astrophysicist and veteran of several decadal survey committees, Michael Turner, had an enlightening analysis of the difficulties that the 2001 and 2010 astronomy and astrophysics surveys encountered:

First, the community has gotten less homogenous…. If you go back 30 years, everybody saw everybody a couple of times a year, and the community was well-connected and on the same page. Astronomy is much more

25. National Research Council, *Earth Science and Applications from Space: National Imperatives for the Next Decade and Beyond* (The National Academies Press, Washington, DC, 2007).

26. Space Studies Board, *Decadal Science Strategy Surveys: Report of a Workshop* (National Research Council, The National Academies Press, 2007), pp. 2–3.

27. "National Aeronautics and Space Administration Authorization Act of 2008," H.R. 6063, P.L. 110-422, signed 15 October 2008.

28. National Research Council, New Worlds, *New Horizons in Astronomy and Astrophysics* (The National Academies Press, Washington, DC, 2011).

29. National Research Council, *Vision and Voyages for Planetary Science in the Decade 2013-2022* (The National Academies Press, Washington, DC, 2011).

30. National Research Council, *Solar and Space Physics: A Science for a Technological Society* (The National Academies Press, Washington, DC, 2012).

heterogeneous and in my opinion more interesting and exciting!

Next, the projects have gotten more expensive and take longer to build, and so it's not obvious that the decade is a right time unit any more. Agency budgets have been unpredictable and not increasing. It's easy to be a genius when budgets are going up. It's easy to look bad when they are going down. In the 2001 survey,…for some of the projects we endorsed there was no way they were going to get done during the decade or even the next decade. In my mind the big issue here is schedule and readiness—not that cost isn't an important issue—but readiness is even more important. For some of those projects the community was unrealistically led to believe that they were actually ready to go. I think we did a lot better on the readiness and the cost [in 2010], but the money available for new activities at NASA kept shrinking. We got the most detailed information ever from [NASA], however, it changed with time, which was not very helpful. Then of course the big disaster was the [James Webb Space Telescope] overrun.

Finally, we were all set up for just stunning international cooperation…. And then everything unravels sadly, because of budgets on both sides of the Atlantic. On our side, we didn't have enough money to go fast enough for ESA. On their side, they had too much money, and if they didn't [move] fast enough they were going to lose their budgetary authority in the future…. It was kind of the perfect storm.[31]

In late 2012, the SSB and the NRC Board on Physics and Astronomy (BPA) organized another workshop—this time to identify lessons learned from the most recently completed surveys.[32] The workshop involved past survey committee chairs and members, other scientists and engineers, agency representatives, and representatives from the international space research community. Participants examined every aspect of the decadal survey process, including planning, coordination between the NRC and the agencies, the character of recommended goals and priorities, cost and risk assessments, dealing with contingencies, and international perspectives.

SSB chair Charles Kennel opened the workshop by acknowledging the problems with the recently completed surveys and noting that each one had been overtaken by events in some way. Some survey recommendations were already in tatters, and others had already become unaffordable. Workshop co-chair Alan Dressler put things in a brighter perspective by observing that with the decadal surveys "the NRC does something imperfectly that should be impossible."[33] Lennard Fisk's keynote talk and Kennel's closing remarks succinctly captured key conclusions from the workshop. Fisk opened the meeting by posing two rhetorical questions: "Should we abandon our decadal process? Certainly not! Should we try and adapt the decadal process for today's reality? Absolutely!"[34] Kennel noted that he heard plenty of support for continuing the process at its current scope without making it more elaborate, but he also heard arguments for being more explicit about the uncertainties and limitations of the surveys' cost estimates. As for the

31. Turner interview.

32. Chapter 2 of the workshop report, *Lessons Learned in Decadal Planning in Space Science: Summary of a Workshop* (The National Academy Press, 2013), includes a comprehensive discussion of how the 2011 and 2012 surveys were organized and conducted.

33. Alexander document files from the 12 November SSB workshop.

34. Quoted in National Research Council, *Lessons Learned in Decadal Planning in Space Science: Summary of a Workshop* (The National Academies Press, Washington, DC, 2013), p. 3.

bottom line, he emphasized that "nobody said we shouldn't have another decadal survey."[35]

NASA Associate Administrator for Science John Grunsfeld summarized the views of many NASA managers about the risks of overly optimistic decadal survey mission models when he commented on the 2010, 2011, and 2012 surveys as follows:

> Each decadal survey is unique…. Starting with planetary, they took a very risky strategic tack of looking at the budgets that they enjoyed for years and saying, "Well look, if we study a budget option that's flat or declining then that gives somebody the ammunition to do that program, not the more desirable one. So let's assume that we get at least [growth to match] inflation and then [also] prepare for a really big increase…." Later on they then said, "We will add some decision rules in case you don't get that," because it was already clear that that was not the economy we are in. So that's one factor—a realistic budget. We are struggling… where the budgets that were assumed to develop the survey were much too optimistic. [B]oth in planetary and astrophysics they did an experiment where they said, "Let the decadal process actually design missions. Have Aerospace [Corporation] do cost and technical evaluations…. "Basically doing everything that we actually do here for a living in SMD…. [T]he Space Studies Board really didn't have all the team members needed or the time to do it right…. [W]e know from vast experience of over 50 years in the space age that you really don't know what something is going to cost

> until well after you have set the requirements and done the design work and performed a good cost estimate…. What we really need the decadal surveys to focus on is for the community to … prioritize the main science objectives and show through some level of analysis, some level of cost forecasting, and existence proofs of instruments that could answer that science, but then let NASA and the community go back and figure out exactly what their implementation will be once the budget is settled.[36]

In the last part of his comment, Grunsfeld was essentially harkening back to Newell's early guidance for the SSB to provide "broad overall objectives… rather than detailed program formulation."[37]

In addition to NASA concerns over the credibility and utility of decadal survey committees' mission cost estimates, a few members of the scientific community have worried about the risk that the surveys can freeze priorities so that there is no opportunity for timely response to important new discoveries. These critics argue that it is wrong for a single committee, regardless of its size and breadth, to be able to issue a document that takes on "biblical importance," and thereby constrains the future directions of a field.[38]

Given concerns exemplified by Grunsfeld's comments above and by some scientists, the most ambitious and comprehensive examination of the decadal survey process was a study initiated in 2014 by an ad hoc committee that was organized under SSB auspices. The committee's report—"The Space Science Decadal Surveys: Lessons Learned and Best Practices"—was a resounding reaffirmation

---

35. Quoted in National Research Council, *Lessons Learned in Decadal Planning in Space Science: Summary of a Workshop* (The National Academies Press, Washington, DC, 2013), p. 79.

36. Grunsfeld interview.

37. See John E. Naugle, *First Among Equals: The Selection of NASA Space Science Experiments* (NASA SP-4215, NASA History Division, Washington, DC, 1991), ch. 5, p. 72.

38. Luhman interview, 11 November 2014.

of the decadal survey process, but it did offer a number of useful, and feasible, ideas for improving the process and making it more resilient. These ideas included approaches for reviewing the state of the science during the organizational phase of a survey so that the survey committee could begin its work on prioritizing future science goals more quickly and for fostering international discussions of science goals so as to facilitate better coordination towards opportunities for international cooperation. The report was unequivocal in saying that decadal surveys should not abandon the practice of recommending priorities for both a discipline's science goals and the missions or programs needed to pursue the goals.[39]

The committee devoted much of its attention to the issue of obtaining realistic cost estimates, and it recommended that survey committees utilize a two-phase cost and risk assessment in which candidate missions would be run first through a coarse "cost-box" analysis before subjecting fewer candidates to a more in-depth analysis. In using this approach, the committee also recommended that most missions so analyzed be clearly understood to be reference missions rather than high-fidelity design assessments. Future survey committees would devote their most intense efforts to understanding the very largest candidate missions where unforeseen cost growth or technical hurdles could have seriously disruptive effects on a discipline as a whole. The 2015 committee report also made a strong case for the importance of surveys that "provide clear decision rules and decision points that will effectively establish cost caps, with the intent of triggering reconsiderations of the mission and the possibility, or necessity, of rescoping its science capability."[40]

Mid-Course Assessments Track the Decadal Surveys

The 1991 decadal survey for astronomy and astrophysics, which was prepared under the leadership of Princeton astrophysicist John Bahcall,[41] was remarkably successful. By the middle of the decade following the report, the survey's major recommendations for space activities either had been accomplished or were well on the way. Most notably, development of the top-priority large mission, the Space Infrared Telescope Facility, had started, and advanced technology activities for important future missions were in progress. At the same time, NASA was beginning to implement strategic planning requirements called for in the new GPRA legislation, and so the agency needed guidance about what scientific priorities should guide NASA's planning for the end of the decade. Consequently, NASA asked the SSB to update the scientific priorities that had been outlined in the 1991 astronomy decadal survey and, thereby, provide a mid-decade review and an up-to-date basis for NASA's next space science strategic plan. The SSB, jointly with the Board on Physics and Astronomy, organized an ad hoc Task Group on Space Astronomy and Astrophysics to do the job, and their report was issued in 1997.[42] Recognizing the special status of decadal surveys in the astronomical community and a high degree of protectiveness on the part of the chair and authors of the survey report, the task group took pains to explain that their effort was "not

39. National Research Council, *The Space Science Decadal Surveys: Lessons Learned and Best Practices* (National Academies of Sciences, Engineering, and Medicine, Washington, DC: The National Academies Press, 2015), pp. 1–6.

40. National Research Council, *The Space Science Decadal Surveys: Lessons Learned and Best Practices* (The National Academies Press, Washington, DC, 2015), p. 6.

41. National Research Council, *The Decade of Discovery in Astronomy and Astrophysics* (National Academies of Sciences, Engineering, and Medicine, National Academy Press, Washington, DC, 1991).

42. National Research Council, *A New Science Strategy for Space Astronomy and Astrophysics* (The National Academies Press, Washington, DC, 1997).

a decadal survey and does not replace the wider-ranging, consensus-building activities associated with the Bahcall report and its predecessors."[43]

Less than half a decade later, as the 2001 decadal survey report for astronomy and astrophysics was nearing completion, the field was exploding (pun noted) with discoveries that would pose new questions about fundamental aspects of physics and cosmology: "What is dark matter? How can dark energy be explained? What caused an apparent acceleration of the expansion of the universe at its earliest moments? Does Einstein's theory of gravity work as well in the presence of intense gravity as it does under more 'normal' circumstances?" Discoveries in other subdisciplines—for example, mounting evidence for the ubiquity of planets around other stars and of massive black holes—were equally copious and exciting. Thus, in only a few short years after publication of the 2001 decadal survey, the scientific core of the field was evolving at an unprecedented pace. A new NRC committee addressed the implications of developments at the interfaces between astrophysics and physics in a 2003 report—"Connecting Quarks with the Cosmos: Eleven Science Questions for the New Century"[44]—that was intended to complement the most recent astronomy and astrophysics decadal survey report by summarizing the new scientific developments and recommending actions that NASA, NSF, and DOE could take to pursue those opportunities. Some astronomers began to ask whether scientific opportunities were moving so rapidly that the basis for recommendations in the 2001 decadal survey deserved to be revisited.

At the same time that the scientific scene was changing at a breathtaking pace, the political and programmatic environment at the relevant federal agencies was also in considerable flux, especially at NASA. The Space Shuttle *Columbia* accident in February 2003 created exceptional stresses, and the conclusions of the Columbia Accident Investigation Board[45] prompted internal and external assessments of NASA's programs and operations. One consequence that was immediately important to astronomy was NASA Administrator Sean O'Keefe's decision to cancel any further Space Shuttle servicing missions to the Hubble Space Telescope.[46]

President George W. Bush introduced his new Vision for Space Exploration[47] in January 2004, and that initiative had important implications for space astronomy, as well as for the rest of NASA's space and Earth science programs. The core of the initiative involved human missions to and on the Moon, which would serve as test beds for later human missions to Mars and elsewhere in the solar system, and a complementary robotic solar system exploration program.

NASA's plans for responding to the Bush vision assumed a growing NASA budget from fiscal year 2005 onward, and the budget for science was divided between "exploration missions," which included planetary science, and "other science activities," into which fell most of astronomy as well as Earth science and solar-terrestrial physics. The message for activities that were lumped in "other science" seemed to be that they would be expected to be good soldiers and tighten their

43. National Research Council, *A New Science Strategy for Space Astronomy and Astrophysics* (The National Academies Press, Washington, DC, 1997), p. 4.

44. Board on Physics and Astronomy, *Connecting Quarks with the Cosmos: Eleven Science Questions for the New Century* (National Research Council, The National Academies Press, Washington, DC, 2003).

45. Columbia Accident Investigation Board, *Report of the Columbia Accident Investigation Board* (National Aeronautics and Space Administration and the U.S. Government Printing Office, Washington, DC, August 2003).

46. But see chapter 16.

47. George W. Bush, "A Renewed Spirit of Discovery: The President's Vision for U.S. Space Exploration," The White House, January 2004.

belts while the exploration effort gathered steam. NASA's budget–chart makers even assigned a dull grey shade to the band depicting other science at the bottom of the chart while other elements of the budget, all of which were implied to be relevant to exploration, were displayed in colored bands in the year-by-year budget projection.[48] The concept of a balanced science program, which had been advocated by countless advisory bodies and which aimed to permit all discipline areas to make progress, seemed to have gone out the window. It was enough to give more than a few astronomers a case of the willies.

Bush appointed the Commission on Implementation of United States Space Exploration Policy, chaired by former senior DOD and aerospace industry executive Edward "Pete" Aldridge, to recommend research, development, and management strategies to implement the vision.[49] The Aldridge report included a "notional science research agenda" that provided some reassurance by explicitly incorporating scientific themes and objectives that compared well with the scientific themes of the 2001 astronomy and astrophysics decadal survey. The fact that astronomer Neil deGrasse Tyson, as well as geochemist Laurie Leshin, lunar geologist Paul Spudis, and planetary scientists Maria Zuber were members of the commission probably made a difference. Nevertheless, scientists outside NASA began to worry about how NASA managers would embrace the new exploration priorities and how NASA's response would impact community priorities for the future.

Budget requests in ensuing years would reinforce those worries. When the Bush initiative was announced in 2004, the total NASA budget was projected to grow robustly by around 5 percent per year through fiscal year 2007.[50] However, those increases never materialized, and at the same time continuing costs to operate the Space Shuttle and complete construction of the International Space Station pushed previously expected budget windfalls farther out into the future. (See chapter 16's discussion of the SSB "Balance" report for more.)

The Committee on Astronomy and Astrophysics, which was a joint standing committee of the SSB and BPA, concluded that this stew of rapidly developing scientific advances and alarming changes inside NASA called for a review of the progress made since the last decadal survey as well as an evaluation of whether any changes in direction were appropriate. When the review idea was first broached, there were immediate concerns from some members of the recent survey committee and its parent boards, the SSB and the BPA. In particular, they worried that a review by a committee not as broadly based, as inclusive, or as deliberative could not be as credible. More risky, in this view, was the possibility that such a review could actually propose revisions to the decadal survey priorities. A review that proposed new or different priorities just a few years after the decadal survey was completed could threaten long-term community buy-in and scientific stability for the survey. Others countered that refusing to take a look at whether the thoroughly debated survey priorities were still timely seemed unnecessarily defensive and tantamount to according the survey scriptural status.

The two parent boards overcame the decadal survey protectors' reservations and crafted an acceptable study charge so that the verbosely titled Committee to Assess Progress Toward the Decadal

---

48. See chart #14 of the NASA Administrator's FY 2005 budget summary presentation available at *http://www.nasa.gov/pdf/55522main_FY05_Budget_Briefing020304.pdf*.

49. President's Commission on Implementation of United States Space Exploration Policy, *A Journey to Inspire, Innovate, and Discover* (U.S. Government Printing Office, Washington, DC, June 2004).

50. NASA Administrator's FY 2005 budget summary presentation, *http://www.nasa.gov/pdf/55522main_FY05_Budget_Briefing020304.pdf*, 3 February 2004, chart #14.

Vision in Astronomy and Astrophysics could be appointed in 2004. The committee, chaired by C. Megan Urry of Yale University, included members of the recent survey committee, the Quarks-with-the-Cosmos committee, and other senior leaders in U.S. astronomy. Their report highlighted ways in which program priorities from the decadal survey would address important new scientific findings, and it concluded that recent advances "do not require that the NRC reexamine the [decadal survey] report or undertake an in-depth mid-course review of the scientific goals or recommended priorities."[51] The report also emphasized the concept of balance—in terms of tools, ranging from computer modeling and theory to major facilities and space missions, and in terms of size, ranging from small to large projects—as many advisory committees had throughout NASA's (and the NACA's!) history. The report was relatively mild in terms of raising explicit concerns about the community's confidence in NASA's stewardship of the decadal survey recommendations and rather vague regarding specific actions that were recommended.

The important point for the 2005 progress assessment report was that it broke new ground. The Committee on Astronomy and Astrophysics initiative to conduct a review of progress halfway between decadal surveys and to consider Agency responsiveness was a seminal event. Midterm reviews subsequently became regular formal events that were enshrined in law and applied across the space and Earth sciences. They generally followed the 2005 approach of adhering to the priorities that were laid out in the prior decadal survey and assessing agencies' progress in implementing those priorities. And as we shall see, the fact that they involved performance evaluations, rather than just recommendations of goals, made them more likely to stimulate controversy.

Mid-Decade Reviews Go Mainstream

By 2005, the NRC had conducted five decadal surveys in astronomy and astrophysics and had broken new ground with surveys in planetary science, solar and space physics, and Earth science from space. Both the pace of important new scientific discoveries and the time scale over which NASA's budget and programs were buffeted began to pose new problems for the staying power of major recommendations from the decadal surveys. At the same time, given the fact that Congress had embraced the decadal surveys as important sources of guidance on Agency priorities, members of Congress began to ask for a way to monitor NASA's responses to the surveys' recommendations. When the new astronomy and astrophysics progress review appeared in early 2005, it apparently helped set a broader process in motion.

Subsequently, Congress passed and the President signed the NASA Authorization Act of 2005, which included specific direction to NASA to have

> [t]he performance of each division in the Science directorate of NASA... reviewed and assessed by the National Academy of Sciences at 5-year intervals

and to

> transmit a report to the Committee on Science of the House of Representatives and the Committee on Commerce, Science, and Transportation of the Senate—(1) setting forth in detail the results of any external review...; (2) setting forth in detail actions taken by NASA in response to any external

51. National Research Council, *Review of Progress in Astronomy and Astrophysics Toward the Decadal Vision: Letter Report* (The National Academies Press, Washington, DC, 2005), p. 8.

TABLE 11.3.   Complete list of decadal survey reports and midterm assessment reports through 2016 (All reports are available via The National Academies Press, Washington, DC, at *http://www.nap.edu/.*)

Astronomy and astrophysics decadal surveys
Ground-Based Astronomy: A Ten-Year Program (1964)
Astronomy and Astrophysics for the 1970s (1972)
Astronomy and Astrophysics for the 1980s (1982)
The Decade of Discovery in Astronomy and Astrophysics (1991)
Astronomy and Astrophysics in the New Millennium (2001)
New Worlds, New Horizons in Astronomy and Astrophysics (2010)
Planetary science decadal surveys
New Frontiers in the Solar System: An Integrated Exploration Strategy (2003)
Vision and Voyages for Planetary Science in the Decade 2013–2022 (2011)
Solar and space physics decadal surveys
The Sun to the Earth — and Beyond: A Decadal Research Strategy in Solar and Space Physics (2003)
Solar and Space Physics: A Science for a Technological Society (2012)
Earth science and applications decadal surveys
Earth Science and Applications from Space: National Imperatives for the Next Decade and Beyond (2007)
Earth Science and Applications from Space 2017 (expected 2017)
Decadal survey midterm reviews
Review of Progress in Astronomy and Astrophysics Toward the Decadal Vision (2005)
A Performance Assessment of NASA's Astrophysics Program (2007)
Grading NASA's Solar System Exploration Program (2008)
A Performance Assessment of NASA's Heliophysics Program (2009)
Earth Science and Applications from Space: A Midterm Assessment of NASA's Implementation of the Decadal Survey (2012)

review; and (3) including a summary of findings and recommendations from any other relevant external reviews of NASA's science mission priorities and programs.[52]

Thus, the midterms became law. The SSB subsequently organized midterm reviews that were published in space astronomy in 2007, solar system exploration in 2008, solar and space physics in 2009, and Earth science and applications from space in 2012. Table 11.3 lists all of the decadal surveys and midterm reviews produced through 2016.

Although all the program assessments were responsive to the congressional mandate, they were not cut out with the same cookie cutter. One aspect that they all shared was a gloves-off approach to how the review committees judged the government's performance in responding to the recommendations of their respective decadal surveys. NRC reports have often been known for their temperance and kid-gloves presentation

---

52. National Aeronautics and Space Administration Authorization Act of 2005, Public Law 109–155, 30 December 2005, 119 Stat. 2917.

of critical points of views. The midterms may have taken the same kind of traditionally polite approach, but they were still quite explicit about findings of federal failings to respond to the recommendations of the decadal surveys. And the review committees were not afraid to point the finger at parts of the Administration outside NASA or at Congress.

The first assessment in response to the 2005 Authorization Act was the 2007 astronomy and astrophysics report, "A Performance Assessment of NASA's Astrophysics Program." Coming only a couple years after the first attempt at a midcourse review, the 2007 report was considerably more explicit. While concluding that NASA's 2003 program plan to act on advice from both the 2001 decadal survey and the 2003 Quarks-with-the-Cosmos report was appropriately responsive, the report went on to say that realities of execution had curtailed progress and that NASA's subsequent 2006 plan would lead to further erosion. The report emphasized that "NASA's Astrophysics Division does not have the resources to pursue the priorities, goals, and opportunities"[53] in the decadal survey and the "Quarks" report. The committee made several recommendations, including one regarding a recurring theme of nearly every advisory committee and report—namely, that NASA needs a balanced and diversified portfolio of large and small missions and investments in technology development, data analysis, data archiving, and theory.

Owning to the fact that the report was prepared during the time when NASA's internal advisory structure was in disarray (see chapter 12), the report also tackled the problem of NASA communications with the outside community by recommending the following:

NASA should consider changes in its advisory structure to shorten the path between advisory groups and relevant managers so as to maximize the relevance, utility, and timeliness of advice as well as the quality of the dialogue with advice givers…. Currently advice of all kinds—from the high-level policy and strategic advice needed by NASA's administrator and senior management to the more tactical expert advice needed by science managers—is transmitted vertically through the NASA Advisory Council to the administrator and then down to the relevant managers. Direct two-way connections between advisory committees and managers would foster several important goals, including timely provision of and access to input tailored to the needs of the managers at each level, strengthened communication between NASA and the scientific user community, and greater flexibility for the NASA Advisory Council to focus on issues of policy and high-level agency strategy. NASA might also wish to reconstitute informal management operations working groups to enable science managers to quickly and effectively obtain expert advice on specific issues. The committee suggests that a continual dialogue between vested parties will produce the most effective outcome, especially in circumstances when difficult choices may be required.[54]

The 2008 evaluation of NASA's solar system exploration program took a more quantitative approach to program assessment. The committee evaluated NASA's progress against the 2003 decadal survey and a complementary 2006 NRC report that had examined NASA's Mars program

---

53. National Research Council, *A Performance Assessment of NASA's Astrophysics Program* (The National Academies Press, Washington, DC, 2007), p. 2.

54. National Research Council, *A Performance Assessment of NASA's Astrophysics Program* (The National Academies Press, Washington, DC, 2007), pp. 41–42.

architecture, and it gave a real report card with letter grades (A through F) plus trending assessments to each of the major elements of the program. The report gave the overall planetary science program a B but indicated that the state of the program was worsening over time, saying "on its current course, NASA will not be able to fulfill the recommendations of the solar system exploration decadal survey."[55] When the committee looked at individual flight programs, it gave the Mars program an A but gave some other flight programs—small Discovery-class principal-investigator-led missions and large flagship missions—a D. In what looked like a classic case of the law of unintended consequences, subsequent to the NRC review NASA took money from the healthy Mars program and bolstered activities that were rated more poorly. While outside observers saw this was a case of cause and effect, NASA officials disputed that and said the budget decisions had already been made when the NRC assessment was published. Nevertheless, the midterm review grades provided NASA officials with cover when they rebalanced budget allotments at the expense of the Mars program. NASA Administrator Mike Griffin defended the cuts to the Mars program, saying that it had become too bloated.[56] The outsiders' view was captured by one former SSB member who later noted that one doesn't achieve excellence by taking money from a strong program and giving it to a weak program so that they both become mediocre.

The 2009 heliophysics program review mapped NASA's program against the decadal survey's seven topical chapters and then used the practice adopted by the planetary scientists of giving letter grades to how NASA was responding to recommendations in each of those areas. This midterm review was probably the most negative evaluation to date, and that turned out to have a real, and possibly unexpected, impact. The review committee's bottom line was that,

> Unfortunately, very little of the recommended NASA program priorities from the decadal survey's Integrated Research Strategy will be realized during the period (2004–2013) covered by the survey. Mission cost growth, reordering of survey mission priorities, and unrealized budget assumptions have delayed or deferred nearly all of the NASA spacecraft missions recommended in the survey. As a result, the status of the Integrated Research Strategy going forward is in jeopardy, and the loss of synergistic capabilities in space will constitute a serious impediment to future progress.[57]

The committee gave most of the seven elements into which they divided the heliophysics program a C grade and even gave NASA an F for its attention to how the program connected to other scientific disciplines. Grades for individual flight projects and other specific program elements were not especially severe, with the evaluation granting four As, six Bs, three Cs, and only one D. The report also looked ahead at lessons that should be considered in planning the next decadal survey, and it provided specific recommendations about how to improve the next survey.[58]

---

55. National Research Council, *Grading NASA's Solar System Exploration Program: A Midterm Review* (The National Academies Press, Washington, DC, 2008), p. 4.

56. Griffin remarks at Space Studies Board meeting, 2 May 2006, SSB archives, Washington, DC. Also see transcript of Griffin speech to Goddard Space Flight Center employees on 12 September 2006, p. 2, *http://www.nasa.gov/pdf/157382main_griffin-goddard-science.pdf*.

57. National Research Council, *A Performance Assessment of NASA's Heliophysics Program* (The National Academies Press, Washington, DC, 2009), p. 2.

58. National Research Council, *A Performance Assessment of NASA's Heliophysics Program* (The National Academies Press, Washington, DC, 2009), pp. 3–9.

The heliophysics performance review report landed at NASA with a splat—it was not happily received. The earlier planetary science review was nearly as critical, but NASA's planetary science chief was said to have accepted it as a wake-up call, which he sought to embrace and use to his advantage. However, NASA heliophysics division officials appeared to take the review as more of a personal attack. Others at NASA, while not going as far as taking the report personally, nevertheless agreed that the report appeared to go overboard in its negative tone. While no one outside NASA disagreed that the Agency program had serious problems, not all of which were of NASA's making, there were independent views that the tone of the report was unnecessarily pejorative.

Were it not for a change in NRC policies after implementation of FACA section 15, the heliophysics performance review might have gone to NASA with fewer sharp edges and a tone that would have not have been viewed as confrontational. Up until the early 2000s, the SSB conducted an informal review of all reports prepared under its auspices before a committee's draft report went out for formal peer review. For each report, a small group of board members would be assigned to read the draft report and then lead a discussion of the report with the authoring committee chair during a board meeting. The process added a little time to the overall report schedule, but it often exposed issues that the report authors had overlooked and were wise to reconsider. Because of conflict-of-interest policies implemented simultaneously with NRC compliance with FACA, the board no longer could hold such discussions.

Compounding the problems with the helio-physics report, the SSB recognized belatedly that it had not given the committee adequate staff support and guidance. Consequently, the SSB also took away some lessons about how to work to make assessments more likely to be constructive and less likely to drive NASA straight up the wall.

The final performance assessment in the SSB's first round after the congressional call for regular reviews addressed NASA's response to the 2007 decadal survey for Earth science and applications from space. The 2012 report, which employed qualitative assessments rather than letter grades, started positively with kudos for NASA:

NASA responded favorably and aggressively to the 2007 decadal survey, embracing its overall recommendations for Earth observations, missions, technology investments, and priorities for the underlying science. As a consequence, the science and applications communities have made significant progress over the past 5 years.[59]

But the committee moved quickly to its major concerns about the robustness and long-term outlook of the U.S. program, saying that, "The nation's Earth observing system is beginning a rapid decline in capability as long-running missions end and key new missions are delayed, lost, or canceled." The review was very clear that NASA was not solely to blame:

Congress's failure to restore the Earth science budget to a $2 billion level [at which it was operating in fiscal year 2006] is a principal reason for NASA's inability to realize the mission launch cadence recommended by the survey.... The 2007 decadal survey's recommendation that the Office of Science and Technology Policy develop an interagency framework for a sustained global Earth observing system has not been implemented. The committee concluded that the lack of such an implementable and funded strategy has become a key, but not

59. National Research Council, *Earth Science and Applications from Space: A Midterm Assessment of NASA's Implementation of the Decadal Survey* (The National Academies Press, Washington, DC, 2012), p. 2.

the sole, impediment to sustaining Earth science and applications from space.[60]

Thus, while earlier midterm reviews in other fields had acknowledged that problems were not always under NASA's control and that NASA sometimes had to try to make the best of a difficult situation, the Earth science assessment was the first to be explicit about how other parts of the government had to share some blame and responsibility. The Earth science budget subsequently did enjoy modest improvements, and by 2015 NASA funding for Earth observation satellite programs appeared to have stabilized, albeit at levels still below what the survey committee had hoped to see. NASA began to prepare many of the recommended space missions for launches in 2017 and beyond, especially via the innovative use of small, low-cost spacecraft and instruments on the International Space Station. And with the help of congressional prodding, the Obama administration prepared a National Strategy for Civil Earth Observations in 2013[61] and a National Plan for Civil Earth Observations in 2014.[62]

Assessing the Assessments

The 2012 SSB-BPA decadal survey workshop examined experience with the midterm reviews as well as the decadal surveys themselves. There was wide agreement that the midterms were an important vehicle for stewardship of the surveys and that they could have value for Congress, the Administration, and the scientific public, as well as NASA. The reviews provided recognition and

measures of progress as well as relevant advice about needed corrective actions.

Views about the merits of the midterm reviews have not always been glowingly positive. NASA officials, in particular, have sometimes complained that the assessment reports were prone to criticizing the Agency for failures or inactions beyond NASA's control, especially when budget constraints limit the capacity to act. For example, senior Science Mission Directorate manager Paul Hertz put the problem as follows:

> … several of the mid-decade reviews that have been done so far have said, "You're doing a terrible job because you don't have enough money." That's not helpful. The Earth science one said, "Well, within the money you have, you're doing a reasonable job of prioritizing and responding." That is helpful. So, even with the same instructions when they tell us that we don't have enough money, [they should] know that we don't actually have control over how much money we get. I don't get to pick my budget. So if a review committee tells me, "You didn't get the money that the decadal survey thought you were going to [get], and you haven't done what they said they were going to do because of that, and therefore, you get a failing grade," it's true but not helpful.[63]

Hertz did acknowledge that statements in midterm review reports sometimes can be directed at audiences other than the science program managers. A finding about inadequate budgets can be an effort by the review committee to press senior NASA

60. National Research Council, *Earth Science and Applications from Space: A Midterm Assessment of NASA's Implementation of the Decadal Survey* (The National Academies Press, Washington, DC, 2012), p. 3.

61. National Science and Technology Council, National Strategy for Civil Earth Observations (Executive Office of the President, Washington, DC, April 2013).

62. Office of Science and Technology Policy, *National Plan for Earth Observations* (Executive Office of the President, Washington, DC, 18 July 2014).

63. Hertz interview, pp. 7–8.

leadership or OMB or Congress about a problem. Then, to the extent that those other decision makers take the priorities of the decadal survey seriously and have the ability to redirect resources, a midterm review conclusion about the impacts of budgets can be helpful in the end.

In view of the state of NASA's own advisory committees at the time of the workshop (see chapter 12) and concerns about the charters and clout of the SSB standing committees when operating under NRC FACA constraints (see chapter 9), people saw an especially important role for the midterms in monitoring Agency progress and interpreting the surveys in the face of rapidly changing programmatic environments. However, there have been doubts about whether the midterms alone can provide timely stewardship in today's dynamic environment. One congressional staff member who follows NASA programs closely had this to say about the midterm assessment reports:

> They are not my go-to document.... I still think we need some sort of interim ... conversation about where things are and what's the constellation of factors that are influencing the implementation of the decadal.... I think that the midterms are providing it, but I wonder if that's the right vehicle and maybe an every two or three-year conversation rather than an every five-year that's an actual report.[64]

Of course, that more regular role of monitoring progress against the recommendations of the decadals was once filled by the SSB's standing committees until they were put on a tighter leash.

The workshop discussions drew the line at changing scientific priorities via the midterm reviews, both because the midterms lacked the broad community involvement upon which the decadals were based and because scientific advances are not likely to support changing priorities in as

short a time as five years. On the other hand, the workshop exposed a lot of sentiment for adapting decision rules that a survey might have proposed for dealing with programmatic exigencies. The midterms were also viewed as the perfect time to begin planning for and improving the next decadal survey.

Astronomer Marcia Rieke summarized the situation from her perspective, having served on several decadal survey committees:

> I think the value is that science happens at a pretty rapid pace sometimes. For example, if you go back and look at Astro2010 [the 2010 astronomy and astrophysics decadal survey] there were a number of questions posed in there that could not be answered and were recognized as unanswerable.... And there were several science areas that we realized were moving sufficiently rapidly that there ought to [have been] a mid-decade look at whether, for example, technology development funds ought to be re-vectored in midstream. And we were thinking [that] if there's limited technology development funds, why not to take a look mid-decade and see how has the science evolved. How have the technologies for these kinds of missions evolved, and where do we think the greatest opportunity is? And the Astro2010 explicitly said we need to take a look at these questions mid-decade ... but mid-decade reviews may be needed just because circumstances and the science behind things changes so quickly that waiting a full 10 years may not be serving the community well. That said, these are still going to be done with the notion that you don't change mission priorities, ... that you don't revisit the whole scene, that you have the specific focused task to look at how the sciences and technologies have evolved and how is the implementation

---

64. Whitney interview.

going and should the implementation be tweaked in some way.[65]

Why the Decadals Work

The decadal science strategy surveys have enjoyed remarkable acceptance, respect, and staying power. Even though their recommendations have often been overly optimistic and their execution has taken longer than the decade for which they have been framed, both NASA and Congress have tended to view them as the best advice available. Nearly all space flight program initiatives recommended by the surveys in the 1990s or beyond have been adopted or carried on for study and later selection. The statement quoted at the opening of this chapter by Congressman John Culberson, Chair of the House Commerce, Justice, and Science Appropriations Subcommittee, may have established him as a leader of the survey fan club. One year later, Culberson doubled down on his enthusiasm for the decadals, encouraging the NSF to also embrace the process and saying,

> I'm very impressed with the work…the National Academies have done in their decadal surveys, and that's why I included language in our 2016 bill to ensure that NASA follows the decadal recommendations…. [The decadal surveys allow] us as members of Congress to recognize what the priorities are of the scientific community and their best objective judgment, and fund those priorities and make sure they're carried out….[66]

This record of success can be ascribed to several key aspects of the surveys. First, the broad participation by a substantial fraction of the relevant research community and the intense deliberations that lead to the surveys' conclusions provide a kind of heft that makes them very difficult to discount or disregard. (Fig. 11.2 provides a simple illustration of the differences in approaches between a typical NRC advisory study and a typical decadal survey.)

A survey committee's membership is drawn from a broad cross section of the relevant research community—including not only scientists but also engineers and experts with management and policy experience—so that there are ample opportunities to correct for persons who might be pushing a single agenda or who might not be expert in all the dimensions of the work at hand. Furthermore, by being convened under the aegis of the National Academies, the committees legitimately benefit from the stature and reputation for independence for which the Academies have been known. Policymakers recognize that the results of the surveys represent about as good a community-wide consensus as can be obtained. Just as importantly, the broad participation generates buy-in across the community so that researchers feel a sense of ownership in the survey results and are usually likely to stand behind the results.

Second, the recommendations in the survey reports are derived from a fundamental scientific assessment that first defines a set of scientific goals from which implementation priorities are derived. The surveys don't first ask, "What do we want to build?" or "How much money do we expect?" and then build a program around those estimates. Of course, in the cold light of day it's hard to imagine that such considerations don't enter into committee members' thinking, but the logic for the survey conclusions is built first on the science. The more carefully and coherently that train of scientific arguments is built, the more successful the

65. Rieke interview, p. 4.

66. House Commerce, Justice, and Science Appropriations Subcommittee hearing, 16 March 2016, quoted in FYI: *The Bulletin of Science Policy News*, No. 34, 17 March 2016, American Institute of Physics.

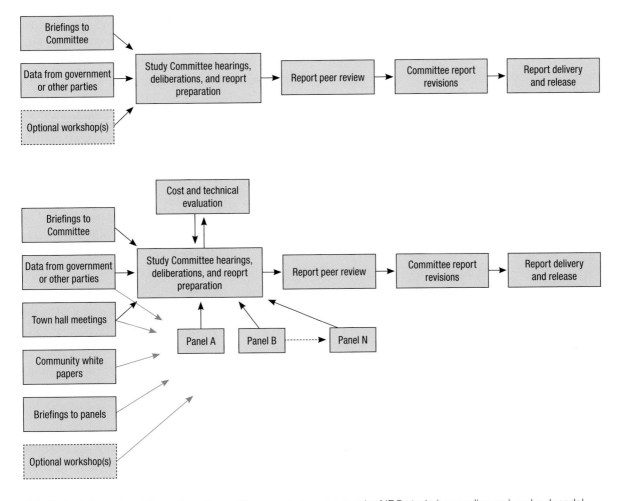

FIGURE 11.2 Notional illustration of key differences between a regular NRC study (upper diagram) and a decadal survey (lower diagram)

final result will be. So the survey committees first ask, and ask their colleagues, "What have been the major scientific developments over the past decade? What are the most pressing scientific problems to be tackled in the coming decade? What do we need to do to make progress in answering those questions?" Thus, they begin by following Newell's original call for "broad overall objectives."[67] Having then filled in the scientific outline, they proceed to

translate the scientific strategy into an implementation strategy.[68]

The third powerful attribute of the surveys is that they do recommend specific priorities and recommend implementation actions in priority order. To do so requires the committees to make difficult choices, from which there are inevitably winners and losers. Recent surveys have also proposed decision rules, which recommend how NASA should

---

67. See John E. Naugle, *First Among Equals: The Selection of NASA Space Science Experiments* (NASA SP-4215, NASA History Division, Washington, DC, 1991), ch. 5, p. 72.

68. The recommended programmatic strategies are often used as standards against which to measure program performance as discussed in chapter 8.

weigh decisions when unforeseen implementation problems arise or other issues force managers to make tradeoffs or choose between alternative paths.[69] Thus, the surveys demonstrate a sense of seriousness about the recommendations and a willingness on the part of the scientific community to take ownership of their recommendations. Of course, having such an explicit recommended strategy certainly gives decision makers and managers a basis from which to work if they so choose. They also appreciate the fact that having such a solid outside set of recommendations often provides excellent cover that permits them to point to a decadal survey when justifying a decision.

A logical question to ask is, "Given the success of the decadals in the space sciences, can the process be as useful for other scientific and technical fields outside of NASA's scientific interests?" The list above of success factors—broad community participation and consensus, foundation built on fundamental scientific goals, rank-ordered priorities, and consideration of approaches for dealing with unforeseen problems—is a big list. Consequently, decadals are a major effort to accomplish. Agencies and scientific communities need to be willing and able to commit the time, energy, and resources to make a decadal survey successful.

The more a decadal survey is directed at a relatively contained ensemble of sub-disciplines and communities, the easier and more tractable the effort is likely to be. A relatively homogeneous agency mission and stakeholder community should be a ready candidate for a decadal survey if it will have the attributes noted above. However, as mission and stakeholder diversity increase—for example, by combining scientific research with service or operational or regulatory roles—the endeavor can become increasingly complex. This kind of diversity especially impacts the outreach and consensus-building aspects of a survey.

Finally, one might ask whether a decadal survey approach would be an appropriate way to tackle a major, but so far unmentioned element of NASA's program. That is, "Is the decadal survey process applicable to the area of human spaceflight?" The discussion above would suggest not for at least two reasons. First, the *mission* of human spaceflight is not at all narrowly defined or distinct, and one might argue that the mission is not well defined at all. Efforts to define a clear set of goals or a singular rationale for human space flight[70] have struggled and have usually ended up with diverse purposes that include national security, technology, international relations, science, education, and others. That is a lot for a decadal survey to get its arms around. Second, the *community* for human spaceflight is probably too narrow. It consists mostly of elements of NASA—notably Johnson Space Center, Marshall Space Flight Center, and Kennedy Space Center—plus the aerospace firms that support those centers and build the necessary hardware. No larger community exists in the way that it does for the space sciences, where scientists, technologists, and students pursue their work in many academic, private sector, and government laboratories. On the other hand, the SSB and the ASEB did jointly conduct the first decadal survey covering the *scientific* aspects of human spaceflight

---

69. An example of a decision rule might be "If budget problems arise, first de-scope or delay major missions; then, if necessary, delay small and moderate-scale missions, and preserve R&A resources as the highest priority." For a good discussion of decision rules, see National Research Council, "The Space Science Decadal Surveys: Lessons Learned and Best Practices" (The National Academies Press, Washington, DC, 2015), pp. 74–78.

70. For example, see National Research Council, "Pathways to Exploration: Rationales and Approaches for a U.S. Program of Human Space Exploration" (The National Academies Press, Washington, DC, 2014); National Research Council, "NASA's Strategic Direction and the Need for a National Consensus" (The National Academies Press Washington, DC, 2012); and National Research Council, "America's Future in Space: Aligning the Civil Space Program with National Needs" (The National Academies Press, Washington, DC, 2009).

in 2010, and that survey report was issued in 2011.[71] The NASA office responsible for managing life and physical science in the low-gravity environments of laboratories on the International Space Station appeared to be striving to respond as positively to the survey recommendations as limited budgets would permit.

Returning to the decadals for the space sciences, the addition of the mid-course reviews in 2005 served to enhance the chances for success and reinforce the utility of the surveys. By having a mid-decadal assessment of the government's response to the surveys, there was some continuing attention and follow-up so as to reduce the likelihood that the survey reports were not permitted to fade away through neglect or misuse. The midterms also provide a means for the research community to interact with the government to respond to changes in the programmatic environment that might require corrective actions, changes in decision rules, or other implementation adjustments, all within the scientific priorities and general principles that were set forth in the survey report. Thus, the institution of the midterms served to help provide robustness to the survey process even as the overall programmatic and political climate became more complex and challenging for federally sponsored science.

As the next chapter will show, the midterms became especially important when NASA's own in-house committees were not able to operate with full authority.

---

71. National Research Council, "Recapturing a Future for Space Exploration: Life and Physical Sciences Research for a New Era," Washington, DC, The National Academies Press, 2011.

CHAPTER 12

A NASA Advisory Council under Stress

During NASA's early history, the NASA Advisory Council (NAC) and its predecessors served at the pleasure of the NASA Administrator, and the council's agenda and level of engagement also largely reflected the Administrator's interests. That tradition remained in place as the century turned over in 2001, but the Administrators' interests in the early 2000s took a worrisome turn.

When Dan Goldin was Administrator, he was an ardent user of the external advisory process. One of Goldin's last interactions with the NAC before he left NASA was to approve the formation of an International Space Station Management and Cost Evaluation (IMCE) task force led by former NASA and aerospace industry executive Thomas Young. The NAC IMCE's independent, expert review was highly critical of NASA's management and financial controls of the program, referring to deficiencies as being inexcusable.[1]

Waning Influence

Sean O'Keefe, who had served as comptroller and chief financial officer of the Department of Defense, as Secretary of the Navy, and as Deputy Director of OMB, succeeded Goldin in late 2001. O'Keefe brought credentials in government management and budgeting; therefore, he was counted on to get his arms around the unabated and uncertain growth of Space Station costs. However, O'Keefe had no discernible prior exposure to the science community or its culture. Many scientists viewed O'Keefe's interest in courting the outside community for advice and guidance as shallow at best.

Lennard Fisk, who served as an ex-officio member of the NAC by virtue of being chair of the SSB, was skeptical of O'Keefe's interest in outside advice:

> O'Keefe did not want NAC advice. He wanted to make sure they only talked about totally irrelevant things. And if you challenged him, it was sort of bizarre. He would come into every meeting, and he would go through this flowery speech about how wonderful we were for giving our time and all that sort of stuff, the same speech every time. And then a couple of times... I raised a question. I forgot what the subject was, but he just practically stormed out of the room. I guess I was there to just say flowery things. It wasn't a real advisory structure of any substance. Some of that was also driven by FACA. Everything had to be said in

---

1. Letter from NAC Chair Charles F. Kennel to NASA Acting Administrator Daniel R. Mulville, "NASA Advisory Council Findings from the International Space Station Management and Cost Evaluation (ICME) Task Force," 19 December 2001. The full report is available at *http://history.nasa.gov/youngrep.pdf*.

the open. Therefore there was a great deal of sensitivity about saying anything.[2]

Former NAC chair Charles Kennel saw the role of the NAC as having been important during the years of turmoil over the Space Station (e.g., via the IMCE task force) but being diminished after the Space Shuttle Columbia accident in 2003:

> [T]he NASA Advisory Council during that time became a rather pathetic observer.... We could begin to feel that we were being kept at arm's length.
>
> Sean O'Keefe did appoint Fred Gregory, who was Deputy [Administrator] at that point, to liaise with us. And Fred brought us news, but basically it was clear that the decision on the program then was being made in very closely held hands. They tried various ideas on us to see if they made sense to us, but I never had the sense of how things were developing. So, maybe our reactions were okay, but I didn't think we played a very big role.[3]

O'Keefe left NASA in early 2005 after reorganizing to pursue President Bush's Vision for Space Exploration, and he was succeeded in April 2005 by Michael Griffin. In contrast to O'Keefe, whose professional background was in management and administration, Griffin earned advanced degrees in engineering and physics and worked for most of his career in the aerospace arena. Prior to becoming Administrator, he held senior management positions at the Johns Hopkins University Applied Physics Laboratory, Orbital Sciences Corporation, DOD, and NASA (where he was Associate Administrator for Exploration from 1991 through 1993). Griffin was firmly committed to implementing the vision and to meeting, or even accelerating, its goals to develop new Constellation

transportation systems to replace the Space Shuttle and to return astronauts to the Moon.

Griffin's NAC

Not long after taking the Administrator's job, Griffin turned his attention to how the NAC could assist in his efforts to build Constellation. He disbanded the existing NAC and changed its composition and structure. He kept former chair Charlie Kennel as chair of the NAC Science Committee and the only carry-over member. Kennel is an accomplished theoretical plasma physicist who has also served in senior leadership positions, including executive vice chancellor of UCLA, NASA Associate Administrator for Mission to Planet Earth, and director of the Scripps Institute of Oceanography. Griffin appointed Apollo-17 astronaut and former U.S. Senator from New Mexico, Harrison "Jack" Schmitt, as the new NAC Chair. Schmitt, who holds a Ph.D. from Harvard in geology, was the only scientist to walk on the Moon. Given his Apollo experience, one might not be surprised that Schmitt came to the NAC as a vigorous advocate for human missions to the Moon. Likewise, many of the new NAC members shared backgrounds that made them sympathetic to the humans-to-the-Moon initiative.

Griffin restructured the reporting relationships of the NAC and its committees. Before this time (see chapter 6), each NAC committee (e.g., the Space and Earth Sciences Advisory Committee, etc.) reported to the NAC and also provided advice to the relevant program Associate Administrators. And each committee had discipline subcommittees that reported to the main committee and also, at least informally, advised the relevant discipline division chiefs. In the restructuring, the discipline subcommittees were suspended and the main committee was only permitted to provide its advice up

---

2. Fisk interview, p. 16.

3. Kennel interview, p. 6.

the chain to the NAC, where the NAC would forward it to the Administrator when and if it saw fit. The program Associate Administrators and division leaders were left out of the loop.

Griffin contended that the changes were needed because NASA was receiving sometimes-conflicting advice from too broad a spectrum of advisory entities. He felt that one consequence of that was that NASA managers weren't being held accountable to make their own decisions as responsible public officials.[4] He also felt that with so many advisory avenues there was too little attention paid to integrating across disciplines and too much room for dueling goals and priorities being influenced by the loudest advocates. With the new structure, Griffin intended to ensure that NASA management was more directly a part of the advisory conversation and that the NAC would play a more significant peer review role as advice trickled up from lower advisory committees.[5]

Kennel watched as scientists on NAC and in the larger community tried to voice concerns over priorities being pushed for human space exploration at the expense of science, and he concluded that,

[T]hey didn't exactly work out at all with the science community. By that time, the life and microgravity sciences program had been completely eviscerated. There were rants against certain darlings of the science program that seemed, to us, irrational. In fact, there was an attempt to cut the astrobiology program by more amount of money than any other science program, and we didn't understand that. There began to develop a hostile

relationship between the science part of the NASA Advisory Council, with which I was involved, and the rest of it, which had been reconstructed along the lines to build the *Constellation* program.[6]

Schmitt saw the conflict as a case of some members trying to overturn the Bush administration's new Vision for Space Exploration and, thereby, straying well beyond the NAC's proper charge:

The Science Sub-committee…kept coming back with advice counter to the presidential policy, and that wasn't our job. We weren't supposed to be advising the President; we were supposed to be advising Mike Griffin on how to implement the President's policy.[7]

Given the NAC scientists'—Wesley Huntress of the Carnegie Institute of Washington and Eugene Levy of Rice University—unwillingness to play along with NASA's approach, Schmitt persuaded Griffin to dismiss them from the NAC, and Griffin did so in August 2006. Kennel resigned a few days earlier. In a letter to the NAC, Griffin assailed Huntress and Levy as having conflicts of interest and caring more about the interests of the scientific community than of NASA.[8] Huntress described Schmitt's approach to leading the NAC, and a major source of tension, as follows:

[He] controlled the agenda very strictly, did not want to hear dissenting opinions, [and] did not want to hear that science was getting harmed. Every attempt that we made in

4. Griffin remarks at Space Studies Board meeting, 2 May 2006, SSB archives, National Research Council, Washington, DC.

5. Griffin interview. Griffin also outlined his views in considerable detail in a 12 September 2006 speech at the Goddard Space Flight Center. See *http://www.nasa.gov/pdf/157382main_griffin-goddard-science.pdf*.

6. Kennel interview, pp. 6–7.

7. Schmitt interview.

8. Letter from Michael Griffin to the NASA Advisory Council, 21 August 2006 (reproduced at *http://www.spaceref.com/news/viewsr. html?pid=21810*). Also see Andrew Lawler, "NASA Chief Blasts Advisors," Science Magazine, 22 August 2006, *http://www. sciencemag.org/news/2006/08/nasa-chief-blasts-advisors*.

our little science committee to bring something forward for recommendation just got
slapped down.[9]

When Griffin and Schmitt reconstituted the
Science Committee, the new committee quickly
developed an adversarial relationship with the NASA
Headquarters science staff. Huntress recalled that,

> The decadals meant nothing to these folks…
> as if the decadals were irrelevant. It was really
> hard on the AA and the staff, because these
> [NAC] committees were trying to dictate to
> them what their programs should be.[10]

The realization of this new system dismayed
many in the space science community. Fisk
described two examples of how the system operated, both in early 2007, to the SSB. First, the
NAC Science Committee brought forward a resolution proposing to restore the cuts to the research
and analysis (R&A) program by taking some
money from flight programs. The resolution was
killed by the NAC chair. Then shortly later, the
committee offered a resolution to endorse NASA's
Earth science program. That resolution met the
same fate.[11]

Marcia Smith described the impact of the
revised approach in colorful (or bland, if you prefer)
terms: "[A]ll the grain keeps getting pounded out
of the recommendations as they work their way. So
it's just white flour by the time it gets up to the
Administrator."[12]

Fisk assessed the impact of the change in starker
terms:

[T]his, I think, was one of the most destructive
things that ever happened to NASA science…
it was just the beauty of that advisory structure, given the connections to the community,
given the vertical chain of information for the
management. I mean it was just destroyed, and
it was something that was built up successfully
over 40 years by that point.[13]

Earlier reductions in the NASA Headquarters
staff made the effects of limitations in access to
outside advisors more acute than it might have
been otherwise. Under Administrator Goldin, the
size of the Headquarters staff had been reduced
from somewhat more than 2,000 positions in the
mid-1990s to less than 1,000 in 1999; and the staff
count had only recovered to around 1,300 by 2005.
With the reduced staff to manage a program that
was every bit as broad and complex as it was in the
1990s, NASA managers had their hands full, and
they needed to be able to rely on outside experts as
sounding boards and avenues to sample the views
of the scientific community even more than before.

Edward Weiler recalled that the view from
inside NASA mirrored what outsiders such as
Smith and Fisk saw:

> So the bottom line is that was a really dark
> day for the advisory system. The NASA I
> grew up with had an incredibly strong advi-
> sory system—starting with MOWGs going
> up to division committees and then SSAAC
> and NAC and having the Academy, at least
> in astronomy, and having decadals and
> CAA[14]—to a point where we had nothing.

---

9. Huntress interview, p. 13.

10. Ibid.

11. Alexander document files from 5 March and 28 June 2007 SSB meetings, respectively.

12. Smith interview, p. 21.

13. Fisk interview, p. 15.

14. Committee on Astronomy and Astrophysics of the SSB.

OSS had no advisory group; the SSAAC was cut off at the limbs because it advised Griffin and it didn't advise the AA technically. And we had no active CAA at that time. That was kind of a bad period.[15]

Budget issues became a major source of alarm within the space research community and tension between NASA and scientists on the NAC. When the Bush Vision was announced in 2004, the Agency's overall budget was projected to grow faster than the rate of inflation through fiscal year 2007 and then level off when NASA anticipated that funds would become available for new activities after the Space Shuttle was retired in 2010. The projections called for a robust budget for space and Earth science that would grow from about $5.5 billion in 2004 to about $7 billion in 2009.[16] However, when NASA submitted its fiscal year 2006 budget request to Congress in early 2005, the optimistic prior projections ran smack into reality.

Administration priorities such as deficit reduction and funding for homeland security and the war in Iraq made NASA's rosy expectations unsustainable. NASA was under relentless pressure from OMB to live with a budget that would constrain the number of remaining Space Shuttle flights and retire the Shuttle by 2008.[17] NASA's total 5-year budget growth projection was reduced significantly compared to a year earlier, with the largest portion of the reduction ($3.1 billion) coming from science. Now the space and Earth science budget profile showed a drop from fiscal year 2005 to 2006, followed by one-percent annual growth thereafter, corresponding to a likely loss in buying power from 2006 onward due to inflation.[18] A considerable fraction of the reductions to science funding represented transfers to deal with continued Space Shuttle and International Space Station funding shortfalls, while the higher priority exploration program was expected to sustain smaller proportional cuts. In terms of total budget levels for NASA, Griffin felt that his hands were tied, because he had no choice but to find ways to live with the reduced figures that he inherited when he arrived as Administrator.[19] On top of the external (to space science) pressures on the budget, cost growth in a number of large Science Mission Directorate flight missions[20] further limited the office's flexibility to make adjustments.

The way in which NASA proposed to implement the cuts to its science program budget made the situation even more alarming.[21] New mission starts were deferred, the launch rate for small Explorer-class missions was approaching historical lows, and investments in new technologies for future missions were reduced. Across-the-board 15 percent reductions in R&A were particularly perplexing, because scientists consistently considered this element of NASA's science programs to be crucial. R&A grants, especially to university researchers, provided a key means for translating space

15. Weiler interview, p. 9.

16. NASA Administrator O'Keefe's fiscal 2005 budget presentation. "NASA FY 2005 Budget," 3 February 2004 at *http://www.nasa.gov/pdf/55522main_FY05_Budget_Briefing020304.pdf*. See charts 10, 13, and 14.

17. In fact, the last Shuttle flight occurred in July 2011.

18. NASA Administrator O'Keefe's fiscal year 2006 budget presentation. "NASA FY 2005 Budget," 7 February 2005 at *http://www.nasa.gov/pdf/107495main_FY06_AOK_pres.pdf*, chart 6. Also National Research Council, *An Assessment of Balance in NASA's Science Programs* (The National Academies Press, Washington, DC, 2006) p. 10.

19. Griffin interview.

20. Among the projects that were in cost and schedule trouble were the James Webb Space Telescope, the Stratospheric Observatory for Infrared Astronomy airborne telescope, the DAWN asteroid mission, and the Mars Science Laboratory surface rover mission.

21. See Space Studies Board, *An Assessment of Balance in NASA's Science Programs* (National Research Council, The National Academies Press, 2006), for a more detailed discussion.

mission data into scientific understanding, providing the scientific foundation for future research, and training students in space research and development. A plan to cut funding for astrobiology research to less than half of its fiscal year 2005 level was especially vexing. Astrobiology—studies regarding the chemical and biological origins of life in the solar system and beyond—spanned the interfaces between traditional disciplines to constitute an exciting new direction for space science.

While space scientists had good cause for worry, the microgravity life and physical sciences—i.e., research to be conducted in Space Station laboratories—were put on life support. The budget for these areas was reduced by a factor of three, dropping from about $900 million in fiscal year 2005 to about $300 million in 2006 and beyond. Such cuts could be expected to severely reduce the use of the Space Station as a research laboratory, postpone or delete critical biomedical research needed to reduce risks to long-term human spaceflights, immediately cancel support for hundreds of students and post-docs, and drive many researchers away from the field.

NASA's Associate Administrator for Science, former astronaut Mary Cleave, retired in April 2007 and was replaced by planetary scientist Alan Stern. Although he was only on the job for one year, Stern worked to begin funding restorations for R&A and small flight missions. Stern's successor, Edward Weiler, continued to push for reallocations to the budget.

The cuts to science budgets were fundamentally tied to the need to find ways to fund Space Station development and support the remaining Space Shuttle flights. Thus, there was a cultural mismatch between consideration of the interests of the scientific community, which viewed itself as the customer of the science program, and the customers of the Space Station/Shuttle program,

which were basically NASA and its industry contractors. Space scientists saw external advice as a crucial way of operating, while the NASA-industry community responsible for Station and Shuttle saw no need for external advice.

Consequently, Griffin's budget decisions, which stimulated much of the controversy, reflected a serious misreading of the scientific community's priorities and expectations about relationships with NASA. This became clear in a May 2006 meeting between Griffin and the SSB, during which Griffin candidly explained that he viewed R&A to be welfare for university professors and their students, who put their own interests ahead of national interests. He said that he would have expected scientists to prefer a new spaceflight mission over R&A and was surprised to hear so many views to the contrary. Further, Griffin viewed scientists as contractors who *worked for* NASA—a perspective quite different from the scientists who always saw themselves as *partners with* NASA.[22] But he told the board that he was willing to listen. One cannot help but wonder whether the treatment of NASA's science budget might have played out differently if there had been more open and continuing dialog between the Agency's leadership and the scientific community.

Lingering Impacts

Griffin left NASA at the end of the Bush administration, and, in July 2009, former astronaut Charlie Bolden succeeded him as Administrator. Kenneth Ford, the founder and CEO of the Florida-based Institute for Human & Machine Cognition, had taken over as NAC chair when Schmitt resigned in October 2008. He led the NAC until 2011, when Bolden appointed Steve Squyres, a highly respected planetary scientist from Cornell University, to become chair.

---

22. Administrator Griffin also outlined his views in considerable detail in a 12 September 2006 speech at the Goddard Space Flight Center. See *http://www.nasa.gov/pdf/157382main_griffin-goddard-science.pdf*.

The constrained reporting structure for NAC committees that had been instituted under Griffin remained largely unchanged through 2013. Committees and subcommittees could only formally convey their advice up the advisory body chain. Consequently, program division directors and associate administrators could hear the advice as it was being framed, but they could not cite the advice or use it to explain decisions (e.g., in interactions with congressional committees) unless the advice successfully made its way out of the NAC to the Administrator and back down the NASA management pipeline. Given that the NAC had many issues to consider, much relevant advice that would be useful for senior managers' decision making never made it through the NAC's high-level filter.

Squyres described the system that he inherited as being an impediment to the overall effectiveness of the NAC:

> And every single recommendation, every single finding from every committee had to flow through the NAC and had to flow through the Administrator. And so, for example, let's say a science committee has some advice that really is advice for [NASA Associate Administrator for Science] John Grunsfeld. It's not advice for Charlie [Bolden]; it's advice for John…. We wound up spending so much of our time on committee business and so much of our time on issues that were not the big issues facing the agency but instead were the ones facing individual AAs and so forth. It really kind of stood in the way of us doing some of the things that I think the Council really should be intended to do.[23]

The old Management Operations Working Groups also became endangered species. In their place, NASA formed ad hoc "analysis groups" to deal with more tactical topics that arose. The analysis groups were not chartered under FACA as formal subcommittees of NAC committees or subcommittees; they were charged to gather individual opinions from their members, rather than consensus views of the whole group. They were permitted to prepare white papers from the group so long as they did not include recommendations. Then, the collected opinions of analysis group members were forwarded upward to the relevant NAC committees.[24] A few NASA managers continued to fly below the formal advisory system radar by using MOWG-like rump committees, thereby following an old tradition of finding a way to do what seemed sensible in spite of seemingly irrational rules. Nevertheless, for observers who remembered the good old days with MOWGs feeding subcommittees that fed higher-level committees and thus providing useful, timely advice to management levels along the way, the jury was still out.

The NAC and its committees had always been viewed on Capitol Hill as being more a creature of NASA and less independent than their NRC counterparts, and the upheaval in advisory architecture and membership made them seem even less influential. As of 2013, Marcia Smith found the whole process rather toothless:

> I must say, these last several years where I have been listening in on the NAC committee meetings, I have been disappointed at just how ineffectual they are, and how much people pull their punches when push comes to shove. So you get these great discussions and people are absolutely willing to say whatever is on their mind. But when it comes to the end of the meeting and they are writing down their recommendations that they want

---

23. Squyres interview.

24. While the analysis groups were primarily intended to help forward ideas from the scientific community to NASA, they also helped promote communications across the community and to relevant NRC committees.

to forward to the full NAC, everybody pulls their punches. They all want to reach consensus and "yada, yada, yada." Then whenever they come up with [a conclusion] that goes to the full NAC, "Oh no, we can't say that. Oh, we said that a year ago, we don't need to say it again." And what actually gets sent to the Administrator is really hardly worth the paper it's printed on. And then NASA takes it and at the next NAC meeting, they report "Well, NASA did not accept your advice on this and they did not accept your advice on that." And so you wonder what the point is. It does provide a good forum for people to vent, but they don't seem willing to take that extra step and actually put words on paper, except in very rare instances.[25]

Fresh Air?

In late 2013, Administrator Bolden and NAC chair Squyres began to institute changes that would restore the council's effectiveness. In addition to adjustments to the NAC's committees, task forces, and membership structure, the advisory relationships were being brought back to an arrangement that more nearly matched earlier approaches. In November 2013, NASA announced that "In addition to Council recommendations that are now only provided to the Administrator, the Council and its standing committees will also be encouraged to send specific recommendations to NASA Mission Directorate Associate Administrators."[26] Under the revised arrangement, Squyres expected that NAC standing committees would "only come to the Council and they only come to Charlie when they've got an issue that cuts across the agency or there's sufficient importance that they really want to spend a silver bullet."[27]

The two subcommittees of the NAC Science Committee that employed analysis groups—planetary science and astrophysics[28]—did connect their activities with the analysis groups by ensuring that the analysis group chairs also served on the subcommittee. Thus, one problem that had handicapped the NAC for nearly a decade appeared to be near solution.

Squyres felt that the analysis groups developed into an effective platform for hearing from the scientific community:

They serve an important function. They do provide a forum in which the community can gather together. The way you become a member of one of the analysis groups is you show up at the meeting, that's it. Nobody gets chosen; there's no selection process; it's self-selecting.[29] The people who have the resources and the time to show up … and they voice their opinions. If you go and you listen to one of these meetings, you get a pretty good sense of what's the pulse of the community on this issue or that issue.[30]

---

25. Smith interview, p. 19.

26. See *http://www.nasa.gov/content/nasa-advisory-council-reorganizes-for-greater-effectiveness/*.

27. Squyres interview.

28. In early 2016, there were planetary science AGs in extraterrestrial materials curation and analysis, lunar exploration, Mars exploration, outer planets, small bodies, and Venus exploration; and there were astrophysics AGs for the Cosmic Origins, Exoplanets, and Physics of the Cosmos programs.

29. Members of the relevant disciplinary communities are usually well aware of these plans via newsletters, informal information exchanges, etc.

30. Squyres interview.

Proving, perhaps, that any good idea can be undermined by an ardent bureaucracy, NASA officials announced in early 2015 that since the advisory groups were no longer formally affiliated with the NAC or its subunits, they could no longer meet without arranging for every individual meeting to be treated as a conference. However, thanks to new constraints that the administration had imposed in response to widely publicized lavish spending and abuses of conferences by other agencies,[31] NASA had adopted highly conservative documentation and approval requirements on all Agency participation in conferences. The net result was that each advisory group meeting would need to be justified, organized, approved, and documented as a separate ad hoc event. According to one NASA manager, the administrative and logistical work load for analysis group activities would triple compared to when they were handled as informal sources of input to NAC subcommittees. Furthermore, because there were restrictions on the number of NASA employees permitted to attend conferences, the new arrangement made it more difficult for NASA people to hear from outside scientists who would attend the meetings. Consequently, their linkage to NASA's advisory activities and their capacity to give officials scientific community input on programmatic issues could become even more tenuous and arduous, as well as costly.

Concerns about the operation and effectiveness of the NAC did not escape congressional attention. In April 2014, some members of the House Committee on Science, Space, and Technology proposed to include language in the 2014 NASA Authorization bill that would change the structure and expand the authority of the NAC to make it more like the National Science Board, which has power over the NSF that is more akin to a corporate

board of directors. While the proposal for NSB-like changes did not survive, the bill was subsequently modified to call for a study of the effectiveness of the current council and for recommendations of possible changes:

SEC. 707. NATIONAL AERONAUTICS AND SPACE ADMINISTRATION ADVISORY COUNCIL.

(a) STUDY.—The Administrator shall enter into an arrangement with the National Academy of Public Administration to assess the effectiveness of the NASA Advisory Council and to make recommendations to Congress for any change to—

(1) the functions of the Council;

(2) the appointment of members to the Council;

(3) qualifications for members of the Council;

(4) duration of terms of office for members of the Council;

(5) frequency of meetings of the Council;

(6) the structure of leadership and Committees of the Council; and

(7) levels of professional staffing for the Council.

In carrying out the assessment, the Academy shall also assess the impacts of broadening the Council's role to advising Congress, and any other issues that the Academy determines could potentially impact the effectiveness of the Council. The Academy shall consider the past activities of the NASA Advisory Council, as well as the activities of other analogous federal advisory bodies in conducting its assessment.[32]

---

31. The stringent travel constraints at NASA were imposed as part of an administration-wide clamp-down after scandals over a General Services Administration conference in Las Vegas in 2010. See *https://www.washingtonpost.com/politics/gsa-chief-resigns-amid-reports-of-excessive-spending/2012/04/02/gIQABLNNrS_story.html*.

32. H.R.4412 – National Aeronautics and Space Administration Authorization Act of 2014, 113th Congress (2013–2014).

That version of the Act passed in the House of Representatives on 9 June 9 2014 by an impressive 402 to 2 vote. The Senate then assigned the bill to the Committee on Commerce, Science, and Transportation on 19 June, where it languished as did so many other pieces of potential legislation in 2014. After another unsuccessful try in 2015, the NASA Transition Authorization Act of 2017 did include the provisions when it was enacted in March 2017.

The NAC in Context

Throughout NASA's history, the NASA Advisory Council, or something resembling it, has been a fixture in the Agency's overall approach to gathering outside expert advice. NASA's predecessor, the NACA, was formally established around an advisory committee. The concept was continued, in an embryonic form, in NASA's first years to balance and complement the role of the National Academy of Sciences and the Space Science Board. From the 1960s through the 1990s, the NAC, its predecessors, and its committees provided a forum for discussions between NASA's leadership and experts from the space community about NASA policies, priorities, and tactics. The degree to which the NAC became involved in important issues varied with each Administrator's preferences and the style of the NAC chair, but it was always there.

The NAC, and its specialized committees, survived a rebooting experience in the 2000s. When a NASA Administrator sought to downplay the NAC's role or to shape its priorities, the overall effectiveness of the council suffered. The effects were obvious to the larger space research community, and the community responded to press NASA for changes. Those changes, reflecting the resilience of a system that has been proven over decades, appear to be taking hold to some degree in the 2010s. The next chapter takes a look at whether NASA's advisory culture and history has been unique or whether it is simply a test particle in the larger universe of federal research agencies.

CHAPTER 13

Comparing NASA's Advisory Culture with Other Agencies

Needless to say, NASA is not the only agency that invites and receives external advice. There are roughly 1,000 FACA committees;[1] more than 400 NRC committees and boards;[2] and an unknown number of temporary ad hoc committees advising the federal government at any time. Perhaps half of the FACA committees are proposal peer review panels, especially at NIH and NSF, but still there is a lot of advising going on. So it makes sense to ask the following questions: How do NASA's advisory processes and culture compare with those in other similar agencies? Does NASA do things differently? Is it more or less engaged? Is its approach exceptional or typical? An unscientific attempt to address those questions follows.

National Science Foundation Advisory Structure

The top of the advisory structure for the National Science Foundation (NSF) is the National Science Board (NSB), which is the highest-level policy advisory body for the NSF.[3] However, it is also the formal, legislatively established, operating entity for the NSF, and thus it is much more than just an advisory body. NSB memberships are presidential appointments, and NSF officials don't enjoy the same degree of flexibility to accept or ignore NSB guidance that is the case for purely advisory bodies. NASA has no corresponding managing entity that oversees Agency policy and operations to the extent that the NSB does for the NSF.

The NSB regularly produces reports on the state of U.S. science and engineering research, education, and workforce development that are broader in scope and deeper in their analysis than what has typically come from the NSB's nearest NASA counterpart, the NAC. It also has tackled specific strategic issues (e.g., portfolio content) and tactical issues (e.g., execution of peer review) for which independent outside advice was needed.

The NSF has a FACA advisory committee for each of its seven technical directorates, for example the Advisory Committee for Mathematical and Physics Sciences, and they are formed by and provide advice to the corresponding NSF assistant

---

1. According to a 2009 CRS report (Wendy R. Ginsberg, "Federal Advisory Committees: An Overview," CRS report R4052, Congressional Research Service, Washington, DC, 16 April 2006), there were 917 active committees advising 50 agencies in fiscal year 2008.

2. The 2014 National Academies Report to Congress (see *http://www.nationalacademies.org/annualreport/*) states that the institution published more than 400 reports that year; hence, one can expect there to have been more than 400 advisory committees in place that year.

3. See *http://www.nsf.gov/nsb/* for full information about the NSB.

director.[4] Thus, the directorate committees are roughly comparable to the NASA FACA committee that is chartered under the NAC to provide advice regarding activities of the Science Mission Directorate.

Each directorate also has a Committee of Visitors that meets every three years to review the directorate's proposal peer review and selection processes.[5] These committees have been described as filling a watchdog role for which there is no obvious counterpart at NASA. Former NSB member and veteran of several Committee of Visitors reviews Louis Lanzerotti lauded the process:

> [The Assistant Directors] would call in a group to … see that the review process was performing as it should be, and whether the decision-making was according to the reviews.… [O]ne would see who is reviewing these proposals, and whether that was the right set of reviewers, and whether the decision making by the program manager was consistent with the reviews.… I found that really very, very constructive in terms of how they manage their programs.[6]

In the past, the NSF also utilized committees that advised the discipline division directors within a directorate, but those bodies were dissolved when the Clinton administration directed a reduction in the number of advisory committees as part of its reinventing government initiative. Thus the NSF advisory structure partially mirrors the NASA advisory structure under Administrator Griffin, in the sense that advice starts at a relatively high level in the organization and flows upward through the highest-level advisory body, with no lower discipline-specific advisory groups. At times in the past, connections between the NSB and division-level, disciplinary issues have been tenuous at best.

Part of the logic for the NSF advisory process is that NSF is different, because it is not a mission-driven agency like NASA and DOE. Instead, because NSF responds predominately to proposal pressure, it is an agency that is "driven by the genius of the scientific community."[7] The vast array of proposal peer review panels give NSF ample tactical advice. Consequently, in this view, the NSF needs less guidance about *what* to do as compared to *how* it's being done. If a new layer of subcommittees was added below each of the division committees that could just lead to unneeded micromanagement. From this perspective, the visiting committees address the really important issues that benefit from an outside look.

Not everyone has been convinced by these arguments. Some observers who have interacted at length with both agencies argue that by not having lower-level discipline-oriented advisory bodies, advice that eventually works its way up to the NSB and to NSF leadership is inevitably diluted. Astronomer and student of national science policy Kevin Marvel put it this way:

> It limits the range of comment of any single directorate advisory committee on any one topic. So if we're looking at it from astronomy, at the most we only have three reps on this body, and they can only say so much, and any report that the internal advisory committee releases can only have so much content to go into astronomy. Whereas if you had a complete division-based advisory structure, as they

---

4. For a full list of NSF FACA committees, see *http://www.nsf.gov/about/performance/dir_advisory.jsp*.

5. For information about NSF Committees of Visitors, see *http://www.nsf.gov/about/performance/dir_advisory.jsp*; for a description of the NSF peer review process, see *http://www.nsf.gov/bfa/dias/policy/merit_review/*.

6. Lanzerotti interview, pp. 11–12.

7. Turner interview.

used to have, then that advisory body would be responsible for advice pertaining specifically to that division and pass that advice up to the next higher level, which it could then get amalgamated and ultimately given to the Director.[8]

Claude Canizares drew on his experience on both NSF and NASA committees to describe a committee culture that often couldn't see the forest for the trees:

The MPSAC [Mathematical and Physical Sciences Advisory Committee], at least when I was on it, felt almost like [my] early days… with SESAC, where you would just have a bunch of people representing their areas, trying to juggle things so that they could get a better seat at the table. They are always the haves and the have nots. The physicists have much bigger budget than astronomy, but also particularly than math or chemistry. And there were always materials scientists who would come in and argue that they are much more relevant because they produce products.[9]

Former NSB and SSB member Mark Abbott raised a possibly more fundamental point. Abbott noted that there can be a gap between advisory committees' broad strategic advice and advice about how to execute:

[S]ometimes the advice is a little bit disconnected between the process that NSF puts in place for formulating a vision of where they want to go versus the kind of day-to-day proposal pressure…. I can understand why people

see that sometimes you get the high-level stuff from a science board or maybe a standing committee, but then you get all of this advice when every six months a whole raft of proposals comes in. Where does the NSF get something in between vision and day-to-day funding decisions?

I think that's sometimes problematic … because they don't have a real standing committee. The committees at the directorate level have to see so much. They really do come in, and it's Death by PowerPoint, and they make a report and off they go. It's hard to make that crosswalk between vision and sort of an implementation strategy and the tactics that are down at the program level.[10]

The NSF has sometimes formed ad hoc advisory entities to obtain strategic and tactical advice that might otherwise have come from discipline-oriented standing committees. A notable example is the senior review that the Division of Astronomical Sciences first organized in 2005. The review, which was recommended by the 2001 astronomy and astrophysics decadal survey and which was modeled after NASA's senior reviews of space science mission operations (see chapter 10), examined the balance in support of NSF ground-based astronomical facilities. The review panel, which was established as a subcommittee of the FACA committee for the Directorate for Mathematical and Physical Sciences, recommended priorities for continued operations as well as recommendations for budget reductions and even facility closures.[11]

Worries about increasingly constrained budgets that motivated the 2005 senior review did not

8. Marvel interview, pp. 9–10.

9. Canizares interview, pp. 9–10.

10. Abbott interview, pp. 2–3.

11. Senior Review Committee, "From the Ground Up: Balancing the NSF Astronomy Program" (Division of Astronomical Sciences, National Science Foundation, Arlington, VA, 22 October 2006), *https://www.nsf.gov/mps/ast/seniorreview/sr_report_mpsac_updated_12-1-06.pdf.*

moderate; in fact, the outlook worsened, so the 2010 decadal survey recommended another review. Consequently, the NSF organized what was termed a portfolio review in 2011. The broader portfolio review examined the entire astronomical sciences program, including not only facilities but also activities such as research grants, laboratory and computational research, workforce development, and education. Thus, the committee's comprehensive report[12] resembled a recommended strategic plan for the division that assessed community needs; alternative budget scenarios; and priorities, capabilities, investments, and disinvestments for the period 2015 to 2020, all in the context of priorities from the 2010 decadal survey.[13] While the portfolio review certainly delivered specific advice that responded to its charge, occasional portfolio reviews are not substitutes for regular advice to help bridge long-term vision and shorter-term issues of program execution.

One notable outcome of the 2005 senior review was a recommendation to drastically reduce funding for, and potentially close, the Arecibo Observatory, which is home to the world's largest single-aperture radio telescope and which is most familiar to the public via its role in popular fiction and movies such as the James Bond movie *GoldenEye* and *Contact*, the movie based on Carl Sagan's book of the same name. NSF began to implement the senior review recommendation, but supporters of Arecibo mounted rescue efforts and convinced Congress, and the government of Puerto Rico, to provide enough funding to keep the observatory alive.[14] One factor that probably helped persuade the NSF to continue funding Arecibo was a NRC report on near-Earth asteroid (NEO) hazard assessments and mitigation.[15] That report made a clear recommendation for an Arecibo role in radar detection and characterization of NEOs. However, the NSF astronomy program portfolio review in 2011, a similar review conducted for the NSF Division of Atmospheric and Geospace Sciences in 2015, and the 2016 National Academies midterm review of NSF and NASA astronomy programs[16] again gave the observatory a low priority;[17] by 2016 Arecibo again appeared to be on the chopping block.[18]

In addition to its own internal advisory bodies, the NSF uses the NRC for independent advice. The NSF has always been a sponsor of the astronomy and astrophysics decadal surveys, and the foundation supported the decadal surveys for solar

12. Portfolio Review Committee, *Advancing Astronomy in the Coming Decade: Opportunities and Challenges* (Division of Astronomical Sciences, National Science Foundation, Washington, DC, 14 August 2012).

13. The NSF's Atmospheric and Geosciences Division Geospace Section formed an ad hoc committee to conduct a similarly broad portfolio review of its program in 2015. See *http://www.nsf.gov/geo/ags/geospace-portfolio-review-2015/fact-sheet-gs-portfolio-review-june2015.pdf*.

14. For a thorough discussion of the issues surrounding the support of the Arecibo Observatory, see Christine M. Matthews, "The Arecibo Ionospheric Observatory," CRS report R40437, Congressional Research Service, Washington, DC, 23 February 2012.

15. National Research Council, *Defending Planet Earth: Near-Earth Object Surveys and Hazard Mitigation Strategies* (The National Academies Press, Washington, DC, 2010).

16. National Academies of Sciences, Engineering, and Medicine, *New Worlds, New Horizons: A Midterm Assessment*, (The National Academies Press, Washington, DC, 2016).

17. Portfolio Review Committee, "*Investments in Critical Capabilities for Geospace Science, 2016 to 2025*" (Advisory Committee for Geosciences, National Science Foundation, Arlington, VA, 14 April 2016) *https://www.nsf.gov/geo/adgeo/geospace-review/geospace-portfolio-review-final-rpt-2016.pdf*.

18. See Nadia Drake, "Uncertain Future for Earth's Biggest Telescope," National Geographic.com, 4 June 2016, *http://phenomena.nationalgeographic.com/2016/06/04/uncertain-future-for-earths-biggest-telescope/*. For the NSF "Notice of intent to prepare an Environmental Impact Statement and initiate Section 106 consultation for proposed changes to Arecibo Observatory operations," see Federal Register Notices, vol. 81, no. 99, 23 May 2016, p. 32349. Also available in Alexander document file, NASA History Division, NASA Headquarters, Washington, DC.

and space physics and for planetary science when they were initiated by the SSB. NSF program managers have sought consistently to be responsive to decadal survey recommendations, but budget constraints have often stretched the time scales on which they have been able to act. The NSF also has engaged the NRC for advice on specific topics via ad hoc NRC study committees, including those of the SSB. In general, NSF officials have a reputation for trying very hard to be responsive to recommendations from NRC committees. This may reflect the culture of the NSF in which the members of the staff see an obligation to be responsive to needs and ideas from the scientific community. Thus, one might argue that the NSF turns to the NRC to meet its needs for translation between vision and implementation.

However, Marvel noted that a significant consequence of the NSF committee architecture was that there was no simple linkage between NSF internal advisory activities and incoming discipline-specific advice from the National Academies:

[W]hen the community's reports come through the National Academy, like the astronomy and astrophysics decadal surveys, … there is no internal match. So it basically falls to the division staff to advocate the recommendations of the survey within the agency, as there are no real other champions. Obviously the few people at the directorate level are going to know of the recommendation reports from the Academy and make them known, but that's just a couple of voices drowned out by the voices from the other divisions within the given directorate. And so I think it's harder for advice from the Academy, at least from the astronomy perspective, to get into the NSF chain…. It's always seemed to me … that the division leadership seems blocked out or

wedged out from any serious discussion about strategy for their division.[19]

Department of Energy Scientific Programs

Because it is a mission-driven agency, one might expect the U.S. Department of Energy (DOE) to be particularly similar to NASA. The DOE Office of Science has six program offices—Advanced Scientific Computing Research, Basic Energy Sciences, Biological and Environmental Research, Fusion Energy Sciences, High Energy Physics, and Nuclear Physics—each of which has its own FACA-chartered advisory committee.[20] Each committee has a subcommittee, called a Committee of Visitors, which conducts triennial assessments of the processes by which the office selects and funds research and of the quality of that research. The Office of Science also relies on the NRC, especially the Board on Physics and Astronomy (BPA), for external advice in a manner similar to how NASA utilizes the SSB.

The Nuclear Science Advisory Committee (NSAC) that advises the Office of Nuclear Physics is an interesting case because it is shared with and also advises the NSF via the NSF Mathematics and Physical Sciences Directorate. Thus, one might consider this arrangement to be an example of a matrix management approach in which a single committee looks across two agency's programs in the same field. NSAC appears to have a history of producing more formal, and more readily publicly available, reports than its counterparts at NASA. NSAC has prepared long-range plans for a national program in nuclear science at intervals of about every five to seven years, and these plans are developed via a process with substantial community engagement that is similar to the SSB decadal survey process.

19. Marvel interview, p. 10.

20. For information about DOE FACA committees, see *http://science.energy.gov/about/federal-advisory-committees/*.

BPA has used these long-range plans as input to NRC decadal surveys for nuclear science.[21] As an indication of the effectiveness of the NSAC, the decadal surveys have more often than not largely endorsed the NSAC strategic plans.

The High Energy Physics Advisory Panel (HEPAP) also advises both DOE and NSF. Its subcommittee, the Particle Physics Project Prioritization Panel (P5) has been an important influence in strategic planning for the Office of High Energy Physics. P5 has employed its own version of the decadal survey process in which the Division of Particles and Fields of the American Physical Society has managed a series of meetings and workshops to obtain broad community input, and then P5 has translated that scientific input into recommended DOE priorities. P5 is not established under FACA, so its recommendations are forwarded to HEPAP for concurrence and submission to the DOE. Thus, the resulting strategy shares many attributes of the SSB decadal surveys, but it lacks the degree of independence that comes from an effort conducted entirely under the auspices of the National Academies. Nevertheless, the fact that at a 22 May 2014 hearing of the Energy Subcommittee of the House Science, Space, and Technology Committee the P5 report[22] earned enthusiastic bipartisan support suggests that the arrangement has served DOE well.[23]

Michael Turner summarized his view of the DOE committees' performance:

> And I would say they are a model for managing with FACA Committees. I didn't mean to imply the word perfect; I didn't mean to imply that they get it all right. But I think that

the [committees] that I'm aware of (HEP and Nuclear Science) have done a very good job. They're getting the community input, and they give the agencies advice that they can actually use.

And he noted that there are pros and cons to the DOE approach:

> Unlike an NRC report where you ask the Academy to do something, and then you don't get to hear what's going on inside, on the FACA committee side you do. But you lose the independence. But I think the advantage, if you're looking for the pluses, is that you've got the agency keeping the committee focused on the task.[24]

At the risk of oversimplifying the situation, one might conclude that while DOE utilizes both its own internally established FACA committees and external NRC advisory bodies, it relies more substantively on the former than NASA does and consequently receives advice that may be more operationally specific but also more under DOE control and less independent than is the case for NASA.

In 2014, DOE's Fusion Energy Sciences Advisory Committee (FESAC) got itself into a kerfuffle that illustrates how sometimes agency control can backfire. In response to congressional direction, the committee was asked to recommend investment priorities as part of a ten-year strategic plan for the department's Fusion Energy Science program. When the committee's report was released, it drew immediate flak from many

21. See, for example, Board on Physics and Astronomy, *Nuclear Physics: Exploring the Heart of Matter* (National Research Council, The National Academies Press, Washington, DC, 2013).

22. Particle Physics Project Prioritization Panel, *Building for Discovery: Strategic Plan for U.S. Particle Physics in the Global Context* (U.S. Department of Energy, Washington, DC, May 2014).

23. Richard M. Jones, "Upbeat Hearing on P5 Report" (FYI: The AIP Bulletin of Science Policy News, American Institute of Physics, No. 109, 17 June 2014), *https://www.nsf.gov/mps/ast/seniorreview/sr_report_mpsac_updated_12-1-06.pdf*.

24. Turner interview.

members of the fusion science community. Critics charged that the committee failed to gather sufficiently broad scientific community input and that report was not representative of the views of the fusion research community. Critics also argued that the composition of the committee's strategic planning panel was unbalanced in a way that put academic researchers at a disadvantage compared to scientists and facilities at national laboratories. Scientists from university-based fusion laboratories had been excluded from the report-drafting panel due to DOE lawyers' concerns over conflicts of interest. The vice-chair of the planning panel was quoted as saying that the DOE's treatment of conflict of interest was much more stringent than what would have been expected of an NRC committee. When it came time for FESAC to vote on whether to approve the planning panel's report, only nine of FESAC's 23 members were deemed conflict-of-interest-free and able to vote.[25] Thus, charges about the committee's lack of inclusiveness and balance made the report vulnerable from the outset.

A Joint NSF-NASA-DOE Advisory Committee

Agencies most often establish advisory committees at their own initiative, but occasionally the push comes first from other directions. The Astronomy and Astrophysics Advisory Committee is an interesting example of the latter, in which the push came from the White House Office of Management and Budget, Congress, and then the NRC—and in which three agencies ultimately became sponsors of the committee. But let's begin at the beginning.

In early 2001, the George W. Bush administration submitted its fiscal year 2002 budget request to Congress, and as administrations often do in the name of efficiency, the proposal included the idea for a potential reform. Specifically, the budget document suggested that maybe the management of U.S. research in astronomy could be more effective if all responsibilities then under the NSF and NASA were merged and assigned to NASA. In order to pursue the idea, the administration called for formation of a "Blue Ribbon Panel" to assess the issues and recommend options for handling federally sponsored astronomical research.[26]

NSF and NASA duly (but probably not gladly) accepted the charge to arrange an evaluation of the idea, and they jointly asked the NRC to form a committee for the task. The NRC Committee on the Organization and Management of Research in Astronomy and Astrophysics was very much a blue ribbon committee, chaired by former aerospace industry executive Norman Augustine and populated by a small who's who in U.S. astronomy and science policy. It began its work in mid-2001 and released its final report in late 2001.[27]

The NRC committee concluded that NSF and NASA each had unique, important, and effectively managed roles and, therefore, responsibilities should not be consolidated in one agency. However, committee members were surprised to learn that the relevant sitting NASA associate administrator and NSF assistant director had never even met to discuss possible collaboration between the two agencies or other matters of common interest. Consequently, the committee called for better coordination and an integrated strategy for U.S. astronomical research. The committee

---

25. For a more comprehensive description of the FESAC report and reactions to it, see article by Michael Lucibella, "Fusion Research Runs into Turbulence," *APS News*, Vol. 23, no. 10, American Physical Society, November 2014, *http://www.aps.org/publications/apsnews/201411/fusion.cfm*.

26. Executive Office of the President, *A Blueprint for New Beginnings: A Responsible Budget for America's Priorities* (U.S. Government Printing Office, Washington, DC, 2001), p. 161.

27. National Research Council, *U.S. Astronomy and Astrophysics: Managing an Integrated Program* (The National Academies Press, Washington, DC, 2001).

recommended that the government establish an interagency planning board and a multiagency advisory committee that would provide external input to the planning board.[28] Congress liked the idea of an advisory committee that would look at cross-agency planning and coordination and included provisions for the advisory committee in the NSF Authorization bill for 2002.[29] The legislation directed NSF and NASA to establish such a committee—the Astronomy and Astrophysics Advisory Committee (AAAC)—to monitor and advise on coordination of astronomy programs and to report to Congress annually. Administration of committee activities was assigned to NSF. Two years later, in 2004 authorization language for DOE, Congress added DOE astronomy programs to the advisory committee's purview.[30] Thus, the original OMB interest in possibly consolidating management of federal astronomical research in one agency morphed into formation of a FACA committee charged to look across agency programs on a routine basis—providing a fine illustration of the idea that "If no action is evident, then form a committee instead."

In its early years of activity, the AAAC (sometimes fondly referred to as "aack," pronounced as if the speaker were choking) was visibly active in promoting support for the recommendations of the 2001 astronomy and astrophysics decadal survey on Capitol Hill, and the committee continues to prepare an annual report to Congress and the agencies that includes discussion of the status of implementation of decadal survey recommendations. The concerns expressed by the 2001 NRC committee over the effectiveness of interagency coordination do appear to have been resolved, and the

AAAC's 2015 annual report lauded the agencies for having increased their cooperation and coordination.[31] However, the committee is not often the agencies' first choice for advice, particularly because the AAAC's charter focuses on activities at the intersections of the agencies' programs rather than the astronomy programs of individual agencies. Instead, NASA, NSF, and DOE more often tend to look to their own FACA committees or to committees of the NRC for specific advice. This case of a matrix management arrangement for an advisory committee may be less successful both because of the narrowness of its charge and the fact that the agencies have other committees on which to rely.

Astronomer Marcia Rieke had her own reservations about the AAAC:

There is some weirdness in the AAAC in that some of what they do looks duplicative of agency advisory committees…. And in the law setting up the AAAC is a phrase that they're supposed to monitor what happens with the decadal survey, and I have to say quite honestly that gives the NRC some heartburn, because it's not clear what that means. Why is there yet another group doing that? But there haven't been any particular crossed swords over differing recommendations. That's certainly another forum where agencies can get advice. I think at one point in time when the AAAC was first constituted, there was a real concern about the NSF stewardship of ground-based astronomy and whether or not NASA should just take it over entirely. And I think the AAAC was meant to be more of a group formed in response to

---

28. National Research Council, *U.S. Astronomy and Astrophysics: Managing an Integrated Program* (The National Academies Press, Washington, DC, 2001), pp. 4–5.

29. National Science Foundation Authorization Act of 2002, Public Law 107-368, 19 December 2002.

30. Department of Energy High-end Computing Revitalization Act of 2004, U.S. Congress, Public Law 108-423, 30 November 2004.

31. Astronomy and Astrophysics Advisory Committee, *Report of the Astronomy and Astrophysics Advisory Committee* (National Science Foundation, Washington, DC, 15 March 2015) *http://www.nsf.gov/mps/ast/aaac/reports/annual/aaac_2015_report.pdf.*

some of those thoughts. And maybe now it's not clear whether their existence needs to be continued, but at the moment it is.[32]

National Oceanic and Atmospheric Administration

NOAA has a number of advisory bodies that are chartered under FACA. Most of them are charged to provide advice and oversight regarding various aspects of the agency's mission (e.g., weather, climate, marine fisheries, and hydrographic services), which encompasses operational services, regulatory, and scientific research roles. NOAA's Science Advisory Board (SAB) is probably the closest cousin to NASA's FACA-chartered space and Earth science advisory committees. In contrast to NASA's science committees, whose members are drawn largely from the research community, the membership of the SAB tends to be representative of the broad range of NOAA services customers and therefore more diverse. From time to time the SAB has produced letter reports (e.g., on draft strategic plans), and it has empaneled standing or ad hoc working groups that have prepared a steady stream of topically focused advisory reports. The Board formally reviews working group reports for approval and subsequent submission to the agency.[33]

Many outside observers who have been familiar with both agencies have noted, however, that NOAA tends to be less open to using its formal FACA committees than NASA and that the committees have been less pervasive and have had relatively less influence at NOAA compared to their NASA or NSF counterparts. The difference

is probably attributable to several factors, including the fact that NOAA's regulatory and service responsibilities add dimensions that are absent at NSF and NASA. NOAA officials may also feel that they have fewer resources to expend on an advisory structure than their sister agencies. Finally, one gets a sense that NOAA is culturally rather less open to outside advice. NOAA has less in-house institutional capability compared to NASA, which draws on in-house expertise via the substantial technical staffs at the NASA field centers. Consequently, NOAA may be more prone to simply comply with direction from other elements inside the administration (e.g., the Department of Commerce and OMB) rather than to turn to the outside for advice. The situation is further complicated by recent political controversies over climate change issues that have led to some congressional pressure for NOAA to be more open to advice from industry sectors where climate policies may have an impact.

In contrast to NOAA's use of standing FACA committees, the agency has vigorously embraced input from ad hoc expert advisory committees when they have been created to tackle a particular problem. One notable example was the Independent Review Team (IRT) chaired by former SSB co-chair and long-time advisor to NASA and DOD, as well as NOAA, Tom Young. The IRT was set up to review NOAA's environmental satellite program management in 2012 and 2013, and the team's report pulled no punches, saying, for example, that Department of Commerce and NOAA oversight of the programs was "dysfunctional and not [providing] value added."[34] NOAA officials made prompt efforts to act on the advice from Young's team. NOAA Administrator Kathryn Sullivan

32. Rieke interview, pp. 3–4.

33. For information about the NOAA SAB, see *http://www.sab.noaa.gov/*.

34. NOAA NESDIS Independent Review Team, "NOAA NESDIS Independent Review Team Report," NOAA, National Environmental Satellite, Data, and Information Service, 20 July 2012, available at *http://www.spacepolicyonline.com/pages/images/stories/NESDIS_IRT_Final_Report.pdf* and at *http://science.house.gov/sites/republicans.science.house.gov/files/documents/NESDIS_IRT_Final_Report.pdf*.

colorfully, but appreciatively, described the IRT's assessment as having "wirebrushed" the agency's management approach.[35]

Lou Lanzerotti described a similar experience when he led an ad hoc effort to examine NOAA's space weather program:

> My experiences with NOAA are mostly phone calls that I have received from various NOAA executives and administrators who ask various questions on some issue or other. Or if NOAA wants to do something, like when they wanted to look at the National Space Weather Program, they put together a committee with an outside contractor who managed the process. That gave us a lot of independence…. It was very heartening to see that kind of independence provided, with no torquing at all. NOAA deserves credits in that particular instance for the way they handled the assessment of the space weather program.[36]

NOAA also has turned to the NRC from time to time to seek advice on specific, focused topics. For example, in 2001, NOAA's National Environmental Satellite, Data, and Information Service (NESDIS) asked the NRC to provide advice on improving the transitioning of NASA research and technology development into NOAA's operational services. Three boards — the SSB, the Aeronautics and Space Engineering Board, and the Board on Atmospheric Sciences and Climate — teamed to organize a study committee that issued its report to NOAA and NASA in 2003.[37] That report, and vigorous congressional prodding, led to the formation of a joint NASA-NOAA transition office to implement many of the NRC's recommendations.

A particularly interesting case of one advisory committee trumping the advice of another followed the 2008 report prepared by a committee jointly organized by the SSB and the Board on Atmospheric Science and Climate. NASA and NOAA asked the committee to provide advice about how to recover lost climate measurements when NOAA's meteorological satellite program was restructured to deal with serious development problems in the mid-2000s. The NRC established priorities for measurements needed for climate research and recommended a strategy to mitigate the impact of instrument payload reductions that had been proposed to remedy ballooning satellite system costs and schedule delays.[38] NOAA did its best to follow the committee's recommendations and even received a budget plus-up to cover the costs of some of the recommended restorations. However, one of the principal recommendations from Tom Young's independent review team mentioned above was that NOAA badly needed to stick to its core mission — weather — and not dilute its efforts on other tasks that would distract attention and sap budgets. Consequently, NOAA, and the administration, followed the Young team's advice and stripped the new satellite systems of climate sensors.

The work of the 2012 independent review team is illustrative of how NOAA sees the relative roles of the SAB and NRC committees on one hand and ad hoc advisory bodies on the other. Former Assistant Administrator for Satellite and Information

---

35. Comments during 18 March 2015 hearing of the House Appropriations Subcommittee on Commerce, Justice, and Science (quoted in *http://www.spacepolicyonline.com/news/noaas-sullivan-pfo-new-way-to-buy-satellites-after-wirebrushing-from-tom-young-panel*).

36. Lanzerotti interview, p. 11.

37. National Research Council, *Satellite Observations of the Earth's Environment: Accelerating the Transition of Research to Operations* (The National Academies Press, Washington, DC, 2003).

38. National Research Council, *Ensuring the Climate Record from the NPOESS and GOES-R Spacecraft: Elements of a Strategy to Recover Measurement Capabilities Lost in Program Restructuring,* (The National Academies Press, Washington, DC, 2008).

Services Mary Kicza noted that "the FACA committees and the NRC committees tend to be more strategic, [while ones like] the very focused Young committee tend to be more tactical."[39]

NOAA co-sponsored the SSB's 2003 decadal survey for solar and space physics[40] and the 2005 decadal survey for Earth science and applications from space.[41] While NOAA officials have usually voiced an interest in responding positively to the surveys, the results have been mixed. NOAA has been less responsive to the recommendations from the decadal surveys compared to NASA and NSF. This has been partially a consequence of ongoing NOAA budget difficulties, but NOAA's hesitant response can also be traced to NOAA's need to focus on its core operational and service missions.

Kicza made it clear that scientific advice has to be viewed in the context of NOAA's multiplicity of customer needs:

> NOAA has to first and foremost provide continuity of observations. They cannot disrupt the level of capability that is provided to and depended upon by the public. That is always a first priority. Within and beyond that, we work to move forward, given the recommendations from the research community — balancing that against the needs of the operational community. It's a triumvirate input that has to be considered — the operational requirement, the research opportunities, and what can be done within the budget envelope that we can afford.[42]

However, former SSB member and chair of the 2012 decadal survey for solar and space physics Dan

Baker noted that there is another angle on NOAA's, and other agencies', willingness to embrace outside scientific advice. Namely, when multiple agencies are on the receiving end and when the advice includes recommendations about relative agency roles and responsibilities, turf battles and budget envy can gum up the works. Baker saw this as his committee tried to address the nation's space weather program:

> [T]here was a lot of maneuvering with NASA, with NOAA, with NSF, all for somewhat different reasons as to what agencies should be involved, what should be the tasks assigned, and what should be the charge for each of those.... It has become more and more of a problem that agencies want to opt out.... [L]ots of problems … have arisen because of this kind of sibling rivalry between agencies. NSF is a very much favored agency within the government, but it doesn't have as large a budget; the overall NSF budget is comparable to what is spent just on space and Earth science in NASA. And so I think there is a fair amount of resentment that sort of develops from that budgetary imbalance. Also NOAA, I think, resents the fact that they don't have all the technical knowledge and management capability that NASA does, and so they have to go sort of hat-in-hand to NASA, to design, procure, manage and ultimately launch … the space programs that they rely on within [the National Environmental Satellite, Data, and Information Service].[43]

39. Kicza interview.

40. National Research Council, *The Sun to the Earth — and Beyond: A Decadal Research Strategy in Solar and Space Physics* (The National Academies Press, Washington, DC, 2003).

41. National Research Council, *Earth Science and Applications from Space: National Imperatives for the Next Decade and Beyond* (The National Academies Press, Washington, DC, 2007).

42. Kicza interview.

43. Baker interview, pp. 3–4.

NASA in Context

Based on the cursory survey summarized above, one can still draw some general conclusions about how NASA's advisory culture has compared with that of other R&D agencies. Many observers have found NASA's openness and willingness to invite and listen to outside advice to be especially notable. Of course advice is just advice, not direction, and NASA has declined to accept and implement advice on occasions when the agency preferred, for any of a multitude of reasons. But on the whole, NASA has gotten high marks for its efforts to actively engage the outside community as advisors. Claude Canizares reflected on his experience with NASA, NSF, DOE, and others, saying, "Well there may be some of you-love-what-you-know in this, but I felt that at the time that I was in the advisory process, both at the NASA side and the Academy side, that the interactions between the advisory structure and the agency were about as good as you could hope for."[44]

NASA has also appeared to turn to the National Academies more often and more regularly than most of its sister agencies. According to former Congressional Research Service space expert Marcia Smith, "I think that NASA used the National Academies more, at least more than I was aware of the other agencies using it."[45] The tradition began with the formation of the SSB before NASA was formally put to work, and it has continued under an uninterrupted series of contracts to engage the SSB and its committees to study a panoply of topics.

On the other hand, Len Fisk noted that NASA's advisory culture and processes have been becoming more similar to and less distinct from those of other agencies:

I suspect that what NASA does today is more similar to what other agencies do. I think this sort of pervasive advisory structure, you know at all levels and connected to each other and all that stuff, was a unique NASA construct. It was not duplicated by anybody else. And, so NASA has returned to the norm in some sense. That's unfortunate, because I don't think it's as good as what NASA did. But I think you probably go to other agencies and find that in some ways a disjointed structure. I mean there are advisory committees all over the government, but if you don't wire them together effectively, then they are less effective than they would be.... I think the ones that NASA has probably have their counterparts in other agencies.[46]

There are a number of reasons for NASA's apparent trending towards becoming more like the rest of the pack. First, the enactment of GPRA meant that all agencies had to prepare regular strategic plans and performance evaluations. Thus, some of what NASA did in the 1980s with advisory body assistance or input became more nearly the norm across the government in the 1990s. Second, the National Academies' response to enactment of FACA section 15 measurably impacted the NRC's ability to respond quickly or to call directly and immediately on standing bodies such as the SSB and its standing committees to respond to urgent needs for independent external advice. That change translated directly into limitations on the kinds of advice that the Academies could provide. From an internal NASA perspective, the restructuring of the NAC and its committees under Administrator Griffin, including dissolution of discipline subcommittees and MOWGs, led to a concomitant

---

44. Canizares interview, p. 9.

45. Smith interview, p. 1.

46. Fisk interview, p. 23.

reduction in the ability of NASA's internal advisory bodies to provide timely substantive attention to tactical issues about which NASA managers needed advice.

NASA's Marc Allen summarized the situation succinctly as follows:

> So you have this really strange thing that occurred starting the second half of the 2000s decade where you had two parallel advisory systems — both staffed with the cream of the crop in the U.S. [scientific] investigator community — both of which had been hamstrung in different ways by the very legislation that was supposed to improve the advisory system process.[47]

In short, an advisory culture that had been viewed by many as amongst the best in the federal R&D sector began to slide towards being similar to all the rest and even began to appear more advice-averse as NASA entered its sixth decade.

There has been one very important exception to this trend—namely, the decadal surveys and mid-decade evaluations. Allen observed the growing clout of the decadal surveys from inside NASA:

> [I]n fact the Academy became much stronger. But it didn't become stronger on the basis of small studies. Its decadal surveys became incredibly powerful…early in the 2000s…. [T]hese reports became increasingly large and complex…. And so the decadal surveys began

to become increasingly programmatic. And this really meant that instead of a source of advice, they became almost like religious texts. In fact, provisions concerning how they should be used, how they should be structured, and how they should be conducted began to appear in congressional report language and even in statute.[48]

NASA has consistently and energetically supported the decadal survey process and has responded as vigorously as budgets, unforeseen technical and programmatic obstacles, and politics have allowed. The Agency provided funds to expand the coverage of the surveys to include all space and Earth science disciplines and to expand the depth of the surveys to include program cost and technical risk assessments. Ironically, NASA's broad support of the surveys has helped make the agency less exceptional in the sense that other agencies—including NSF (which, of course, was a customer of the very first decadal survey in the 1960s), NOAA, DOE, and the Air Force Office of Scientific Research—also now support the surveys. Nevertheless, the NRC decadal surveys and midterms remain a particular bright spot in NASA's advisory ecosystem.

The next chapter concludes Part II's survey of advisory activities in the second half of NASA's lifetime by summarizing what has persisted in the advisory environment going back to the NACA's days, as well as what has evolved over time in response to changes in the policy and programmatic environment.

---

47. Allen interview, 7 May 2014, p. 5.

48. Allen interview, 7 May 2014, p. 5.

wasn't frankly what people wanted to hear or didn't think they could afford or wasn't money they wanted to spend in science as opposed to other priorities of the administration.[2]

But the overall advisory environment for space and Earth science remained generally supportive, in spite of the actions or body language of the Agency's or Administration's senior leadership. Science managers who dealt with the program day-in and day-out, and who made the hard decisions about program execution, continued to consult with and consider advisors from the outside research community.

Strength and Independence of the Modern Space Studies Board

The clout of the original Space Science Board was due, in part, to the stature of the National Academy of Sciences. The Board also benefited from relative freedom from NASA controls and from institutional bureaucratic or procedural constraints. The National Academies' stature and reputation for independence and expertise remain as strong as ever. The institution works hard to protect those attributes and the image that they sustain. Congressional interest in independent, expert advice remains relatively strong as demonstrated by continuing legislative calls for NASA to obtain or follow the National Academies' advice. However, while respect for the stature and independence of the SSB and its sister bodies remains, many observers both inside NASA and in the scientific community believe that the earlier freedom from bureaucratic and procedural constraints has diminished. In the opinion of those stakeholders, some NRC policies and procedures that were introduced during the institution's response to FACA section 15 have been a backwards move in terms of agility, flexibility, and general responsiveness (see chapter 9).

Evolution of NASA's Internal Advisory Committees

As one would expect, just as the SSB's committee structure and operating policies have evolved over the years, so too have those of NASA's internal committees. The enactment of the Government Performance and Results Act (GPRA) helped formalize a basis for NASA advisory committees' roles in assisting with program office strategic planning and performance evaluation. However, the most profound change came with Griffin's reorganization of the NASA Advisory Council and its committees (see chapter 12). Management Operations Working Groups—the lowest and often most directly accessible elements of the advisory food chain—were largely disbanded; discipline subcommittees lost their formal, direct access to NASA science discipline division directors; and all committee advice had to be funneled up through the NAC to the Administrator. MOWGs and science subcommittees were replaced with ad hoc entities that NASA dubbed "analysis groups," which could only report findings rather than render recommendations and which could not formulate consensus views to be relayed to NASA managers. Thus, what the Administrator saw as a more orderly and integrated process many other participants saw as a system evolving towards filtered advice, diluted impact, and compromised trust.

The restructuring of NASA's internal advisory apparatus also had a practical effect on the tools and information that were available to help science managers do their jobs. During Daniel Goldin's time as Administrator, he oversaw a reduction in the size of the NASA Headquarters staff by more than a factor of two. Consequently, individual program managers had more tasks to juggle and less time to devote to each one. Those circumstances made access to good outside advice especially important, even crucial, but access to

---

2. Weiler interview, p. 14.

such advice through NASA committees became constrained.

Such changes would have very naturally and quickly made the SSB and its committees and sister boards even more important and powerful as they would be called upon to fill the gaps created by the weakening of the internal advisory committee system. However, the more-or-less concurrent post-FACA changes in the SSB's agility left NASA to try to pick between two imperfect choices for ways to get advice.

Division of Labor between the NRC and NASA's Internal Committees

Perhaps one of the most enduring characteristics of the advisory ecosystem has been a widely accepted understanding of the relative roles and relationships between the NRC and NASA's internal committees. The NRC provides strategic advice and recommends long-range scientific priorities. NASA's committees provide tactical advice and recommendations about how to implement the NRC scientific priorities. Certainly there have been, and always will be, overlaps and exceptions. But this big picture of the division of labor has survived since it was articulated by Newell and Naugle beginning in 1958 and on into the early 1970s. Some five decades later, NASA's science office head, John Grunsfeld, held the same view in 2014:

> The NASA Advisory Council is…what I think of as tactical advice. Whereas for strategic advice I think of longer-term deliberation, of much broader engagement of the community, and some time for fermentation, and that's what the National Research Council Space Studies Board does….[3]

Dan Baker shared the long accepted view about the division of responsibility between NASA and NRC advisory committees, but he felt that the system was broken:

> Looking back [to the NASA science advisory structure of the 1980s and 1990s], there were internal advice panels that were almost always populated heavily by people from outside, who knew about management, who knew about how projects and programs are carried out. And so there you had very natural tactical advice that … really had to be listened to…. And then you had the very appropriate strategic advice being given by groups like … the Space Studies Board — they have the long-term, big picture. You had the tactical advice where anytime something was questioned or it was maybe going off the rails, you could get really good quick feedback from knowledgeable people. And I think … the whole advice apparatus of the nation was well served by that. There came a time when that internal advice especially was not appreciated, not wanted by administrators and associate administrators. So I think that the disbanding of that internal advisory apparatus has been very detrimental to the whole space program. I think the NASA Advisory Council is only a pale shadow of what internal advice used to be.[4]

Baker added that while in the early 2010s the NASA advisory functions had been partially restored to their older arrangements, he still saw impacts on both the NASA and the NRC elements of the advisory ecosystem:

> [M]ore and more is being asked of the Academies and the NRC to provide tactical advice. I don't think the Academies should

---

3. Grunsfeld interview.

4. Baker interview, p. 7.

be doing this, and they are not well suited to be doing this. It's really important that we as a nation look at how academia and industry and government really work together and how one gets appropriate advice fed back into the agencies and how that advice is dealt with.… [W]hen this advisory apparatus gets out of whack and when you try to get the boards to deliver immediate, instantaneous, tactical advice it just doesn't work.… [T]hen we end up again with agencies that are desperate to get community buy-in; they are trying to do it through the NRC, because they are not getting it from the internal advisory apparatus. They start to resent the slowness, and they start shooting from the hip or they start criticizing the strategic advice of the decadals. I think this undercuts the decadal surveys, and you get into a negative feedback loop here on all of these things where the Academies and the NRC and the whole decadal process begins to be questioned. You think you need more quick answers. [T]he whole advisory apparatus … needs to be restored to its appropriate balance between internal, strong, and very responsive internal advice and broader, longer-term, strategic advice from the right parties.[5]

Value of FACA

The enactment of FACA created a helpful set of standards for federal agencies' use of advisory committees. It created an orderly management process, and it ensured public access to advisory activities. Thus, FACA was successful in its early implementation. But problems arose. In particular, NASA found ways to press, if not abuse, the provisions of the Act. By declining to separately charter the science committees and subcommittees, and instead

making them subservient to the NASA Advisory Council, and by applying particularly restrictive constraints on committee membership conflict of interest, NASA lawyers (even if they had prudent objectives) made it difficult to add legitimate experts to its science advisory bodies.

After enactment of FACA section 15, which applied to the National Academies, the NRC found ways to complicate its own procedures. The law requires that

> The Academy shall make its best efforts to ensure that (A) no individual appointed to serve on the committee has a conflict of interest that is relevant to the functions to be performed, unless such conflict is promptly and publicly disclosed and the Academy determines that the conflict is unavoidable, (B) the committee membership is fairly balanced as determined by the Academy to be appropriate for the functions to be performed, and (C) the final report of the Academy will be the result of the Academy's independent judgment. The Academy shall require that individuals that the Academy appoints or intends to appoint to serve on the committee inform the Academy of the individual's conflicts of interest that are relevant to the functions to be performed.[6]

The NRC interpreted these provisions for ensuring balance and objectivity to mean that standing boards and committees could not be permitted to author advisory reports, because the members had not been empaneled to provide advice on a topic that had not been defined in advance of their appointment to the standing body. In earlier times, the breadth and depth of the membership of the SSB and of its standing committee were accepted as strong reasons to qualify those bodies for many tasks within their areas of expertise. Consequently,

5. Baker interview, pp. 7–8.

6. "Federal Advisory Committee Act Amendments of 1997," Public Law 105-153, 111 Stat. 2689 (1997).

they often undertook studies that produced letter reports or full-length advisory reports on topics for which they were already informed and viewed as experts, and they did so relatively quickly. Under the revised policy, the full appointment process had to run its course before a newly appointed committee, even with the same membership as the standing committee, could go to work. While this procedure permitted the NRC to argue that it had been very diligent about avoiding conflicts of interest, it also made the study process more time-consuming and led standing committee members to doubt whether they had a meaningful role to play in the advisory ecosystem. The loss of flexibility on the part of standing boards and committees to respond relatively quickly to government officials' need for advice likely also contributed to greater government interest in alternative forms of NRC interactions such as workshops and informal roundtable discussions.

Environment of Constructive Tension

The constructive tension between the scientific community and NASA that was a constant ingredient of relationships in the early years of the space age has persisted undiminished. Scientists continue to press the Agency, sometimes with ambitions that border on naively optimistic, to support a robust science program. And NASA managers usually strive to be as responsive as budgetary, programmatic, and political realities permit. The tension has been less evident when times have been good—for example, when science budgets were growing in the late 1980s. But relationships have become more stressed whenever advice has seemed to be ignored or blocked. Nevertheless, the advisory process has both leveraged the tension and often helped moderate it.

The character and extent of the tensions also tend to reflect the leadership styles of the principals. In the mid- and late 1980s, Administrator James Fletcher understood the culture of the scientific community and knew how to stay open to community views, just as he had during his first tour as Administrator in the 1970s. Although the scientific community may have been unfamiliar to Richard Truly, Fletcher's successor, Truly trusted his science head, Len Fisk, to maintain ties with the community and largely deferred to Fisk on matters of using outside scientific advice. Thus, relationships were relatively cordial during the late 1980s. In contrast, Administrators O'Keefe and Griffin in the 2000s were more familiar with the defense industry community with which they had interacted, and they tended to see the scientists as contractors rather than partners. This heightened the tension during their tenures at NASA's helm.

A second kind of tension became rather more prominent in NASA's second three decades, and that is the tension associated with NRC studies conducted at congressional direction. Congress has been inclined to step in and call for an independent assessment from the National Academies when the members or their staffs have been concerned about whether they could trust the agency to be forthcoming or to do the right thing. Marcia Smith emphasized that federal agencies do not welcome advisory studies that are forced on them:

> If Congress asks for a study, they [the funding agency] are going to resist anything that it says, because they resent being required to spend their resources on something that Congress asked for. They consider it an unfunded mandate, they didn't want the advice, they didn't want to pay for the advice, and they are being forced to do it, because the Congress said so.[7]

---

7. M. Smith interview, p. 13.

While such congressionally mandated studies often have been hard for NASA officials to swallow, they can also put the NRC in an awkward position when the NRC's customer sees the NRC as an adversary rather than a constructive partner. Of course, NASA is not a monolithic institution in which everyone shares identical views on all issues. So we can add another dimension to the tension—namely, the likelihood that on some issues there are people inside NASA who might welcome the contrary positions articulated in a mandated NRC report. Palace politics have always been an element of the way large institutions operate, and that's not different here. In any case, chapter 16 will explore examples of congressionally mandated NRC studies in some detail.

Need for Leadership

Chapter 6 described a deeply rooted advisory ecosystem that provided significant benefits for space and Earth sciences in NASA's first three decades. But it was showing signs of stress thanks to austere budgets, unpredictable NASA decision making, and a series of accidents that had grounded America's entire space launch system. Thus, there was an urgent need for leadership that could help reinforce the inherent strengths, restore vitality, and provide forward stability.

All the major stakeholders responded in their own way. In the late 1980s, NASA's Office of Space Science and Applications instituted a strategic planning process that communicated a clear sense of priorities. The office subsequently created the senior review process that utilized outside advice to optimize resources to be applied to ongoing space science flight missions. And then in the early 2000s, NASA and the SSB worked together to expand and apply the decadal survey process to all space and Earth science disciplines. The SSB recognized that some form of stewardship was needed

between surveys and introduced decadal midterm reviews beginning in the mid-2000s. The SSB also recognized that the surveys needed to improve their cost and technical realism and introduced more in-depth technical assessments for new mission candidates in the late 2000s.

Congress also took some meaningful actions over the same period. First, although the 1993 Government Performance and Results Act and its 2010 update, the GPRA Modernization Act, were not explicitly directed at the advisory process, the legislation formalized government agency strategic planning and performance reviews and, thereby, provided a natural opening for NASA's advisory committees to participate. Congress was quite explicit about its expectations for using outside advice in the NASA Authorization Act of 2005, which directed NASA to "draw on decadal surveys and other reports in planetary science, astronomy, solar and space physics, earth science, and any other relevant fields developed by the National Academy of Sciences."[8] The 2008 authorization bill went farther in codifying the use of decadal surveys and their incorporation of cost and technology assessments and decision rules for coping with unexpected developments:

SEC. 1105. NATIONAL ACADEMIES DECADAL SURVEYS.

(a) In General – The Administrator shall enter into agreements on a periodic basis with the National Academies for independent assessments, also known as decadal surveys, to take stock of the status and opportunities for Earth and space science discipline fields and Aeronautics research and to recommend priorities for research and programmatic areas over the next decade.

(b) Independent Cost Estimates – The agreements described in subsection(a) shall include independent estimates of the life

---

8. "National Aeronautics and Space Administration Act of 2005," Public Law 109–155, 30 December 2005, 119 Stat. 2895.

cycle costs and technical readiness of missions assessed in the decadal surveys whenever possible.

(c) Reexamination – The Administrator shall request that each National Academies decadal survey committee identify any conditions or events, such as significant cost growth or scientific or technological advances, that would warrant NASA asking the National Academies to reexamine the priorities that the decadal survey had established.[9]

And to mangle metaphors beyond recognition, the scientific community comprised a third leg of the stool by continuing to support advisory efforts with extraordinary investment of energy and effort. Scientists served, often tirelessly and without remuneration, on NASA committees, National Academies bodies, and ad hoc panels to translate their expertise and experience into advice, in spite of the short-term hiccups in the system. This effort and the countless hours that community members invested have amounted to an enormous off-the-books contribution to the national space research enterprise.

How well has it worked? When did it work well, and why? Were there advisory duds that still offer useful lessons? The chapters to follow in Part 3 will begin to explore those questions.

---

9. "National Aeronautics and Space Administration Act of 2008," Public Law 110–422, 15 October 2008, 122 Stat. 4779.

CHAPTER 15

Case Studies: Advice Requested by NASA

The preceding chapters' tour through NASA's scientific advisory history provides a framework through which to review the impacts of the process and a backdrop against which to examine some of the notable successes and failings of the system. The decadal surveys have become the signature products of the National Academies' advice to NASA, and also NSF and NOAA, regarding goals and priorities in astronomy and astrophysics, solar system exploration, solar and space physics, and Earth science and applications from space. Chapter 11 discusses their origins, strengths, and successes in considerable detail. But the cumulative body of advisory work developed by National Academies bodies, especially the SSB, for NASA is much larger than the decadals alone. And NASA's own internal advisory committees also have contributed in important, and sometimes more practical, ways. So when looking at the history of all this effort, what can we learn about what has succeeded, what has fallen flat, and why?

This chapter takes a deeper look at a few case studies of advisory efforts that were commissioned by NASA and that can serve as informative examples of the process. We look first at studies carried out by NASA committees, then at activities conducted by NRC bodies.

Internal NASA Advisory System Examples

With relatively few exceptions, NASA's internal advisory bodies have operated as standing committees (or the equivalent) that have offered advice on a continuing basis when NASA officials or the committee members have perceived a need. That advice usually has been developed quickly—often during the course of a single meeting—and has been framed in a relatively ad hoc, topic-by-topic fashion. The senior reviews described in chapter 10 are a notable exception in which committees of external experts have been organized periodically to carry out a systematic scientific evaluation and provide views that have informed major operational decisions.

The sections below look at four other examples of major undertakings by internal committees created by NASA—the Great Observatories brainstorming group, the Earth System Sciences Committee (ESSC), the Discovery Program definition group, and the Mars Program Independent Assessment Team (MPIAT). They are useful illustrations of how NASA turned to outside experts to help define and advocate new scientific efforts or restructure ongoing programs. Three were ad hoc efforts; the ESSC was a formally chartered FACA committee.

THE GREAT OBSERVATORIES BRAINSTORMING GROUP: When Charlie Pellerin became Director of Astrophysics at NASA Headquarters in 1983, the Space Telescope (later to become the Hubble Space Telescope) was under construction for a planned mid-1980s launch. The 1982 astronomy and astrophysics decadal survey had given a high priority to a large x-ray telescope, the Advanced X-ray Astrophysics Facility (AXAF, later to become the Chandra X-ray Observatory), as the next major space astronomy mission, but AXAF had not yet been given a go-ahead at NASA. At the same time, a vocal advocacy group was making a case for a new large telescope to operate at infrared wavelengths, and astrophysicists were also beginning to dream about a large telescope to measure cosmic gamma rays. Supporters of each proposal touted the strengths of their particular candidate over the alternatives, but none of these concepts had been able to gather enough steam to secure a development budget or a place in the new-start queue. Pellerin recalled that at the time, "The big popular story was that the Congress keeps asking 'Why do you need so many telescopes?'"[1]

Pellerin adopted a two-pronged strategy to deal with the challenge. The first was to find a way to couch the proposals, not in terms of building one or another space telescope, but in terms of what were the most fundamentally interesting questions about the universe and how would measurements at different wavelengths resolve them. The second was to find a way to communicate the fundamental scientific value of different space observatories in terms that were unencumbered by the complex technical jargon that was so much of astronomers' everyday language but Greek to policy makers. Pellerin and his staff pulled together a group of accomplished scientists as an informal, ad hoc advisory committee that would flesh out his plan. He recruited Cornell University astronomer Martin Harwit, who was then holding a visiting fellowship at the National Air and Space Museum, to chair the group, and they assembled for a rather unconventional meeting at the Goddard Space Flight Center.[2]

The 3 January 1985 meeting began with discussions of the top-level unanswered questions in astrophysics and cosmology. Then Pellerin threw his group of heavy hitters a curve. He recalled the meeting as follows:

> [T]hen I said, 'Okay…I've got crayons and magic markers and paper. I want you to take each one of these topics and write [it] on top of the paper. Go around the room and make me cartoons as to how the missions could work together synergistically to answer these questions'…So they had these guys—I mean these are the top people—on their hands and knees on the floor doing these pictures with the crayons. And at the end of the day Martin gathered them up and had a friend…get this into a brochure…. It was the Great Observatories brochure.[3]

The name "Great Observatories" actually emerged shortly after the brainstorming and cartooning session. Pellerin recalled meeting with Harvard astrophysicist George Field, who had just chaired the 1982 astronomy and astrophysics decadal survey, and explaining that Pellerin was stumped about what to call the program outlined

---

1. Pellerin interview, p. 6.

2. Harwit provided his own firsthand account of this event in his book, *In Search of the True Universe: The Tools, Shaping, and Cost of Cosmological Thought* (Cambridge University Press, New York, NY, 2013), pp. 234–238.

3. Pellerin interview, pp. 6–7. The brochure is reproduced (in black and white) in Logsdon, John M., ed., with Amy Paige Snyder, Roger D. Launius, Stephen J. Garber, and Regan Anne Newport. *Exploring the Unknown: Selected Documents in the History of the U.S. Civil Space Program, Volume V, Exploring the Cosmos.* (NASA SP-4407, NASA History Division, Washington, DC, 2001), pp. 703–730.

in the new brochure. Field replied, "Why don't you call it the Great Observatories?"[4]

The concept of a Great Observatories program that integrated a suite of separate space observatories into a synergistic whole was a great success. It created a coherent story for how multiple measurements at different wavelengths could address some of the most important, and fascinating, problems in modern science. It brought competing factions together to support one another for a common scientific good. And by means of the Great Observatories comic book the concept could be communicated clearly and non-technically to audiences ranging from members of Congress to schoolchildren. The program name became a household word, at least in the space community.

Al Diaz, who was helping manage planetary science programs at the time and who later held a number of senior positions with management responsibilities for the observatories, was typical of the concept's admirers:

It was an elegant plan. It was something that you could actually understand… to cover the electromagnetic spectrum outside of the influence of the atmosphere and take full advantage of the space capability.[5]

Pellerin made an effort to avoid letting the brochure trivialize the science. He recalled that his group of crayon-wielding experts supplemented their lay-reader presentation with inserts for more scientifically informed readers by adding

little boxes where smart guys, smarter than me in physics and more specialized, could put down the arguments with some equations that [I could use with] an observer who was critical

of this. I could go toe to toe with the other scientists if I had to.[6]

The ad hoc Great Observatories brainstorming group subsequently morphed into an informal advisory committee — the Astrophysics Council — for Pellerin in his role as Astrophysics Director. It performed first as a Management Operations Working Group and later as a subcommittee of the NASA Space Science and Applications Advisory Committee (see chapter 5). This group served as a forum for debate on issues that Pellerin wanted to try out on leaders in the astrophysics community, and consequently, it was a continuing platform for obtaining advice about the program. Pellerin took pride in being able to recruit several Nobel Laureates to participate in the Council, thereby adding a special degree of stature to the group and also remarkable clout. Pellerin recalled that on several occasions he was able to call on them to help contact senior Agency officials to advocate on behalf of the program.[7]

All four elements of the Great Observatories — Hubble Space Telescope, Chandra X-ray Observatory, Compton Gamma Ray Observatory, and Spitzer (infrared) Space Telescope — were eventually highly successful missions. Hubble and Compton had already entered development phase when Pellerin's group first met, and Chandra and Spitzer subsequently won approval from NASA and Congress. The birth of the Great Observatories concept and its successful advocacy began when NASA convened the 1983 ad hoc gathering of outside experts and sought their advice.

EARTH SYSTEM SCIENCES COMMITTEE: As chapter 5 described, NASA officials in the early 1980s recognized the opportunity to build both

4. Pellerin interview, p. 9.

5. Diaz interview, p. 9.

6. Pellerin interview, p. 8.

7. Pellerin interview, p. 13.

a foundation and a rationale for a space-based Earth observing system. Growing support for such a system came from several sources, including productive workshops on the subject of global change and of studies of the global-scale intersections of the geosciences and ecology, encouragement from the Space Science and Applications Advisory Committee, Associate Administrator Burt Edelson's interest in establishing an international presence in space applications, and NASA Deputy Administrator Hans Mark's encouragement. NASA's Director of Earth Science Shelby Tilford arranged for formation of an Earth Systems Science Committee under the auspices of the NASA Advisory Council. The committee of 16 members was chaired by National Center for Atmospheric Research Director Francis Bretherton. The committee's meetings often included ex officio participation by liaison members and observers from other interested government agencies and the NASA field centers, so the committee's deliberations were generally open and inclusive.[8] Working over a period of more than five years, the committee articulated a compelling scientific definition and rationale for studying the Earth as a system and developed a set of recommendations on how to carry out such a study.

One of the committee's most notable and enduring products was the so-called Bretherton diagram that appeared in the committee's report. The diagram illustrated the complex web of interactions between external forces (from the Sun and volcanoes), responses and interactions between the physical climate system (the atmosphere, oceans, and land) and biogeochemical cycles (chemistry of the troposphere, oceans, and terrestrial ecosystems), and their collective impact on and response

to human activities.[9] Thus, this holistic perspective and the committee's substantive report had a major impact on creating a major new thrust in studying the Earth as a complex, interactive system, and it provided a scientific basis for NASA's Earth Observing System program, which began in 1991. Perhaps equally importantly, the committee helped change the way that Earth scientists from different sub-disciplines saw their field.

Len Fisk, who inherited responsibility for initiating the EOS program when he became Associate Administrator, described the ESSC report as follows:

I think its impact was enormous... it spawned... [and] really sort of cemented this concept of Earth system science. At the time most Earth scientists viewed themselves in a disciplinary way, whether they were meteorologists or ice people or oceanographers or something. But the sort of enlightened people, the people that were starting to think about the future, said that the real problems are at the interfaces between these things. [T]hat gave birth to Earth system science as a subject... I think it was in many ways one of the seminal events that got the whole concept... in the community's mind as the thing that had to be done.[10]

Eric Barron, an oceanographer who joined the Penn State faculty in 1986, and who subsequently has served in many scientific and academic leadership positions, recalled his impressions about the importance of the report:

The Bretherton Committee's Report... spurred all sorts of different activities and focal points,

---

8. See Earth System Sciences Committee, *Earth System Science, Overview: A Program for Global Change* (NASA Advisory Council, NASA, Washington, DC, May 1986) p. 48.

9. Earth System Sciences Committee, *Earth System Science, Overview: A Program for Global Change* (NASA Advisory Council, NASA, Washington, DC, May 1986).

10. Fisk interview, pp. 1–2.

including changing how advice was given to the federal government, particularly in the National Academy of Sciences. What you saw emerging was a Climate Research Committee out of the National Academy of Sciences, the Board on Atmospheric Sciences and Climate, the Committee on Global Change Research … you had those three groups, and then some others, that all began to interact within the same arena … I view those committees as the ones that stepped in following the Bretherton Report specifically to look and evaluate many different programs.[11]

Thus, observers both inside and outside the Earth sciences have credited NASA's Earth System Sciences Committee with having a major impact on the direction of the field. And for NASA, it led to the definition, development, and launch of a series of Earth observing satellites that also largely defined NASA's role in the U.S. Global Change Research Program.[12]

DISCOVERY PROGRAM ADVISORY COMMIT-TEES: NASA formed the Solar System Exploration Committee under auspices of the NAC in 1980 (see chapter 5) in order to respond to political and budgetary factors that threatened the very existence of the planetary science program. It was successful in the short term by providing some evidence that the community was getting its act together and coming up with a scheme for delivering good science more cost-efficiently than in the past. But it was not especially successful over a longer term, because the committee's proposal to build two series of standard spacecraft designs—Planetary Observer and Mariner Mark II—both proved to be impractical and still costly. Thus, when former Jet Propulsion

Laboratory cosmo-chemist Wes Huntress became Director of Solar System Exploration in 1992, he faced the possibility of a five-year or longer gap in planetary mission activity beginning in the late 1990s. He needed to find a way to increase the number and rate of flight opportunities and to make the program more affordable.

One of Huntress' top objectives when he took the helm of the Solar System Exploration Division was to start a program of low-cost planetary missions that could be built and launched more frequently than in the past and that could be worked into the budget in hard times as well as good times. His idea was initially controversial because he proposed to create a program of missions that would be led and managed by individual principal investigators who would be selected through open competition. This approach was well entrenched in the space astronomy and space plasma physics communities where the Explorer program of low-cost, competed, principal-investigator-led missions had become a mainstay. The planetary sciences community, on the other hand, was accustomed to providing instruments that were then integrated onto large facility-class spacecraft by a NASA field center, such as the Langley Research Center for the Viking Mars landers and the Jet Propulsion Laboratory for many planetary missions. Thus, the conventional wisdom, encouraged by JPL, was that planetary missions were too big for NASA to give full development responsibility to a single lead scientist outside NASA and too costly to be feasible.[13]

Huntress patiently turned conventional wisdom around by challenging members of the community to convince *themselves* that a new idea would or wouldn't work. He formed two ad hoc advisory committees—one for science and one for engineering—and charged them to evaluate the low-cost

11. Barron interview, NASA "Earth System Science at 20" Oral History Project, 1 July 2010, p. 6.

12. For a concise history of the program, see National Research Council, *Earth Observations From Space: History, Promise, and Reality (Executive Summary)* (The National Academies Press, Washington, DC, 1995), pp. 4–6.

13. Huntress interview, pp. 5–6.

mission concept in depth and to specify what attributes would be needed to make it work. He asked the science panel, "Can you do decent science with a spacecraft that is limited in scope and has only a few instruments on it … instead of these big Christmas trees you are used to?"[14] The engineering panel included people who had significant familiarity with low-cost missions (particularly from the Naval Research Laboratory and the Johns Hopkins University's Applied Physics Laboratory) as well others who were known skeptics of the small-mission proposal. Huntress recalled how he got the results that he hoped for:

> And I just let them go at it and have the NRL folks and the APL folks kind of teach everybody how to do low-cost spacecraft and people experienced in planetary teach the low-cost spacecraft guys what the idiosyncrasies of doing planetary are. And so we spent a couple of years convincing our science community 'Yeah, maybe this will work.' The scientists liked the idea of the missions being PI-led and proposed, and the engineering community became convinced that you could do low-cost planetary mission.[15]

By the end of 1992, NASA had transformed the two committees' deliberations into the Discovery program, and the first Discovery mission—the Near Earth Asteroid Rendezvous mission—was successfully launched in February 1996. Eleven missions were launched, with only one failure, through December 2012. The planned 2016 launch of a twelfth mission (to land on Mars) was scrubbed (but rescheduled for 2018) due to development problems with the French seismometer that was intended to be a key instrument on the

mission. Overall, however, Discovery proved to be a great scientific and strategic success, a source of genuinely innovative approaches, and a critical element of NASA's solar system program. Its origins can be traced to the foresight of NASA managers who conceived a revolutionary solution to a serious gap in the Agency's set of tools for solar system science and who knew that the best way to sell the idea to the community was to engage the community in scrutinizing the idea and fleshing it out. From an advisory process perspective, two keys to Huntress' success were that he gave his teams adequate time to debate and work through the problem and that he picked people for the job in whom he was confident about their willingness to listen to competing viewpoints.[16]

MARS PROGRAM INDEPENDENT ASSESSMENT: When Dan Goldin became NASA Administrator in April 1992, he was concerned that NASA science missions had grown too large, too complex, and too costly. Consequently, he became a passionate advocate for endeavors that would be faster, better, and cheaper, and the phrase became Goldin's mantra as he pushed the Agency and its programs to move to larger numbers of smaller missions developed on fixed schedules and at lower costs. The faster-better-cheaper approach also emphasized expanded technological innovation, streamlined management with greater delegation to lower levels, and a higher tolerance of technical risk.

Faster-better-cheaper had some notable early successes, including Mars Global Surveyor, which incorporated some aspects of the idea, the Near Earth Asteroid Rendezvous, which was the first Discovery-class mission, and the Mars Pathfinder lander with its successful airbag lander and highly popular Sojourner rover. Nevertheless, the concept

---

14. Huntress interview, p. 6.

15. Huntress interview, p. 6.

16. For a more extensive history of the origins of the Discovery Program, see Michael J. Neufeld, "Transforming Solar System Exploration: The Origins of the Discovery Program, 1989–1993," *Space Policy*, vol. 30, pp. 5–12, 2014.

also had its highly visible stumbles. Mars Climate Orbiter failed to go into orbit at Mars in September 1999 due to a navigation error, which resulted from an error in converting propulsion thrust from Newtons to foot-pounds. Mars Polar Lander failed to land safely in December 1999. A postmortem analysis determined the most likely cause of the mishap was premature termination of the engine firing prior to the lander touching the surface, causing it to strike the planet at a high velocity.[17] The Mars Polar Lander spacecraft carried a pair of small technology development probes, called Deep Space 2, that were intended to detach from the Mars Polar Lander and penetrate Mars' surface, but they also failed for unknown reasons.

Understandably alarmed by the rash of failures and determined to fix the Mars program as quickly as possible, Goldin and his Associate Administrator for Space Science, Ed Weiler, recruited space program veteran Tom Young to lead an ad hoc Mars program independent assessment team. Young was a retired senior executive of Martin Marietta Aerospace and Lockheed Martin, and he had served earlier in a number of important NASA positions, including Viking Program Mission Director, NASA Headquarters Planetary Program Director, and Director of the Goddard Space Flight Center. He would later serve as chair of the International Space Station Management and Cost Task Force for Goldin and chair of the two independent review teams for NOAA mentioned in chapter 13.

A diverse group of experienced industry and government aerospace managers as well as several planetary scientists filled out Young's 17-person team. Their charge called for the team to review the three failed missions and three similar successes (Mars Global Surveyor, Pathfinder rover, and the Deep Space 1 technology testing mission), examine the roles and relationships of key mission participants (as well as the relationships between their institutions), oversee separate Mars Polar Lander and Deep Space 2 failure reviews, identify lessons learned, and provide advice that would be relevant to future missions. The team began its work on 7 January 2000, and they met their remarkably tight deadline by delivering their report to Goldin on 14 March only slightly more than two months later.

In what became typical of all advisory activities carried out under Young's leadership, the report was explicit and direct. It reaffirmed that Mars exploration was important and challenging, and it went on to conclude that the U.S. space community has what it takes to do it successfully and that the FBC approach is viable if properly applied. The team found that "there were significant flaws in the formulation and execution of the Mars program"[18] that included lack of discipline and of defined policies and procedures, failure to understand prudent risk, an unwillingness at JPL to push back when Headquarters-imposed cost or schedule constraints were dangerously tight, and an overall focus on cost instead of mission success. The report identified numerous best practices from successful missions and areas for future attention regarding project management responsibility and accountability, testing and risk management and decision making, adequate budgeting, and institutional relationships, as well as others.[19]

Goldin shouldered the responsibility for the problems, saying that he pushed too hard, cut

17. Private communication from G. Scott Hubbard to the author. For an extensive account of these Mars missions, see Erik M. Conway, *Exploration and Engineering: The Jet Propulsion Laboratory and the Quest for Mars* (Johns Hopkins University Press, Baltimore, MD, 2015).

18. Mars Program Independent Assessment Team, *Mars Program Independent Assessment Team Summary Report*, (NASA, Washington, DC, 14 March 2000), p. 12, available at *http://engineer.jpl.nasa.gov/mib/MarsProgram_2000_mpiat_summary.pdf*.

19. For press accounts of the Young report and NASA's response, see Keith Cowing, "NASA Reveals Probable Cause of Mars Polar Lander and Deep Space-2 Mission Failures," SpaceRef.com, 28 March 2000; Warren E. Leary, "Poor Management by NASA Is Blamed for Mars Failure," NYTimes.com, 29 March 2000; William Harwood, "NASA orders sweeping changes after Mars failures," Spaceflight Now, 29 March 2000.

budgets too much, and created an environment in which managers could not succeed.[20]

Weiler used the Young report to restructure the Mars program, starting with appointment of Ames Research Center executive Scott Hubbard as Headquarters Mars Program Director and clarifying lines of responsibility and authority between Headquarters and the Jet Propulsion Laboratory, where the program was implemented. With the benefit of the independent assessment team's advice, Weiler, Hubbard, and JPL were able to get the program back on track so that NASA enjoyed seven straight Mars mission successes starting with Mars Odyssey launched in 2001, and continuing through the Curiosity Mars Science Laboratory launched in 2011, and the Mars Atmosphere and Volatile Evolution orbiter launched in 2013.[21]

External NASA Advisory Examples

NASA has often also turned to the NRC to carry out an advisory study on behalf of the agency. The cases below are illustrative of such efforts in which the Space Studies Board organized committees to advise NASA about a specific topic or area. In one case—a Mars rock symposium—the activity was actually a joint effort between the SSB and NASA's internal FACA committee.

SPACE TELESCOPE SCIENCE INSTITUTE REPORT:[22] In the early 1970s, NASA and space astronomy advocates in the scientific community were trying to build a case for starting development of the Large Space Telescope. While most of the activity focused on design studies for the proposed flight hardware, NASA officials also began to consider approaches for operating the telescope once it could be launched. The mission was expected to have a 10-to-15-year lifetime during which it would operate as a facility that would serve many users and produce unprecedentedly large volumes of data. Thus, the post-launch scientific aspects of the program would be formidable and would include activities such as evaluation of proposals for obtaining observing time, establishing observing priorities, scheduling telescope operations, and generally serving as the primary interface with the scientific community.

Two competing concepts emerged, and they generated lots of heated debate. NASA's initial preference was for scientific operations to be co-located with the engineering control center for the spacecraft and telescope at a NASA facility. This was the strong, basically unyielding, preference of officials at the Goddard Space Flight Center to which management responsibility for development of the telescope scientific instruments and for flight mission and data operations had been assigned. Outside astronomers could play an advisory role, but Goddard people were convinced that their experience with earlier multiuser astronomy missions, in which NASA had end-to-end control and in which outside astronomers participated as guests, demonstrated that that was the way to go.

On the other hand, outside astronomers in the broader scientific community were equally convinced that scientific operations of the telescope should be outside NASA's control. Many in the scientific community felt that NASA could not be trusted (See the discussion of tensions between NASA and the Astronomy Missions Board in chapter 3.) to work fairly on behalf of all astronomers

---

20. Matthew Fordahl, "NASA Chief Blames Self for Botched Missions," ABC News, Pasadena, CA, 30 March 2000, Alexander doc files, NASA History Division, NASA Headquarters, Washington, DC.

21. For more on faster-better-cheaper and the Mars mission failures as a business school case study, see Sean Silverthorne, "Mission to Mars: It really *Is* Rocket Science" (Working Knowledge, Harvard Business School, 1 March 2004), available at *http://hbswk.hbs.edu/item/mission-to-mars-it-really-is-rocket-science*.

22. A thorough discussion of the origins of the Hornig report appears in Robert W. Smith, *The Space Telescope: A Study of NASA, Science, Technology, and Politics* (New York, NY: Cambridge University Press, 1989), ch. 6, pp. 187–220.

or to remain committed to the long-term scientific value of the telescope. So the astronomers' alternative was an independent scientific institute that would be managed by an outside organization such as a consortium of universities. This concept was not especially new. For example, in 1966 the Ramsey Science Advisory Committee had recommended a NASA lunar science institute (see chapter 3), and that idea subsequently led to creation of the Lunar Science Institute that was initially managed by the National Academy of Sciences through Rice University and then, beginning in 1969, by a new consortium of universities—Universities Space Research Association. The concept was also familiar to astronomers who had experience with the Association of Universities for Research in Astronomy (AURA) through which the Kitt Peak National Observatory complex of telescopes was managed for the NSF.

Thus, by the mid-1970s, the terms of a battle were clearly drawn. Would scientific aspects of the telescope's operations be controlled by NASA along with the rest of the telescope's operations—possibly with some advice from participation by the scientific community—or would science operations be separate from the traditional functions of the space mission control center and controlled by an independent scientific organization? Astronomers outside NASA strongly adhered to the latter, and some NASA managers began to warm to that approach as well. But others, especially at Goddard, held fast to the former, NASA-controlled approach. Noel Hinners, who was then serving as Associate Administrator for Space Science, already had his hands full dealing with challenges posed by the program's budget, a political fight to gain congressional approval for the program, and continuing resistance from those astronomers who thought the project was too costly compared to the ground-based facilities with which they had always worked.

He didn't need another battle with the scientific community at this time. Consequently, Hinners arranged for the Space Science Board to organize a study to examine possible institutional arrangements for the scientific use of the telescope.[23]

Donald F. Hornig, who had just stepped down from being president of Brown University, was selected to chair the study committee. Hornig was a Harvard-trained chemist who had been a group leader in the Manhattan Project and who had served as science advisor to President Lyndon Johnson from 1964 to 1969. The 17-person committee included experts who had experience with the operation of national research centers, including astronomers who had experience with space astronomy missions and others who were experienced with the operation of both national and privately funded, ground-based, astronomical facilities. The committee met for information collection sessions in Washington, DC, and at Goddard, and then they gathered for a two-week work session at the NAS study center in Woods Hole, MA. The luxury of having a study committee together for two straight weeks of discussion and report writing (free of e-mail and cellphones) would be a rare luxury now, but it was not uncommon in the 1960s and 1970s.

The committee's report—"Institutional Arrangements for the Space Telescope"—was a remarkably thorough assessment of plans for the Space Telescope, experience with other space and ground-based observatories, factors relevant to whether an institute was needed, and options for the structure of an institute. The committee's core recommendations were unequivocal:

- The productive use of the ST depends upon the safe, reliable operation and maintenance of the spacecraft and its associated communications and data-processing

23. For a good view of Hinners' thinking about the institute, see Hinners' interview by Rebecca Wright for the NASA Headquarters Oral History Project, 19 August 2010, pp. 3–4.

systems, and upon the quality of the astronomical research that is conducted with it.

- Whereas the operation of the ST and its associated systems is best carried out by NASA, optimum scientific use of the ST requires the participation of the astronomical community.
- An institutional arrangement, which we call the Space Telescope Science Institute (STSI), is needed to provide the long-term guidance and support for the scientific effort, to provide a mechanism for engaging the participation of astronomers throughout the world, and to provide a means for the dissemination and utilization of the data derived from the ST.
- We recommend that the STSI be operated by a broad-based consortium of universities and nonprofit institutions…. The consortium would operate the institute under a contract with NASA.
- We recommend that the policies of the STSI be set by a policy board of about ten people representing the public interest, as well as the astronomical community and the broader scientific community. The quality and independence of the policy board is essential to the success of this enterprise.[24]

The report went on to discuss recommended scientific and operational functions, structure, governance, staffing, facilities, arrangements for interactions with NASA, and location of the institute. NASA largely accepted the Hornig committee's recommendations and incorporated many of the ideas from the report in the procurement solicitation document for an institute. After a competition to choose an organization to create and manage

the institute, NASA selected AURA, and the Space Telescope Science Institute (STScI) was established in 1981. STScI now sits in Baltimore, adjacent to the Johns Hopkins University campus and less than a one-hour commute from Goddard.

The institute has been enormously successful, something about which both astronomers and NASA officials agree. Ed Weiler, who served for a long time as NASA Headquarters Program Scientist for Hubble before becoming science Associate Administrator, was effusive about the impact of the Hornig report and the success of its recommendations:

> That's actually a good example of some early advice that was not only followed for Hubble but then followed forever. It wasn't a decadal, but, boy, did it have an impact on the community, you bet! And the Institute has been a tremendous success, despite what a few people might say, in terms of bringing in the community and making Hubble a national, frankly international, presence.[25]

The Hornig report nicely illustrates an advisory effort that met NASA's needs and provided actionable advice that had a significant lasting impact. NASA's Noel Hinners wanted a way to resolve the conflict between Goddard and the astronomy community, he wanted independent guidance on how to maximize the long-term scientific value of the Space Telescope program, and he wanted to be able to build a positive relationship with the community that would shore up their willingness to be advocates for the program. Hinners probably also wanted cover; he had a good idea of what he wanted to do, but having a National Academy of Sciences committee behind him made his future decisions much more palatable.

24. National Research Council, *Institutional Arrangements for the Space Telescope: Report of a Study at Woods Hole, Massachusetts, July 19–30, 1976* (The National Academies Press, Washington, DC, 1976), p. vii.

25. Weiler interview, p. 11.

MARS ROCK EVENTS: The continent of Antarctica is a great place to look for meteorites, because they stand out distinctly in its pristine environment of bare white ice fields and they lay undisturbed for long periods of time. In December 1984, NSF-sponsored meteorite hunters discovered a specimen that had a major impact on an aspect of NASA science and, for a while, seemed destined to profoundly impact science much more broadly.

Named ALH84001 for its discovery site in the Allen Hills region of Antarctica, the nearly 2 kilogram rock was one of a class of meteorites that most likely came from Mars, because it contains gases whose composition is very much like the composition of the Martian atmosphere. On 6 August 1996, NASA scientist David McKay and collaborators published a paper[26] that reported that they had found electron microscopic and chemical evidence of fossil Martian micro-organisms in ALH84001. Needless to say, discovery of life on Mars—even primitive life that might have been extinct for a few billion years—would be a really big deal.[27]

Responses to the reported discovery were prompt and dramatic. McKay had given a heads-up to NASA Associate Administrator Wes Huntress, who alerted his boss, NASA Administrator Dan Goldin, who alerted the White House. President Bill Clinton commented on the discovery as he departed the White House for a trip on 7 August:

> Like all discoveries, this one will and should continue to be reviewed, examined and scrutinized. It must be confirmed by other scientists…. First, I have asked Administrator Goldin to ensure that this finding is subject to a methodical process of further peer review and validation. Second, I have asked the Vice President to convene at the White House before the end of the year a bipartisan space summit on the future of America's space program. A significant purpose of this summit will be to discuss how America should pursue answers to the scientific questions raised by this finding…. If this discovery is confirmed, it will surely be one of the most stunning insights into our universe that science has ever uncovered. Its implications are as far-reaching and awe-inspiring as can be imagined. Even as it promises answers to some of our oldest questions, it poses still others even more fundamental.[28]

To respond to Clinton's call to convene a space summit to consider how the nation should explore the implications of the ALH 84001 paper, Huntress turned to his principal advisory bodies—the internal FACA-charted Space Science Advisory Committee (SSAC) and the external Space Studies Board. He asked SSAC chair Anneila Sargent and SSB chair Claude Canizares to organize a workshop that would involve a diverse group of experts to dig into the state of knowledge of the origins of the universe and life and everything in between and ponder future research directions regarding these questions.[29] In less than three months, Canizares and Sargent pulled some 40 scientists together to meet, discuss, and prepare a briefing for Vice President Al Gore. A subgroup of the workshop organizers and participants met with the Vice President in early December for a lively discussion

26. David McKay et al., "Search for Past Life on Mars: Possible Relic Biogenic Activity in Martian Meteorite ALH84001," *Science*, 273, (5277), 924–930, 6 August 1996.

27. For an extensive discussion of the Mars rock story see Kathy Sawyer, *The Rock from Mars: A Detective Story on Two Planets* (Random House, New York, 2006).

28. "President Clinton Statement Regarding Mars Meteorite Discovery," White House press release, Office of the Press Secretary, 7 August 1996.

29. NASA/National Research Council, "The Search for Origins: Findings of a Space Science Workshop" (Space Policy Institute, George Washington University, Washington, DC, 28–30 October 1996).

of what the nation might consider regarding studies of life in the universe.

Canizares recalled the effort:

We pulled together quickly a panel of really quite remarkable people…I believe we collectively came up with this idea of an *origins* thrust, and for us origins wasn't just looking for life around other stellar systems. It was literally…pretty much all of space science. And it was saying, 'Really this is a piece of a much, much bigger quest.' And it was kind of a plea for trying to look rationally at the whole thing and not only start looking for life in meteorites.

Then we prepared this briefing book…[for the Vice President, and] we had a session with him where we all went to the Indian Treaty room. I think it went on for an hour and a half, and he left. Then he came back as everybody was standing around to ask more questions. He was very engaged.

I think in the end the origins became one subset for NASA, so it kind of distorted what we were trying to say. But some of the spirit I think stayed there, and it at least put things into a context.[30]

Huntress emphasized the impact of the SSB-SSAC workshop and briefing to Vice President Gore:

It had the strongest effect of anything that NRC did while I was AA. The rest of it was kind of in background—'we need you to make sure we are doing our kind of science'—that kind of stuff. This one was important.

And then when the response to the [Mars] rock came, I was summoned up to OMB by [the NASA programs branch head] Steve Isakowitz, and he said, 'Okay, now what are going to do about this.' I laid out what we

called the Origins Program on the table for him. Origins had already been part of our strategic planning process, and we were trying to draw a thread through all of the disciplines in space science having to do with the origins of life and looking for life…. You know how hard it is to get new [research and analysis] money for the agency. So I put a line item for astrobiology in the budget, and he liked that. And so the ultimate result was that we got a new R&A line called astrobiology, and that allowed us to bring the biologists back into the program over time. It really worked well.[31]

McKay's paper was controversial when it first appeared, and it has remained controversial ever since. Many other experts put forth arguments questioning the conclusions, and McKay steadily sought to rebut the skeptics. While the final verdict on whether ALH84001 does or does not hold evidence of past Martian life forms may not have been rendered, the event was a major milestone for NASA and an interesting example of roles of its outside advisors. First, the "Mars rock symposium," as the effort became known, illustrated that advisory bodies could act quickly—in just four months in this case—in response to a compelling government need. Second, the character of the activity was unique. It was initiated at the direct request of the White House, it was very much a joint effort between NASA's internal advisory committee and the SSB, and NASA played a substantive role in preparation of the briefing materials for the Vice President that came out of the effort. No one appeared to worry about one body's independence with respect to the other. This kind of collaboration was probably possible because the activity did not produce formal advice; rather, it represented the collective opinions of a group of distinguished individuals. Thus, the two advisory

---

30. Canizares interview, pp. 6–7.

31. Huntress interview, pp. 11–12.

bodies were fulfilling responsibilities to promote communications between the government and the scientific community. In the end, those communications—from outside advisory bodies to the Vice President and to OMB—provided a highly credible foundation upon which NASA was able to build a substantial new program in astrobiology and to make the concept of origins an integrating theme for much of the space science program.

CONNECTING QUARKS WITH THE COSMOS:

There are many interesting examples of advisory studies giving a push to certain scientific areas and to missions or mission sets. One stems from a 1999 request by NASA Administrator Dan Goldin to the NRC Board on Physics and Astronomy to examine science opportunities and to recommend a strategy for research at the intersections of fundamental physics and astronomy. That is, what are the key areas where elementary particle physics and cosmology share intellectual frontiers, and how should we exploit them? The BPA, with assistance from the SSB and funding from NASA, NSF, and DOE, organized the Committee on the Physics of the Universe to carry out this task. There were some initial apprehensions that this study would stray into competition with related decadal surveys. NRC committees are notoriously protective of their conclusions and their immutability—"Once handed down, thou shalt not meddle!" Consequently, the committee took pains to declare its intention to complement the most recent surveys in astronomy and astrophysics and in physics[32] and to build on the priorities identified by those studies.[33]

The final report—"Connecting Quarks with the Cosmos: Eleven Science Questions for the New Century"[34]—outlined an interesting set of fundamental science questions that could capture imagination and capitalize on the rapid advances being made in contemporary physics and astronomy. (One has to wonder whether they tried to keep the list to ten and failed, but then decided against going for an even dozen.) Then the report identified future projects that could help attack the questions.

Michael Turner, who chaired the committee, recalled the effort fondly:

The legacy is twofold: first, the enormous effort focused on dark matter, dark energy and the CMB [cosmic microwave background], both in the astronomy community and in the physics community. Second, our approach has been copied a lot: First identify the science. This is so important for discovery science. At the end of the day, what discovery science is all about are the big questions you're asking. And if all you are telling the agencies, Congress, and the people is the projects you want to build and not the big questions you are struggling to answer, you're in trouble in discovery science. Because at the end of the day, your strongest suit is wonderment about the universe and our big mysteries…. It's now been copied, everybody starts with the science questions…. And I think what's important is that the questions that we are asking, trying to answer, anyone can understand them…. So I think that's what we did; we all of a sudden made that popular.[35]

---

32. National Research Council, *Physics in a New Era: An Overview and Astronomy and Astrophysics in the New Millennium* (both from the National Academy Press, Washington, DC, 2001).

33. Board on Physics and Astronomy, *Connecting Quarks with the Cosmos: Eleven Science Questions for the New Century* (National Research Council, The National Academies Press, Washington, DC, 2003), p. ix.

34. Board on Physics and Astronomy, *Connecting Quarks with the Cosmos: Eleven Science Questions for the New Century* (National Research Council, The National Academies Press, Washington, DC, 2003).

35. Turner interview.

The committee's approach of starting with the big scientific questions—painting an understandable picture of the intellectual frontiers and then building the arguments for important next steps in research from there—was the same approach that Charlie Pellerin's great observatories brainstorming group employed. And just as was the case for Pellerin, Turner's committee outlined ideas that had great scientific appeal.

Kevin Marvel recalled that the Turner report and its emphasis on the science questions had unintended consequences with respect to the preceding astronomy decadal survey:

The 2001 [survey] report really waned in influence around 2006. I think that was partly due to the release of…the Quarks to the Cosmos[36] report…. And when Quarks to the Cosmos came out, oh man, everybody wanted to talk about Quarks to the Cosmos instead of the decadal survey. And the reason for that was that Quarks to the Cosmos didn't have a shopping list in it. By shopping list I'm not being pejorative; it's just that's our range of priorities of things that the community needed. And some people are much happier with [no shopping list] because, they knew what the scientific priorities were, but they weren't being told how much it would cost to fulfill those scientific priorities. And so I think that especially the people on the Hill like that more than actually having a dollar amount tagged to a particular thing.[37]

Indeed, the committee's report was initially a big hit. The White House Office of Science and Technology Policy formed the Interagency Working Group on the Physics of the Universe to prepare a plan to act on the committee's recommendations and to advise government officials about budgetary priorities related to the report.[38] The fundamental science questions that the Quarks report outlined were enduring ones. Many of them found their way into the major scientific themes that emerged in the 2012 decadal survey for astronomy and astrophysics.

Although the 2003 report placed its major emphasis on important science questions, it closed with a chapter that addressed efforts that federal agencies could and should make to attack those questions. It gave a special nod to two NASA missions that were in the early stages of planning—the Constellation-X x-ray observatory (Con-X) and the Laser Interferometer Space Array (LISA) for gravitational wave detection, both of which had been cited in the astronomy decadal survey. The report also endorsed a DOE-backed space mission—the Super Nova Acceleration Probe (SNAP)—that would investigate evidence for dark energy. SNAP wasn't mentioned in the 2001 survey, but it had strong DOE interest.[39] All three future space missions survived, albeit in different guises. None of them managed to break the mission and budget approval barrier, due mostly to problems not of their making, but they continued to stay alive and high in the queue for future space astrophysics initiatives.

36. In spite of the fact that the report title uses the phrase "Quarks *with* the Cosmos," it has become popularly known as "Quarks *to* the Cosmos" or Q2C.

37. Marvel interview, pp. 4–5.

38. See Interagency Working Group on the Physics of the Universe, *A 21st Century Frontier of Discovery: The Physics of the Universe* (National Science and Technology Council Committee on Science, Executive Office of the President, Washington, DC, February 2004).

39. Board on Physics and Astronomy, *Connecting Quarks with the Cosmos: Eleven Science Questions for the New Century* (National Research Council, The National Academies Press, Washington, DC, 2003), ch. 7.

The two NASA mission candidates were part of a larger NASA program called Beyond Einstein[40] that also included two of the Great Observatories — the Compton Gamma Ray Observatory and the Chandra X-ray Observatory — and others. Con-X's blessing by the Turner committee was not enough to propel it into new-start status, partly due to its likely high cost at a time when NASA was still struggling to deal with the costs of the James Webb Space Telescope. NASA moved to join forces with the European and Japanese space agencies (ESA and JAXA) and to replace Con-X with U.S. participation in a European-led International X-ray Observatory (IXO) project. The 2012 astronomy and astrophysics decadal survey ranked LISA as the number 3 priority for large space missions, followed by IXO in the number four slot. However, when IXO failed to win a go-ahead in an ESA competition for new missions, it was back to the drawing board again with ESA initiating a new study of an Advanced Telescope for High Energy Astrophysics (Athena) to replace IXO. NASA kept the phone lines to ESA open and continued plans about potential ESA-NASA collaboration on Athena with a possible launch in the late 2020s. ESA placed LISA next in the queue of large space missions after Athena and initiated a test mission, called LISA Pathfinder, that was launched in December 2015 to demonstrate critical technologies needed for the LISA gravitational wave detection science mission. NASA took on a junior-partner role with ESA on LISA Pathfinder, just as it did on Athena.[41]

SNAP, which was intended to study the expansion of the universe via measurements of supernovae, had its own metamorphic history. After being initially proposed by the DOE, it was superseded by the Joint Dark Energy Mission (JDEM), which was the product of on-again-off-again discussions of a collaborative NASA-DOE project that was to include the SNAP measurements. Neither SNAP nor JDEM were granted a priority in the 2010 astronomy and astrophysics decadal survey, but the survey did give top priority to a Wide Field Infrared Survey Telescope (WFIRST) that would incorporate a version of the JDEM instrumentation and accomplish many of the scientific objectives of JDEM. Then in 2012, NASA announced that the National Reconnaissance Office — the U.S. spy satellite agency — had offered components for two unused, 2.4-meter diameter, space telescopes to NASA. Both a NASA and an NRC ad hoc science panel declared the proposed gift — dubbed the Astrophysics Focused Telescope Assets, or AFTA — to be well-suited for accomplishing WFIRST's scientific mission. However, the NRC panel cautioned that the immaturity of aspects of the WFIRST-AFTA design concept posed too great a technical and cost risk unless and until NASA could complete further technology development and design assessments to demonstrate that the mission could be accomplished at an acceptable cost.[42] NASA initiated preliminary studies of a WFIRST-AFTA mission concept in hopes that formal mission development could conceivably begin in the late 2010s.[43]

Turner recalled how the Quarks report also had an impact on DOE:

And the other legacy of it would be on the DoE side. DoE at the Office of High Energy

---

40. NASA's Beyond Einstein program was subsequently renamed the Physics of the Cosmos program.

41. For more details, see Peter B. de Selding, "Lisa Pathfinder's success boosts likelihood of future gravity-wave observatory" (SpaceNews.com, 7 June 2016), available at *http://spacenews.com/lisa-pathfinders-success-boosts-likelihood-of-future-gravity-wave-observatory/*.

42. National Research Council, *Evaluation of the Implementation of WFIRST/AFTA in the Context of New Worlds, New Horizons in Astronomy and Astrophysics* (The National Academies Press, Washington, DC, 2014).

43. Presentation by Paul Hertz, NASA Astrophysics Division Director, to the SSB Committee on Astronomy and Astrophysics, 30 March 2016, Alexander document folder, NASA Headquarters Archives, Washington, DC.

Physics used to be "accelerators are us." And now they also have the Cosmic Frontier [program], so they have completely bought into dark matter, dark energy, [cosmological] inflation, as part of their scientific agenda. And I think Quarks to the Cosmos was the foot in the door. They realized that their mantra is not "accelerators are us," although accelerators are an important tool. Their mantra is, "We are looking to understand, at the most basic level, matter, energy, space, and time."[44]

It shouldn't be especially surprising that when NASA received scientific advice that the Agency had explicitly requested the advice was usually welcomed and likely to have an impact. The cases described above are notable examples of situations where there was a particularly interested customer or patron inside the Agency, as well as a particularly strong advisory group to respond to NASA's request. But there have been other occasions in which someone outside NASA set the advisory effort in motion regardless of whether there was any interest inside the Agency. The next chapter will look at a few examples of these independently instigated studies and examine their mixed record of success or failure.

44. Turner interview.

CHAPTER 16

Case Studies: Advice Initiated from Outside NASA

In order to assess the impact of external scientific advice to NASA and to try to understand why efforts succeeded or failed, we need to distinguish between advice that NASA sought and advice that NASA may not have wanted, or at least not requested. Chapter 15 examined some case studies of advisory activities that NASA initiated and that were carried out by NASA committees or by NRC bodies at NASA's request. Now we turn to some that were conducted by the NRC at the request of Congress or simply at the NRC's own initiative.

Congressionally Mandated Reports

Congress occasionally has directed NASA to obtain external advice, and then the Agency has been obligated to seek the advice regardless of whether or not Agency officials really wanted it. Sometimes the request originates with a single member of Congress who wants the Agency to hear from outside experts about a pet issue. On other occasions the request may be in response to input from members of the scientific community.[1] And, of course, members of Congress and their staffs sometimes feel that NASA needs to be forced to pay attention to an issue, and they use mandates (either in

legislation itself or in reports that accompany legislation) to get NASA's attention.

Congressionally mandated advisory studies are not often welcome at NASA, as former Congressional Research Service space expert Marcia Smith has made clear:

> Unless there is something really worthwhile in that report, and considering it takes 18 months to 24 months to get the report out and by then things may have changed at NASA, then I think they are pretty much not going to pay attention to it, they are going to find reasons to ignore it.[2]

Ed Weiler, confirmed this view, saying, "Ones that tend to be the least useful are the ones demanded by Congress that we didn't ask for."[3]

Nevertheless, a congressional call for an advisory study is powerful, especially when the call is incorporated in or accompanies enacted legislation. Such studies get done. The 2005 study on options for extending the life of the Hubble Space Telescope (HST) and the 2006 report on imbalances in NASA's science budgets are particularly interesting examples.

---

1. Although there is a popular perception that SSB chairs lobby Congress for mandated studies, the author found that to be rare when he was interacting regularly with the chairs from 1998 to 2006.

2. Smith interview, p. 13.

3. Weiler interview, p. 3.

EXTENDING THE LIFE OF THE HUBBLE SPACE TELESCOPE: The disastrous loss of the Space Shuttle Columbia and its seven crew members in February 2003 prompted much soul searching and reassessment of the U.S. space program, both inside and outside NASA. Those examinations led to an expanded emphasis on flight safety, development of a capability for in-flight Shuttle inspections and possible repairs, provisions for having a second Shuttle ready to conduct a rescue mission if needed, and a general increase in conservatism about the use of the Shuttle. HST had been launched via the Shuttle in 1990 and designed to be serviced by later Shuttle visits, of which there were four between December 1993 and March 2002. A fifth servicing mission had been planned for late 2005. However, in January 2004, NASA Administrator Sean O'Keefe canceled the next servicing mission, saying that for safety reasons there would be no more Shuttle flights to HST.[4]

There was an immediate outcry from the astronomical community and even from the general public.[5] Kevin Marvel recalled an unusual measure of public interest that appeared via a deluge of letters to the American Astronomical Society from elementary school classes around the country: "I know the congressional offices also received these letters.... So the school children of America

spoke."[6] The astronomers picked up an important ally in Senator Barbara Mikulski of Maryland who had an interest because two key HST institutions—the Space Telescope Science Institute and the NASA Goddard Space Flight Center—were in her state and because she chaired the Senate appropriations subcommittee that handled NASA's budget. Mikulski argued that O'Keefe was wrong to make his decision unilaterally.[7]

Ed Weiler had played major roles in the development and operation of HST throughout his career, but he acknowledged that O'Keefe had been in a tough spot:

> I understood why he made the decision he made, because he was responsible for the lives of astronauts. He lived through seeing those seven astronauts tragically killed. You know, if I had to make a decision back then about do we plan a servicing mission, I might have made the same decision. Luckily I didn't have to make the decision. But I understood his decision.[8]

Nevertheless, if something wasn't done to replace aging components on the telescope, it would be expected to die in a few years. The engineering team at Goddard, which had been responsible for designing hardware used on the Shuttle servicing

---

4. Steven Beckwith, "Servicing Mission 4 Cancelled" (Space Telescope Science Institute, quoted by Space Ref.com 16 January 2004), available at *http://www.spaceref.com/news/viewsr.html?pid=11615*; Warren E. Leary, "NASA Chief Affirms Stand On Canceling Hubble Mission" (New York Times, 29 January 2004), available at *http://www.nytimes.com/2004/01/29/us/nasa-chief-affirms-stand-on-canceling-hubble-mission.html*.

5. For example, see Richard Tresch Feinberg, "Hubble Supporters Fight Back," Sky and Telescope, 23 January 2004, *http://www.skyandtelescope.com/astronomy-news/hubble-supporters-fight-back/*; Brian Berger, "Canceled Hubble Repair the First Victim of New NASA Vision," *Space News*, 26 January 2004, p. 6; and New York Times editorial, "Premature Death for the Hubble," 29 February 2004.

6. Marvel interview, p. 7.

7. See Leonard David, "The debate over Hubble" (from Space.com quoted at Science & Space, CNN.com, 24 January 2004), available at *http://www.cnn.com/2005/TECH/space/01/24/hubble.funding/*; Keith Cowing, "NASA's Hubble Space Telescope: A Fate Far From Certain" (SpaceRef.com, 14 March 2004), available at *http://www.spaceref.com/news/viewnews.html?id=937*; and Richard Tresch Fienberg, "Senator Vows to Fight for Hubble" (Sky & Telescope Magazine, 23 January 2005), available at *http://www.skyandtelescope.com/astronomy-news/senator-vows-to-fight-for-hubble/*.

8. Weiler interview, p. 5.

missions, immediately began to explore robotic alternatives for visiting HST.

In March 2004, Senator Mikulski directed NASA to engage the NRC for an independent evaluation of options for extending the life of HST, including Shuttle- and robotic-servicing as well as optimization of ground operations, and for an assessment of whether the scientific gains to be expected from any viable options would be worth the risk involved.[9] The SSB and the Aeronautics and Space Engineering Board jointly organized a study committee and recruited physicist Louis Lanzerotti to serve as chair.

The organizers made a considerable effort to ensure that the panel was a blue-ribbon committee in the truest sense and that its members would bring the highest level of stature and expertise to the effort. Lanzerotti was not an astronomer, but he had been involved in space research throughout his career, had been chair of both NASA's SESAC and the SSB, and had served on the National Science Board and two White House commissions regarding U.S. space policy. Perhaps more importantly, he was respected as a straight shooter who could be absolutely trusted to aim to do the right thing. Marcia Smith described him as follows:

> Lou really has an unimpeachable record…. And I don't think anyone questioned whether he was being fair or not, so he was the perfect choice to lead that committee, technically competent … full of integrity.[10]

The committee membership included former senior engineering and management experts from NASA, the Department of Defense, and industry, including former HST program leaders; robotics and risk assessment experts; three former Shuttle astronauts, including two who had flown on HST missions, plus former NASA Administrator Richard Truly; two former senior Shuttle program leaders; and three distinguished astronomers, including two Nobel Prize winners.[11] The 20-member committee was larger than typical NRC committees, and that size enabled the group to divide its tasks into manageable chunks, dig into each in depth, and then subject potential findings and conclusions to independent scrutiny in plenary discussions.

At a congressional hearing in April, O'Keefe had said that the prospects for carrying out a robotic servicing mission were looking more promising than NASA officials had first believed, and he was optimistic that this could be an alternative to a Shuttle servicing mission.[12] Then in June, NASA announced that it would formally solicit proposals for using a space-borne robot to service Hubble as an alternative to a Shuttle mission.[13]

The process of organizing the Lanzerotti committee began in April. There was considerable pressure to provide a report quickly—some officials asked for results as early as September—so that NASA could make technical and budget decisions before they would be too late to execute. The committee met for the first time in early June and prepared an interim report, at NASA's request, in mid-July. The interim report basically said that

---

9. "Senators ask NASA to seek another opinion on Hubble" (USA Today, 11 March 2004), available at *http://usatoday30.usatoday.com/news/washington/2004-03-11-hubble-senate_x.htm#*.

10. Smith interview, p. 6.

11. Space Studies Board and Aeronautics and Space Engineering Board, Assessment of Options for Extending the Lifetime of the Hubble Space Telescope: Final Report, National Research Council, The National Academies Press, Washington, DC, 2005), pp. 137–144.

12. Brian Berger and Leonard David, "NASA: Robotic repair of Hubble 'promising'" (Space.com, 27 April 2004), also available at *http://www.cnn.com/2004/TECH/space/04/27/hubble.repairsII/index.html*.

13. NASA Office of Public Affairs, "NASA Considering Robotic Servicing Mission to Hubble," NASA press release 04-173, 1 June 2004.

HST was worth saving, that there were significant uncertainties about the feasibility of robotic servicing, and that NASA should take no actions that would preclude a Shuttle servicing mission until the committee completed its assessment.[14]

The committee's final report was completed and briefed to NASA and to congressional officials in the first week of December and released to the public on 8 December. The 160-page NRC report included a discussion of the HST system, its past and potential future scientific accomplishments, technical assessments of likely system lifetimes and of the feasibility of robotic servicing, considerations relevant to Shuttle servicing, and a benefit-risk assessment of servicing options. The report concluded that NASA should send the Space Shuttle to service HST and that robotic servicing was not recommended. The committee explained that while there were too many technical uncertainties pertaining to the readiness and risk of robotic options, a Shuttle mission to HST was not significantly more risky than Shuttle missions to the International Space Station, which NASA planned to do at least 25 more times. The committee did not rule out eventual use of a robotic system to take HST out of orbit at the end of its life and send it on a controlled re-entry.[15]

It was a tough pill for O'Keefe to swallow, but the report was well received on Capitol Hill and in the scientific community and expansively treated in the media. In addition to coverage in many major daily papers and news broadcasts, the *New York Times* even published an editorial that cited the Lanzerotti report's "unusually blunt assessment," characterized NASA's arguments for favoring Shuttle missions to the Space Station rather than to Hubble as "a sham," and urged NASA to get on with an astronaut flight to rescue Hubble.[16]

Ed Weiler, who was then serving as Director of the Goddard Space Flight Center, saw immediate impacts from the report:

> It was very strong impact, because all the money that Hubble had was going toward getting ready for a robotic servicing mission.... We had hardware and lots of hardware; robots were already built; their containers were being built. Our project manager was going nuts and building things and spending money, I might add. So when the report came out, and more importantly when [future NASA Administrator Michael] Griffin was in place, we immediately switched gears.[17]

As one might expect for such a complex and potentially controversial issue, not everyone was pleased with the outcome. Al Diaz, who was Goddard Director when the study was initiated and then Associate Administrator for Science when the report was delivered to NASA, felt that by foregoing robotic servicing of Hubble, the Agency missed an opportunity to extend Hubble's life indefinitely and to build robotic servicing capabilities that NASA would need in the future:

> I really do think that we could have extended the life of Hubble and used it on a continuing basis if we just made the investment in developing the robotic servicing capability.... I believe that it was not only possible but reasonable to think about developing the capability.[18]

---

14. Space Studies Board and Aeronautics and Space Engineering Board, *Assessment of Options for Extending the Lifetime of the Hubble Space Telescope: Final Report* (National Research Council, The National Academies Press, Washington, DC, 2005), pp. 116–125.

15. Space Studies Board and Aeronautics and Space Engineering Board, *Assessment of Options for Extending the Lifetime of the Hubble Space Telescope: Final Report* (National Research Council, The National Academies Press, Washington, DC, 2005).

16. "A Blow to NASA's Hubble Rescue," *New York Times* editorial, 12 December 2004.

17. Weiler interview, p. 5.

18. Diaz interview, p. 6.

O'Keefe resigned in February 2005, approximately two months after the Lanzerotti committee delivered his report, and he was succeeded in April by Michael Griffin. During Griffin's first year on the job, NASA made good progress in demonstrating a capability to have a second Shuttle ready to launch a rescue mission and for crews to make on-orbit repairs to a damaged orbiter. When Congress passed the NASA Authorization Act for 2005,[19] it included language calling for a Shuttle mission to HST so long as it would not compromise astronaut safety. In October 2006, Griffin reversed O'Keefe's decision and announced that NASA would fly one more Shuttle servicing mission to HST.[20]

Griffin later said that the NRC report had no impact on his decision to approve another Shuttle servicing mission, and that he had made his own decision independently after having led an assessment of robotic options for Goddard Space Flight Center officials before he became Administrator.[21] Nevertheless, the NRC report certainly provided ammunition for Senator Mikulski who pressed to see the telescope refurbished one more time.

The final HST servicing mission in May 2009 turned out to be a roaring success. The Shuttle crew installed two new science instruments and upgraded two others. They also installed replacement batteries, new gyroscopes, a command and data-handling unit, and made other fixes. Consequently, estimates of the likely extension of the telescope's lifetime ranged from at least 2015 to possibly the end of the 2010s decade.[22]

The HST committee effort was notable on many fronts. First, the NRC succeeded in recruiting a uniquely distinguished group of experts to serve. Uniformly, when people were contacted and asked to consider participating, they acknowledged the importance of the study in a national scientific context and agreed to commit their time because the task was important to the U.S. space program and to science. Second, the task was controversial, technically complex, and tinged with political interests. Consequently, it demanded that the committee's deliberations be technically credible and completely objective. And perhaps most challenging, the committee had to complete its work in a short time. They rose to that challenge and delivered their advice in less than eight months—a span that amounts to near-record time for NRC studies.

BALANCE IN NASA'S SPACE AND EARTH SCIENCE PROGRAMS: President George W. Bush's January 2004 announcement of his Vision for Space Exploration was both a response to the impacts of the catastrophic Space Shuttle Columbia accident nearly one year earlier and an articulation of a new U.S. civil space policy. As chapter 11 explains, it emphasized both human and robotic exploration missions, and it assumed a growing NASA budget to pay for the proposed initiatives. However, the administration's fiscal year 2005 budget proposal to Congress raised some immediate concerns when it separated NASA science into areas that were directly related to the exploration vision—mainly planetary science—and practically everything else,

---

19. NASA Authorization Act of 2005 (P.L. 109-155), enacted in December 2005.

20. NASA News Release, "NASA Approves Mission and Names Crew for Return to Hubble," release 06-343, 31 October 2006, available at *http://www.nasa.gov/home/hqnews/2006/oct/HQ_06343_HST_announcement.html*.

21. Griffin interview. Also see "Transcript of NASA Administrator Nominee Michael Griffin's Confirmation Hearing 12 April 2005" (Spaceref.com, 13 April 2005), available at *http://www.spaceref.com/news/viewsr.html?pid=16155*.

22. For a thorough account of the Hubble servicing episode, see the appendix titled "The Decision to Cancel the Hubble Space Telescope Servicing Mission 4 (and Its Reversal)" by Steven J. Dick in *Hubble's Legacy: Reflections by Those Who Dreamed It, Built It, and Observed the Universe with It*, edited by Roger D. Launius and David H. DeVorkin (Smithsonian Institution Scholarly Press, Washington DC, 2014).

including astronomy (except for searches for Earth-like planets around other stars), space plasma physics, and Earth science, which were deemed "other science." Alarm bells quickly sounded as people in the scientific community and their congressional supporters became wary of this partitioning. Consequently, Congress inserted language in its explanatory report to the fiscal year 2005 appropriation bill, requiring

> the National Academies' Space Studies Board (SSB) to conduct a thorough review of the science that NASA is proposing to undertake under the space exploration initiative and to develop a strategy by which all of NASA's science disciplines, including Earth science, space science, and life and microgravity science, as well as the science conducted aboard the International Space Station, can make adequate progress towards their established goals, as well as providing balanced scientific research in addition to support of the new initiative.[23]

Neither NASA Administrator Sean O'Keefe nor his successor Michael Griffin were particularly anxious to get outside advice that might challenge the administration's plans, but NASA duly asked the NRC to conduct the required review. The SSB produced an initial report in 2005 that served as a partial response. It recommended a set of principles for NASA to use in making decisions about science to be pursued under the new exploration vision.[24] For all practical purposes, the answer was, "Let science be your guide, and follow the decadal surveys and their counterparts." While the principles and accompanying guidance that the Board outlined in its report reinforced ideas that were fundamentally important to the scientific community, the report had little tangible impact. At least one congressional staff member skewered the report, saying that it was devoid of specific, actionable recommendations and that "except as a repository of a few useful aphorisms and a source of undiscussed ideas contained in other studies … it's worthless."[25] Luckily for the SSB, they had another time at bat in which to try to provide sharper guidance.

The SSB had explained to the congressional appropriations committees that it would complete its task by reviewing a set of research and technology development plans that Administrator O'Keefe had commissioned as part of NASA's implementation of the exploration vision. However, when Michael Griffin succeeded O'Keefe as Administrator, Griffin modified the planning process and the expected NRC review of the suite of research and technology plans was abandoned.

When NASA's fiscal year 2007 budget proposal went to Congress in February 2006, the alarm bells about NASA's treatment of science under the vision sounded even more loudly. The prior assumptions for a growing NASA budget did not materialize, commitments and costs for operating the Space Shuttle and completing the International Space Station remained, and planned budget increases for new human space exploration systems and for science were sharply reduced. Consequently, the new budget would have the space and Earth sciences losing ground against inflation and having $3.1 billion less to spend over the five-year period 2007 to 2011 than had been proposed a year earlier.[26]

---

23. Conference Report on H.R. 4818, Consolidated Appropriations Act, 2005, H. Rept. 108-792, p. 1599.

24. Space Studies Board, *Science in NASA's Vision for Space Exploration* (National Research Council, The National Academies Press, Washington, DC, 2005).

25. E-mail, "Re New NRC report on Science and Space Exploration," from Paul Rehmus (Congressional Budget Office) to Joseph Alexander (Space Studies Board), 11 February 2005, available in Alexander document file, NASA History Division, Washington, DC.

26. For more discussion of the FYs 2005 and 2006 budget issues, see chapter 12.

After seeing the details of how NASA proposed to reallocate science budgets, the SSB elected to complete its congressional charge to "develop a strategy by which all of NASA's science disciplines…can make adequate progress towards their established goals, as well as providing balanced scientific research in addition to support of the new initiative"[27] with a new report.

The report—"An Assessment of Balance in NASA's Science Programs"[28]—is an interesting example of how the NRC could leverage a congressionally mandated task to provide advice that NASA would probably not have preferred to hear but that was clearly responsive to earlier congressional concerns. The report was prepared by an ad hoc committee composed of the members of the SSB plus one additional expert,[29] and it drew on input from the Board's disciplinary standing committees, thereby quickly tapping the full range of expertise and experience available to the SSB.

The conclusions in the report were particularly concise, direct, and critical of the proposed NASA budget for 2007:

Finding 1. NASA is being asked to accomplish too much with too little. The agency does not have the necessary resources to carry out the tasks of completing the International Space Station, returning humans to the Moon, maintaining vigorous space and Earth science and microgravity life and physical sciences programs, and sustaining capabilities in aeronautical research.

Finding 2. The program proposed for space and Earth science is not robust; it is not properly balanced to support a healthy mix of small, medium, and large missions and an underlying foundation of scientific research and advanced technology projects; and it is neither sustainable nor capable of making adequate progress toward the goals that were recommended in the National Research Council's decadal surveys.[30]

The report was highly critical of NASA's decision to reduce science budgets, apparently so as to provide some funding to the administration's human space exploration initiative in a less-robust-than-expected fiscal environment. In particular, the SSB analyzed budget trends for several years before the Bush initiative and their projections for future years and then presented explicit summaries of the impacts of the budget proposals on the likely health of NASA's basic research programs, discipline by discipline. Among the largest impacts, according to the SSB analysis, was a deep cut to the astrobiology program that had been stimulated by the earlier Mars rock events and that had grown to become a significant new element of the space sciences.

NASA Administrator Mike Griffin explained that NASA faced serious budgetary problems with completion of the International Space Station and the costs of the winding down of the Space Shuttle program, both of which had been substantially underfunded.[31] He acknowledged that the cuts damaged the science program, but said there

27. Conference Report on H.R. 4818, Consolidated Appropriations Act, 2005, H. Rept. 108-792, p. 1599.

28. Space Studies Board, *An Assessment of Balance in NASA's Science Programs* (National Research Council, The National Academies Press, Washington, DC, 2006).

29. The report was the last one prepared by the SSB itself after the NRC ruled that, due to FACA conflict of interest concerns, standing boards could not author reports.

30. Space Studies Board, *An Assessment of Balance in NASA's Science Programs* (National ``Research Council, The National Academies Press, Washington, DC, 2006), p 2.

31. Griffin remarks at Space Studies Board meeting, 2 May 2006, SSB archives, National Research Council, Washington, DC.

was nowhere else to turn to find budgetary relief. With respect to the cuts to basic research activities, and especially astrobiology, Griffin said that it had been his personal judgment that they were less important than support for flight missions and that academic scientists are too often protective of research grants because of their own self-interests. Nevertheless, Griffin said he was willing to listen to the views of the scientific community.

The 2006 report had an interesting reception. Congress responded positively, and the report certainly caught attention from the press. House Science Committee Chairman Sherwood Boehlert issued a statement saying,

> The Academy report bears out what I have been saying since the Administration budget was released in February and what witnesses argued at the Science Committee's March 2 hearing on NASA's science programs: NASA's proposed fiscal 2007 budget provides inadequate funding for earth and space science and in particular gives short shrift to the smaller projects that are necessary to keep science progressing and to train new scientists. I think the Academy report gets it exactly right.[32]

According to members of the staff of the House Science committee, there was already bipartisan support for a balanced NASA science portfolio, and so while the report wasn't a game changer, it reinforced those views. Most importantly, it provided a basis for helping congressional appropriations committee staff members to be supportive of budget restorations.[33]

Journalists who followed NASA and U.S. space science had similar takes on the report. Story headlines included "Criticism of NASA science budget grows,"[34] "Study finds money gap at NASA grows,"[35] "Academy of Sciences bemoans budget limits,"[36] "NASA underfunded, panel reports,"[37] and perhaps most provocatively, "NASA's lunar leap may put other projects in a tailspin."[38]

Beyond early reactions to the NRC report, it's a little hard to see where there were specific, tangible responses. NASA space science officials felt that their hands were tied, and their immediate reaction was to say, "We have our orders." For example, Paul Hertz, who was then Science Mission Directorate Chief Scientist, described their situation as follows:

> [A]s a NASA employee member of the administration, I have huge opportunities to advocate within the system for what I think is the right thing to do, budget-wise and programmatically.... But once a decision is made at any of those levels, it's my job to implement that decision even if it's the exact opposite of what I advocated. So you understand this balancing act that we do.... That was a time where, for one reason or another, the decision that was made had a specific impact on the science community. I believe that Mike Griffin said in public ... that he didn't like the

32. House Science Committee Press Office, "Boehlert Statement on National Academy Report on NASA's Science Budget," Press Release, U.S. House of Representatives, Washington, DC, 5 May 2006.

33. Goldston interview.

34. Maggie McKee, "Criticism of NASA science budget grows" (*Daily News, New Scientist*, 4 May 2006), available at *https://www.newscientist.com/article/dn9110-criticism-of-nasa-science-budget-grows/*.

35. Warren E. Leary, "Study Finds Money Gap at NASA" (*New York Times*, 5 May 2006).

36. Nell Greenfield-Boyce, "Academy of Sciences Bemoans NASA Budget Limits" (Morning Edition, National Public Radio, 5 May 2006).

37. Guy Gugliotta, "NASA Underfunded, Panel Reports" (*Washington Post*, 5 May 2006).

38. Mark Carreau, "NASA's lunar leap may put other projects in a tailspin" (*Houston Chronicle*, 5 May 2006), available at *http://www.chron.com/news/nation-world/article/NASA-s-lunar-leap-may-put-other-projects-in-a-1901027.php*.

system we had where scientists advised the government on how much money we should send to scientists. He thought that was like industry advising us on how much money we should spend on industry[39].... So he was not interested in the kinds of advice that might come out of that Balance report. And we in the Science Directorate already knew it. We could've written that Balance report ourselves because it definitely aligned with what we thought appropriate priorities were for handling budget reductions.[40]

Nevertheless, Mary Cleave, who had to cope with the budget cuts as Associate Administrator for Science at the time, felt that the Balance report was useful to her in trying to explain the impacts to interested members of Congress and to lay the groundwork for recovery.[41] When Alan Stern succeeded Cleave in 2007, he began to rectify some of the cuts to the space science base, and he had Griffin's support in making those adjustments. Ed Weiler continued to restore critical funding when returned to headquarters to replace Stern as Associate Administrator in 2008. Perhaps the report's most important longer-term impact was to provide both NASA science managers and the scientific community with a set of arguments to keep the issue of balance and programmatic critical mass in front of congressional and OMB staff members and some key members of Congress so that they would not let the issue pass without attention. Lamentably, the report's first finding about NASA being expected to do too much with too little received basically the same response as many other advisory reports that said the same thing — no relief.

Self-Initiated Advisory Efforts

Since the late 1980s, the costs of SSB advisory activities for NASA were covered by means of a task-order contract that provided core funding for five-year intervals. The core funding included routine operating costs such as staff support, expenses for regular meetings of the Board and its standing committees, and work associated with preparation of letter reports and several study reports annually. Major efforts above and beyond that level of effort were covered by adding extra tasks to the contract. This core funding arrangement allowed for the Board and its committees to initiate new studies, and therefore, it gave the SSB considerable flexibility. Rather than needing to wait for a specific NASA request, the units could initiate study efforts on topics of their own choosing so long as they were within the general range of responsibilities for the Board.[42] As earlier chapters have indicated, many letter reports and a series of regular study reports emerged from the Board under this arrangement. Let's look at some examples of how this option played out.

AN EXPERIMENT IN SETTING PRIORITIES: It's interesting to examine advice that no one sought explicitly but for which everyone might agree there was a need. The Space Studies Board embarked on a search for a version of that holy grail in 1992 — namely, to see if a scientific advisory group such as the SSB could devise a method to reach consensus on priorities *across* scientific disciplines. The results of the Board's efforts were remarkable for the fact that in the end the conclusion was basically "We tried and failed."

---

39. Griffin made his position clear on multiple occasions, perhaps most thoroughly at a speech to Goddard Space Flight Center employees on 12 September 2006; available at *http://www.nasa.gov/pdf/157382main_griffin-goddard-science.pdf*.

40. Hertz interview, p. 9.

41. Cleave interview.

42. After about 2001, NASA specified that the SSB could no longer initiate its own studies without prior approval.

their value, despite skepticism about them in the more established scientific fields.[48]

After NASA formally requested the study called for by the Senate, the SSB formed the Committee on the Future of Space Science, which was led by former IBM Vice President for Science and Technology John Armstrong. Armstrong's steering group formed subordinate task groups for each of the three main elements of the congressional request—alternative organizations, research prioritization, and technology. The prioritization task group was chaired by Roland Schmitt, former President of the Rensselaer Polytechnic Institute, and the group's membership had no overlaps with the membership of Dutton's priorities task group. The final study report included substantial recommendations on a National Institute for Space Science (*Don't do it.*), responsibilities of the NASA Chief Scientist (*Strengthen them.*), technology development (*NASA needs a strategy.*), and several management issues, as well as recommendations on science prioritization. On the latter subject, the report made crisp recommendations about the importance of scientific considerations in setting program and mission priorities for space research. It emphasized that science should be a factor at all levels of decisions, but it recognized that as priority-setting progresses to involve successively broader areas of activity, the extent of participation by scientists may decrease and the necessary participation by senior Agency management will increase.[49]

In hindsight, the two studies—the SSB's frustrating experiment in cross-discipline priority setting and the Armstrong committee's report on managing the space sciences—had significantly different impacts. The former demonstrated, to

quote Claude Canizares who was SSB chair when the latter report was published, "[prioritizing] across different disciplines ... [is] very, very difficult to do."[50] But beyond that, efforts to employ a quantitative methodology have never taken hold, and the report is largely forgotten. The latter report, on the other hand, made it clear to the scientific community that while there were compelling arguments for keeping scientific considerations and the scientific community involved in the process of setting broad program priorities, scientists can only be part of the solution as the questions move up the institutional food chain. Perhaps more importantly, the Armstrong report met Senator Mikulski's need for ammunition to ensure that Goldin's new organizational structure did not compromise the scientific integrity and vigor of NASA's science program.

SPACE PHYSICS PARADOX REPORT: In the 1980s and 1990s, two standing committees of two different boards worked together as a federated body to provide advice to NASA and the NSF. Both the SSB's Committee on Solar and Space Physics (CSSP) and the Committee on Solar Terrestrial Research (CSTR) of the Board on Atmospheric Sciences and Climate shared concerns over research about the Sun, the Sun's influence on interplanetary space, and the space environments of the Earth and other planets. The two committees routinely collaborated to develop coherent lines of advice to the two agencies that were principal sponsors of research in those areas. When the two committees embarked on a study that went beyond their usual scientific range of interests and dug into what the study report acknowledged to be "administrative, managerial, and funding"[51] aspects of the agency's programs, they may have not realized how

---

48. U.S. Senate Committee on Appropriations, Subcommittee on VA, HUD, and independent agencies, report accompanying NASA's FY 1994 appropriation.

49. Space Studies Board, *Managing the Space Sciences* (National Research Council, The National Academies Press, Washington, DC, 1995).

50. Canizares interview, p. 3.

51. National Research Council, *A Space Physics Paradox: Why Has Increased Funding Been Accompanied by Decreased Effectiveness in the Conduct of Space Physics Research?* (The National Academies Press, Washington, DC, 1994), p. ix.

far they were straying into what a scientific advisory body should view as terra incognita.

Over the decade leading up to the study, research funding had grown significantly, and so had the size of the research community. In 1991, at the request of the SSB, the two committees had prepared an assessment of the NSF and NASA programs that was quite positive about recent scientific progress, but the report indicated that progress on prior NRC programmatic recommendations had been slow and that support for small programs such as research grants had eroded.[52] Thus, the central question for the committee — the space physics paradox — was "Why has increased research funding been accompanied by decreased effectiveness in the conduct of space physics research?"[53] Or to put it in slightly different words, "If funding has improved, why isn't everyone happy?"

The "Paradox" report dug into the big-science-little-science debate that was active at the time and asked whether a move towards more and more large programs was causing the erosion of small research activities that the committee referred to as "the base-funded program." The report analyzed trends in research funding, community demographics, proposal demand and success rates, mission and experiment development times and consequent flight rates, and various administrative costs. The authors concluded that, in spite of overall budget increases over the prior decade, a number of factors had sapped the impact of the increases. They attributed the problem to increases in time consumed in proposal preparation and review, university overhead costs, and reliance on big programs that were intrinsically more complex and slower to implement. They also dinged the agencies and the research community for failing to produce effective strategies and priorities that would support more realistic decision making. The report presented a set of four relatively broad recommendations for the agencies and the community:

1. Increase the size of the base-funded research program,
2. Adjust the portfolio to increase the proportion of small programs,
3. Set more realistic priorities in anticipation of limited future resources, and
4. Streamline program management.[54]

These may have been perfectly reasonable ideas, but when the report landed at NASA, it was a more or less immediate flop. NASA officials considered its conclusions to be self-serving and its recommendations to be too short on specificity to be useful. George Withbroe, a veteran solar astrophysicist who was NASA's Director of Space Physics at the time, found the report to be far afield from what he viewed as appropriate territory for NRC committees:

It was basically, or what it read to me as, an argument for a WPA program[55] for space physics, rather than "Here's the exciting science we want to do. Here are our priorities. Here's how to do it." The whole tone was WPA program; that's the way I read it. And that's not, in my mind, what the Academy should be doing. The Academy should be defining exciting science and priorities among scientific programs and not trying to say "Here's how you keep

---

52. Committee on Solar Terrestrial Research and Committee on Solar and Space Physics, Assessment of Programs in Solar and Space Physics (National Research Council, National Academy Press, Washington DC, 1991).

53. National Research Council, *A Space Physics Paradox: Why Has Increased Funding Been Accompanied by Decreased Effectiveness in the Conduct of Space Physics Research?* (The National Academies Press, Washington, DC, 1994), p. i.

54. National Research Council, *A Space Physics Paradox: Why Has Increased Funding Been Accompanied by Decreased Effectiveness in the Conduct of Space Physics Research?* (The National Academies Press, Washington, DC, 1994), pp. 77–79.

55. The Work Projects Administration employed millions of unemployed people for public works projects during the Great Depression of the late 1930s and early 1940s, and it has since become a metaphor for "make-work" programs.

space physicists employed in the most cost-effective way." What they are doing is what's most important, not how they're employed. Are they doing exciting science? That's what the government is paying for…. There wasn't any science in the report.[56]

The two authoring committees—CSSP and CSTR—did act on their own advice in one way. The "Paradox" report had recommended that "the space physics community establish realistic priorities across the full spectrum of its scientific interests," and the two committees issued a new scientific strategy for the discipline in 1995[57] that began with a thorough discussion of the scientific underpinnings and goals for the field and then translated them into recommended implementation priorities.

Perhaps the work that went into the report was needed to provide an analytical basis for the priorities that emerged from the new science strategy, but as an advisory product, the "Paradox" report became notable for its poor reception at NASA.

———

The brief discussions of advisory efforts in the previous two chapters, and in earlier chapters as well, might make interesting history, but they could have a bigger lasting value if they can teach us something about what particular attributes or approaches make the advisory process successful. Why have some advisory studies had a significant impact when others have not? The next chapter digs into that question.

56. Withbroe interview.

57. National Research Council, *A Science Strategy for Space Physics* (The National Academies Press, Washington, DC, 1995).

CHAPTER 17

Assessing the Impacts of Advisory Activities: What Makes Advice Effective

The long history of interactions between NASA and its scientific advisory groups provides a rich experience base from which to try to learn how and why some advisory efforts have been successful and why others have fallen flat. Earlier chapters have mentioned many relevant examples. Chapter 2 highlights some notable early reports from the Space Science Board and its committees, and chapters 3 and 5 sketch parallel, complementary activities by NASA's internal advisory committees during NASA's first three decades. Chapter 10 describes the relatively more recent role of senior review panels formed by NASA that have influenced NASA decision making, and chapter 11 summarizes the institutionalization of NRC decadal strategy surveys and mid-decade progress assessments that have become pivotal in space research planning and priority setting. Finally, chapters 15 and 16 provide a more extensive discussion of a few notable advisory efforts.

Can one make sense out of this ensemble of examples? What common attributes or recurring themes can one discern that help distinguish between effective efforts and run-of-the-mill communications? In nearly all of the examples, their degree of success has depended on four factors that characterize the advice and the advisory process (Figure 17.1):

- Client interest or need,
- Actionability,
- Content and packaging, and
- Execution and follow-up.

To be sure, not every case study is likely to exhibit fully all of these characteristics. And there will always be exceptions or contradictions where an advisory effort will deviate from this prescription and still be successful and important. Nevertheless, the discussion that follows is a synthesis of what the majority of cases seem to teach us.

Not surprisingly, most of these success factors are relatively obvious in hindsight—they're not profound, they're common sense. But it's worthwhile to heed the words of renowned science fiction author Isaac Asimov, who wrote, "It is the obvious which is so difficult to see most of the time. People say 'It's as plain as the nose on your face.' But how much of the nose on your face can you see, unless someone holds a mirror up to you?"[1] So let's take a look at what the history of advisory efforts tells us.

Client Interest or Need

The first key to effectiveness is whether the advisory effort has an accepted purpose and an intended recipient or client who needs and wants advice. Is

---

1. Isaac Asimov, "The Evitable Conflict" (*I, Robot*, Bantam Books, New York, NY, mass market reissue, 2004), pp. 243–244.

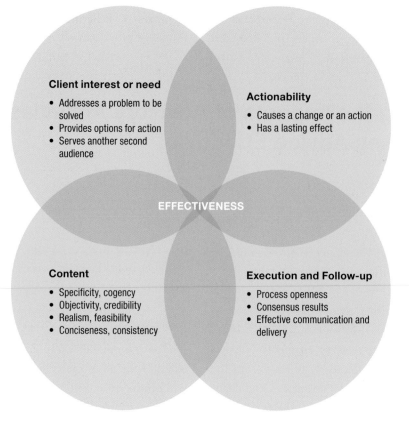

FIGURE 17.1 Key factors for effective advice

there a problem that needs to be solved or a decision that needs to be made? Does an agency need to define a way forward, or is there a question that calls for independent expertise? If the answer to any of these questions is "yes," then outside advice may be appropriate. But need may not be sufficient. There also has to be a receptive audience that is willing to accept the advice or a third party that can influence a response.

The decadal surveys are especially good examples of advice to a waiting and receptive audience. Once the astronomers demonstrated the strengths of the decadal survey approach from the 1960s through the 1990s, NASA and congressional officials welcomed decadals for all areas of space science. The surveys satisfied a clear desire for consensus priorities that had the backing of the broad research community. Likewise, NASA science program managers wanted the senior reviews

of space science mission operations, because they wanted science-based assessments that could guide decisions about which missions to continue and which ones to phase down in the face of constrained budgets.

All the advisory efforts discussed in chapter 15 were requested by interested government recipients, and all succeeded in meeting the customer's need. Charlie Pellerin wanted help articulating a scientific case for the Great Observatories; Hans Mark, Burt Edelson, and Shelby Tilford wanted the scientific community to help define a major role for NASA in studying global change; Wes Huntress wanted scientists and engineers to help frame a low-cost planetary exploration flight program or show why it couldn't be done; and Dan Goldin and Ed Weiler certainly wanted help to arrest the failures in NASA's Mars program. So in each case, they formed an advisory group to address their needs.

Tom Young, chair of the Mars Program Independent Assessment Team, summed up his views on the importance of having a willing and capable audience as follows:

> It's one thing to have a good report and secondly to have someone to deliver it to who knows what to do with it.... There were people who not only knew what to do with it, but were genuinely interested in getting the report and wanting to respond to the recommendations.... A good report was developed, but it would have just been put on a shelf if there had not been competent, capable people to receive the report and integrate the recommendations that we had, and that happened. And I think that happened in a manner that kind of set the stage for the Mars Program moving from what was clearly a low... to what since then has been an extraordinary series of successes.[2]

Similarly, when government officials have turned to the NRC for advice they usually have been anxious to hear it and, therefore, receptive. Noel Hinners wanted a credible outside group to help frame the arguments and define the structure for a science institute for the Space Telescope; both the White House and Congress wanted advice from distinguished scientists on an appropriate response to the putative evidence of Martian life in the Mars rock; and Dan Goldin wanted to find a NASA role in research at the interfaces of fundamental physics and cosmology.

Thus, all of the examples in chapter 15 illustrate the point that advice has a better chance of being used when the recipient wants it and asks for it. Maybe that should be obvious, but it's still important to emphasize.

Sometimes, the advisee doesn't seek or want advice, but a third party does and insists that the process go forward. Often, the advice delivered at the request of a third party turns out to be important. For example, in spite of the NASA Administrator's firm preference to stop future Space Shuttle missions to the Hubble Space Telescope after the Columbia accident, Senator Mikulski insisted on a National Academies review of the issues. The Lanzerotti report helped turn around the decision and pave the way for a very successful extension of the telescope's life. Similarly, top NASA officials had no interest in hearing about the scientific impacts of budget cuts proposed in 2005, but a congressional call for NRC attention ensured that the SSB Balance report would emerge and get an airing.

However, independent advice often falls flat when no one seeks the advice except the advisors themselves. Chapter 16 highlighted two examples of self-initiated advisory products that fizzled. NASA had not asked whether scientists should try to set cross-discipline priorities or what might be a method for doing so, but in the end it didn't really matter. The SSB's near-simultaneous report on "Managing the Space Sciences," which was requested by Congress, produced an alternative perspective saying that as decisions reach higher and wider levels, scientists need to cede the power to other players and other factors. Finally, the Paradox report illustrates the principle that if scientific advisors want to be heard, they would be wise to base their advice on science rather than to stray into what their customer views as its own exclusive area of responsibility.

So the central questions are "Will the effort satisfy a need?" and "Will it respond to an appeal for outside help?" Successful advice begins by recognizing where there is a need, a problem, or a question and then making the advice relevant to that need. Fundamentally, successful advice addresses an itch that needs to be scratched.

---

2. Project Management Institute interview of Tom Young published 7 November 2013 on YouTube, *https://www.youtube.com/watch?v=eiFQIzuFKiw.*

Actionability of the Advice

Of course effective advice has to have more than a receptive recipient or patron. It has to be actionable. One can look at this critical aspect in at least three ways. First, does the advice help lead to a change or action? Second, is the advice timely and available in time to be used effectively? Advisory reports that take longer to prepare than the time scale on which budgets, key personnel, or institutional interests change are not likely to be very useful. Third, does the advice have an appropriately lasting effect? Fleeting ideas don't make much of an impact.

Our poster children for successful reports — the decadal surveys — are distinguished by the fact that government officials have generally worked hard to follow the recommendations. Issues of cost, technological complexity, agency budget realities, programmatic factors, and politics often impact an agency's ability or willingness to implement the recommendations, but the decadals still present a standard by which to measure the utility of outside advice. However, recent decadals have become vulnerable in terms of timeliness, because the budget assumptions on which they were based were out of date by the time the reports were completed. (See chapter 11.)

Many of the examples in the preceding two chapters met the impact test. The Great Observatories, Earth system science, Discovery program, Space Telescope institute, Mars program assessment, Mars rock, and Hubble servicing efforts all led to actions that persisted as long as the need existed. Explicit responses to the NRC Quarks-with-the-Cosmos and Balance reports may be a little harder to identify, but in both cases the reports' authors succeeded in communicating ideas (in the former case) or issues and principles (in the latter case) that remain accepted and relevant today. On the other hand, the SSB's Priorities report and the Paradox report did not lead to visible actions, and so it would be hard to say that they were successes.

Content and Preparation of the Advice

Advice can go to a willing audience and address important issues and still fall flat. How the advice is framed and how it is communicated become very important factors in whether the advice is heard and considered. The most successful cases of advisory activities discussed in earlier chapters share most of the following attributes.

SPECIFICITY: Cogency and specificity are particularly important if advice is going to be useful and effective. Is the advice substantive? Does it include a clear path for action? Is it convincing and compelling? Is it explicit and free of code words or concepts that befog what advisors really intend?

The Hornig report on a Space Telescope science institute, the Discovery program study teams, and the Hubble Space Telescope servicing study all had very explicit and well-argued recommendations on which NASA could act. Decadal surveys are, by their nature, distinguished by their recommendations for explicit priorities.

One speaker at the 26 August 2014 meeting of the SSB Committee on Survey of Surveys made a point about what kind of advice will get the attention of decision makers in OMB as well as in Congress. In essence, the more explicit one can be, the more likely one can have an impact at OMB. Subtle statements don't often work.

OBJECTIVITY AND CREDIBILITY: Advice also needs to be viewed as objective, fair, and credible, and these attributes become increasingly important when the advice addresses uncertain, complex, or controversial topics. Advisors' clout depends upon how people outside the advisory process view the process. Are the advisors really experts? Are they community leaders? Do they have acceptance in the community as being consensus builders?

There can be a fine line between building consensus around the majority views of a community on the one hand and the destructive consequences of arbitrarily freezing out contrary points of view on the other. That's why an advisory group's objectivity, fairness, breadth, balance, independence, and stature are important to gaining acceptance once advice is delivered.

The members of the Hubble servicing study and the Great Observatories brainstorming group were both notable for the stature and expertise of their members. In the former case, the committee was led by a chair whose reputation for evenhandedness and demanding standards was exceptional, and the committee itself brought extraordinary depth of expertise in all the areas that were relevant to the topic. Perhaps the most important and lasting impact of the Earth System Science Committee was its ability to bring a diverse research community together and to forge a consensus in which Earth scientists thought about their fields in a new, integrated way. Of course, the success of the decadals is very much a consequence of the survey committees' reliance on community leaders who undertake a broad outreach effort to build consensus and community ownership of the final product.

Wes Huntress attributed much of the success of the two teams that developed the Discovery program of small planetary science missions to the fact that the members were able to bring the full range of points of view about the concept's feasibility to the debate:

> [D]evelopment of the Discovery program required a great deal of outside advice from not just the science community but from the engineering community as well on how to craft a program that was not in the experience base, or even the desire, of these communities. An advisory group of engineers with members from outside organizations like APL and NRL with experience in low cost missions

had to be brought into the process to counter JPL's flagship-mission proclivities. The science advisory group wrestled with their culture of vying for space on large missions. The crafting of the Discovery program had to deal with a myriad of counter-culture scientific and engineering issues.[3]

Independent outside advice can also play another kind of role. Government science officials often have to make decisions that are likely to be controversial, even though the necessary course is clear. But with or without controversy, there's great benefit to be gained from being able to share ownership of a decision with the scientific community. Consequently, a key value of advice can be to independently confirm and support a direction that officials expect to take. Ed Weiler put the situation succinctly when he said, "I like having air cover; if I were a General I wouldn't attack without air cover."[4] There is a rich legacy of SSB reports that assessed changes that NASA was considering in order to reduce or simplify the scope of planned space missions and where the SSB reviewed and endorsed the proposed NASA changes, thereby granting a blessing on behalf of the broad scientific community. Sometimes reinforcement can be important.

REALISM AND FEASIBILITY: Among the first questions that government officials ask upon receiving advice, even in the most welcoming circumstances, are "Do the recommendations define what actions are needed?; what will it cost to act on the recommendations and can we afford it?; and are the recommended actions within our power and capabilities?" Thus, effective advice has to pass the tests of affordability, achievability, and actionability.

Two of the examples from earlier chapters—the senior reviews of operating space missions and the Discovery program teams—are notable for the

3. Huntress e-mail to the author, 1 November 2013.

4. Weiler interview, p. 15.

fact that they both explicitly address ways to solve a problem by reducing costs. The senior reviews (see chapter 10) start with NASA guidelines for expected budget ceilings or allocations, which are invariably constrained, for a suite of missions, and then they are charged to recommend steps or options to make the overall program fit within those constraints. The Discovery advisory group experience provides an interesting contrast to the Solar System Exploration Committee (SSEC) that tackled affordability issues a decade earlier. The SSEC temporarily arrested the nearly disastrous free-fall of the planetary science program by recommending two new mission classes—Planetary Observers and Mariner Mark II. However, neither scheme proved to be feasible or affordable in practice, and they both went away shortly after initial attempts to pursue them. Discovery, on the other hand, proved to be a continuing success because of its affordability and associated scientific and management strengths.

The Great Observatories brainstorming group was a straightforward example of realism and feasibility. Pellerin asked his advisors to articulate a scientific basis for integrating four astronomical spacecraft into a single unifying framework, and they did so ably and at no added cost to the program. Of course, it helped that Pellerin already had a workable vision.

The decadal surveys are an interesting, and so far unresolved, on-the-one-hand-on-the-other-hand example here. First, each of the surveys issued in 2011 and 2012 included some version of decision rules that advised what to do if unforeseen budget, programmatic, or scientific developments interfered with agencies' ability to implement the recommended priorities. They also often included "tripwires" that described when an agency or the community should reassess priorities in the event that programs ran over their expected budgets or schedules in a way that would impact the health of the rest of the program. These aspects of the surveys were introduced in response to experiences

with implementation of prior survey priorities, and the new measures were viewed as being realistic and responsive to uncertainties about the future. In spite of those efforts, the 2011–2012 surveys all ran into problems due to mismatches between budget scenarios and/or recommended mission cost estimates that were out of line with emerging budget and project realities. Consequently, some of the newer decadals almost immediately found themselves up against a wall with respect to the utility of the decision rules and tripwires.

A classic case of scientific advisory committees losing touch with reality relates to recommendations to reorganize the government. After considering feasible solutions, or perhaps failing to focus on feasible solutions first, many committees lunge for the idea of recommending a reorganization and reassignment of responsibilities within or across government agencies as their preferred solution. Such recommendations rarely, if ever, succeed. The 1985 Space Applications Board report that recommended moving NOAA out of the Department of Commerce (see chapter 2) comes to mind. Advisors who are technical experts usually understand the complexities of technical issues, but perhaps they have trouble appreciating that obstacles posed by established bureaucracies can be even more formidable and beyond the advisors' reach.

The 2001 study on NASA-NSF astronomy programs (see chapter 13) provides an interesting example of a sort. After discovering that the two senior physics and astronomy officials in the two agencies never talked, the committee recommended that the agencies form a coordinating committee for cross-agency programs. Congress put the recommendation into law, and the duly appointed FACA committee continues to operate today in spite of growing uncertainty about its utility and value. Aside from recommending that NASA's and NSF's astronomy programs not be merged (which was certainly a critically important conclusion), the report had little other impact.

CONCISENESS: The appropriate length of an advisory report and the amount of detail that is needed to back up advisors' recommendations can be complicated, but the bottom line is almost always "Keep it crisp, concise, and to the point." Senior agency officials at NASA and OMB and congressional staffers have generally argued that the most useful reports are short, focused, and prompt. Such pieces of advice only include as much data and elaboration as is needed to make the case, and no more. Senior officials don't have time to read long documents, and furthermore, they often don't have time to wait for an answer—or so the story goes.

Let's look at a few examples of conciseness before getting to the exceptions. The letter reports that were prepared by the SSB and its standing committees before 2007 were usually only a few pages long, and they rarely ran over 20 pages. They seldom required discussion of data or analytical efforts to support their conclusions; rather, they often pointed to prior work by the same advisory bodies to underpin the conclusions. The Hornig committee report on Institutional Arrangements for the Space Telescope was loaded with quite specific points about the rationale, roles, and structure of an institute, but the authors covered it all in just 30 pages plus a few appendices. Tom Young's Mars Program Independent Assessment Team distilled their findings down to a 13-page narrative summary and a set of 65 incisive briefing charts.

Under Charles Bolden's tenure as NASA Administrator, the NAC's standing committees followed a prescribed format to forward advice to the NAC. Each recommendation from the committee to the Council included a brief statement of the recommendation, a paragraph summary of the major reasons for the recommendation, and a similar summary of what the committee saw as the potential consequences of no action on the recommendation. If the NAC concurred, the recommendations were sent to the Administrator with the same information as in the committee's report. NASA provided a brief response back to the Council for each recommendation sent to the Agency.

The Mars rock activity did not include a formal report at all. Instead the group of experts that was assembled for the task developed a simple, but handsome, briefing package to advise the White House about the implications of putative evidence of relic life on Mars.

So when might brevity not be a virtue? When a subject is particularly complex or far-reaching, there are clear reasons, indeed there may be compelling needs, for the advice to be accompanied by more detail than can be shoehorned into a brief report. Sometimes detail is necessary to provide an evidentiary basis or in-depth analysis or simply to outline the background for conclusions in adequate detail. There are also occasions when an advisory report is written for multiple audiences, and in those cases the level of appropriate detail may differ from one audience sector to another. This is usually the case for decadal surveys and other major scientific discussions where the advisory report is intended to be read and appreciated both by students and members of the scientific community, who will want substantial scientific detail, and also by program officials and policy decision makers, who will want to get to the bottom-line advice. In these cases, the structure of the advisory report becomes especially important.

The greatest pressure is on the decadal surveys, which need to be sufficiently clear and concise in making recommendations about program priorities so that OMB budget analysts and congressional staffers can turn to the core recommendations for priorities and implementation decision rules. Nevertheless, the reports need to simultaneously develop the scientific and technological basis for those conclusions so that members of the scientific community understand how their survey committee colleagues reached those conclusions and so that scientists can understand how to link proposals for future space missions to the scientific goals outlined in the surveys. Of course, the same depth is important to anyone who wishes to be able to explain it clearly to others.

The authors of the decadals have employed similar approaches to respond to this need for multitasking reports. The 2007 Earth science and applications decadal survey report ran to more than 380 pages, but the text was divided into three parts, which successively presented an integrated strategy, followed by a discussion of recommended missions, and then the collected reports of the survey's individual study panels. The 2010 astronomy and astrophysics survey report, at roughly 260 pages, may have looked lean and mean, but it was accompanied by a roughly 500-page collection of focused panel reports. The 2011 survey report on solar system exploration approached the challenge by providing both a summary of the whole report and a briefer executive summary, all followed by a full report of nearly 300 pages. The 2013 report by the solar and space physics survey committee approached the problem via a report of somewhat more than 320 pages that was divided into a report by the steering committee, with all the priority details, and then a separate part 2 with the reports of the disciplinary panels.

Two other examples are interesting. The Earth System Science Committee, under Francis Bretherton, took its time to complete its work—five years in fact. But the committee didn't make the world wait for its final report. Instead, it first prepared a very succinct summary of the emerging Earth systems science concept that was basically a brochure called an "Overview."[5] It then followed later with a document of about 30 pages—called "A Preview"—that was more or less the equivalent of an extended executive summary. Finally, the full report—"A Closer View"—appeared.[6] The ESSC was working to bring along the relevant scientific communities, and so taking some time to develop

and articulate the arguments in depth was probably a good strategy.

The Hubble servicing report, which Lanzerotti's committee prepared in only about six months, is an example of a different sort. The committee had the daunting task of analyzing all the dimensions of the problem—value of Hubble, projected lifetime of Hubble, maturity and outlook for robotic servicing, outlook for Space Shuttle performance, and absolute and comparative risks—and giving NASA and the Congress a timely assessment. The committee's report did so in a document of only about 110 pages plus appendices. The study was a heroic effort, both in scope and turnaround time, and went well beyond what the NRC can ordinarily accomplish.

The important point here for all the examples of longer advisory reports is not that, given the challenge, scientific advisory committees can filibuster ad nauseam. No one disputes that. Rather, there are times when deeper discussion can be essential, and substantive elaboration counts. When that happens, volunteer advisors can and often do commit extraordinary time and effort to that job. This is also a particularly notable distinction between most NASA FACA committees and committees established via the NRC. The former usually don't have the time or resources to dig into topics with the same depth as the NRC committees, albeit at the expense of a longer NRC gestation time.

CONSISTENCY: Collections of celebrated quotations on the subject of consistency offer many witty and sometimes wise aphorisms, both lauding but often belittling the attribute. So what are advisors to make of consistency? Well, for starters, the National Academies make a big deal of consistency. While there may be no formal policy, there is an expectation that new advice rendered by an

---

5. Earth System Science Committee, *Earth System Science: Overview, a Program for Global Change* (NASA Advisory Council, NASA, Washington, DC, May 1986).

6. Earth System Science Committee, *Earth System Science: A Closer View* (NASA Advisory Council, NASA, Washington, DC, January 1988).

Academy advisory committee will be consistent (or at least not inconsistent) with prior Academies advice on the same subject. This shouldn't be too hard in general; if a committee gets things right the first time, then a later properly reasoned study should get the same answer. NRC committees often cite prior advice in the course of justifying conclusions in a new study. This kind of consistency can have a substantial impact on the credibility of the advice when an audience can see an historical chain of data and reasoning on which new conclusions are drawn. Certainly, the converse situation—advice that changes direction or appears to be unstable—will not instill confidence that today's position won't change again tomorrow. So as a general rule, consistency in advice can be a virtue.

But the environment in which advice is developed and offered isn't static. To the contrary, new scientific or technological developments can lead to compelling new scientific opportunities and possibly new priorities. Likewise, the political and programmatic environment can change and thereby change the boundary conditions that define what is practical and feasible and what is not. For example, a large investment in a project to pursue a high-priority scientific question may become so costly in a newly constrained budget environment that it is either no longer affordable at all or not affordable without doing significant damage to the rest of the scientific program. This is basically the situation in which the organizers of decadal surveys found themselves in the 2010s, and the debate about how to marry consistency and pragmatism became serious. For instance, should future midterm assessments between decadal surveys avoid any tinkering with priorities recommended by the surveys and accept them as gospel? Should new decadal surveys accept priority missions and projects from the prior survey as gospel or should they all be fair game for revision?

Certain key aspects of the decadal surveys and their predecessors have been highly consistent from one version to the next. For example, the major

scientific goals articulated by the authors of SSB discipline-oriented science strategy reports in solar system exploration and in solar and space physics that were issued in the decades before decadal surveys were introduced in those areas comprise a reasonably consistent train of scientific priorities. Fundamentally all NRC science strategy reports going back to the beginning and all parallel advisory documents from NASA's internal committees have emphasized a handful of critical issues concerning the health and robustness of the space sciences. These recurring themes have included the need for a balanced portfolio of small, mid-sized, and large missions; balance between investments in missions and facilities and in basic research and enabling technology; vigorous flight rates that reduce gaps between missions; and development of the technical workforce to sustain a strong space research program. Thus, one can readily find threads of consistency in advisory history even while practical realities and new scientific discoveries have caused priorities and approaches to evolve and adapt over time.

Execution and Follow-Up

The fourth key factor in influencing the effectiveness of advice—after considering audience interest and the utility and the content of the advice—relates to the process itself. "How was the advice developed and delivered; was the process open and consultative; did it emerge from serious deliberation and did it represent a clear consensus; and was it communicated appropriately?" These aspects of the execution of the advisory process all depend heavily on having an established process and a strong chair or other leader of the group of advisors.

Both NASA's own committees and the National Academies have processes that have been established over decades, as earlier chapters have explained. The NASA process follows FACA requirements, which include providing for balanced advisory group composition, open meetings and deliberations, and a committee structure that is established or reaffirmed every few years by the NASA Administrator. In the case of the NASA senior reviews, the panel participants, who are drawn from the relevant scientific communities and who have relevant breadth of expertise, work from explicit NASA guidelines about the envelope in which the budgets for operating missions must fit. The NRC process follows the dictates of FACA section 15, as interpreted by the NRC, including a rigorous committee member appointment process that follows FACA and institutional guidelines and a rigorous peer review process for its advisory reports. The NRC process stands in contrast to NASA's own for its internal committees, not only because it may be more rigorous but also because it is usually, and significantly, more time-consuming and slower to deliver answers. The most successful advisory products also have had systematic approaches for gathering data, information, and outside points of view.

The Hubble Space Telescope servicing committee is a particular example of where the commitment of the committee members had a key impact. Indeed, the importance of the topic was critical to being able to recruit such a distinguished study committee. In describing the study to the SSB at its March 2004 meeting, SSB chair Len Fisk told the Board that this would "be a defining moment for the current Board" and that they needed committee members who would have "the highest level of stature and expertise" and who would "play it straight."[7] Here the SSB and the NRC succeeded.

Strong chairs have been crucial to many important advisory activities, and indeed, most of the particularly successful advisory studies highlighted earlier benefited from having strong chairs at the helm. The best chairs have been able to command respect and to lead their colleagues

to consensus through an approach that has been accepted for its fairness, rigor, and realism. The best chairs also have used an array of tools, including writing op-ed columns and arranging private meetings with members of Congress, to get their message out about the scientific community's views and advice. One particularly active past chair has referred (positively) to these tools as opportunities for "misbehaving," but so long as the chair respects the integrity of the advisory institution and knows where to draw a line, a chair who isn't afraid to push the envelope can have an extraordinary impact. The business of chairing an advisory activity can be time-consuming, especially in NRC studies, and so it requires genuine commitment.

Marcia Smith emphasized the singular importance of a chair for an NRC study as follows:

[T]he key to almost everything is the chair of the committee. And if you have a chair who is really widely respected to begin with, the committee members are going to defer to that person and that person is going to know how to get a decent consensus and, yet, still have strongly worded recommendations. So I think the chair of the committee has a lot of influence on what actually comes out even through the review process.[8]

Tom Young, who himself has earned an extraordinary reputation as a leader of important advisory studies, recalled the impact of one legendary member of the SSB in the 1970s, Caltech geophysicist Jerry Wasserburg, who led the Board's Committee on Planetary and Lunar Exploration. Young felt that the committee's influence was largely a consequence of the fact that Wasserburg stayed engaged with NASA leadership, especially the Administrator.[9]

7. Alexander document file from 16 March 2004 SSB meeting.
8. M. Smith interview, p. 20.
9. Young interview, p. 1.

In his 1992 book, *The Advisors: Scientists in the Policy Process*,[10] Bruce Smith makes an important point about how the committee chair plays a crucial role in an environment in which high-level policy makers often get most of their input orally:

> The chairman's role is so critical in part because of the almost exclusively oral tradition that operates in the higher reaches of the federal government. Policy makers in general read almost nothing beyond the short summaries and briefing papers prepared by staff. They derive their impression of the advisor's message from what the chairman tells them or from oral updates of the panel's progress given them by staff.... Thus the personal interaction between the official and the advisors—most commonly the chairman of the formal committee—remains the critical variable.

This may be a bit of an overstatement as far as NASA science advice is concerned, because such advice is often directed to more than a single official. Nevertheless, the communications impact of the committee chair remains especially important.

Finally, our list of key success factors must include follow-up. An advisory group's work is rarely completed just by tossing its advice over to a government official and declaring success. The advisory ecosystem is sufficiently complex and multifaceted that more often than not there are multiple audiences—not only agency program managers and senior officials but also other executive branch staff members, members and staff from Congress, and the research community—that have a stake in the implications and implementation of the advice. Consequently, the most effective advisory groups ensure that there are provisions for communicating their advice widely.

Follow-up also can involve longer-term stewardship of the advice. For example, most of the members of Pellerin's Great Observatory brainstorming group stayed engaged when the group morphed into the Astrophysics Council, and members of Bretherton's Earth System Science Committee built momentum throughout the scientific community for the committee's new way of looking at the Earth sciences. In what has been typical for many independent advisory studies, Tom Young testified at a congressional hearing about the results of his team's Mars program assessment, and the chair and several members of the Hubble Space Telescope servicing committee gave extensive congressional briefings about their findings. The chair of the 1991 decadal survey for astronomy and astrophysics, John Bahcall, took his job so seriously that he famously committed himself to watch after the survey's recommendations for the full decade following its completion. In contrast, advice that has been shipped quietly to "current occupant" has rarely had any impact.

Does Advice That Fails to Meet These Tests Sometimes Still Have an Impact?

As chapter 16 illustrated, there are times when the immediate recipient of advice may not welcome it or even want it at all, but developing advice on the subject at hand may be important and impactful nonetheless. The 2005 report "Assessment of Options for Extending the Life of the Hubble Space Telescope" and the 2006 report "An Assessment of Balance in NASA's Science Programs" are relevant examples of this point. In the case of the former, the NASA Administrator had already decided on a course for Hubble that would not use the Space Shuttle, but pressure from Senator Mikulski gave the Agency no choice but to seek a wider independent assessment. The SSB's Balance report made recommendations that would be hard, if not impossible, for mid-level NASA science officials to

---

10. Bruce L. R. Smith, *The Advisers: Scientists in the Policy Process* (The Brookings Institution, Washington, DC, 1992), ch. 9, p. 190.

implement on their own. But in this case, the report was addressed to a wider audience that included Congress; thus, the report helped build a wider base of support for remedies to science budget cuts that the science office was able to administer in the ensuing years.

The second of the four keys to success described above emphasized that advice needs some specific utility or value, but sometimes there can be long-term value even when there is no specific short-term impact. Additionally, sometimes the value of the advice can emerge slowly when given a chance. The Quarks-with-the-Cosmos report is a case in point (see chapter 15). When the report was published in 2003, it was lauded for its science-first approach, but its highlighted space missions never got to the head of the queue. Nevertheless, the broad ideas of organizing part of NASA's and DOE's astrophysics programs around the interfaces between fundamental physics and cosmology struck a chord that was embraced in the OSTP Physics of the Universe report,[11] and that persisted in NASA's Beyond Einstein program, which then morphed into the Agency's Physics of the Cosmos program. The Quarks report's favorite space missions are like the character named Not-Dead-Fred early in Act 1 of the musical *Monty Python's Spamalot*—they're not dead yet.

What Leads to Failure?

Besides analyzing the attributes of successful advisory efforts, one can look at whether there have been notable aspects of unsuccessful attempts to provide advice. The obvious answer is that efforts that don't embrace the success factors above will be candidates for failure. But let's examine a few examples in more detail.

LACK OF AN INTERESTED SPONSOR OR PATRON: The 1994 Paradox report is an example of an advisory study for which there was no government customer or recipient who wanted the advice. As chapter 16 explains, the SSB initiated the study pertaining to NASA and NSF programs in solar and space physics because of concerns voiced by members of that research community about declining robustness of the field in spite of apparently healthy agency budgets. While many of the study report's recommendations were fundamentally sound, they strayed into management and administrative areas that NASA officials viewed as being inappropriate for the NRC. Thus, the report offered advice that NASA didn't seek or especially want. Furthermore, the report struck the same NASA officials as being whiny and self-serving.

SUPERFICIALITY: Advice that lacks substantive or actionable recommendations is usually on a short path to oblivion. As the discussion above has noted, advice recipients want to see a clear plan for action and a sense that taking action has the potential for a beneficial impact. The SSB's 1995 Priorities report was unable to meet those tests because the study committee was unable to convince itself or others that the committee's approach to producing viable cross-disciplinary priorities was workable. As chapter 16 indicated, the best that the committee could do was to reaffirm that the general priority-setting criteria that the SESAC Crisis report had outlined nearly a decade earlier were appropriate but that, alas, the actual task of establishing cross-discipline priorities would not be easy. To their credit, however, the SSB and its priorities committee were willing to say so and go on to other, more tractable issues.

The SSB's 2005 report on science in the context of the Bush Vision for Space Exploration

---

11. Interagency Working Group on the Physics of the Universe, *A 21st Century Frontier of Discovery: The Physics of the Universe* (National Science and Technology Council Committee on Science, Executive Office of the President, Washington, DC, February 2004).

(see chapter 16) was notable for its high principles and lack of hard-hitting conclusions. After at least one congressional staff member skewered the report, the SSB had another chance to try to provide sharper guidance. That second at-bat produced the 2006 Balance report, which had a better long-term impact.

PREACHY OR PEDANTIC STYLE OR SUBSTANCE: Certainly a good way to handicap even sound advice is to deliver it in a fashion that annoys the recipient. While neither the Paradox report nor the Science in Exploration reports cited above were intended to be preachy, they struck some important readers that way. As the discussion above just explained, that style and lack of new substance helped lead to those reports being largely ignored.

OBSOLESCENCE: Delivering advice after the need has passed or when the clock is running out on time available to act is a surefire route to irrelevance. This is a problem that is less of a risk for NASA's internal committees, where the interactions between advisors and advisees can be more direct and where NASA can exercise more control. On the other hand, it has been a persistent threat to the effectiveness of NRC advisory activities.[12]

The SSB's 2004 report, "Plasma Physics of the Local Cosmos," is a notable example of an advisory report that only marginally survived its long gestation period. The study was conceived in 1999 when the Board's Committee on Solar and Space Physics sought to prepare a report that would discuss and assess the character and state of science at the interfaces between space plasma physics and related areas of astrophysics and laboratory plasma physics. The study was also intended to assess the adequacy of resources to support work in these areas and to develop programmatic recommendations for the future. After beginning the study and even writing a draft report, the study was put on hold while the committee helped organize the first decadal survey for solar and space physics. After the decadal survey was completed in 2003, the report that had its roots in 1999 was resurrected, and it finally appeared in 2004.[13] Because the decadal survey report had included resource priority recommendations for the whole program for both NASA and NSF, the 2004 report only addressed the scientific aspects of the original charge and included no recommendations. Thus, while the report may have had value for scientists and students interested in plasma physics, its ultimate advisory value was modest at best.

A 1995 *Science* magazine article[14] described the NRC's efforts to cope with government officials' desire for timely advice and prompt responses to requests for advisory studies, on the one hand, and the often-conflicting demands imposed by the institution's standards for quality and its administrative procedures. The article's author, Andrew Lawler, compared two studies—one that was completed in just seven months and a second, which required execution of a new contract with NASA, that took 17 months from the time of NASA's request (or 11 months from the time of contract award) to report delivery. The latter study (see the chapter 16 discussion of the congressionally mandated Future of Space Science study) stretched over a two-year span from the time of the Senate request for advice.

---

12. To be realistic, the NRC is not always in full control of factors that affect timeliness. Delays in government contract awards, conflicting schedules and priorities of key committee members, inaccessibility of necessary data or information, and even departure of government officials who requested a study can seriously impact the timely utility of a report.

13. Space Studies Board, "Plasma Physics of the Local Cosmos" (National Research Council, The National Academies Press, Washington, DC, 2004).

14. Andrew Lawler, "NRC Pledges Faster Delivery on Reports to Government," *Science*, vol. 270, p. 22, 6 October 1995.

More recently, Marjory Blumenthal, who was a long-time NRC board director before becoming Associate Provost at Georgetown University, wrote about the urgent need for the NRC to become more responsive to government demands for timely advice. On the occasion of the 150th anniversary of the National Academy of Sciences, Blumenthal argued that the time had come for the institution to become "more nimble." She added,

> As politics become more contentious, policy-makers are seeking faster advice, and organizations that offer advice are proliferating. Twenty-first-century realities demand that the NAS provide expert advice more quickly and do a better job at explaining its value.[15]

Advice versus Advocacy versus Special Pleading

It is natural, and for that matter important, for someone on the receiving end of advice to ask whether the advice is objective and credible. Likewise, others who might want to assess the advice may well ask whether the advice represents the special interests of the advisors or the broader scientific and programmatic context of the subject of the advice. To put the issue in different words, When does advice become advocacy? Is advocacy necessarily a bad thing? And when does advocacy become special pleading?

First, almost all advisory studies have an element of advocacy. Former Chief of Staff of the House Committee on Science David Goldston has pointed out that the space community is such a small community that basically everyone has an interest in the outcome of the advice that it provides and that even the authors of the decadals have an interest in benefiting from the effort.[16]

No one expects a decadal survey committee to say, "This scientific field isn't worth it; don't pursue it." Instead, the surveys are organized on the premise that they address important scientific areas that are worthy of support. Thus, the members of a survey committee are, at a basic level, advocates for the field. That should be accepted as given when viewed in the context of the breadth of the subject about which they are charged to advise. There have been exceptions that we'll get to shortly, but in general, advocacy isn't necessarily a bad thing in and of itself. Special pleading, on the other hand, can occur when its proposers take a position so narrowly that objectivity is lost. One can argue that when advocacy becomes special pleading, it is no longer credible as advice. That should be a no-brainer.

Two characteristics help distinguish the former from the latter. The first relates to the breadth of the topic of the advice (and of the advisors) and the diversity of possible advisory conclusions that could be presented. For example, all decadal surveys span a broad range of sub-disciplines and topics within their particular scientific field. Astronomers weigh the importance of studying stars, novae, dust, galaxies, and many other kinds of cosmic bodies, and they consider a great range of both ground-based and space-borne tools to conduct their studies. Solar system exploration survey committees consider competing arguments for research on rocky planets in the inner solar system; icy gas giants in the outer solar system; and a host of primitive bodies and material such as comets, moons, asteroids, and interplanetary debris. Those committees also assess the merits of focusing the research from differing perspectives such as geology, geophysics, atmospheric science, or plasma physics. The surveys for solar and space physics and for Earth science have a similarly daunting range of perspectives and areas of concentration to consider. In

---

15. Marjory S. Blumenthal, "Move with the times," *Nature*, vol. 494, p. 423, 28 February 2013.

16. Goldston interview.

RELATIONSHIPS: NASA's relationships with its own committees and NRC committees have always been different, and the differences have affected both the way the two advisory entities have operated and how their products have been viewed by the outside world.

The SSB had considerable freedom to define the tasks of its self-initiated studies until NASA required prior approval for all new SSB tasks beginning in the 2000s. More generally, however, the tasking for NRC studies has reflected mutual agreement between NASA and the NRC, which has allowed the NRC complete independence to select and appoint study committee members. On the other hand, NASA officials select the members of internal advisory bodies and define their tasks.

Once an advisory activity is under way, the degree of independence is also different for NASA committees and NRC committees. FACA regulations require a NASA official to sit in on all of its FACA committee meetings and deliberations. That official has authority to "call, attend, and adjourn committee meetings [and] approve agendas."[8] Thus, NASA officials remain continuously informed about the committee's progress. In contrast, NRC committees expect to operate entirely independently of NASA once a formal advisory study has begun, and the Agency has no control of or insight into the committee's deliberations outside of what the general public sees during FACA-mandated, open committee meetings until the study is completed. To be clear, the firewall applies to access by NASA and the public to internal NRC committee discussions as a committee debates conclusions in a formal advisory study. General information-gathering meetings and informal discussions by standing boards and committees are always open.

While the extent of NASA's control over its own committees vis-à-vis NRC committees affects their relative independence, the difference in how FACA regulations dictate the openness of committee deliberations can impact the directness and candor of the advice the advisory bodies deliver. When NRC committees deliberate to reach consensus, they are permitted to conduct their discussions in closed sessions. However, all NASA FACA committee discussions and deliberations must be conducted in sessions that are open to the public. For the NASA committees, this can lead to the watering down of a committee's advice that Marcia Smith saw in the operations of the NASA Advisory Council (see chapter 12).

NASA officials' occasional misunderstandings of this difference in operating independence have led to some interesting experiences. A prime example was the case described in chapter 2 when NASA Administrator Fletcher appealed to NAS President Philip Handler to not appoint Richard Goody as SSB chair and Handler completely ignored Fletcher's entreaty.

NASA officials' also may have misread the independence of Academy studies during the run-up to the Lanzerotti committee's study on options for extending the life of the Hubble Space Telescope. At about the same time that the committee was being organized, SSB Chair Len Fisk had gone to a NASA Advisory Council meeting in Houston, and he had asked the Chief of Staff to NASA Administrator O'Keefe if he could hitch a ride back to Washington on the Administrator's plane after the meeting. Fisk saw that as an opportunity to meet O'Keefe and strike up a relationship. Let Fisk pick up the story here:

> [O'Keefe] comes back, and he welcomes me with open arms.... And it turns out O'Keefe wants to convince me that he is right about Hubble and the servicing... his idea was that he had to convince me that he was entirely

8. NASA Advisory Council Charter, approved by NASA Administrator Charles F. Bolden, Jr., 21 October 2015, available at *http://www.nasa.gov/sites/default/files/atoms/files/nac_charter_renewal_2015_tagged.pdf.*

correct and so on. I listened patiently and sipped my scotch all the way home.[9]

Fisk never relayed the conversation to Lanzerotti, and aside from helping recruit committee members, Fisk let the committee do its own thing.

Another instructive example of the relative independence of NASA and NRC committees comes from the operation of the NASA Advisory Council when Michael Griffin was Administrator. Chapter 12 recounted the abrupt retirement of three scientist-members of the NAC in 2006 when they ran crossways with Griffin and the NAC Chair Jack Schmitt. The scientists had been vocal about the deleterious impacts of cuts to NASA's science program budgets, and that line of advice was not welcome at the highest levels of NASA.[10] The members of the NAC serve at the pleasure of the Administrator, and so Griffin was within his rights to remove the unwelcome members. However, the episode exacerbated strains between NASA and the scientific community and undermined the credibility of the NAC process.

By way of contrast, there is a formal process for incorporating minority positions in NRC advisory reports. Study committee chairs and staff members work hard to help a committee reach consensus—maybe occasionally at the cost of watering down some conclusions—but when agreement becomes impossible, the contrary views are included.

The flip side of independence is accessibility. NASA committees are generally more accessible to NASA officials, and they offer more options for interactions. An especially notable example from the distant past was NASA's Management Operations Groups (MOWGs, see chapter 4), which were exempt from FACA and which worked intimately with NASA managers and program scientists. Ed Weiler recalled that "they [were] almost part of the staff. I mean your MOWG chair was like your best buddy." Charlie Pellerin gave the system his highest praise, saying, "I don't think there's any system anywhere to get as close to this aspect of customers in any business I've ever seen."[11] Lamentably, MOWGs no longer exist at NASA, and the analysis groups that succeeded them are not permitted to give formal consensus advice. Nevertheless, Grunsfeld's comments quoted above illustrate the close, informal relationships that NASA still expects with its internal committees.

Just to muddle the picture a bit, there are instances where NASA officials and NRC committees have been able to straddle the line between independence and accessibility, albeit in the now distant past. Charlie Pellerin recalled how he was able to work closely with his Academy advisors, especially the decadal survey committee, in the 1980s:

> By the way, I think things worked very differently for me than the way they work today. I was hand-in-glove with all these things that the Academy was doing. We talked to each other all the time about what was going on. Today it seems that people—division directors—are more likely to go off and let these boards just complete. But for everything of that nature, I liked working with the outside team all along.... And so [decadal survey committee chair] George Field would consult with me on everything, because what they understood was that they need to make recommendations that were programmatically achievable.... I had

9. Fisk interview, p. 17.

10. See David Kastenbaum, "Budget Cuts Trigger NASA Resignations" (National Public Radio, All Things Considered, transcript, 18 August 2006), available at *http://www.npr.org/templates/story/story.php?storyId=5671708*; Andrew Lawler, "NASA Chief Blasts Advisors" (Science Magazine, 22 August 2006), available at *http://www.sciencemag.org/news/2006/08/nasa-chief-blasts-advisors*.

11. Weiler (p. 18) and Pellerin (p. 5) interviews, respectively.

very, very close dialogue with the leadership in our community.[12]

Former science Associate Administrator Al Diaz offered an important alternative way of looking at the differences between NASA's committees and NRC committees, and this is a key point. He described the relationships not in terms of how NASA viewed them but from the perspective of how the two sets of advisory bodies appear to view the relationships. Diaz recalled that the two different perspectives also led to different levels of stress or cohesion when he was leading the program:

This goes back to this question about whose resources are they that NASA is using to do science missions. I think there was a very clear belief in the NRC that these are resources that are being entrusted to NASA to benefit the scientific community. The MOWGs and the [NASA] advisory committees were involved in advising NASA on how to conduct what were clearly NASA missions. And as a consequence I think there was a much better working relationship between the internal advisory committees and NASA itself.[13]

Finally, it's fair to ask whether any advisory relationships have been truly independent or whether there is always an element of allegiance or dependence that influences advisory conclusions. Certainly, advisors' recommendations often have aligned with NASA's preferences. For example, the SSB's 1975 endorsement of the Large Space Telescope[14] and the astronomy and astrophysics decadal survey endorsements of an x-ray observatory in 1982[15] and an infrared observatory in 1991[16] (see chapter 11) coincided with NASA managers' hopes. There also have been cases in which advisor-agency relationships would be considered cozy in today's world. For example, consider the participation of senior NASA officials in SSB meetings in the early 1970s mentioned in chapter 2 or Pellerin's description above of his coordination with the decadal survey committee chair in the early 1980s.

On the other hand, the history of advisory relationships provides ample examples of when advisors have taken contrary views and challenged the Agency. Consider Goody's appointment as SSB chair in spite of Fletcher's objections (chapter 2), SSB pans of draft NASA strategic plans (chapter 8), Earth science decadal survey criticism of the U.S. Earth observations program (chapter 11), the SSB Balance report (chapter 16), the HST Shuttle servicing mission report (chapter 16), and others. Usually the contrary findings do reflect the positions of the scientific community even when they are not what NASA might prefer, and that's the proper task of advisors.

The important point is that advice that agrees with the Agency does not necessarily mean that advisors are not independent. Neither NASA nor advisors make up their ideas ab initio. They all stem from ideas born in the scientific community, polished and developed via community and Agency discussions, and then tested to see what rises to the top. NASA listens and advisors listen. While no doubt there have been exceptions, outside advisors have largely sorted out priorities independent of what NASA has requested, even when

12. Pellerin interview, p. 2.

13. Diaz interview, p. 7.

14. National Research Council, *Opportunities and Choices in Space Science* (The National Academies Press, Washington, DC, 1975), p. 40.

15. National Research Council, *Astronomy and Astrophysics for the 1980's, Volume 1: Report of the Astronomy Survey Committee* (The National Academies Press, Washington, DC, 1982), p. 15.

16. National Research Council, *The Decade of Discovery in Astronomy and Astrophysics* (The National Academies Press, Washington, DC, 1991), p. 3.

the resulting viewpoints agree. The advisors' job has usually been to review, assess, and recommend. History shows that when done well, that process has added value because the job was conducted by people who were objective and not directly under NASA control. When they agreed with NASA, it was often because NASA already had been doing its job well.

OPERATIONAL FACTORS: Practical differences in the way internal and external advisory bodies conduct their work can have a significant impact on the overall advisory process. Perhaps the two most important factors translate into time and money.

The issue of turnaround time has popped up time and time again. Chapter 17 highlighted the effects of timely delivery on the utility of advice, and Grunsfeld's comments above illustrate how NASA prefers to go to its own committees when a prompt answer is needed. NASA can turn to its internal standing committees essentially immediately or at least put an issue before them at their next regularly scheduled meeting. Then the committee can respond at once, so long as the Agency's provisions for vetting advice through the NAC can be handled (see chapter 12).

One disadvantage of the NAC Science Committee's near-real-time approach to advisory activities is that it rarely has time to dig into topics in depth and to substantively assimilate and integrate what it hears from its disciplinary subcommittees. This was evident, for example, in an extended discussion at a Science Committee meeting in July 2012. Members of the committee were debating how to handle recommendations from some of its subcommittees about a perennial issue—i.e., relative priorities and balance between small and large spaceflight missions in an overall science program. After considerable give and take that led to tabling

the question, committee members expressed frustration that the meetings lacked time for adequate investigation and deliberation.[17]

The SSB always has had to first ensure that adequate funding for a study was available and to secure formal go-ahead approval from the NRC Governing Board, and those steps could take weeks or months. After the NRC's adoption of FACA section 15 compliance procedures that practically prohibited standing boards and committees from providing advice (chapter 9), NRC studies also were required to go through a formal process of nominating and appointing an ad hoc study committee before the work could begin. Then, once an NRC study committee completed a draft consensus report, there was a period, usually a few weeks to a few months, for independent peer review of the report conducted under the auspices of the NRC Report Review Committee.[18]

NASA committees, on the other hand, rarely add the independent review stage for advice developed by the committee. The process of vetting committee and subcommittee recommendations by the NAC that was introduced under Administrator Griffin could be viewed as an independent review stage, but the process is quite different from NRC report review. NRC studies, which are very probably more rigorous than NASA committees' quick-response advice, come at a cost of turnaround time that is often measured in months.

The other significant operational factor is monetary cost. NRC advisory activities are conducted under a contract that covers the costs of travel and logistics for committee meetings, salaries and benefits for the NRC staff members who organize and support all aspects of the studies, and production of the study reports. A typical 18-month NRC study conducted by a 12-person committee can easily cost half a million dollars. On the other hand, the

17. NASA Advisory Council Science Committee meeting minutes for 23–24 July 2012, available at *https://smd-prod.s3.amazonaws.com/science-green/s3fs-public/mnt/medialibrary/2012/10/22/NAC_Science_Committee-July2012-Minutes-121018-FINAL.pdf.*

18. For a description of the National Academies study process, visit *http://www.nationalacademies.org/studyprocess/index.html.*

operations of NASA's internal committees require a smaller staff load; the time span per piece of advice is shorter; there is no report review phase for the staff to coordinate; advisory report production is often, but not always, a smaller aspect of the activity; and some internal administrative costs are absorbed in other administrative budgets that are not labeled as being related to advisory activities. Budgeting for internal NASA committee activities is probably easier to plan and control, because the NASA committees can be constrained to a prescribed budget while demands for NRC may pop up at any time during a budget year. Consequently, there is a net cost advantage for NASA committees compared to NRC committees.

Ed Weiler summarized the choices posed by the differences in timeliness and cost when he was science Associate Administrator as follows:

> I have two views. I have the rational side of me and irrational side of me. The irrational side of me: why does it take the Academy two years to make an obvious decision…? On the other hand, I can't believe that, and I also say the reason the Academy reports are so respected is because they are done carefully. If you want it quick, you will pay for quick, and it won't be very good…. Sure, the Academy is expensive, but you pay…. And if it takes a little longer, it's worth it.
>
> Now there are times, and this is a problem we have had a lot, in which we need a decision quickly. And one then has to ask the question is it really a strategic decision or tactical, because the definition of tactical is quickly…. [W]e were never in my time able to crack that nut as to what happens to the things that don't really fall into the decadals, and they were probably a little higher level than [NASA's FACA committee]. What's that middle ground?[19]

STATURE AND CREDIBILITY: The extent to which audiences are inclined to respect and accept outside advice often depends on perceptions of the stature of the advisors and the credibility of the advice. Stature depends on both tangible factors, such as advisors' seniority, experience, and recognition, and on intangibles such as institutional reputation. Both NASA and the NRC strive to select members of advisory groups who bring the relevant tangible credentials to the enterprise. NASA probably engages more relatively junior scientists on its lower-level committees and analysis groups. Len Fisk has often joked that NASA's internal committee structure offered a career path for advisors, starting with membership in MOWGs and progressing upward to division-level subcommittees, then to the committee to advise the Associate Administrator, and ultimately to the NAC.[20]

NRC committees and reports have an edge in the intangibles because of their association with the National Academies. The same edge applies to NRC advice when it comes to credibility. Thanks to the rigor with which NRC advice is developed and peer-reviewed and its association with the reputation of the Academies, NRC reports are often viewed as being more credible compared to advice from NASA committees, which have to overcome a burden of skepticism because of their association with NASA.

Weiler recalled that during his time as Associate Administrator for Space Science in the late 1990s his NASA committee chairs didn't pull their punches:

> When I was AA I had some pretty independent SSAC chairs. I had Steve Squyres and Anneila Sargent. Anneila sent me some letters that I didn't necessarily want to get; she was probably one of the most independent of the people I had. Steve was a close second. I didn't

---

19. Weiler interview, p. 12.

20. Fisk interview, p. 4.

However, Agency lawyers have become increasingly rigorous in their approach to dealing with perceptions of conflicts of interest. In contrast with his experience through the 1990s, Len Fisk described an example of NASA's conflict-of-interest approaches in the 2000s when he served as an ex-officio member of the NAC by virtue of his being the chair of the SSB:

> I think they made good use of FACA in the sense of using it for their purposes. I mean they over-interpreted the FACA laws. The FACA law … had been in existence for a long time, since 1972. It didn't interfere with anything that you and I did when we were there. But they decided to interpret it in the most outrageous of ways. There was a case where they had this young professor [who] was a good guy, but he got in all sorts of trouble because he authored a statement on the bad things about cutting the R&A [research and analysis] program, which was going on at the same time. And the lawyers decided he was not entitled to do this [because] he had an R&A grant.[29]

NASA's shift from using its old informal advisory MOWGs, which were not considered to be subject to FACA regulations because their advice pertained to specific program operations rather than to policy or decision making, was another important change in the internal advisory committee landscape. The new analysis groups that replaced the MOWGs were also established outside of formal FACA constraints, but they were not permitted to provide formal advice or any kind of consensus views. They could only develop *findings* and report the opinions of individuals rather than of the group as a whole. As chapter 12 describes, this change undercut one of the major strengths of NASA's prior network of advisory bodies. NASA

Administrator Bolden modified the policy in late 2013 to permit NAC committees to communicate advice directly to their program Associate Administrators as well as to the NAC, and that provided a partial solution but not a return to the more highly integrated advisory network of earlier times.

Nevertheless, NAC chair Steve Squyres saw two important advantages to the analysis group arrangement:

> They do provide a forum in which the community can gather together…. If you go and you listen to one of these meetings, you get a pretty good sense of what's the pulse of the community on this issue or that issue…. At the same time they are completely unfettered by FACA, which is a good thing in some ways…. I've heard some people argue that they would love to see the AGs be a formal part of the advisory process, and my response has always been, "You don't want to deal with FACA. Trust me, you don't want to deal with FACA." I mean … FACA exists for a very good reason. But at the same time it makes conducting the business of a group very much more complicated. And so I think the AGs serve a useful function in that they give the community a voice…. They are very town-meeting–like. When we did the [NRC decadal survey in planetary science] we had a number of ways in which we reached out to the community…. [We] had what we called town-hall meetings. So we would go to a [scientific society] meeting … and there would be hundreds of people in the room and we'd go on for hours. And it was a chance for people to get up and have their say…. And the AGs serve a similar role. The decadal once every 10 years is very much a strategic function; the AGs sort of provide a similar venue in a tactical timeline.[30]

---

29. Fisk interview, p. 16.

30. Squyres interview.

After amendment of the FACA legislation in 1997 to expand the law to cover NRC advice to the government, the NRC began to implement changes in its procedures intended to prevent advisory committee conflicts of interest. These changes developed more or less concurrently with NASA's apparent tightening of conflict-of-interest controls. As earlier chapters have discussed, NRC officials moved to prevent standing boards and committees from authoring advisory reports unless they were independently chartered for the subject of the new report. Coming during the same period that the science committee and its subcommittees under the NASA Advisory Council were being restrained from advising program officials without first sending their advice through the NAC for clearance meant that NASA science program officials had no one to turn to for expert answers to questions on a short time scale. Instead, the whole advisory infrastructure went into a sort of slow motion.

Former Associate Administrator for Science Alan Stern saw that change in the way both bodies operated as being more significant than any intrinsic differences between the two advisory tracks:

> [M]y experience more or less practically, runs from '89 to '07, during which I saw a strong temporal evolution in how much less direct and much more restricted [were] the types of commentary, the way that people interacted with committees, the way that conflict of interest was perceived and actually mitigated. I think all those things from my perspective are the strongest signal, if you will, versus whether they were internal or external.[31]

Informal Advice

There is a form of advice that straddles the line between informal and formal and that depends almost entirely on personal relationships. Chapter 17 noted how an advisory committee chair plays a particularly important role in ensuring that advice has an impact. A chair's or key committee member's relationship with a senior official on the receiving end of the advice has often been pivotal in this sense, and in some notable cases, that relationship has helped make the advisory process uniquely effective. Charlie Pellerin recalled how intense debates with his most outspoken committee member enhanced the advisory process, "[We] would go nose to nose, so nothing short of fisticuffs, but at the end of the day we liked each other."[32] When he was a senior manager of the astrophysics program, Ed Weiler also valued a similarly close relationship with the chair of the SSB Committee on Astronomy and Astrophysics in the 1990s:

> [We] were like close buddies, even though we were independent of each other, and would meet on the Hill in little restaurants and have private conversations about what was going on, and that was a really, really tight relationship I had to CAA.[33]

One of the most interesting examples of close and effective working relationships comes from the 1980s when Tom Donahue was SSB Chair and Frank McDonald was NASA Chief Scientist. The two were scientific colleagues who had interacted often throughout their research careers. Donahue had been elected to the National Academy of Sciences in 1983, and McDonald was elected in 1986. Although Donahue's SSB was often sharply

---

31. Stern interview, p. 2.

32. Pellerin interview, p. 8.

33. Weiler interview, pp. 12–13.

critical of NASA, he and McDonald stayed in very close touch. While it might be a stretch to say that they collaborated, they certainly coordinated in preparing formal communications between NASA and the NRC. That coordination is evident in a careful reading of Administrator Beggs' 1984 letter requesting an SSB long-range study of space science in the period 1995 to 2015 (see chapter 2) and in a subsequent 1984 Beggs-to-Donahue letter[34] in which Beggs confirmed their prior conversation in which he committed to protecting funds for space science and applications.

Perhaps the most important characteristic of these examples of close relationships between advisors and advisees is that they rested on a solid balance of respect, cooperation, and independence.

All of the discussion of science advice to NASA up to this point has focused on formal mechanisms, mainly via committees created either by NASA or the NRC. But the situation is not quite that simple, especially because there have always also been informal efforts by individuals or independent ad hoc groups. Most of them have taken on more explicit advocacy roles and have not tried to present themselves to be otherwise. Even though such efforts have wrapped themselves in the cloth of "What's good for NASA science," at their core they have been lobbying activities. To put it in terms of the discussion of advice versus special pleading in chapter 17, they fail the breadth test.

Let's look at two especially notable cases. The first example relates to sustained advocacy for what may be the longest-running gestation history of a single satellite mission. Two physicists—George Pugh from MIT in 1959 and Leonard Schiff from Stanford in 1960—came up with an idea to test

aspects of Einstein's theory of general relativity using a space-based gyroscope. Schiff and his Stanford colleagues William Fairbank and Robert Cannon submitted a proposal to NASA in 1962 to build a satellite that could carry out the experiment, and the proposal was funded in 1964 to begin to develop the technologies that would be needed to make the satellite experiment possible. The project was anointed "Gravity Probe B"[35] or GP-B in 1971.[36]

Fairbank had recruited physicist Francis Everitt to join the Stanford team in 1962, and Everitt became leader of the GP-B effort in 1981, as the project was transitioning from its status as a technology R&D effort to the early stages of a real flight project. GP-B was finally launched in 2004.

That the mission had to follow a four-decade path from conception to technology R&D to entry in the flight mission queue and eventual launch was due to at least two factors. First, the requisite technology was so challenging that much of it had to be invented in the course of the project. This included a satellite-within-a-satellite so that the main system could be isolated from effects of drag due to residual atmosphere and solar pressure at the satellite's orbit, a thermos-bottle-like container that would keep the system to within 2 degrees of absolute zero, and four fused-quartz golf-ball-size gyroscope spheres that would be the most perfectly round objects ever made. If the spheres really had been golf balls, the dimples would have had to be less than 40 atoms deep. After the Space Shuttle Challenger accident in 1986, the original spacecraft design that had been intended for launch from the Shuttle had to be downsized to be compatible with a launch on an expendable rocket.[37]

34. James M. Beggs to Thomas M. Donahue, 9 May 1984 letter in reply to 5 March 1984 letter from Donahue, NAS Archives, Washington, DC.

35. Gravity Probe A was a test of the gravitational redshift effect by flying a hydrogen maser clock in orbit and comparing it to an identical clock on the Earth's surface in 1976.

36. The Stanford University web site for GP-B has much information about the project, including a thorough history of its inception, all available at *http://einstein.stanford.edu/index.html*.

37. See the Stanford University Web site for GP-B at *http://einstein.stanford.edu/index.html*.

GP-B's second obstacle, beyond the technological hurdles, was that the mission lacked a champion either in NASA or in the outside scientific community beyond the Stanford team. The scientific thrust of the mission did not fit comfortably in any of space science's traditional subdisciplines such as astrophysics or space plasma physics. GP-B was never directly included or addressed in any decadal survey. It was like a probably brilliant but eccentric uncle at a family reunion. It couldn't be ignored, but it was hard to understand and didn't quite seem to fit in.

Francis Everitt became the driving force that ensured that GP-B couldn't be ignored, and furthermore, that the project would not die. He was an advocate extraordinaire—almost a fixture on Capitol Hill and in the halls of NASA Headquarters and OMB, where he would argue tenaciously about the merits of GP-B. After being on the receiving end of Everitt's penetrating stare and quiet eloquence as he enumerated points about fundamental scientific importance, technological accomplishment, scores of doctorate degrees earned, and hundreds of undergraduate and high school students touched, it was hard for anyone to ignore GP-B.

As the cost for GP-B grew over time, to eventually reach more than $700 million, NASA tested the project's staying power and Everitt's perseverance many times. There were regular project milestone reviews, an ad hoc review by outside scientists commissioned by Len Fisk in 1991, and an SSB review of the project in 1995, all of which gave it passing grades.[38] Due, in part, to GP-B's esoteric nature and the cost growth that accompanied the continuing technical challenges, NASA sought to cancel the program on three occasions between 1989 and 1995. Thanks in no small measure to Everitt's effective interactions with Washington, DC, policy makers, especially in Congress, GP-B stayed alive.[39]

The successful 2004 launch gave the Stanford team good reason to celebrate, but the celebration was rather short-lived. Unexpected system noise and unexpected wobble in the gyroscope rotors created major problems with analysis of the flight data. In fact, after the mission passed its nominal operating lifetime without producing convincing results, an astrophysics senior review ranked GP-B dead-last, putting it in the number 10 slot out of 10 missions being reviewed.[40] That could have spelled a bitter end, but Everitt once again found a way to save the day. First, he obtained modest private funding that NASA and Stanford agreed to match to keep the data analysis going temporarily, and then he obtained a substantial award from the King Abdulaziz City for Science and Technology in Saudi Arabia. With that funding, the team was able to identify and remove the effects of the wobble and complete the data analysis. In 2011, the team announced that GP-B had confirmed the general relativity theory's predictions of the gravitational distortion of space-time.[41]

GP-B's damsel-in-distress survival story is a remarkable example of how an independent advocate, undergirded by competent technical

---

38. See National Research Council, "Review of Gravity Probe B" (The National Academies Press, Washington DC, 1995). The review committee did not reach consensus, but instead found that a majority of its members favored completing the project while a minority felt that the mission was too narrowly focused compared to other scientific missions.

39. Dennis Overbye's "52 Years and $759 Million Prove Einstein Was Right," available at *http://www.nytimes.com/2011/05/05/science/space/05gravity.html?_r=2&ref=science*.

40. See Jeff Hecht, "Gravity Probe B scores 'F' in NASA review" (New Scientist, 20 May 2008), available at *https://www.newscientist.com/article/dn13938-gravity-probe-b-scores-f-in-nasa-review/*; "Gravity Probe B comes last in NASA review" (21 May 2008), available at *http://physicsworld.com/cws/article/news/2008/may/21/gravity-probe-b-comes-last-in-nasa-review*.

41. Andrew Grant, "Final chapter published in decades-long Gravity Probe B project: Details sum up tests confirming Einstein's general relativity," *Science News*, vol. 188, no. 13, 26 December 2015, p. 7; Dennis Overbye, "52 Years and $759 Million Prove Einstein Was Right," available at *http://www.nytimes.com/2011/05/05/science/space/05gravity.html?_r=2&ref=science*; Robert Lee

and management expertise, can work outside the nominal advisory system. Everitt received little help from the mainstream community, but he succeeded in keeping his ideas alive in an environment that didn't know quite how to deal with it.

Our second example of out-of-the-loop advice that was successfully delivered to NASA as advocacy is the Alpha Magnetic Spectrometer (AMS). The AMS story is different from GP-B in that it took considerably less time to accomplish, but it's similar in that it addresses equally esoteric science for which there was no champion in the mainstream space science community, and it succeeded in large measure thanks to impressive sales efforts by its principal advocate.

Nobel Prize winning MIT physicist Sam Ting went to NASA Administrator Dan Goldin in 1994 to propose an experiment to search for antimatter signatures in high-energy cosmic rays in space. Goldin was enamored of the idea of having a Nobel Laureate using the International Space Station (ISS), and so he bypassed NASA's long-standing practice of submitting any spaceflight science project to independent peer review. Instead Goldin committed to fly the AMS on the Space Station. One of Ting's selling points was that he could draw on a team of hundreds of scientists from more than a dozen countries and that the partners, including the U.S. Department of Energy, would pay for the

instrument so that NASA only had to cover the launch cost.[42]

A test version of the AMS instrument was flown on the Space Shuttle in 1998, and the full-up instrument was slated to be launched on another Shuttle flight to the Space Station in the early 2000s. After the Shuttle Columbia accident in 2003, launch plans were delayed, and at one point NASA took the AMS completely off the Shuttle launch manifest. This was a time when some credible critics questioned whether this rather speculative experiment was worth the cost and the impact on the overall NASA Shuttle program. The Bush White House's Office of Management and Budget was adamantly opposed to adding a Shuttle flight to deliver the AMS hardware. Ting reacted energetically to the threats to prospects for AMS's launch to the Space Station, and members of Congress, especially in the Senate, responded by directing NASA to add a flight for the AMS in the post-accident Shuttle manifest. The nearly 7,000 kg AMS magnet and detector assembly was subsequently launched and installed in 2011. It continues to operate as of this writing.[43]

The experience with AMS, like the one with GP-B, illustrates the fact that regardless of the weight of tradition and stature that are integral to NASA's advisory ecosystem, there are still independent routes by which NASA can be influenced to

---

Hortz, "Good Thinking Einstein: Researchers Spent $750 million—and 52 Years—Affirming the Theory of Relativity," *Wall Street Journal*, 5 May 2011, available at *https://www.wsj.com/articles/SB10001424052748703849204576303393134261736*; Eugenie Samuel Reich, "Troubled probe upholds Einstein: General relativity vindicated, but was the mission worth it?," *Nature Magazine*, vol. 473, 10 May 2011, pp.131–132, available at *http://www.nature.com/news/2011/110510/full/473131a.html*.

42. For good summaries of the scientific and political history of AMS, see Nature Magazine, "Particle physics: Sam Ting's last fling," *Nature*, vol. 455, 5 October 2008, pp. 854–857), available at *http://www.nature.com/news/2008/081015/full/455854a.html*; Dennis Overbye, "A Costly Quest for the Heart of the Cosmos," New York Times, 16 November 2010, available at *http://www.nytimes.com/2010/11/17/science/space/17dark.html?_r=0*; and Charles P. Pierce, "Samuel Ting's space odyssey," *Boston Globe Magazine*, 10 April 2011, available at *https://www.bostonglobe.com/magazine/2011/04/09/samuel-adventure-space-odyssey-unlocking-deepest-billion-university-nearly-decades-mysteries-universe-later-physicist-hatched-plan-finally-bold-experiment-space/EqmSUjLVuDmZTjgV9Xo7NK/story.html*.

43. For information about early results from the experiment, see CERN (European Organization for Nuclear Research) press release, "Latest measurements from the AMS experiment unveil new territories in the flux of cosmic rays, " 18 September 2014, available at *http://press.cern/press-releases/2014/09/latest-measurements-ams-experiment-unveil-new-territories-flux-cosmic-rays#overlay-context* and NBC News, "AMS Space Experiment Sees Hints of Dark Matter Particles," 18 September 2014, available at *http://www.nbcnews.com/science/space/ams-space-experiment-sees-hints-dark-matter-particles-n206411*.

act. Although not always as dogged or esoteric as the advocacy for GP-B and AMS, such freelance appeals to NASA and to Congress for priority and support were common into the mid-1980s. The introduction of a space and Earth science–wide NASA strategic planning process under Lennard Fisk in the late 1980s and then the subsequent adoption of decadal survey planning across all disciplines in the 2000s helped tamp down those efforts. One long-time congressional space policy expert noted that there seemed to be fewer individual end runs around the established, community-based planning system:

> The other thing that [decadals have] been helpful with is [that] I haven't seen as much in recent years of the interested company, interested researcher, interested university pushing their own project or [a] subgroup of the science community saying "I've got this important project, and I can't get NASA interested in it." And I just haven't seen as many of those … over the last five years…. I think the decadals had a positive impact on that, because … it's easier to say "Well, how come you're not in the decadal?" and you'll get "Well, it's a different area that kind of fell through the cracks and it wasn't…." But you don't hear that much anymore.[44]

This chapter has looked back over previous discussions of the advisory process to compare three different systems or approaches: formally chartered bodies established by NASA, formally chartered bodies established by the National Research Council, and informal contacts between individuals and government officials. While there are some relatively clear distinctions between the two formal systems, the distinctions are not absolute or universal. Furthermore, all three approaches have their own relative advantages and handicaps, and so when an agency official has a choice of which alternative approach to use, the choice is often a matter of a customer's needs.

NRC advisory committees, including those of the Space Studies Board, have often proven preferable when the advice depends on in-depth analysis, strategic or long-term perspectives, a nearly impeccable pedigree, and the highest degree of independence. NASA's own committees have been well suited to tasks that depend on a quick response, direct interaction, and guidance on more tactical or operational topics. In recent years, both systems have appeared to grow more rigid in their handling of conflicts of interest, all in the name of FACA. Informal advisory contacts offer the greatest flexibility and freedom from procedural constraints, but they lack the power of advice developed in public view by multiple experts who integrate a balanced range of perspectives to reach consensus.

The next chapter takes a step back to look at the big picture. What can we learn from nearly 60 years of NASA's use of outside scientific advice? What have been its overall strengths and weaknesses?

---

44. Obermann interview.

CHAPTER 19

The Big Picture — Lessons Learned

All of the history, case study examples, and summaries of recurring themes in the pages up to now might make for an interesting diversion for a few dedicated space policy wonks, but they do have a more ambitious purpose. Let's take a step back and ask a few big questions: Why (or when) does, or should, an agency such as NASA seek outside scientific advice? What good is the process or the advice? Has it really made a significant impact and, if so, in what way? This chapter will take one last look at what one might learn from the past as a springboard to contemplate the future.

Why Seek Outside Advice?

Nearly sixty years of experience with NASA's sometimes-testy-but-more-often-cordial relationships with outside scientific advisory groups provide good reasons to nurture the process. First, it's simply a fact that a relatively small group of dedicated managers, even very scientifically and technologically smart ones, cannot have all the answers about how to plan, organize, and execute an enterprise as complex as space research. The task has too many dimensions and too many unknowns and alternative paths, and the pace of new developments is moving too rapidly to keep up without outside perspectives. It is a business where two heads *are* often better than one. This is not an argument that negates former NASA Administrator Griffin's point that as public officials agency managers must

be ultimately responsible and accountable for their decisions. The point is that getting good outside advice does improve the product.

Second, there is also a fundamental question to consider: Should the government seek advice that essentially helps *manage* science? (i.e., Can or should science be *planned*?) The discussion of advice to the NSF in chapter 13 noted that there are proponents of a basic research program in the NSF that is less constrained by outside advice and more guided by the innovative thinking of individual members of the scientific community. However, for mission agencies such as NASA or DOE, or NOAA, the situation is different. Mission agencies have to weigh large capital investments and commitments to both long development times and long operational lifetimes, all in the context of constrained budgets. Consequently, these agencies have no choice but to plan and manage the scientific undertakings they support. Given that reality, it is much better to have outside scientific advice available to the agency managers as they, and Congress, make decisions about priorities and allocations of resources.

Third, the processes of inviting and delivering outside advice have been powerful means of promoting communication between NASA, which is responsible for mounting the nation's civil space program, and the scientific community, which plays the principal role in conducting the scientific research. Indeed, it works both ways. Scientists better understand NASA as a consequence of their interactions via the advisory process. Consequently, the outside scientific community is more likely to take ownership of Agency decisions and Agency programs, because the members have had a role in helping influence the decisions and programs. Even in hard times, the decisions are more likely to be accepted.

In a sense, the process of getting outside scientific advice creates the benefits that competition creates for customers in the private sector. That is, because NASA is the dominant, and very nearly only, provider of programs in space science in the United States, there are no substantial competitors in the marketplace for customers to make comparisons in terms of quality or efficiency or relevance. Consequently, the process of inviting and considering independent advice helps keep NASA focused on its customers—the scientific community—from whom the advice flows. This is the point that Pellerin made when he said, "I don't think there's any system anywhere to get as close to this aspect of customers in any business I've ever seen"[1] (see chapter 6).[2]

Finally, to be pragmatic, the advisory process provides top cover. In an environment that can be contentious or politically tinged, an agency official can be in a stronger position when the official's actions are backed up with credible, independent, expert advice. Recall former NASA science Associate Administrator Ed Weiler's observation, "I like having air cover; if I were a General I wouldn't attack without air cover."[3]

There is an aspect of the process of obtaining outside scientific advice, at least in the NASA system, that is hard to categorize but impossible to ignore. Namely, it's possibly the best bargain in town. Some of the nation's most distinguished and experienced scientists, engineers, and technologists are willing to donate their time at no cost to the government, except for their travel expenses, to provide their knowhow and ideas for the betterment of the space program. MIT astrophysicist and administrator Claude Canizares made the point clearly: "I don't think the public really knows that the scientific community is actually providing a huge amount of pro-bono consulting advice to the government."[4]

What Has Advice Accomplished?

Given those reasons to pursue outside scientific advice, it makes sense to ask whether the system has delivered on expectations. The collection of cases in earlier chapters does offer positive answers to that question. They include examples of advice that propelled major scientific accomplishments, created opportunities for the United States to play international leadership roles, underpinned arguments to secure government policy-maker support, and garnered international respect.

The decadal surveys may have been lauded to the point of exhaustion, but the fact remains that this course of advisory activities has had an indelible impact on the direction of U.S. space science. Their power lies in the broad participation and input drawn from the relevant scientific community, reliance on a set of fundamental scientific questions as a foundation for program recommendations, and consensus recommendations on explicit priorities for future Agency programs. In essence, this approach is an application of the principles of peer review to the highest level of scientific planning.

However, the impacts of an active advisory process go beyond the decadals. Starting with the

---

1. Pellerin interview, p. 4.

2. The author is grateful to one of the NASA History Division's peer reviewers for highlighting this point.

3. Weiler interview, p. 15.

4. Canizares interview, p. 15.

earliest SSB science strategy reports in the 1960s (see chapter 2) and complementary efforts such as the NASA Astronomy Missions Board's long-range plan for space astronomy in 1969 (see chapter 3), outside advisors have defined programs that made U.S. space research a major success story. Each scientific field has moved forward in amazing ways by leveraging the combined talents resident in the scientific community and NASA to pursue the recommendations of advisory groups to advance scientific frontiers. Examples of important programmatic milestones abound, both in terms of their scientific impact and their evidence of international leadership roles. The cases discussed in earlier chapters, such as the conception and eventual realization of the Great Observatories, the impetus for Mission to Planet Earth, and the kick to start the Discovery Program are just the tip of the iceberg. The unique kind of partnership between NASA and the scientific community in which NASA has been open to outside advice and the community has been willing to commit time, energy, and ideas to frame the advice has been a critical factor in enabling this record of accomplishments.

Attention from, and action by, senior administration and congressional policymakers provides a relatively tangible measure of the effectiveness of advisory activities, and here there is ample positive evidence. Congress has embraced the use of decadal surveys, midterm progress assessments, and senior reviews and has folded them into legislation, thereby mandating that those advisory products be used regularly. Congress used the 2004 Hubble Space Telescope servicing report as ammunition to direct NASA to give serious consideration to a Shuttle flight to extend the telescope's life, and the 2006 Balance report gave congressional staffers clear arguments for restorations of science budget cuts in 2007.

Outside advisory activities have sometimes played a lifesaving role by evaluating, and occasionally devising, options for restructuring programs that were in trouble so that they could be rescued and put back on track. Such was the case with assessments of proposed reductions in scope of the Advanced X-ray Astrophysics Facility (later launched as the Chandra X-ray Observatory),[5] the Cassini mission to Jupiter,[6] and the Space Infra-Red Telescope Facility (later launched as the Spitzer Space Telescope),[7] all in the 1990s, as well as the Mars Program Independent Assessment[8] and an evaluation of reductions to the Next Generation Space Telescope (now called the James Webb Space Telescope) in 2001.[9] In every case, an independent outside assessment of proposed corrective actions helped decision makers agree to move ahead after reshaping programs that had become too complex or too costly.

Of course, advisory committees' revival efforts have not always succeeded in riding in at the last minute to rescue the damsel in distress. Notable efforts that fell short include NASA committees' appeals to save the U.S. spacecraft for the International Solar Polar Mission in the 1980s[10]

5. National Research Council, *On the Advanced X-ray Astrophysics Facility: Letter Report (1993)* (The National Academies Press, Washington, DC, 1993).

6. National Research Council, *On the Restructured Cassini Mission: Letter Report* (The National Academies Press, Washington, DC, 1992).

7. National Research Council, *On the Space Infrared Telescope Facility and the Stratospheric Observatory for Infrared Astronomy: Letter Report* (The National Academies Press, Washington, DC, 1994).

8. National Research Council, *Assessment of Mars Science and Mission Priorities* (The National Academies Press, Washington, DC, 2003).

9. National Research Council, *Scientific Assessment of the Descoped Mission Concept for the Next Generation Space Telescope (NGST): Letter Report* (The National Academies Press, Washington, DC, 2001).

10. Alexander document files, NASA HRC.

and then calls to save the Comet Rendezvous and Asteroid Flyby mission in 1990.[11] Both missions ultimately were canceled. These examples remind one that scientific advisors are mere mortals after all, and that scientific arguments are not the only relevant considerations for big program and budget decisions. Experience with the Solar System Exploration Committee in the 1980s provides an example of how advisors can deflect a crisis temporarily but not necessarily for the long term. The SSEC was able to help avert Reagan administration attempts to kill NASA's planetary science program by crafting an apparently more affordable approach, but their Planetary Observer and Mariner Mark-II spacecraft lines proved infeasible and the program had to be rescued again with the help of Huntress' Discovery program teams in the 1990s.

Finally, the fact that the broad participation of outside advisory groups in the United States is much respected in the international research community provides an independent measure of the impact of the system. Ed Weiler described how he saw this in his dealings with ESA: "When they talk about doing priorities [they say] 'Well maybe we should adopt some of the methods of the National Academy of Sciences in the U.S.'"[12]

Can NASA's Experience Be Readily Transferred to Other Agencies?

With the exception of the comparisons between NASA and other agencies in chapter 13, all of our attention up to this point has been focused on NASA's advisory process. But before turning to look at what the future might hold for NASA, it makes sense to detour briefly to the question of whether lessons from NASA's experience are applicable to other agencies. Certainly the factors cited above that characterize most cases of effective

advising should be more broadly applicable, and maybe even universally so.

If one accepts that NASA's advisory experience has been largely a success story, then the question to ask is what kinds of tests one might apply to see if the NASA approach is transferable. First, NASA has the advantage of a long tradition of working with outside advisors. That aspect of the Agency's culture has been important in helping weather the inevitable tensions between NASA and the scientific community that have appeared from time to time. In a different environment where that tradition is not already part of the culture, players may need to be especially sensitive to how to create and sustain an atmosphere of openness to advice. Agency officials will need to be able to gain the trust of the stakeholder community. One way to test for this trust is to ask if the advisory process leads to decisions for which the stakeholder community shares a sense of ownership—"Whether we like it or not, we know the agency heard our advice, and we understand its decision."

Second, NASA's experience should be most applicable in other government settings when the issues are free of political spin and when the process is nonpolitical. When scientists and engineers attack technical questions, even ones that have societal or political implications, their approach is most often based on evidentiary measures rather than beliefs. When special interests or concerns about representing interest groups may overshadow scientific considerations, then the utility of NASA's experience as a model becomes less straightforward.

Third, NASA has used a range of advisory fora, including formal internal bodies established under FACA, internal ad hoc committees, and formal external committees established by the National Academies among others. All agencies have the same ability and authority to engage outside

11. National Research Council, *On the Scientific Viability of a Restructured CRAF Science Payload: Letter Report* (The National Academies Press, Washington, DC, 1990).

12. Weiler interview, p. 12.

advisors, and all agencies have done so. The choice of which platform to use will depend on several factors. When an issue is urgent and an agency needs a quick response to a (usually) tactical or operational question, then an internal body is most likely to be the way to go. When the issue requires a body with a particularly high level of expertise and recognition — i.e., the blue ribbon committee — the National Academies do not necessarily have a monopoly on the approach, but they are most often likely to be the best option. The same probably also applies when the advisory process needs to be (and needs to be viewed as) especially independent and/or able to deal with a particularly contentious technical issue.

The next chapter turns attention back to NASA and takes a look forward at some issues, relationships, challenges, and fundamental principles that are likely to affect the advisory process in the future.

CHAPTER 20

The Big Picture — Future Challenges

Earlier chapters' tours of NASA's advisory history should be able to open a window through which to peer into the future. Given past experiences and trends, can one count on the process working as well in the future, or are there obstacles to be anticipated and overcome? How might, or should, the advisory ecosystem adapt to be an asset to space research in the future? Finally, are there any fundamental principles that need to be heeded going forward? This chapter will deal with each of those questions, more or less in order.

Future Advisory Ecosystem Challenges and Threats

Chapter 6 introduced the idea of a NASA science advisory ecosystem and described it in terms of six key aspects at the end of NASA's first thirty years. Chapter 14 revisited those perspectives and examined how they had evolved as NASA approached its 60th year. Let's take another look, this time in terms of what contemporary or emerging stresses might affect the future.

CULTURE OF ACCEPTANCE OF OUTSIDE ADVICE IN AN ENVIRONMENT OF CONSTRUCTIVE TENSION: These two factors—openness and conflict—are so interrelated that they are best considered together as two sides of the same coin. Chapter 1 noted that involving outside expert advice was woven into the very fabric of NASA's predecessor, the NACA, and that independent experts played key roles in the early framing of a national space research program before NASA was established. Later chapters traced the continuing influences on NASA's approach to building a space and Earth science program. Dan Baker put this aspect of NASA's culture in metaphorically genetic terms:

> My belief is that in the very DNA of NASA the government-academic partnership was sort of built in. I think a lot of the founders ... recognized that it was just absolutely crucial to the vitality of the disciplines to have this strong academic involvement, the constant refreshment and turnover. And so this aspect got built into NASA's very being.... And in fact I think that the lack of ... a natural way to include the academic advice and insight and review, really has been detrimental to many non-NASA agencies. The different government agencies, institutions, all suffer arteriosclerosis to some extent or another. But I think it's hastened in the case where you have this insular attitude.[1]

Likewise, constructive tension has been an enduring element of NASA's relationship with its

---

1. Baker interview, p. 6.

scientific advisors and the broader scientific community. Such tensions were evident all the way back to NACA days; they appeared in the earliest SSB efforts and in the 1966 Ramsey committee's proposal to provide management guidance to NASA; and they charged the atmosphere during conflicts with the Astronomy Missions Board and the Lunar and Planetary Missions Board in the late 1960s (see chapter 3). Homer Newell's advice to James Fletcher in 1971 to nurture a climate of openness, stay true to prior commitments, and establish close communications and working relationships with outside advisory bodies was precipitated in part by tensions between NASA and its advisors.[2]

As chapter 19 noted, outside advice and criticism provide a kind of market competition in a situation where there is only one source—NASA—of goods or services. When there are multiple offerors, competition pushes suppliers to meet or exceed customers' expectations. Since NASA is fundamentally the only supplier of opportunities for space science, the scientific advisory process pushes NASA to respond.

Al Diaz observed that one reason for the tension stemmed from how the scientific community appeared to view its relationship with NASA:

[I]t was more than simply the community advising NASA. It was really the community determining what the course of the program should be and NASA being the trustee that provided the capability to get it done. And while NASA was dedicated to achieving mission success—it really wasn't [NASA's] program, it was the community's program.[3]

Scientists have always set the bar high and pushed the Agency to do more and to move faster than has generally been possible with the resources NASA has been able to secure. And at times, scientists have been particularly critical of the Agency and even naïve about what they can influence and what NASA can control. But by and large, the relationship has been positive and productive.

Two issues—one longstanding and another rather recent—are relevant to this relationship. The first relates to the questions of how much advice is too much advice and where the line should be drawn between when the scientific community should expect to have a say and when NASA should be left to proceed on its own. NASA Administrator Mike Griffin raised this issue in his dialog with the scientific community over his expectations of advisory bodies during the debates over science budgets in 2005 (see chapter 12). He argued that as public servants, NASA managers had to be expected to take responsibility and be accountable for their decisions and not become reliant on advisors to tell them what to do.[4]

Lennard Fisk drew a line in 1988, when he developed a strategic plan for NASA's science program that was based on scientific priorities from the SSB and its committees, but he considered responsibility for translating those science goals into program plans and priorities to be NASA's job. According to Fisk,

The strategic plan was, of course, based upon Academy reports. It had its footprints there. So you could say that was the influence that the Academy reports had on the NASA strategic plan—a foundation for the strategic plan. At no point did we ask the Academy to review the strategic plan and to comment on it.[5]

2. "Relations with the Scientific Community and the Space Science Board," Homer E. Newell memo to James C. Fletcher, 3 December 1971, Historical Reference Collection folder 4247, History Division, NASA Headquarters, Washington, DC.

3. Diaz interview, p. 2.

4. Griffin interview.

5. Fisk interview, pp. 20–21.

In fact, this is basically the same conclusion that the SSB reached in its 1995 report on managing the space sciences (see chapter 16) when it concluded that as the span of a decision expands from being relevant to a single discipline to affecting the full program, the decision-making process moves beyond being purely scientific.[6] It may be fine for scientific advisors to articulate their views on the scientific aspects of a decision, but they need to understand that the final decision will rest on integrating across other dimensions as well.

Furthermore, even if all the advice that flows to NASA is somehow relevant, the mere appearance of too much advice can compromise the advisory ecosystem. Michael Griffin's restructuring of the NASA Advisory Council directly reflected his opinion that NASA officials were getting too much advice from too many, sometimes conflicting, directions. Science policy expert Kevin Marvel saw evidence of a similar attitude in his interactions with congressional staffers: "And one joke that I heard a staffer say at one point is 'The Academy produces a report every day, which one am I supposed to read?' So they are a little bit jaded."[7] Although Marvel was describing congressional reactions to the totality of NRC advisory reports and not just ones for NASA, the idea is still relevant: Can the advisory system dilute its utility and impact by saturating the audience? At what point will the targets of advice just stop listening?

Such concerns may reflect a mismatch between perceptions and reality. In the years 2013 to 2015, the SSB delivered only half as many advisory reports (13) as it did between 2003 and 2005 (26). Part of the reason for the drop may be the tightening of NASA budgets, which constrains funds available for advisory studies along with

everything else, as well as a growing sense inside NASA that less advice is needed. Since the enactment of the National Academies amendments to FACA in 1997, there has also been an increase in government requests across the NRC for *convening activities* (e.g., workshops), which do not require organizing a formal advisory committee, instead of study committees to prepare consensus reports.[8] In any case, this is something that the scientific community and the advisory mechanisms that it uses need to consider.

The second, more recent and more troubling, issue relates to the propensity of high-level government officials outside NASA's science office to ignore outside advice. Ed Weiler observed that after the early 2000s OMB officials were less inclined to be responsive to advice from the National Academies and were possibly even covertly disdainful of decadal survey priorities.[9] A senior congressional science committee staff member had a similar impression, noting that OMB had become less attentive to outside advice, especially when the advice was contrary to what OMB wanted. This staffer added that OMB didn't want to hear advice that the Administration felt it couldn't afford to implement.

Tom Young, who has accumulated vast experience in leading and assessing space programs, saw this development as a serious threat to space research:

The one thing that's different today…is the interaction with the Administration. Largely OMB [and] to a lesser extent OSTP are much more involved today. There is no question but today, for all organizations including NASA, the epicenter of power, if that's the way to say

6. National Research Council, *Managing the Space Sciences* (The National Academies Press, Washington, DC, 1995).

7. Marvel interview, p. 3.

8. Peter D. Blair, "The evolving role of the U.S. National Academies of Sciences, Engineering, and Medicine in providing science and technology policy advice to the U.S. government" (*Palgrave Communications* 2, Article number: 16030, 7 June 2016).

9. Weiler interview, p. 14.

it, is really more at the OMB level, than it is at the NASA level.... [I]t complicates interactions with the outside scientific community, because there is such a strong influence on the civil space program from arenas where science is not necessarily the priority, but other factors play. Starting towards the end of [the 1990s] — and it's been true both for the republican administration and now the democratic administration — there's a new player. I happen to think it's stronger today than ever... there's a new player who's playing a much broader role. As a result, I actually think that the capabilities of organizations like NASA, and NOAA too, are not playing as significant a role in leadership of the civil space program. I assume it's because the OMB et al. has usurped that role.... And my personal view is that it's a negative trend.[10]

OMB has always been a major player in ensuring that agency programs and budgets reflect and implement administration priorities. That responsibility, of course, engenders tensions as OMB ultimately recommends approval or disapproval of agency proposals and sometimes even gives an agency specific policy direction. The new aspect of the tension seems to be about who controls the priorities and the message embodied in NASA's science program. Should scientific considerations and the scientific community play a major role in determining the scientific content and priorities? If so, then scientific advisory bodies should be nurtured and heard. Or should the administration have control and expect that its priorities define the directions of the science program? In that case, perhaps the scientific community should be humored but kept in check.

The fundamental problem, even in the likely case that the answer falls in between those two alternatives, is that when decisions are made in

NASA, outside advisors and NASA still can have a dialog about the situation. But when the decisions and priorities are set at and handed down from outside NASA (i.e., at OMB as Tom Young observed) then there is no opportunity for dialog with the scientific community. Such seemed to be increasingly the case starting in the late 2000s.

THE SSB, NASA'S INTERNAL COMMITTEES, AND FACA: Four other factors — (1) the power of the SSB, (2) evolution of NASA's committees, (3) the division of labor between the two, and (4) the impacts of FACA — have become so closely coupled that they also are best considered together. Three issues tend to dominate the picture. First, budgetary and programmatic environments appear to be more dynamic and to be changing much more rapidly than in the past. It has become very hard for advice with a decadal horizon to cope with five-year budgets that change in one year. Even the midterm reviews that are now conducted between decadal surveys may be occurring at intervals that are too long to keep up with the pace of changes in the programmatic and political landscape.

Second, flat or even declining budgets extended into the 2010s. How does an advisory process adapt to be responsive to a changing environment where past optimistic assumptions or options appear to be dead on arrival? Ed Weiler described this as an especially important time for good outside advice: "Now that the budget is really getting tighter I would argue that the need for tactical and strategic advice is even greater."[11]

Third, FACA has turned out to be a fine example of the law of unintended consequences. The legislation was meant to improve the transparency of the advisory process, and while that has happened, implementation of FACA has also limited the efficacy of the advisory process. Agency lawyers' conservative approaches to complying with

10. Young interview, p. 8.

11. Weiler interview, p. 15.

conflict-of-interest constraints seriously handi-capped NASA's internal committees in the 2000s. In examining scientific advice all across the fed-eral government, Bruce Smith has written about the problem of overly zealous conflict-of-interest protections:

> [C]onflicts of interest in the narrow sense are a vastly overstated danger for most advisory committees. The group dynamics of commit-tees of distinguished citizens mitigate against any member seeking to influence government policy to advance narrow personal or institu-tional interests. The clash of different interests and perspectives ensures that no single narrow interest will dominate a committee's delibera-tions. Moreover the concept behind FACA is that the public interest is protected through competition among points of view and that the decision makers benefit from the inter-change and know when and whether to accept advice from outsiders.
>
> The government should not of course be beholden to, or overly dependent on, any group of advisers. Ever more stringent rules and regulations do not, however, contribute to the goal of protecting the public interest. Rather, the search for the last ounce of pro-tection by assailing the advisory apparatus all too often is a sideshow that merely confuses the public and feeds the populist illusion that all government is corrupt. The inner check of professionalism rather than the legislature acting as external policeman is the better route to high ethical standards and good perfor-mance in the executive branch.[12]

At NASA, managers' traditional internal source of tactical advice nearly ground to a halt in the 2000s. Earlier chapters have noted that the bound-aries between internal tactical advice and external NRC strategic advice have never been rigid and that the NRC has offered programmatic advice on many occasions. But in what some have called a perfect storm, the NRC's implementation of FACA section 15 put new constraints on whether and how NRC committees could continue to respond to urgent requests for advice. New procedural requirements prolonged the turnaround time in which the SSB might respond to an important question identified either by NASA or the Board itself. Letter reports in particular, which had often been prepared to address an urgent, narrowly focused issue, were eliminated except in rare cir-cumstances. Furthermore, the policy effectively emasculated the Board and its standing commit-tees, which were no longer permitted to provide advice themselves. In effect, the NRC committees found themselves hamstrung.

In Dan Baker's opinion, recent expectations about the division of labor between internal NASA committees and the NRC have become misaligned:

> I think more and more is being asked of the … NRC to provide tactical advice, which I don't think it should be doing and it's not well suited to be doing. I think it's really important that we as a nation look at how … one gets appro-priate advice fed back into the agencies and how that advice is dealt with. But it fundamen-tally starts with making sure that you have got good internal advice for tactical matters and that you have got a very strong and deliberate kind of strategic advice from the … Academies and from the [NRC] boards.… [W]hen that gets out of whack and when you try to get the boards to deliver immediate, instantaneous, tactical advice it just doesn't work.[13]

---

12. Bruce L. R. Smith, *The Advisers: Scientists in the Policy Process* (The Brookings Institution, Washington, DC, 1992), p. 198.

13. Baker interview, p. 7.

In essence, Baker was calling for a return to a division of roles that is closer to Newell's original call for the SSB to concentrate more on "guiding principles...rather than a detailed program formulation."[14] (See chapter 1.)

NEED FOR LEADERSHIP: The final element of the advisory ecosystem involves leadership and how participants in the advisory process contribute to the overall leadership of U.S. space and Earth science. There are plenty of examples of how strong and timely leadership has made a difference. Consider the vision and insight of senior NASA science leaders such as Noel Hinners, who saw the value of creating the Hornig committee to formulate an approach for a Space Telescope Science Institute; Charlie Pellerin, who focused the imaginations of some top astrophysicists on how to market the Great Observatories concept; Shelby Tilford and Burt Edelson, who established the Bretherton committee that transformed the future of Earth observations from space; Len Fisk, who framed the first science strategic plan; and Wes Huntress, whose Discovery mission study teams defined a new and enormously successful approach to planetary science missions. On other occasions NASA leaders took actions that ensured that engagement of outside advisors would become a regular, recurring process. For example, consider Guenter Riegler, who devised the senior review process; Wes Huntress and Carl Pilcher, who initiated regular SSB reviews of NASA science strategic plans; and Ed Weiler, who expanded decadal surveys to cover all space science.

Members of Congress, and their key staffers, understood the value of regular advisory activities, and they played a leadership role by providing a formal legislative mandate for the expanded decadal surveys, midterm progress reviews, and mission operations senior reviews.

As these pages have mentioned earlier, the scientific community plays a critical leadership role by serving on advisory bodies. The process is a tremendous bargain for NASA and the U.S. taxpayer, because hundreds of top experts in space science and technology serve as consultants without being compensated by the government for their time. Regardless of whether their service is entirely altruistic or out of self-interest, the members of NASA's and the NRC's committees and task forces lend their experience and expertise to analyzing complex issues and crafting recommendations for ways to ensure that space and Earth science activities address the most compelling scientific questions of the day and do so effectively.

In spite of the strengths and benefits of stakeholder leadership noted above, there are some worrisome soft spots and vulnerabilities. They hint that the system may not be as robust or effective in the future as it was in the past. We will look at them as follows, in ascending order of complexity:

1. transience of congressional familiarity with the advisory system,
2. increasing workloads and diminished availability of volunteer advisors,
3. committees' ability to do their jobs, and
4. the NRC's business model.

The first concern has been around forever, so one must simply acknowledge it and compensate. Both the members of key congressional committees and their staffs have a relatively high turnover rate, and so there is a need for continuous education about space research and about the character and role of outside advice. It's not unusual for a new member of one of the congressional space committees to never have heard of a decadal survey or the NAC. And the same can be true for many new, extremely bright but green, political science majors

---

14. See John E. Naugle, *First Among Equals: The Selection of NASA Space Science Experiments* (NASA SP-4215, NASA History Division, Washington, DC, 1991), ch. 5, p. 72.

who join the Hill staff. Consequently, NASA, its advisory entities, and the scientific community all need to regularly explain how the scientific community interacts with the Agency and how outside advice gives decision makers access to independent, expert perspectives. The need is even more acute at a time when public support for science and the concept of using measurements and data to test a hypothesis or establish a factual foundation are increasingly vulnerable due to the politicization of the acceptance of science. The tradition of openness to outside advice is sustained by corporate memory inside NASA, but that kind of corporate memory is much less prevalent in the halls of Congress.

The second problem pertains to the availability of members of the scientific community to serve on advisory bodies. Space research professionals have become increasingly busy and therefore less able or inclined to take on substantive responsibilities on NASA or NRC committees. The typical university professor's plate is already full with teaching, graduate student mentoring, serving on university committees, preparing new research proposals, contributing to journal article peer reviews and agency research proposal review panels, and of course, conducting his or her own research projects. Experts from industry and government laboratories have their own comparably demanding set of "day-job" responsibilities. For relatively junior scientists, all these roles become essential metrics on their résumés as they compete for permanent jobs and tenure. For more senior scientists, the demand for their time just increases. Consequently, recruiting good candidates to serve on advisory committees has become a real challenge.

Serving on a single NASA or NRC advisory committee might entail at least three trips per year to meetings of a few days each, and serving as a committee chair will often require twice as many trips in order to represent the committee in the next body up the advisory chain. NRC study committee members are expected to spend additional time outside of meetings helping prepare their committee reports. The very productive one- or two-week

"summer studies" of the 1960s and 1970s have become virtually impossible.

There is also a danger of advisor fatigue — that is, if too many advisory committee activities are undertaken, the scientific community can become exhausted by being asked to donate too much time and energy. The net result of this situation is that many members of the research community find themselves becoming too busy to take on volunteer roles as members of advisory bodies. Committee organizers continuously struggle to recruit the best-qualified candidates and to coerce the members that they do recruit to meet commitments on study deadlines. (The recruitment problem was exacerbated when NASA committee members felt that they were reined in under the restructuring of the NASA Advisory Council committee system and when NRC standing committees felt that they were disenfranchised by NRC FACA policies that prevented standing boards and committees from writing advisory reports.)

One key attribute of an advisory project can neutralize the problem of recruiting very busy people, and that is when the advisory task is widely understood to be especially important. The higher the visibility and the greater the potential impact on space research, the easier it becomes to secure participation by the best people. For example, this was the case for the study on alternative approaches to extending the life of the Hubble Space Telescope where the NRC succeeded in forming an extraordinarily capable committee. The decadal surveys are another prime example of where members of the community are willing to commit large blocks of their time to the effort because they consider the surveys to be crucial to the future of their fields.

The third leadership problem area relates to whether NASA's internal and external advisory bodies are properly empowered to do their respective jobs. Earlier chapters have often lamented the structural and procedural changes in both the NAC and the NRC that have impacted their ability to fill NASA's needs. Changes to NAC committee and subcommittee reporting relationships that were introduced in the 2000s compromised the value of subsidiary advisory units to Agency managers below the level of the Administrator or Associate Administrator, especially on tactical issues. Nearly simultaneously, the NRC FACA-compliance policies made it practically impossible for NRC committees to pick up the slack, especially given the NRC's more deliberate pace driven by its long-standing standards for in-depth analysis and report peer review. Ed Weiler saw this as a problem from inside NASA:

> So that's still a hole in the system. Where do you get that kind of—maybe when we use the word "advice" we are making the mistake, but "input"—where do you get that input that's semi-strategic and semi-tactical but leans more toward the quick and dirty?[15]

As recently as 2015, the NRC committee to review lessons learned from recent decadal surveys found that the system was still dysfunctional: "The current advisory structure does not adequately provide for short-term tactical advice on strategic programs."[16] Dan Baker's comment above points to the need for each player to do its job. The remarkable successes of Tom Young's independent review teams on NASA's Mars program (see chapter 15) and on NOAA's environmental satellite program (see chapter 13) demonstrate that outside experts can provide timely, actionable tactical advice. But one has to ask why that can be accomplished only by ad hoc groups and not by long-standing bodies of the NAC or the NRC.

The fourth, and probably knottiest, problem on the advisory leadership horizon can be captured in one question: Does the NRC need a new business model? Evidence of the problem comes in at least two forms. First, government officials seem to be increasingly anxious for faster and more readily available outside advice that they can use to address important problems that demand more immediate solutions. NRC officials point to increasing requests for workshops and roundtables rather than traditional advisory studies, because the former can be produced relatively quickly. However the NRC is careful to note that workshops and roundtables lack the strengths that come from formal consensus conclusions and reports that carry the full advisory imprimatur of the National Academies.[17] That is, a government agency cannot point to a workshop report as the formal position of the National Academies. While the Lanzerotti committee's review of options for extending the lifetime of the Hubble Space Telescope did produce a solidly argued consensus report in a relatively short time, one must ask "Why did it have to be such a heroic effort that it cannot often be replicated?"

The other aspect of the problem that may argue for a new business model for the NRC relates to the possibility that NRC managers have become so driven by the business side of the institution (i.e., keeping the cash flowing) that its advisory activities risk being diluted by producing too much product. Board directors are almost constantly thinking about how to keep their staffs employed and how to generate enough business to keep their units financially stable. Consequently, there can be temptation to propose or accept advisory tasks that cannot reasonably satisfy chapter 17's criteria for effective advice. The NRC's Governing Board Executive Committee reviews and approves every proposal for a new study activity, and so there is a

---

15. Weiler interview, p. 13.

16. National Research Council, *The Space Science Decadal Surveys: Lessons Learned and Best Practices* (National Academies of Sciences, Engineering, and Medicine, The National Academies Press, Washington, DC, 2015), p. 3.

17. Workshop reports usually contain no recommendations, findings, or statements of consensus, and they typically include a statement that the views contained in the report are those of individual workshop participants and do not necessarily represent the views of the workshop participants as a whole, the planning committee, or the NRC.

mechanism for filtering out low-priority, low-added-value projects. However, given that NRC board directors are generally more substantively knowledgeable about a particular agency's programs and interests than a typical governing board member, an adept board director could slip an earnestly argued proposal through the review process even when the proposal might not pass a chapter-17 test.

Senior leaders at the National Academies are well aware of these issues, and they have attempted to address them. In addition to making government agency officials more aware of a menu of faster advisory products such as workshop reports, which can summarize the individual opinions of collected experts but not present more formal consensus recommendations, the NRC has revisited so-called fast-track studies. In one approach to speed an advisory study, the entire information collecting and deliberative phase of a study was compressed to a single meeting. This occurred in 2013 following a Presidential Executive Order regarding firearm violence and a subsequent request from the Centers for Disease Control for the National Academies to recommend a research agenda on public health aspects of firearm related violence—and to complete the effort in three months. The expert committee established for the task held a single meeting that included a two-day public workshop followed by a two-day session to prepare the committee's report. After going through a full NRC peer review, the report[18] was completed on time. In a second fast-track approach, all elements of the NRC collaborated to shorten the time required at the startup and concluding stages of a study—including, for example, contract negotiations, committee formation and appointment, and report peer review—so that those phases could be

accelerated while not attempting to rush the committee's deliberations towards consensus conclusions in response to its charge. An example of this kind of fast-track study was a 2014 study to evaluate U.S. signals intelligence practices at the request of the Office of the Director of National Intelligence, which was operating under Presidential direction to quickly address issues raised by the unauthorized release of data collected by the National Security Agency. By pulling out all stops to get the effort under way quickly and keep it moving briskly, a study committee was able to begin work in June 2014, meet over a four-month period, and deliver its report by the end of the calendar year.[19] Thus, the institution proved again that the Lanzerotti committee's Hubble study wasn't a fluke, but that it does take a serious effort to change the culture to accomplish fast-track studies. The 2013 and 2014 cases are notable for the fact that both of them were in response to requests that originated in the White House. That kind of backing does get an institution's attention.

The National Academies are also making efforts to create a more stable funding environment at a time when funding from traditional sponsors, and the government in general, appears to be especially tight. Throughout most of the institution's recent history, funding for advisory activities has come from a few federal agencies, particularly the Departments of Defense, Transportation, and Health and Human Services, and the National Science Foundation. According to Bruce Darling, Executive Officer of the NRC, the institution's leaders are making efforts to become more engaged with other agencies, especially ones that have not turned to the National Academies much in the past, and also to increase private sector support,

18. Committee on Priorities for a Public Health Research Agenda to Reduce the Threat of Firearm-Related Violence, *Priorities for Research to Reduce the Threat of Firearm-Related Violence* (Institute of Medicine and National Research Council, The National Academies Press, Washington, DC, 2013).

19. Committee on Responding to Section 5(d) of Presidential Policy Directive 28: The Feasibility of Software to Provide Alternatives to Bulk Signals Intelligence Collection, *Bulk Collection of Signals Intelligence: Technical Options* (Computer Science and Telecommunications Board, The National Academies Press, Washington, DC, 2015).

which has historically been below 20 percent of the institution's total revenue.[20] One interesting potential source of new funding stems from a precedent set by legal settlements after the 2010 Deepwater Horizon oil rig explosion and oil spill in the Gulf of Mexico. As part of the settlement, the National Academies are administering a 30-year, $500 million activity to address issues regarding oil system safety, human health, and environmental resources.[21] NRC and government officials have had discussions about whether the Gulf Research Program might be a model for how the Academies could serve in other cases where the government takes action to seek recovery from environmental abuses and can benefit from expert scientific and technical oversight.

In working to help move forward on new ways for the National Academies to meet the government's needs for independent scientific and technical expertise, Darling made it clear that while he and other NRC leaders will be willing to experiment selectively to find new and improved approaches and products to serve the institution's mission, they would go into such experiments only when they could be confident that the National Academies' standards for quality and independence would not be compromised. This very probably means that the federal government will have to accept that there will always be limits to what the NRC can deliver and that when an agency needs a technical answer to a tactical question "immediately or sooner," the answer will have to come from somewhere else.

The Advisory Ecosystem of the Future

Our analysis of NASA's use of outside scientific advice up to this point has sought to extract some

lessons about the strengths, impacts, and challenges inherent in the process. Now we turn briefly to what may lay ahead. Let's examine four likely factors that will influence the future:

1. The decadal surveys will continue to play fundamentally important roles and set a standard for outside advice, but they will need to evolve to stay relevant and useful.
2. Continuing, and possibly accelerating, internationalization of space and Earth science programs will call for advisors to pay more explicit attention to international perspectives.
3. Certain recurring themes that have characterized outside advice throughout NASA's history will be just as important in the future as in the past; they cannot be ignored.
4. Every stakeholder has a leadership role, all of which depend on staying true to a few key principles.

Let's look at each of those four factors in turn.

DECADAL SURVEYS. As chapter 11 explained, the SSB's 2015 review of experience with the most recent decadal surveys concluded that "[T]he decadal survey process has been very successful. Indeed, decadal surveys set a standard of excellence that encourages the hope that similar processes could be applied more widely across the nation's science programs. While it has no major flaws, the survey process can, and should, improve and evolve. The remarkable record of decadal surveys makes the committee optimistic that useful changes can and will be made."[22] The changes that were recommended for future surveys included ways to provide state-of-the-science assessments that could give survey committees a running start on their prioritization of future science goals, approaches for

---

20. Darling interview.

21. For information about the Academies Gulf Research Program, see *http://www.nationalacademies.org/gulf/index.html*.

22. National Academies of Sciences, Engineering, and Medicine, *The Space Science Decadal Surveys: Lessons Learned and Best Practices* (The National Academies Press, Washington, DC, 2015), p. 6.

weighing program proposals against more realistic budget scenarios than in past surveys, and ways to sharpen decision rules that could help agency managers respond in the event that large programs run into trouble and threaten to create havoc for an entire program.[23]

One of the most problematic aspects of the decadal surveys conducted in the early 2010s revolved around the cost and technical evaluation (CATE) process that consumed lots of energy and effort by both the survey participants and NASA but that too often was either misinterpreted or overtaken by events. No one seems to doubt the importance of such a process. For example, former planetary science survey committee chair Steve Squyres put his belief in the need for CATEs quite directly:

> I'm a huge fan of the CATE process. The way I would put it is that we do these audacious things where we fling these spacecraft out into the universe and we try to do nearly impossible things. And plans like that really should be devised by people who are by nature optimists, because … you need optimists who are going to have the vision. But your costing should be done by pessimists.[24]

While agreeing that CATEs are necessary elements of decadal surveys, the 2015 SSB report made three key points about how the process of identifying and evaluating future mission concepts should evolve:

- [D]ecadal surveys, in pursuit of ever more accurate cost estimates, may dig too far into implementation details…. [M]issions described in the survey's recommendations might best be considered as "reference missions," except for the concepts that have been studied for many years—where committees explicitly state their intention to recommend a specific implementation approach.[25]

- Future CATEs could…initially run a much larger number of candidate missions through a faster but coarser "cost-box" analysis, to provide a sense of scale for initial consideration. This extra step would reserve the full-CATE process for missions that are likely to become part of the recommended program—that is, those that require more detailed estimates.[26]

- [A] reliable CATE process is crucial for the largest, most ambitious missions…where cost growth can threaten the health of a whole set of activities over a discipline, and beyond…. [F]uture surveys [should] exercise greater attention and care in assessing and recommending potentially "discipline disrupting" programs.[27]

INTERNATIONAL PERSPECTIVES. Research in space and Earth science has always been an international endeavor. The first post-Sputnik U.S. efforts were tied to the International Geophysical Year, and NASA soon forged partnerships with many other countries. Currently active international

---

23. National Academies of Sciences, Engineering, and Medicine, *The Space Science Decadal Surveys: Lessons Learned and Best Practices* (The National Academies Press, Washington, DC, 2015), pp. 3–6.

24. Squyres interview.

25. National Academies of Sciences, Engineering, and Medicine, *The Space Science Decadal Surveys: Lessons Learned and Best Practices,* (The National Academies Press, Washington, DC, 2015), p. 4.

26. National Academies of Sciences, Engineering, and Medicine, *The Space Science Decadal Surveys: Lessons Learned and Best Practices,* (The National Academies Press, Washington, DC, 2015), p. 6.

27. Ibid.

cooperative agreements in NASA's Science Mission Directorate number in the hundreds. While the United States was clearly the international leader in the space sciences well into the 1970s and early 1980s, the scope and competence of other nations' space science programs have grown steadily. Other nations are quite capable of carrying out major science missions entirely on their own.

Advisory committees have generally been cognizant of the international dimensions of their topics. The SSB serves as the U.S. National Committee of the Committee on Space Research (COSPAR) of the International Council for Science, which is the principal international scientific body for communication about and promotion of space research. The SSB also has long maintained liaison with the European Space Science Committee, which is the closest analog to the SSB in Europe. However, international considerations have not been major factors in the advisory ecosystem.[28] Some recent decadal surveys did arrange to obtain perspectives from outside the United States. For example, the 2007 Earth science and applications survey had a European scientist on the steering committee and non-U.S. scientists on two of the survey's topical panels,[29] and the 2011 planetary science survey had European scientists on two of its topical panels and also enlisted two European report peer reviewers.[30]

Nevertheless, one can argue that long-range scientific planning demands an even greater awareness of international points of view. As proposed future space missions become increasingly complex and costly, they will also become impossible for a single nation to afford and conduct. Comprehensive observations of the Earth from space, future advanced space telescopes, and Mars sample return missions are notable examples of where scientific goals may exceed the grasp of any one space agency. If that is so, then international cooperation will offer the only way forward. Therefore, planning for such ambitious international projects must consider international input and participation in the planning process. How, then, should this consideration affect the advisory process?

There are several obstacles to integrating international input into planning for the space sciences. First, there is no close counterpart to the NRC Space Studies Board in other nations and no counterpart to the independently developed, broadly based decadal surveys. Individual space agencies have their own planning processes that involve outside scientists, but the results do not often carry the same political clout as the decadals do in the United States.

Secondly, the planning cycles of other national space agencies are almost always out of phase with those at NASA. The same problem usually exists with respect to decadal surveys in the United States and science planning abroad. NASA's John Grunsfeld found that this was a particularly tough problem in trying to do joint planning with the European Space Agency:

> Right now they have their *vision* process, we have our decadal surveys, and they are out of phase by five years. We have talked about, "Well, is there any advantage to syncing them up and cooperating?" The answer is that [my ESA counterpart] has enough challenge trying to get 20 or more member countries ... all to agree to work together on the same time scale. Not that it is cantankerous, but it is difficult.

28. For three notable exceptions, see the SSB reports "U.S.-European Collaboration in Space Science" (1998), "Approaches to Future Space Cooperation and Competition in a Globalizing World: Summary of a Workshop" (2009), and "Review of the MEPAG Report on Mars Special Regions" (2015), all from the National Academy Press, Washington, DC.

29. National Research Council, a *Earth Science and Applications from Space: National Imperatives for the Next Decade and Beyond"* (The National Academies Press, Washington, DC, 2007), pp. v–ix.

30. National Research Council, *"Vision and Voyages for Planetary Science in the Decade 2013–2022"* (The National Academies Press, Washington, DC, 2011), pp. v–vi and xi.

Trying then to incorporate something out of the European Union, out of the European Space Agency context, with the U.S., which has its own big communities and struggles, would be nearly impossible.[31]

Astronomer Marcia Rieke saw the phasing problem with the Europeans firsthand when she served on the 2010 astronomy decadal survey committee:

But the fact of the matter is then when it comes time to do something like a decadal survey or they do their planning, they are not done at the same time. There isn't a convenient way to coordinate things. What happened to [the 2010 astronomy and astrophysics survey] is a good example where our [priority] numbers two and three required European cooperation or collaboration at fairly deep levels. And because the Europeans didn't choose either one of those next … there we are out on the street.[32]

Rieke concluded that, given the difficulty in synchronizing or coordinating interagency planning, "It may be that one just has to work at the scientist-to-scientist level and come up from the bottom."[33] This view was shared by many of the author's interview subjects.

COSPAR undertook one approach to international grassroots planning in the early 2010s. Groups of scientists prepared a series of scientific roadmaps—covering lunar and planetary exploration, astrophysics, space weather, and Earth science—that were intended to communicate to national space agencies about important scientific opportunities and priorities from an international perspective. The roadmap authors also hoped that they might help inform the deliberations of future decadal survey committees in the United States.[34] It is not yet clear whether this COSPAR initiative will have an impact.

In August 2015 the International Astronomical Union held a two-day session during its triennial General Assembly to promote discussion of issues regarding increased international coordination and cooperation in astrophysics and heliophysics programs. The participants at that meeting agreed that COSPAR's scientific roadmapping approach was appropriate and that international discussions should take into account the priorities identified in various national decadal surveys.[35]

While scientists do often value international collaboration and do collaborate, there are also rather deeply ingrained competitive motivations that can be obstacles to fully open cooperation, even in the advisory process. Marcia Smith saw this in her experience with NRC advisory studies:

From my perspective as someone who is not an astronomer, for example, I think it makes a lot of sense to get the world's astronomy community together just the way you get the U.S. astronomy committee together and figure out what's best to do and who's going to do what. But I do know that astronomers feel personal pride and national pride in being the first to discover something.[36]

Consequently, she found on at least one occasion that the organizers of a long-range planning study committee did not want international people because they viewed them as competitive.

31. Grunsfeld interview.

32. Rieke interview, p. 6.

33. Ibid.

34. Fisk interview, pp. 22–23.

35. For background on the meeting, see *http://astronomy2015.org/focus_meeting_11*

36. Smith interview, p. 25.

It is one thing to work together to identify important scientific priorities and opportunities for international cooperation, but the actual planning of missions is best left to the space agencies. In Grunsfeld's opinion, international collaboration "is very tough for advisory councils or decadal surveys to coordinate, but they can certainly encourage."[37] Former NASA science chief Al Diaz had a similar view, saying that there might "be an international science body that would advise agencies on how to conduct and how to select missions"[38] but that the agencies would not ask such a scientific group to help design the programs. From a U.S. perspective, Claude Canizares also saw the task of promoting an international discussion as being NASA's job:

> There ought to be a regular convening of something like a "space summit." I know that there are international organizations that try to bring some of the right parties together, but I think they are not the best ones to do this. I think NASA should take the lead on that.[39]

In summary, the international picture seems clear on a few points and murky on others. There is general agreement that scientist-to-scientist discussions about scientific goals and priorities that percolate up from the community are the best way to build a scientific consensus about future opportunities for international cooperation. However, the job of designing missions and forging specific partnerships is better left to government space agencies. One can envision a role for advisory bodies, especially at the National Academies, for the former but not the latter. Even when the players make their best efforts, the task will be difficult as long as

planning and project commitment cycles of various nations remain misaligned. That includes the phasing of the decadal surveys in the United States. Given the fact that any ambitious space endeavor is, by definition, a long-term effort, it would make sense for U.S. decadal surveys, and the international scientific community in general, to work to communicate extensively, early, and often to ensure that informed perspectives about international opportunities are delivered to all space agencies.

BASIC RECURRING THEMES OF ADVICE. Certain themes or principles have been woven into nearly every element of outside advice throughout NASA's history. Those themes have become the very foundation for what advisors have urged NASA to do.

1. Priority for scientific quality and merit. Advisors have argued without exception that the first criterion for making decisions and choices about NASA's science program should be driven by scientific merit. This principle was the basis for advice to NASA in the SSB's 1961 letter report[40] (see chapter 2); it has been the starting point for every decadal survey report; and it was the principal theme of the SSB's 2005 report, "Science in NASA's Vision for Space Exploration."[41] As chapter 16 notes, the latter report was a bit of a dud, because it lacked actionable recommendations, but it did repeat and reinforce the principle of making scientific merit a fundamental decision-making criterion. NASA's internal committees also have consistently espoused the same view. For example, the Space and Earth Science Advisory Committee's 1986 Crisis report (see chapter 5) discussed criteria for selecting future

---

37. Grunsfeld interview.

38. Diaz interview, p. 8.

39. Canizares interview, p. 14.

40. National Research Council, "*Policy Positions on (1) Man's Role in the National Space Program and (2) Support of Basic Research for Space Science*" (The National Academies Press, Washington, DC, 31 March 1961).

41. Space Studies Board, "*Science in NASA's Vision for Space Exploration*" (National Research Council, The National Academies Press, Washington, DC, 2005).

research missions and placed scientific merit at the top of its list, saying

> The fundamental purpose of the Space and Earth Science Program is to obtain scientific understanding of the world around us; hence scientific merit and potential scientific contributions must be the dominant values to be assessed.[42]

The Crisis report did go on to add other criteria — specifically, programmatic considerations and societal benefits — but science remained number one.

NASA has been largely responsive to this view and has reflected the advice in practice. For example, the first Office of Space Science and Applications strategic plan in 1988 (see chapter 7) was based on the principle of scientific excellence, and all subsequent science strategic plans either explicitly or implicitly reaffirmed that commitment to scientific merit as a priority.

2. Importance of peer review. The concept of peer review is a fundamental element of scientific research in the United States. By subjecting research proposals and results to critical examination by an independent cadre of scientific experts, the scientific community applies its own, usually rigorous and demanding, version of quality control to the scientific enterprise. Consequently, outside advisors have consistently emphasized that open competition and peer review should be the principal means by which NASA selects scientists to participate in space research missions, and NASA has largely embraced that approach.

The process got off to a shaky start in the years immediately before and after NASA's formation. When the Working Group on Internal Instrumentation of the NAS Technical Panel on the Earth Satellite Program (see chapter 1) recommended experiments to fly on the first Vanguard satellites, the top four priorities included experiments from two of the working group's own members — Herbert Friedman of NRL and James Van Allen — as well as an another experiment by NRL scientist Herman LaGow. Panel member and Vanguard Program science coordinator Homer Newell was Friedman's and LaGow's supervisor. In his book, Naugle describes how extraordinary time pressures subsequently led to a rather chaotic selection process for experiments to fly on Explorer 1 and on the first Pioneer lunar missions, all due to a rush to respond to the successful Soviet Sputnik launches. Almost immediately after its formation in June 1958, the Space Science Board sought to take over future experiment proposal evaluations and selections, and they kicked off the process by issuing a widely circulated invitation to U.S. scientists to propose spaceflight experiments. However, NASA officials were convinced that proposal review and selection were properly NASA responsibilities, and by 1960 NASA put a system in place by which the Agency invited scientific proposals for spaceflight experiments and then organized scientific peer review panels comprised of both outside- and inside-NASA scientists to review the proposals and recommend ones for selection. Naugle describes how that process eventually dealt with the problems of conflicts of interest that colored the early selections for Vanguard, Explorer 1, and the first Pioneers.[43]

After getting an orderly peer review process in place for flight experiments, NASA eventually

42. Space and Earth Science Advisory Committee, "The Crisis in Space and Earth Science: A Time for a New Commitment" (NASA Advisory Council, NASA Headquarters, Washington, DC, November 1986), p. 52.

43. See the discussion "Stress in the Selection Process" in chapter 1 of John Naugle's book *First Among Equals: The Selection of NASA Space Science Experiments* (NASA SP-4215, NASA History Division, Washington, DC, 1991).

moved to apply peer review more broadly to evaluation of all research grant proposals (e.g., for data analysis, ground-based investigations, theoretical studies, and sounding rocket and balloon flight experiments) across the space sciences. The last exception to a totally peer-review-based program was erased in the 1970s, when NASA in-house scientists were required to compete against their non-NASA colleagues in the same process in space science, and in the 1980s, when that approach was applied also to NASA's Earth scientists. The Fisk strategic plan of 1988 and essentially every NASA science strategic plan thereafter have cited peer review as a basic operating principle.

The concept of peer review is integrated even more broadly into the culture of space and Earth sciences, because the advisory process is itself a kind of peer review process. As advisory bodies comprised of science, technology, and policy experts convene to debate potential advice, they challenge one another to ensure that their arguments towards an eventual consensus will stand up under scrutiny from other scientists, government officials, and an interested public. Both NASA's internal advisory committees and committees operating under the aegis of the NRC have explicit policies for dealing with real or apparent conflicts of interest. The process is not perfect, especially because there may always be contrary views when the topic itself is complex or controversial. Nevertheless, the process of information gathering, debate, and convergence towards consensus by a broadly based group of independent experts can provide the government with as good an advisory product as is possible.

3. Balanced portfolio. Advisory body appeals for a "balanced" research program have probably been the most often cited, most open to interpretation, and sometimes most difficult to implement recommendations over NASA's history. The issue of balance goes back to debates over NACA's balance of emphasis on basic aeronautical sciences versus research in support of practical problems in aeronautical engineering. The infant Space Science Board staked out its position in the context of space research in its 1961 letter to NASA (see chapter 2) when it emphasized that a basic research program was essential "quite aside" from NASA's flight projects.[44]

The balance issue in the space sciences, however, has many more facets than just fundamental science versus applications, and it really involves a consideration of several kinds of portfolio mix. First, there is NASA's portfolio of space mission sizes, which range from small individual-scientist-led projects that may cost a few $100 million or less up to major, flagship-class missions that cost billions of dollars. Then there is the question of the proportions of resources going to different classes of research activity, which range from small research project grants in data analysis or theoretical studies, on the one hand, to substantial spaceflight project investments. A more subtle and nuanced aspect of balance involves the relative levels of support and participation by researchers at universities versus researchers at national laboratories and industry. And finally, but in no way least significant, there is the question of balance in terms of relative emphasis and support for different scientific disciplines—e.g., astrophysics versus planetary science versus solar and space plasma physics versus Earth science. All of these dimensions enter into the discussion of balance.

In all of these discussions, balance has never been intended to mean equity. No advisory committee has suggested that NASA take its total budget and divide it equally amongst different components. Rather, advisors have urged NASA to not only avoid putting all its eggs in one basket but to ensure that each element of the program

---

44. National Research Council, "*Policy Positions on (1) Man's Role in the National Space Program and (2) Support of Basic Research for Space Science*" (The National Academies Press, Washington, DC, 31 March 1961).

can remain viable even when some require more resources than others.

Practically every decadal survey report and every SSB review of NASA science strategies have emphasized the principle of balance and have noted its various dimensions. For example, the 2010 astronomy and astrophysics decadal said,

> "Maintaining a balanced program is an overriding priority for attaining the overall science objectives that are at the core of the program recommended by the survey committee."[45]

The 2007 decadal for Earth science and applications from space took a similar view:

> The Earth observation and information system program should seek to achieve and maintain balance in a number of thematic areas in order to support the broad array of demands for Earth information. Balance is required in the types of measurements (research, sustained, and operational), in the sizes and complexity of missions, across science disciplines, and across technology maturity levels.[46]

The 2011 planetary science decadal echoed the same message:

> "[The] prioritized list of flight investigations [has] been judged and ordered with respect to a set of appropriate criteria.... The first and most important was science return per dollar.... The second criterion was programmatic balance—striving to achieve an appropriate balance among mission targets across

the solar system and an appropriate mix of small, medium, and large missions."[47]

There have been occasions when the balance principle has appeared threatened and advisors have raised alarms. For example, in 1969 the Lunar and Planetary Missions Board (see chapter 3) threatened mutiny after the members felt that NASA had abandoned support for small and modest-sized planetary missions in favor of the Administration's interest in big Mars missions. In the early 1970s, astronomers worried about whether the Large Space Telescope would hurt support for smaller, or at least less expensive, ground-based telescopes (see chapter 11). In 2005, scientists feared that President Bush's Vision for Space Exploration would sacrifice astrophysics, space plasma physics, and even Earth science (see chapter 16) in the pursuit of areas that were focused on exploration of the solar system.

Arguments for balance have for the most part been based on long-range strategic considerations. That is, to remain robust and resilient in the face of budgetary or programmatic threats, the program needs a mix of sizes of investments, provisions for ensuring healthy flight rates and new opportunities, resources to enable each scientific discipline to make progress, and means to lay groundwork for both the technologies and the workforce that will be needed in the future. An emphasis on any subset of these at the detriment of others risks compromising program health either in the near term or the long term.

Astronomer Steven Strom noted a societal or cultural argument for balance that goes beyond the cold, pragmatic considerations of investment strategy. When all members of the scientific community

---

45. National Research Council, *"New Worlds, New Horizons in Astronomy and Astrophysics"* (The National Academies Press, Washington, DC, 2010), p. 4.

46. National Research Council, *"Earth Science and Applications from Space: National Imperatives for the Next Decade and Beyond"* (The National Academies Press, Washington, DC, 2007), p. 40.

47. National Research Council, *Vision and Voyages for Planetary Science in the Decade 2013–2022* (The National Academies Press, Washington, DC, 2011), p. 12.

sense that their particular areas of interest are being considered and not being ignored, then NASA can draw on a broader base of support.[48] More people are likely to back the program as a whole, and factional infighting will be less likely to become an impediment. Advisory panels are not oblivious to this perspective, and so consensus recommendations for NASA to attend to the multiple dimensions of balance have been a constant for scientific, strategic, and societal reasons.

LEADERSHIP PRINCIPLES. Finally, our glimpse into the future of outside scientific advice to NASA comes to rest on considerations of leadership. All participants in space research—from policy makers to government managers and administrators to scientists and engineers from academia, government and non-government laboratories, and industry—have leadership roles to play to ensure the success of NASA's use of outside scientific advice. This success, in turn, depends on four key leadership principles.

First, all players need to appreciate that the U.S. space and Earth science program is not NASA's program, and it is not the scientific community's program; it is the nation's program. Homer Newell and John Naugle understood this as they considered the basis for NASA's relationships with advisory committees in the late 1960s and early 1970s (see chapter 3). Ed Weiler's perspective was typical of most science leaders who followed Newell and Naugle: "I always felt that my job as Associate Administrator was to run a national science program.... I never said *NASA space science program*, I said *the nation's space science program*."[49] At the 2012 SSB workshop on decadal surveys (see chapter 11), NASA Chief Scientist Waleed Abdalati noted that while scientists may believe that the space science program belongs to the scientific community because the scientific community uses the advisory process to decide what science is to be done, the scientific community really conducts space research on behalf of the nation.[50] Dan Baker applied this principle to the decadals: "[T]his is advice that is being given to the whole nation. It really is advice that applies as appropriate to all the spacefaring agencies."[51]

Second, by virtue of their different operating approaches and relationships to NASA, external NRC committees and internal NASA committees have distinct and distinctly important roles. Both systems are needed, and their practitioners need to understand and work to meet their different responsibilities. The general division of labor between strategic advice from the NRC and tactical advice from NASA's committees is widely accepted. NRC committees require what John Grunsfeld described as "longer-term deliberation... much broader engagement of the community, and some time for fermentation."[52] They are more likely to be viewed as speaking on behalf of the broader scientific community and to be addressing advice not just to NASA but to all relevant elements of the government. NASA's committees, on the other hand, can respond more quickly to time-critical issues and work more intimately with NASA as their only client.

Each of these two different advisory avenues has its own weaknesses, as well as strengths. The NRC bodies' approaches to preserving independence and imposing strict standards of peer review make it practically impossible for them to deal with

48. Strom interview.

49. Weiler interview, p. 5.

50. National Research Council,"*Lessons Learned in Decadal Planning in Space Science: Summary of a Workshop*" (The National Academies Press, Washington, DC, 2013), p. 72.

51. Baker interview, p 8.

52. Grunsfeld interview.

urgent tactical problems, and that has sometimes frustrated both the advisors and the Agency. For the NASA committees, the tension between providing independent advice versus serving on behalf of NASA has sometimes caused trouble. A notable example was when NAC chair Harrison Schmitt urged Administrator Griffin to dismiss the scientist members of the NAC (see chapter 12), because he felt they were advocating changes to the administration's policy rather than helping implement it.

To be sure, there have been cases where the two kinds of advisory bodies reached well beyond the traditional limits cited above to provide critically important advice. Both the SESAC Crisis report and the Bretherton Earth system science report (see chapter 5) were prepared by NASA committees based on extensive analyses and deliberations. The NRC report on extending the life of the Hubble Space Telescope (see chapter 16) addressed an urgent near-term problem and did so in a remarkably short time. However, it appears that such exceptions are likely to be rare.

Third, the effectiveness of the advisory process needs to be continuously assessed. As the science makes progress, as the political and programmatic environment evolves, and as roles and relationships between elements of the advisory ecosystem change, all the players need to examine the efficacy of the process and ask whether the process itself needs to be modified or sharpened. The series of reorganizations of NASA internal committees from the 1960s through the 1980s reflected NASA officials' views that the committee structure and roles needed to change as NASA's programs progressed. The SSB's continuing evaluations of the decadal survey process have had important impacts on the utility of the surveys, and one can expect further improvements in future rounds. NRC policies and procedures certainly changed in response

to the amendments to FACA legislation, and both the National Academies and NASA are still coping with those changes. Earlier, this chapter argued for a new business model for the NRC, and the organization seems to be making modest progress in that direction. However, whether an institution steeped in history and tradition can keep up with the pace of evolving national needs remains to be seen.

The fourth leadership principle is possibly the most important. Providing and utilizing scientific advice requires partnership. NASA cannot deliver a world-class space research program without sound advice about scientific opportunities and priorities from the research community, participation of U.S. scientists in the enterprise, and supportive budgets and policies from the Congress and the White House. The scientific community cannot make the progress it wants without NASA's direct support in planning and executing a space science research and development program. In addition, Congress cannot ensure that the American people will have a research program that serves the national interest unless it hears and understands the best scientific advice that the nation can obtain. All the players need to understand and embrace a process that is open to ideas, scientifically sound, tested by constructive tensions, and ultimately focused on achievement via partnership.

Earlier chapters have described an advisory ecosystem that has experienced a variety of stresses. Ecosystems often manage to recover from stresses and to emerge as robust as they were before. NASA's advisory ecosystem has demonstrated that capacity in the past, and it should be able to do so in the future. Past conflicts—whether over priorities or resources or authority—have been resolved by players that have been willing to seek consensus, open to embrace partnership, and above all, prepared to exercise leadership.

Bibliographic Essay

To the author's knowledge, this book is the first comprehensive treatment of the history and implications of outside scientific advice to NASA. However, Bruce L. R. Smith's *The Advisors: Scientists in the Policy Process* (The Brookings Institution, Washington, DC, 1992) provides a nice high-level overview of the history of science advice to the government, and it includes case studies from the Department of Defense, the Environmental Protection Agency, the Department of Energy, the Department of State, NASA, and the White House. Smith's emphasis is on the interfaces between science and politics, but he does not dig into the details of the wide array of advisory fora. Also, Peter Blair provides a nice concise summary of the history of the advisory roles of the National Academy of Sciences and recent trends in its roles (Peter D. Blair, "The evolving role of the US National Academies of Sciences, Engineering, and Medicine in providing science and technology policy advice to the US government," *Palgrave Communications* 2, Article number 16030, 7 June 2016).

There are several useful historical treatments of the National Advisory Committee for Aeronautics (NACA). In particular, chapter 1 of *Model Research* by Alex Roland (NASA SP-4130, NASA History Division, 1985) provides an excellent summary of the NACA's origins, and *Orders of Magnitude: A History of the NACA and NASA, 1915–1990* by Roger E. Bilstein (NASA SP-4406, NASA History Division, 1989) covers the NACA's early years and its transition into NASA. A NASA History Division publication, *The National Advisory Committee for Aeronautics: An Annotated Bibliography,* (Monographs in Aerospace History, No. 55, 2014, NASA SP-2014-4555) provides many other useful sources. For coverage of the early evolution of NASA's science programs, Homer E.

Newell's *Beyond the Atmosphere: Early Years of Space Science* (NASA SP-4211, NASA History Division, 1980) and John E. Naugle's *First Among Equals: The Selection of NASA Space Science Experiments* (NASA SP-4215, NASA History Division, 1991) are superb. Both Newell and Naugle discuss relationships between NASA and its internal and external advisory bodies during the Agency's formative years. For a detailed picture of the evolution of the NASA headquarters organization and how NASA's science offices related to the rest of the Agency at different times, one can consult *The Evolution of the NASA Organization*, which was prepared by the NASA Office of Management in 1985; it is available on the NASA History Division Web site at *http://history.nasa.gov/orgcharts/evol_org.pdf*.

An August 1976 paper in the NASA Archives—"The Lunar and Planetary Missions Board"—by University of Virginia professor Barry Rutizer (HHN-138) provides a particularly informative history of the activities of the Lunar and Planetary Missions Board. The NASA Archives also have useful collections of correspondence and documents about NASA's various advisory bodies.

The seven-volume *Exploring the Unknown* documentary history series, which has been prepared for the NASA History Division by John Logsdon and collaborators, has many useful documents that are complemented by incisive introductory essays. The following volumes were particularly helpful for this book:

- Logsdon, John M., ed., with Linda J. Lear, Jannelle Warren Findley, Ray A. Williamson, and Dwayne A. Day. *Exploring the Unknown: Selected Documents in the History of the U.S. Civil Space Program, Volume I, Organizing for Exploration*. NASA SP-4407, 1995.

- Logsdon, John M., ed., with Amy Paige Snyder, Roger D. Launius, Stephen J. Garber, and Regan Anne Newport. *Exploring the Unknown: Selected Documents in the History of the U.S. Civil Space Program, Volume V, Exploring the Cosmos.* NASA SP-4407, 2001.
- Logsdon, John M., ed., with Stephen J. Garber, Roger D. Launius, and Ray A. Williamson. *Exploring the Unknown: Selected Documents in the History of the U.S. Civil Space Program, Volume VI: Space and Earth Science.* NASA SP-2004-4407, 2004.

Several episodes in the history of space science are nicely captured in detail in various pieces. For example, John Logsdon's account of the near death of NASA's planetary program ("The Survival Crisis of the U.S. Solar System Exploration Program") is in Roger Launius' book, *Exploring the Solar System: The History and Science of Planetary Probes* (Palgrave Macmillan, 2012). Robert W. Smith describes the advisory history of the Hubble Space Telescope in *The Space Telescope: A Study of NASA, Science, and Politics* (Cambridge University Press, 1989). Martin Harwit's book, *In Search of the True Universe: The Tools, Shaping, and Cost of Cosmological Thought* (Cambridge University Press, 2013), complements Smith's account and expands on it to cover other space astronomy missions.

The archives of the National Academy of Sciences have relatively complete records of the activities of various National Academies boards and committees. The Web site of the Space Studies Board (*http://sites.nationalacademies.org/SSB/index.htm*) provides a complete list of all SSB study reports going back to 1958 (*http://sites.nationalacademies.org/SSB/SSB_051650#1950s*), and the site includes links to the reports themselves. The SSB also tracks the history of its advisory activities in its annual reports, which are posted at *http://sites.nationalacademies.org/SSB/SSB_051650*. One particularly useful feature of the annual reports is a set of diagrams that display timelines and relationships

for SSB reports in each scientific discipline area. The National Academies Press Web site permits one to search for other National Research Council reports.

"Federal Advisory Committees: An Overview" by Wendy R. Ginsberg (Congressional Research Service, 7-5700, R40520, 16 April 2009) provides a good overview of the Federal Advisory Committee Act history and content.

For advisory committee activities and NASA reactions over the period 1980 through late 1994, the author has also relied on his personal notes. Those notes then cover NRC Space Studies Board activities from early 1998 through about 2012.

Two oral history collections have been helpful to gain insights about some of the key players in NASA science. One is the NASA Oral History Program, for which many interview transcripts are available at *http://www.jsc.nasa.gov/history/oral_histories/participants.htm*. Another is maintained by the Niels Bohr Library and Archives of the American Institute of Physics, which has interview transcripts online at *https://www.aip.org/history-programs/niels-bohr-library/oral-histories*.

Finally, the author conducted interviews with many current and former government officials and with scientists who have been substantively involved in developing scientific advice for NASA. A list of those interviews follows [an asterisk denotes interviews for which a transcript is available in the NASA Oral History program collection.]:

*Mark R. Abbott; Dean and Professor, College of Earth, Ocean, and Atmospheric Sciences, Oregon State University; interview via telephone; 26 March 2014

*Marc S. Allen; Deputy Associate Administrator for Research, NASA Science Mission Directorate; Washington, DC; 9 September 2013 and 7 May 2014

*Daniel N. Baker; Director, Laboratory for Atmospheric and Space Physics, University of Colorado; Boulder, CO; 2 November 2014

Radford Byerly, Jr.; former Chief of Staff, Committee on Science, Space, and Technology, U.S. House of Representatives; Boulder, CO; 3 November 2014

*Claude R. Canizares; Bruno Rossi Professor of Physics and Vice President, MIT; and former SSB chair; Cambridge, MA; 5 December 2013

Arthur Charo; Senior Program Officer, National Research Council; Washington, DC; 8 May 2014

Mary L. Cleave; former Associate Administrator, NASA Science Mission Directorate; Annapolis, MD; 16 July 2014

Bruce B. Darling; Executive Officer, National Research Council; Washington, DC; 16 March 2015

Dwayne A. Day; Senior Program Officer, National Research Council; Washington, DC; 8 May 2014

*Alphonso V. Diaz; Vice President for Financial Affairs and Treasurer, Marymount University, and former NASA Associate Administrator for Science; Washington, DC; 1 August 2014

*Lennard A. Fisk; Thomas M. Donahue Distinguished University Professor of Space Science, University of Michigan, former NASA Associate Administrator for Space Science and Applications and former SSB Chair; Portland, OR; 10 October 2013

*Robert A. Frosch; Senior Associate in Science, Technology, and Public Policy Program,

Harvard University, and former NASA Administrator; Woods Hole, MA; 6 December 2013

Neil Gehrels; Chief of Astroparticle Physics Laboratory, NASA Goddard Space Flight Center; telephone interview; 7 July 2014

David Goldston; Director of Government Affairs, Natural Resources Defense Council, and former Chief of Staff of the House Committee on Science; Washington, DC; 21 November 2014

*Richard M. Goody; Mallinckrodt Professor of Planetary Physics (Emeritus), Harvard University, and former SSB Chair; Woods Hole, MA; 5 December 2014

James L. Green; Director of Planetary Science, NASA Science Mission Directorate; Washington, DC; 8 May 2014 and 7 December 2015

Michael D. Griffin; Chairman and CEO, Schafer Corporation, and former NASA Administrator; Arlington, VA; 20 November 2014

John M. Grunsfeld; Associate Administrator, NASA Science Mission Directorate; Washington, DC; 31 July 2014

*Paul Hertz; Director of Astrophysics, NASA Science Mission Directorate; Washington, DC; 25 November 2013

James F. Hinchman; Deputy Executive Officer, National Research Council; Washington, DC; 9 October 2014

Noel W. Hinners; former NASA Associate Administrator and Chief Scientist; telephone interview; 11 and 17 December 2013

*Wesley T. Huntress; Director Emeritus, Geophysical Laboratory, Carnegie Institution of Washington, and former NASA Associate Administrator for Science; Washington, DC; 4 November 2013

Amy P. Kaminski; Senior Policy Advisor, Office of the NASA Chief Scientist; Washington, DC; 17 March 2015

*Charles F. Kennel; Distinguished Professor of Atmospheric Science, Scripps Institution of Oceanography, former NASA Associate Administrator for Earth Science, former NASA Advisory Council Chair, and former SSB Chair; telephone interview; 20 January 2014

Mary E. Kicza; former NOAA Assistant Administrator for Satellite and Information Services; Washington, DC; 7 August 2014

*Louis J. Lanzerotti; Distinguished Research Professor, New Jersey Institute of Technology, and former SSB Chair; telephone interview; 25 February 2014

Grace Leung; Director of Finance, City of Sunnyvale, CA; telephone interview; 14 August 2014

Janet G. Luhmann; Senior Fellow, Space Sciences Laboratory, University of California at Berkeley; Tucson, AZ; 11 November 2014

*Kevin B. Marvel; Executive Officer, American Astronomical Society; Tucson, AZ, and Washington, DC; 15 October 2013 and 14 July 2014

Ralph L. McNutt; Chief Scientist, Johns Hopkins University Applied Physics Laboratory; Tucson, AZ; 11 November 2014

Michael H. Moloney; Director for Space and Aeronautics, National Research Council; Washington, DC; 15 July 2014 and 18 March 2015

Richard M. Obermann; Democratic Chief of Staff, House Committee on Science, Space, and Technology; Washington, DC; 22 October 2014

Kathie L. Olsen; Founder and Managing Director, ScienceWorks International LLC, former NASA Chief Scientist, and former NSF Deputy Director; telephone interview; 25 August 2014

Joel R. Parriot; Deputy Executive Officer and Director of Public Policy, American Astronomical Society; Washington, DC; 14 July 2014

*Charles J. Pellerin; President, 4-D Systems, former NASA Director of Astrophysics; telephone interview; 23 October 2013

Jeffrey D. Rosendhal; former NASA Assistant Associate Administrator for Space Science and Applications; Washington, DC; 15 November 2013

*Marcia J. Rieke; Regents' Professor of Astronomy, University of Arizona; Tucson, AZ; 11 November 2014

Harrison H. Schmitt; Honorary Associate and Fellow of the College of Engineering at University of Wisconsin-Madison and former NAC Chair; telephone interview; 17 February 2015

*Kathryn S. Schmoll; former Vice President for Finance and Administration, University

Corporation for Atmospheric Research; Boulder, CO; 3 November 2014

Donald C. Shapero; Senior Program Officer, National Research Council; Washington, DC; 17 December 2013

Paul Shawcross; Science and Space Branch Chief, Office of Management and Budget; with Grace Hu and J. D. Kundu, OMB budget examiners; telephone interview; 30 December 2014

David S. Smith; Senior Program Officer, National Research Council; Washington, DC; 15 July 2013

*Marcia S. Smith; Founder and Editor, SpacePolicyOnline.com, and former SSB Director; Washington, DC; 3 September 2013

Steven W. Squyres; James A. Weeks Professor of Physical Sciences, Cornell University, and Chair, NASA Advisory Council; telephone interview; 28 January 2015

*S. Alan Stern; CEO and President, The Golden Spike Company, and former NASA Associate Administrator for Science; telephone interview; 6 August 2014

Ellen Stofan; NASA Chief Scientist; telephone interview; 12 January 2015

Stephen E. Strom; former Chair of the Five College Observatory Astronomy Department, MA, and former member of the scientific staff, National Optical Astronomy Observatory; Tucson, AZ; 6 November 2014

Michael S. Turner; Bruce and Diana Rauner Distinguished Service Professor in Astronomy and Astrophysics, Enrico Fermi Institute, Director, Kavli Institute for Cosmological Physics, University of Chicago, and former NSF Assistant Director for Mathematics and Physical Sciences; Chicago, IL; 11 November 2013

*Edward J. Weiler; former NASA Associate Administrator for Science; Washington, DC; 14 August 2013

Pamela L. Whitney; Professional Staff Member, House Committee on Science, Space, and Technology; Washington, DC; 8 August 2014

Gregory J. Williams; Deputy Associate Administrator for Policy and Plans, Human Exploration and Operations Mission Directorate; telephone interview; 21 February 2014

George L. Withbroe; former Director of the NASA Sun-Earth Connection Division; telephone interview; 25 July 2014

Dan Woods; Director for Strategic Integration and Management, NASA Science Mission Directorate; Washington, DC; 23 March 2015

*A. Thomas Young; former Executive Vice President, Lockheed Martin Corporation, and former SSB Vice Chair; telephone interview; 20 February 2014

Acronyms

AAAC	Astronomy and Astrophysics Advisory Committee
AEC	Atomic Energy Commission
AFTA	Astrophysics Focused Telescope Assets
AIM	Astrometric Interferometry Mission
APL	Applied Physics Laboratory
AMB	Astronomy Missions Board
AMS	Alpha Magnetic Spectrometer
ASEB	Aeronautics and Space Engineering Board
Athena	Advanced Telescope for High Energy Astrophysics
AURA	Association of Universities for Research in Astronomy
AXAF	Advanced X-ray Astrophysics Facility
BPA	Board on Physics and Astronomy
CATE	cost and technical evaluation
COBE	Cosmic Background Explorer
CODMAC	Committee on Data Management and Computation
COMPLEX	Committee on Planetary and Lunar Exploration
Con-X	Constellation-X x-ray observatory
COSEPUP	Committee on Science, Engineering, and Public Policy
COSPAR	Committee on Space Research
COSPUP	Committee on Science and Public Policy
CRAF	Comet Rendezvous and Asteroid Flyby
CRS	Congressional Research Service
CSSP	Committee on Solar and Space Physics
CSTR	Committee on Solar Terrestrial Research
DOC	Department of Commerce
DOD	Department of Defense
DOE	Department of Energy
ELV	expendable launch vehicle
EOS	Earth Observing System
ESA	European Space Agency
ESAC	Earth Sciences Advisory Committee
ESSC	European Space Science Committee
ESSC	Earth System Sciences Committee
EUVE	Extreme Ultraviolet Explorer
FACA	Federal Advisory Committee Act
FESAC	Fusion Energy Sciences Advisory Committee
FUSE	Far-Ultraviolet Spectroscopic Explorer
GLAST	Gamma-ray Large Area Space Telescope
GP-B	Gravity Probe B
GPRA	Government Performance and Results Act
GPRAMA	GPRA Modernization Act
HEAO	High-Energy Astrophysics Observatory
HEPAP	High Energy Physics Advisory Panel
HRC	Historical Reference Collection
HST	Hubble Space Telescope
IGY	International Geophysical Year
IMCE	International Space Station Management and Cost Evaluation
IRT	Independent Review Team
ISPM	International Solar Polar Mission
ISS	International Space Station
IXO	International X-ray Observatory
JAXA	Japanese Space Agency
JDEM	Joint Dark Energy Mission
JWST	James Webb Space Telescope
LGO	Lunar Geoscience Observer
LISA	Laser Interferometer Space Antenna
LPMB	Lunar and Planetary Missions Board
LST	Large Space Telescope

MAO	Mars Aeronomy Observer		P5	Particle Physics Project Prioritization Panel
MEPAG	Mars Exploration Program Analysis Group		PAC	Physics Advisory Committee
MOWG	Management Operations Working Group		PSC	Physical Sciences Committee
MPIAT	Mars Program Independent Assessment Team		RTAC	Research and Technology Advisory Council
MPSAC	Mathematical and Physical Sciences Advisory Committee		RRC	Report Review Committee
NACA	National Advisory Committee for Aeronautics		SAB	Space Applications Board
			SAC	Science Advisory Committee
NAC	NASA Advisory Council		SAFIR	Single Aperture Far Infra-Red observatory
NAE	National Academy of Engineering			
NAPA	National Academy of Public Administration		SDO	Solar Dynamics Observatory
			SDT	Science Definition Team
NAS	National Academy of Sciences		SESAC	Space and Earth Science Advisory Committee
NASA	National Aeronautics and Space Administration		SIM	Space Interferometry Mission
			SIRTF	Space Infra-Red Telescope Facility
NBS	National Bureau of Standards		SMD	Science Mission Directorate
NEAR	Near Earth Asteroid Rendezvous		SNAP	Super Nova Acceleration Probe
NEO	near-Earth asteroid		SOFIA	Stratospheric Observatory for Infrared Astronomy
NESDIS	National Environmental Satellite, Data, and Information Service			
			SPAC	Space Program Advisory Council
NOAA	National Oceanic and Atmospheric Administration		SSB	Space Science Board or Space Studies Board (after 1989)
NRC	National Research Council		SSAC	Space Science Advisory Committee
NRL	Naval Research Laboratory		SSEC	Solar System Exploration Committee
NSAC	Nuclear Science Advisory Committee		SSAAC	Space Science and Applications Advisory Committee
NSB	National Science Board			
NSF	National Science Foundation		STScI	Space Telescope Science Institute
OAO	Orbiting Astronomical Observatory		TPF	Terrestrial Planet Finder
OMB	Office of Management and Budget		UARRP	Upper Atmosphere Rocket Research Panel
OSSA	Office of Space Science and Applications			
			UNH	University of New Hampshire
OTA	Office of Technology Assessment		WFIRST	Wide Field Infrared Survey Telescope

About the Author

Joseph K. Alexander is a space scientist who pursued his research career at the NASA Goddard Space Flight Center. He subsequently served in senior science management and policy development roles at the National Research Council, the Environmental Protection Agency's Office of Research and Development, NASA Headquarters, and the White House Office of Science and Technology Policy. He and his wife, Diana, reside outside Tucson, Arizona.

The NASA History Series

REFERENCE WORKS, NASA SP-4000

Grimwood, James M. *Project Mercury: A Chronology.* NASA SP-4001, 1963.

Grimwood, James M., and Barton C. Hacker, with Peter J. Vorzimmer. *Project Gemini Technology and Operations: A Chronology.* NASA SP-4002, 1969.

Link, Mae Mills. *Space Medicine in Project Mercury.* NASA SP-4003, 1965.

Astronautics and Aeronautics, 1963: Chronology of Science, Technology, and Policy. NASA SP-4004, 1964.

Astronautics and Aeronautics, 1964: Chronology of Science, Technology, and Policy. NASA SP-4005, 1965.

Astronautics and Aeronautics, 1965: Chronology of Science, Technology, and Policy. NASA SP-4006, 1966.

Astronautics and Aeronautics, 1966: Chronology of Science, Technology, and Policy. NASA SP-4007, 1967.

Astronautics and Aeronautics, 1967: Chronology of Science, Technology, and Policy. NASA SP-4008, 1968.

Ertel, Ivan D., and Mary Louise Morse. *The Apollo Spacecraft: A Chronology, Volume I, Through November 7, 1962.* NASA SP-4009, 1969.

Morse, Mary Louise, and Jean Kernahan Bays. *The Apollo Spacecraft: A Chronology, Volume II, November 8, 1962–September 30, 1964.* NASA SP-4009, 1973.

Brooks, Courtney G., and Ivan D. Ertel. *The Apollo Spacecraft: A Chronology, Volume III, October 1, 1964–January 20, 1966.* NASA SP-4009, 1973.

Ertel, Ivan D., and Roland W. Newkirk, with Courtney G. Brooks. *The Apollo Spacecraft: A Chronology, Volume IV, January 21, 1966–July 13, 1974.* NASA SP-4009, 1978.

Astronautics and Aeronautics, 1968: Chronology of Science, Technology, and Policy. NASA SP-4010, 1969.

Newkirk, Roland W., and Ivan D. Ertel, with Courtney G. Brooks. *Skylab: A Chronology.* NASA SP-4011, 1977.

Van Nimmen, Jane, and Leonard C. Bruno, with Robert L. Rosholt. *NASA Historical Data Book, Volume I: NASA Resources, 1958–1968.* NASA SP-4012, 1976; rep. ed. 1988.

Ezell, Linda Neuman. *NASA Historical Data Book, Volume II: Programs and Projects, 1958–1968.* NASA SP-4012, 1988.

Ezell, Linda Neuman. *NASA Historical Data Book, Volume III: Programs and Projects, 1969–1978.* NASA SP-4012, 1988.

Gawdiak, Ihor, with Helen Fedor. *NASA Historical Data Book, Volume IV: NASA Resources, 1969–1978.* NASA SP-4012, 1994.

Rumerman, Judy A. *NASA Historical Data Book, Volume V: NASA Launch Systems, Space Transportation, Human Spaceflight, and Space Science, 1979–1988*. NASA SP-4012, 1999.

Rumerman, Judy A. *NASA Historical Data Book, Volume VI: NASA Space Applications, Aeronautics and Space Research and Technology, Tracking and Data Acquisition/Support Operations, Commercial Programs, and Resources, 1979–1988*. NASA SP-4012, 1999.

Rumerman, Judy A. *NASA Historical Data Book, Volume VII: NASA Launch Systems, Space Transportation, Human Spaceflight, and Space Science, 1989–1998*. NASA SP-2009-4012, 2009.

Rumerman, Judy A. *NASA Historical Data Book, Volume VIII: NASA Earth Science and Space Applications, Aeronautics, Technology, and Exploration, Tracking and Data Acquisition/ Space Operations, Facilities and Resources, 1989–1998*. NASA SP-2012-4012, 2012.

No SP-4013.

Astronautics and Aeronautics, 1969: Chronology of Science, Technology, and Policy. NASA SP-4014, 1970.

Astronautics and Aeronautics, 1970: Chronology of Science, Technology, and Policy. NASA SP-4015, 1972.

Astronautics and Aeronautics, 1971: Chronology of Science, Technology, and Policy. NASA SP-4016, 1972.

Astronautics and Aeronautics, 1972: Chronology of Science, Technology, and Policy. NASA SP-4017, 1974.

Astronautics and Aeronautics, 1973: Chronology of Science, Technology, and Policy. NASA SP-4018, 1975.

Astronautics and Aeronautics, 1974: Chronology of Science, Technology, and Policy. NASA SP-4019, 1977.

Astronautics and Aeronautics, 1975: Chronology of Science, Technology, and Policy. NASA SP-4020, 1979.

Astronautics and Aeronautics, 1976: Chronology of Science, Technology, and Policy. NASA SP-4021, 1984.

Astronautics and Aeronautics, 1977: Chronology of Science, Technology, and Policy. NASA SP-4022, 1986.

Astronautics and Aeronautics, 1978: Chronology of Science, Technology, and Policy. NASA SP-4023, 1986.

Astronautics and Aeronautics, 1979–1984: Chronology of Science, Technology, and Policy. NASA SP-4024, 1988.

Astronautics and Aeronautics, 1985: Chronology of Science, Technology, and Policy. NASA SP-4025, 1990.

Noordung, Hermann. *The Problem of Space Travel: The Rocket Motor*. Edited by Ernst Stuhlinger and J. D. Hunley, with Jennifer Garland. NASA SP-4026, 1995.

Gawdiak, Ihor Y., Ramon J. Miro, and Sam Stueland. *Astronautics and Aeronautics, 1986– 1990: A Chronology*. NASA SP-4027, 1997.

Gawdiak, Ihor Y., and Charles Shetland. *Astronautics and Aeronautics, 1991–1995: A Chronology*. NASA SP-2000-4028, 2000.

Orloff, Richard W. *Apollo by the Numbers: A Statistical Reference*. NASA SP-2000-4029, 2000.

Lewis, Marieke, and Ryan Swanson. *Astronautics and Aeronautics: A Chronology, 1996–2000*. NASA SP-2009-4030, 2009.

Ivey, William Noel, and Marieke Lewis. *Astronautics and Aeronautics: A Chronology, 2001–2005*. NASA SP-2010-4031, 2010.

Buchalter, Alice R., and William Noel Ivey. *Astronautics and Aeronautics: A Chronology, 2006*. NASA SP-2011-4032, 2010.

Lewis, Marieke. *Astronautics and Aeronautics: A Chronology, 2007*. NASA SP-2011-4033, 2011.

Lewis, Marieke. *Astronautics and Aeronautics: A Chronology, 2008*. NASA SP-2012-4034, 2012.

Lewis, Marieke. *Astronautics and Aeronautics: A Chronology, 2009*. NASA SP-2012-4035, 2012.

Flattery, Meaghan. *Astronautics and Aeronautics: A Chronology*, 2010. NASA SP-2013-4037, 2014.

MANAGEMENT HISTORIES, NASA SP-4100

Rosholt, Robert L. *An Administrative History of NASA, 1958–1963*. NASA SP-4101, 1966.

Levine, Arnold S. *Managing NASA in the Apollo Era*. NASA SP-4102, 1982.

Roland, Alex. *Model Research: The National Advisory Committee for Aeronautics, 1915–1958*. NASA SP-4103, 1985.

Fries, Sylvia D. *NASA Engineers and the Age of Apollo*. NASA SP-4104, 1992.

Glennan, T. Keith. *The Birth of NASA: The Diary of T. Keith Glennan*. Edited by J. D. Hunley. NASA SP-4105, 1993.

Seamans, Robert C. *Aiming at Targets: The Autobiography of Robert C. Seamans*. NASA SP-4106, 1996.

Garber, Stephen J., ed. *Looking Backward, Looking Forward: Forty Years of Human Spaceflight Symposium*. NASA SP-2002-4107, 2002.

Mallick, Donald L., with Peter W. Merlin. *The Smell of Kerosene: A Test Pilot's Odyssey*. NASA SP-4108, 2003.

Iliff, Kenneth W., and Curtis L. Peebles. *From Runway to Orbit: Reflections of a NASA Engineer*. NASA SP-2004-4109, 2004.

Chertok, Boris. *Rockets and People, Volume I*. NASA SP-2005-4110, 2005.

Chertok, Boris. *Rockets and People: Creating a Rocket Industry, Volume II*. NASA SP-2006-4110, 2006.

Chertok, Boris. *Rockets and People: Hot Days of the Cold War, Volume III*. NASA SP-2009-4110, 2009.

Chertok, Boris. *Rockets and People: The Moon Race, Volume IV*. NASA SP-2011-4110, 2011.

Laufer, Alexander, Todd Post, and Edward Hoffman. *Shared Voyage: Learning and Unlearning from Remarkable Projects*. NASA SP-2005-4111, 2005.

Dawson, Virginia P., and Mark D. Bowles. *Realizing the Dream of Flight: Biographical Essays in Honor of the Centennial of Flight, 1903–2003*. NASA SP-2005-4112, 2005.

Mudgway, Douglas J. *William H. Pickering: America's Deep Space Pioneer*. NASA SP-2008-4113, 2008.

Wright, Rebecca, Sandra Johnson, and Steven J. Dick. *NASA at 50: Interviews with NASA's Senior Leadership*. NASA SP-2012-4114, 2012.

PROJECT HISTORIES, NASA SP-4200

Swenson, Loyd S., Jr., James M. Grimwood, and Charles C. Alexander. *This New Ocean: A History of Project Mercury*. NASA SP-4201, 1966; rep. ed. 1999.

Green, Constance McLaughlin, and Milton Lomask. *Vanguard: A History*. NASA SP-4202, 1970; rep. ed. Smithsonian Institution Press, 1971.

Hacker, Barton C., and James M. Grimwood. *On the Shoulders of Titans: A History of Project Gemini*. NASA SP-4203, 1977; rep. ed. 2002.

Benson, Charles D., and William Barnaby Faherty. *Moonport: A History of Apollo Launch Facilities and Operations*. NASA SP-4204, 1978.

Brooks, Courtney G., James M. Grimwood, and Loyd S. Swenson, Jr. *Chariots for Apollo: A History of Manned Lunar Spacecraft*. NASA SP-4205, 1979.

Bilstein, Roger E. *Stages to Saturn: A Technological History of the Apollo/Saturn Launch Vehicles*. NASA SP-4206, 1980 and 1996.

No SP-4207.

Compton, W. David, and Charles D. Benson. *Living and Working in Space: A History of Skylab*. NASA SP-4208, 1983.

Ezell, Edward Clinton, and Linda Neuman Ezell. *The Partnership: A History of the Apollo-Soyuz Test Project*. NASA SP-4209, 1978.

Hall, R. Cargill. *Lunar Impact: A History of Project Ranger*. NASA SP-4210, 1977.

Newell, Homer E. *Beyond the Atmosphere: Early Years of Space Science*. NASA SP-4211, 1980.

Ezell, Edward Clinton, and Linda Neuman Ezell. *On Mars: Exploration of the Red Planet, 1958–1978*. NASA SP-4212, 1984.

Pitts, John A. *The Human Factor: Biomedicine in the Manned Space Program to 1980*. NASA SP-4213, 1985.

Compton, W. David. *Where No Man Has Gone Before: A History of Apollo Lunar Exploration Missions*. NASA SP-4214, 1989.

Naugle, John E. *First Among Equals: The Selection of NASA Space Science Experiments*. NASA SP-4215, 1991.

Wallace, Lane E. *Airborne Trailblazer: Two Decades with NASA Langley's 737 Flying Laboratory*. NASA SP-4216, 1994.

Butrica, Andrew J., ed. *Beyond the Ionosphere: Fifty Years of Satellite Communications*. NASA SP-4217, 1997.

Butrica, Andrew J. *To See the Unseen: A History of Planetary Radar Astronomy*. NASA SP-4218, 1996.

Mack, Pamela E., ed. *From Engineering Science to Big Science: The NACA and NASA Collier Trophy Research Project Winners*. NASA SP-4219, 1998.

Reed, R. Dale. *Wingless Flight: The Lifting Body Story*. NASA SP-4220, 1998.

Heppenheimer, T. A. *The Space Shuttle Decision: NASA's Search for a Reusable Space Vehicle*. NASA SP-4221, 1999.

Hunley, J. D., ed. *Toward Mach 2: The Douglas D-558 Program*. NASA SP-4222, 1999.

Swanson, Glen E., ed. *"Before This Decade Is Out…" Personal Reflections on the Apollo Program*. NASA SP-4223, 1999.

Tomayko, James E. *Computers Take Flight: A History of NASA's Pioneering Digital Fly-By-Wire Project*. NASA SP-4224, 2000.

Morgan, Clay. *Shuttle-Mir: The United States and Russia Share History's Highest Stage*. NASA SP-2001-4225, 2001.

Leary, William M. *"We Freeze to Please": A History of NASA's Icing Research Tunnel and the Quest for Safety*. NASA SP-2002-4226, 2002.

Mudgway, Douglas J. *Uplink-Downlink: A History of the Deep Space Network, 1957–1997*. NASA SP-2001-4227, 2001.

No SP-4228 or SP-4229.

Dawson, Virginia P., and Mark D. Bowles. *Taming Liquid Hydrogen: The Centaur Upper Stage Rocket, 1958–2002*. NASA SP-2004-4230, 2004.

Meltzer, Michael. *Mission to Jupiter: A History of the Galileo Project*. NASA SP-2007-4231, 2007.

Heppenheimer, T. A. *Facing the Heat Barrier: A History of Hypersonics*. NASA SP-2007-4232, 2007.

Tsiao, Sunny. *"Read You Loud and Clear!" The Story of NASA's Spaceflight Tracking and Data Network*. NASA SP-2007-4233, 2007.

Meltzer, Michael. *When Biospheres Collide: A History of NASA's Planetary Protection Programs*. NASA SP-2011-4234, 2011.

CENTER HISTORIES, NASA SP-4300

Rosenthal, Alfred. *Venture into Space: Early Years of Goddard Space Flight Center*. NASA SP-4301, 1985.

Hartman, Edwin P. *Adventures in Research: A History of Ames Research Center, 1940–1965*. NASA SP-4302, 1970.

Hallion, Richard P. *On the Frontier: Flight Research at Dryden, 1946–1981*. NASA SP-4303, 1984.

Muenger, Elizabeth A. *Searching the Horizon: A History of Ames Research Center, 1940–1976*. NASA SP-4304, 1985.

Hansen, James R. *Engineer in Charge: A History of the Langley Aeronautical Laboratory, 1917–1958*. NASA SP-4305, 1987.

Dawson, Virginia P. *Engines and Innovation: Lewis Laboratory and American Propulsion Technology*. NASA SP-4306, 1991.

Dethloff, Henry C. *"Suddenly Tomorrow Came…": A History of the Johnson Space Center, 1957–1990.* NASA SP-4307, 1993.

Hansen, James R. *Spaceflight Revolution: NASA Langley Research Center from Sputnik to Apollo.* NASA SP-4308, 1995.

Wallace, Lane E. *Flights of Discovery: An Illustrated History of the Dryden Flight Research Center.* NASA SP-4309, 1996.

Herring, Mack R. *Way Station to Space: A History of the John C. Stennis Space Center.* NASA SP-4310, 1997.

Wallace, Harold D., Jr. *Wallops Station and the Creation of an American Space Program.* NASA SP-4311, 1997.

Wallace, Lane E. *Dreams, Hopes, Realities. NASA's Goddard Space Flight Center: The First Forty Years.* NASA SP-4312, 1999.

Dunar, Andrew J., and Stephen P. Waring. *Power to Explore: A History of Marshall Space Flight Center, 1960–1990.* NASA SP-4313, 1999.

Bugos, Glenn E. *Atmosphere of Freedom: Sixty Years at the NASA Ames Research Center.* NASA SP-2000-4314, 2000.

Bugos, Glenn E. *Atmosphere of Freedom: Seventy Years at the NASA Ames Research Center.* NASA SP-2010-4314, 2010. Revised version of NASA SP-2000-4314.

Bugos, Glenn E. *Atmosphere of Freedom: Seventy Five Years at the NASA Ames Research Center.* NASA SP-2014-4314, 2014. Revised version of NASA SP-2000-4314.

No SP-4315.

Schultz, James. *Crafting Flight: Aircraft Pioneers and the Contributions of the Men and Women of NASA Langley Research Center.* NASA SP-2003-4316, 2003.

Bowles, Mark D. *Science in Flux: NASA's Nuclear Program at Plum Brook Station, 1955–2005.* NASA SP-2006-4317, 2006.

Wallace, Lane E. *Flights of Discovery: An Illustrated History of the Dryden Flight Research Center.* NASA SP-2007-4318, 2007. Revised version of NASA SP-4309.

Arrighi, Robert S. *Revolutionary Atmosphere: The Story of the Altitude Wind Tunnel and the Space Power Chambers.* NASA SP-2010-4319, 2010.

GENERAL HISTORIES, NASA SP-4400

Corliss, William R. *NASA Sounding Rockets, 1958–1968: A Historical Summary.* NASA SP-4401, 1971.

Wells, Helen T., Susan H. Whiteley, and Carrie Karegeannes. *Origins of NASA Names.* NASA SP-4402, 1976.

Anderson, Frank W., Jr. *Orders of Magnitude: A History of NACA and NASA, 1915–1980.* NASA SP-4403, 1981.

Sloop, John L. *Liquid Hydrogen as a Propulsion Fuel, 1945–1959.* NASA SP-4404, 1978.

Roland, Alex. *A Spacefaring People: Perspectives on Early Spaceflight.* NASA SP-4405, 1985.

Bilstein, Roger E. *Orders of Magnitude: A History of the NACA and NASA, 1915–1990.* NASA SP-4406, 1989.

Logsdon, John M., ed., with Linda J. Lear, Jannelle Warren Findley, Ray A. Williamson, and Dwayne A. Day. *Exploring the Unknown: Selected Documents in the History of the U.S. Civil Space Program, Volume I: Organizing for Exploration*. NASA SP-4407, 1995.

Logsdon, John M., ed., with Dwayne A. Day and Roger D. Launius. *Exploring the Unknown: Selected Documents in the History of the U.S. Civil Space Program, Volume II: External Relationships*. NASA SP-4407, 1996.

Logsdon, John M., ed., with Roger D. Launius, David H. Onkst, and Stephen J. Garber. *Exploring the Unknown: Selected Documents in the History of the U.S. Civil Space Program, Volume III: Using Space*. NASA SP-4407, 1998.

Logsdon, John M., ed., with Ray A. Williamson, Roger D. Launius, Russell J. Acker, Stephen J. Garber, and Jonathan L. Friedman. *Exploring the Unknown: Selected Documents in the History of the U.S. Civil Space Program, Volume IV: Accessing Space*. NASA SP-4407, 1999.

Logsdon, John M., ed., with Amy Paige Snyder, Roger D. Launius, Stephen J. Garber, and Regan Anne Newport. *Exploring the Unknown: Selected Documents in the History of the U.S. Civil Space Program, Volume V: Exploring the Cosmos*. NASA SP-2001-4407, 2001.

Logsdon, John M., ed., with Stephen J. Garber, Roger D. Launius, and Ray A. Williamson. *Exploring the Unknown: Selected Documents in the History of the U.S. Civil Space Program, Volume VI: Space and Earth Science*. NASA SP-2004-4407, 2004.

Logsdon, John M., ed., with Roger D. Launius. *Exploring the Unknown: Selected Documents in the History of the U.S. Civil Space Program,*

Volume VII: Human Spaceflight: Projects Mercury, Gemini, and Apollo. NASA SP-2008-4407, 2008.

Siddiqi, Asif A., *Challenge to Apollo: The Soviet Union and the Space Race, 1945–1974*. NASA SP-2000-4408, 2000.

Hansen, James R., ed. *The Wind and Beyond: Journey into the History of Aerodynamics in America, Volume 1: The Ascent of the Airplane*. NASA SP-2003-4409, 2003.

Hansen, James R., ed. *The Wind and Beyond: Journey into the History of Aerodynamics in America, Volume 2: Reinventing the Airplane*. NASA SP-2007-4409, 2007.

Hogan, Thor. *Mars Wars: The Rise and Fall of the Space Exploration Initiative*. NASA SP-2007-4410, 2007.

Vakoch, Douglas A., ed. *Psychology of Space Exploration: Contemporary Research in Historical Perspective*. NASA SP-2011-4411, 2011.

Ferguson, Robert G., *NASA's First A: Aeronautics from 1958 to 2008*. NASA SP-2012-4412, 2013.

Vakoch, Douglas A., ed. *Archaeology, Anthropology, and Interstellar Communication*. NASA SP-2013-4413, 2014.

MONOGRAPHS IN AEROSPACE HISTORY, NASA SP-4500

Launius, Roger D., and Aaron K. Gillette, comps. *Toward a History of the Space Shuttle: An Annotated Bibliography*. Monographs in Aerospace History, No. 1, 1992.

Launius, Roger D., and J. D. Hunley, comps. *An Annotated Bibliography of the Apollo Program.* Monographs in Aerospace History, No. 2, 1994.

Launius, Roger D. *Apollo: A Retrospective Analysis.* Monographs in Aerospace History, No. 3, 1994.

Hansen, James R. *Enchanted Rendezvous: John C. Houbolt and the Genesis of the Lunar-Orbit Rendezvous Concept.* Monographs in Aerospace History, No. 4, 1995.

Gorn, Michael H. *Hugh L. Dryden's Career in Aviation and Space.* Monographs in Aerospace History, No. 5, 1996.

Powers, Sheryll Goecke. *Women in Flight Research at NASA Dryden Flight Research Center from 1946 to 1995.* Monographs in Aerospace History, No. 6, 1997.

Portree, David S. F., and Robert C. Trevino. *Walking to Olympus: An EVA Chronology.* Monographs in Aerospace History, No. 7, 1997.

Logsdon, John M., moderator. *Legislative Origins of the National Aeronautics and Space Act of 1958: Proceedings of an Oral History Workshop.* Monographs in Aerospace History, No. 8, 1998.

Rumerman, Judy A., comp. *U.S. Human Spaceflight: A Record of Achievement, 1961–1998.* Monographs in Aerospace History, No. 9, 1998.

Portree, David S. F. *NASA's Origins and the Dawn of the Space Age.* Monographs in Aerospace History, No. 10, 1998.

Logsdon, John M. *Together in Orbit: The Origins of International Cooperation in the Space Station.* Monographs in Aerospace History, No. 11, 1998.

Phillips, W. Hewitt. *Journey in Aeronautical Research: A Career at NASA Langley Research Center.* Monographs in Aerospace History, No. 12, 1998.

Braslow, Albert L. *A History of Suction-Type Laminar-Flow Control with Emphasis on Flight Research.* Monographs in Aerospace History, No. 13, 1999.

Logsdon, John M., moderator. *Managing the Moon Program: Lessons Learned from Apollo.* Monographs in Aerospace History, No. 14, 1999.

Perminov, V. G. *The Difficult Road to Mars: A Brief History of Mars Exploration in the Soviet Union.* Monographs in Aerospace History, No. 15, 1999.

Tucker, Tom. *Touchdown: The Development of Propulsion Controlled Aircraft at NASA Dryden.* Monographs in Aerospace History, No. 16, 1999.

Maisel, Martin, Demo J. Giulanetti, and Daniel C. Dugan. *The History of the XV-15 Tilt Rotor Research Aircraft: From Concept to Flight.* Monographs in Aerospace History, No. 17, 2000. NASA SP-2000-4517.

Jenkins, Dennis R. *Hypersonics Before the Shuttle: A Concise History of the X-15 Research Airplane.* Monographs in Aerospace History, No. 18, 2000. NASA SP-2000-4518.

Chambers, Joseph R. *Partners in Freedom: Contributions of the Langley Research Center to U.S. Military Aircraft of the 1990s.* Monographs in Aerospace History, No. 19, 2000. NASA SP-2000-4519.

Waltman, Gene L. *Black Magic and Gremlins: Analog Flight Simulations at NASA's Flight Research Center.* Monographs in Aerospace History, No. 20, 2000. NASA SP-2000-4520.

Portree, David S. F. *Humans to Mars: Fifty Years of Mission Planning, 1950–2000.* Monographs in Aerospace History, No. 21, 2001. NASA SP-2001-4521.

Thompson, Milton O., with J. D. Hunley. *Flight Research: Problems Encountered and What They Should Teach Us.* Monographs in Aerospace History, No. 22, 2001. NASA SP-2001-4522.

Tucker, Tom. *The Eclipse Project.* Monographs in Aerospace History, No. 23, 2001. NASA SP-2001-4523.

Siddiqi, Asif A. *Deep Space Chronicle: A Chronology of Deep Space and Planetary Probes, 1958–2000.* Monographs in Aerospace History, No. 24, 2002. NASA SP-2002-4524.

Merlin, Peter W. *Mach 3+: NASA/USAF YF-12 Flight Research, 1969–1979.* Monographs in Aerospace History, No. 25, 2001. NASA SP-2001-4525.

Anderson, Seth B. *Memoirs of an Aeronautical Engineer: Flight Tests at Ames Research Center: 1940–1970.* Monographs in Aerospace History, No. 26, 2002. NASA SP-2002-4526.

Renstrom, Arthur G. *Wilbur and Orville Wright: A Bibliography Commemorating the One-Hundredth Anniversary of the First Powered Flight on December 17, 1903.* Monographs in Aerospace History, No. 27, 2002. NASA SP-2002-4527.

No monograph 28.

Chambers, Joseph R. *Concept to Reality: Contributions of the NASA Langley Research Center to U.S. Civil Aircraft of the 1990s.* Monographs in Aerospace History, No. 29, 2003. NASA SP-2003-4529.

Peebles, Curtis, ed. *The Spoken Word: Recollections of Dryden History, The Early Years.* Monographs in Aerospace History, No. 30, 2003. NASA SP-2003-4530.

Jenkins, Dennis R., Tony Landis, and Jay Miller. *American X-Vehicles: An Inventory—X-1 to X-50.* Monographs in Aerospace History, No. 31, 2003. NASA SP-2003-4531.

Renstrom, Arthur G. *Wilbur and Orville Wright: A Chronology Commemorating the One-Hundredth Anniversary of the First Powered Flight on December 17, 1903.* Monographs in Aerospace History, No. 32, 2003. NASA SP-2003-4532.

Bowles, Mark D., and Robert S. Arrighi. *NASA's Nuclear Frontier: The Plum Brook Research Reactor.* Monographs in Aerospace History, No. 33, 2004. NASA SP-2004-4533.

Wallace, Lane, and Christian Gelzer. *Nose Up: High Angle-of-Attack and Thrust Vectoring Research at NASA Dryden, 1979–2001.* Monographs in Aerospace History, No. 34, 2009. NASA SP-2009-4534.

Matranga, Gene J., C. Wayne Ottinger, Calvin R. Jarvis, and D. Christian Gelzer. *Unconventional, Contrary, and Ugly: The Lunar Landing Research Vehicle.* Monographs in Aerospace History, No. 35, 2006. NASA SP-2004-4535.

McCurdy, Howard E. *Low-Cost Innovation in Spaceflight: The History of the Near Earth Asteroid Rendezvous (NEAR) Mission.* Monographs in Aerospace History, No. 36, 2005. NASA SP-2005-4536.

Seamans, Robert C., Jr. *Project Apollo: The Tough Decisions.* Monographs in Aerospace History, No. 37, 2005. NASA SP-2005-4537.

Lambright, W. Henry. *NASA and the Environment: The Case of Ozone Depletion.* Monographs in Aerospace History, No. 38, 2005. NASA SP-2005-4538.

Chambers, Joseph R. *Innovation in Flight: Research of the NASA Langley Research Center on Revolutionary Advanced Concepts for Aeronautics.* Monographs in Aerospace History, No. 39, 2005. NASA SP-2005-4539.

Phillips, W. Hewitt. *Journey into Space Research: Continuation of a Career at NASA Langley Research Center.* Monographs in Aerospace History, No. 40, 2005. NASA SP-2005-4540.

Rumerman, Judy A., Chris Gamble, and Gabriel Okolski, comps. *U.S. Human Spaceflight: A Record of Achievement, 1961–2006.* Monographs in Aerospace History, No. 41, 2007. NASA SP-2007-4541.

Peebles, Curtis. *The Spoken Word: Recollections of Dryden History Beyond the Sky.* Monographs in Aerospace History, No. 42, 2011. NASA SP-2011-4542.

Dick, Steven J., Stephen J. Garber, and Jane H. Odom. *Research in NASA History.* Monographs in Aerospace History, No. 43, 2009. NASA SP-2009-4543.

Merlin, Peter W. *Ikhana: Unmanned Aircraft System Western States Fire Missions.* Monographs

in Aerospace History, No. 44, 2009. NASA SP-2009-4544.

Fisher, Steven C., and Shamim A. Rahman. *Remembering the Giants: Apollo Rocket Propulsion Development.* Monographs in Aerospace History, No. 45, 2009. NASA SP-2009-4545.

Gelzer, Christian. *Fairing Well: From Shoebox to Bat Truck and Beyond, Aerodynamic Truck Research at NASA's Dryden Flight Research Center.* Monographs in Aerospace History, No. 46, 2011. NASA SP-2011-4546.

Arrighi, Robert. *Pursuit of Power: NASA's Propulsion Systems Laboratory No. 1 and 2.* Monographs in Aerospace History, No. 48, 2012. NASA SP-2012-4548.

Renee M. Rottner. *Making the Invisible Visible: A History of the Spitzer Infrared Telescope Facility (1971–2003).* Monographs in Aerospace History, No. 47, 2017. NASA SP-2017-4547.

Goodrich, Malinda K., Alice R. Buchalter, and Patrick M. Miller, comps. *Toward a History of the Space Shuttle: An Annotated Bibliography, Part 2 (1992–2011).* Monographs in Aerospace History, No. 49, 2012. NASA SP-2012-4549.

Ta, Julie B., and Robert C. Treviño. *Walking to Olympus: An EVA Chronology, 1997–2011*, Vol. 2. Monographs in Aerospace History, No. 50, 2016. NASA SP-2016-4550.

Gelzer, Christian. *The Spoken Word III: Recollections of Dryden History; The Shuttle Years.* Monographs in Aerospace History, No. 52, 2013. NASA SP-2013-4552.

Ross, James C. *NASA Photo One.* Monographs in Aerospace History, No. 53, 2013. NASA SP-2013-4553.

Launius, Roger D. *Historical Analogs for the Stimulation of Space Commerce.* Monographs in Aerospace History, No 54, 2014. NASA SP-2014-4554.

Buchalter, Alice R., and Patrick M. Miller, comps. *The National Advisory Committee for Aeronautics: An Annotated Bibliography.* Monographs in Aerospace History, No. 55, 2014. NASA SP-2014-4555.

Chambers, Joseph R., and Mark A. Chambers. *Emblems of Exploration: Logos of the NACA and NASA.* Monographs in Aerospace History, No. 56, 2015. NASA SP-2015-4556.

ELECTRONIC MEDIA, NASA SP-4600

Remembering Apollo 11: The 30th Anniversary Data Archive CD-ROM. NASA SP-4601, 1999.

Remembering Apollo 11: The 35th Anniversary Data Archive CD-ROM. NASA SP-2004-4601, 2004. This is an update of the 1999 edition.

The Mission Transcript Collection: U.S. Human Spaceflight Missions from Mercury Redstone 3 to Apollo 17. NASA SP-2000-4602, 2001.

Shuttle-Mir: The United States and Russia Share History's Highest Stage. NASA SP-2001-4603, 2002.

U.S. Centennial of Flight Commission Presents Born of Dreams—Inspired by Freedom. NASA SP-2004-4604, 2004.

Of Ashes and Atoms: A Documentary on the NASA Plum Brook Reactor Facility. NASA SP-2005-4605, 2005.

Taming Liquid Hydrogen: The Centaur Upper Stage Rocket Interactive CD-ROM. NASA SP-2004-4606, 2004.

Fueling Space Exploration: The History of NASA's Rocket Engine Test Facility DVD. NASA SP-2005-4607, 2005.

Altitude Wind Tunnel at NASA Glenn Research Center: An Interactive History CD-ROM. NASA SP-2008-4608, 2008.

A Tunnel Through Time: The History of NASA's Altitude Wind Tunnel. NASA SP-2010-4609, 2010.

CONFERENCE PROCEEDINGS, NASA SP-4700

Dick, Steven J., and Keith Cowing, eds. *Risk and Exploration: Earth, Sea and the Stars.* NASA SP-2005-4701, 2005.

Dick, Steven J., and Roger D. Launius. *Critical Issues in the History of Spaceflight.* NASA SP-2006-4702, 2006.

Dick, Steven J., ed. *Remembering the Space Age: Proceedings of the 50th Anniversary Conference.* NASA SP-2008-4703, 2008.

Dick, Steven J., ed. *NASA's First 50 Years: Historical Perspectives.* NASA SP-2010-4704, 2010.

SOCIETAL IMPACT, NASA SP-4800

Dick, Steven J., and Roger D. Launius. *Societal Impact of Spaceflight.* NASA SP-2007-4801, 2007.

Dick, Steven J., and Mark L. Lupisella. *Cosmos and Culture: Cultural Evolution in a Cosmic Context.* NASA SP-2009-4802, 2009.

Dick, Steven J. *Historical Studies in the Societal Impact of Spaceflight.* NASA SP-2015-4803, 2015.

Index